DESTINATION WILDLIFE

DESTINATION WILDLIFE

An international site-by-site guide to
the best places to experience endangered, rare,
and fascinating animals and their habitats

Pamela K. Brodowsky
and The National Wildlife Federation

A PERIGEE BOOK

A PERIGEE BOOK
Published by the Penguin Group
Penguin Group (USA) Inc.
375 Hudson Street, New York, New York 10014, USA
Penguin Group (Canada), 90 Eglinton Avenue East, Suite 700, Toronto, Ontario M4P 2Y3, Canada
(a division of Pearson Penguin Canada Inc.)
Penguin Books Ltd., 80 Strand, London WC2R 0RL, England
Penguin Group Ireland, 25 St. Stephen's Green, Dublin 2, Ireland (a division of Penguin Books Ltd.)
Penguin Group (Australia), 250 Camberwell Road, Camberwell, Victoria 3124, Australia
(a division of Pearson Australia Group Pty. Ltd.)
Penguin Books India Pvt. Ltd., 11 Community Centre, Panchsheel Park, New Delhi—110 017, India
Penguin Group (NZ), 67 Apollo Drive, Rosedale, North Shore 0632, New Zealand
(a division of Pearson New Zealand Ltd.)
Penguin Books (South Africa) (Pty.) Ltd., 24 Sturdee Avenue, Rosebank, Johannesburg 2196, South Africa

Penguin Books Ltd., Registered Offices: 80 Strand, London WC2R 0RL, England

While the author has made every effort to provide accurate telephone numbers and Internet addresses at the time of publication, neither the publisher nor the author assumes any responsibility for errors, or for changes that occur after publication. Further, the publisher does not have any control over and does not assume any responsibility for author or third-party websites or their content.

First edition: April 2009

Library of Congress Cataloging-in-Publication Data

Brodowsky, Pamela K.
    Destination wildlife : an international site-by-site guide to the best places to experience endangered, rare, and fascinating animals and their habitats / Pamela K. Brodowsky and the National Wildlife Federation.
        p.   cm.
    "A Perigee Book."
    Includes index.
    ISBN 978-0-399-53486-7
    1. Endangered species.   2. Wildlife watching—Guidebooks.   I. National Wildlife Federation.   II. Title.
    QL82.B76 2009
    590.72'3—dc22   2008049529

PRINTED IN THE UNITED STATES OF AMERICA

10   9   8   7   6   5   4   3   2   1

Most Perigee books are available at special quantity discounts for bulk purchases for sales promotions, premiums, fund-raising, or educational use. Special books, or book excerpts, can also be created to fit specific needs. For details, write: Special Markets, Penguin Group (USA) Inc., 375 Hudson Street, New York, New York 10014.

For Sarah and Jacob
May you always have wild and wonderful places to explore

ACKNOWLEDGMENTS

With our deepest gratitude we would like to thank the following people whose contributions have made this book possible. For generously sharing their experiences, wisdom, and love for all things wild, special thanks goes to Joe Beck, William Ramroth Jr., Bill Jackson, Amanda Fallon, Lorraine Williams, Sarah Brodowsky, Jonathan Munro, P. J. Dempsey, Thomas Snitch, and Linda Holody.

A very special thank-you goes to our editor and publisher John Duff. His acute attention to detail, his keen eye, and his sheer love for the animal kingdom, have clearly made this book what it is today. For our countless conversations, for taking time out of his own life . . . well beyond business hours, for all he has done and contributed, to him, our sincere gratitude.

The writer is only the first in a series of many people who are involved in the making of a book. It takes the minds and hands of many to create, improve, and mold one's thoughts into what eventually grows from the labor of love of one person into the book you are reading today. With that said, the following "behind the scenes" people rightly deserve their due: Tiffany Estreicher, interior design; Benjamin Gibson, cover design; and Candace B. Levy, our copyeditor, to whom we are forever indebted.

CONTENTS

INTRODUCTION

Destination Wildlife is a book for every eco-explorer, wildlife enthusiast, or armchair adventure traveler—an international site-by-site guide to the best places to experience endangered, rare, and fascinating animals and their habitats on land, in the sea, and sometimes in the air. By necessity this collection is subjective and selective because there are simply too many animals (even of the rare and endangered sort) and too many places worthy of inclusion to fit into a single volume. But the criteria we used are clear: places that are wild and wonderful and that offer something truly distinctive and memorable.

From trekking in search of gorillas in Parc National des Volcans (Volcanoes National Park) in Rwanda or camping among the wild pony herds of Assateague Island National Seashore in Maryland to kayaking alongside the orcas off Alaska's Kenai Peninsula or listening to the howler monkeys in the Costa Rican rain forests, many of the experiences in this book will be familiar to readers but there are many that will be unknown because the opportunities for eco-travel are expanding constantly, even as many fragile places on earth are continuing to be threatened.

This book is intended as a modest introduction to the world of eco-travel and as a guide to bring us face-to-face with the last of many species. But it is also intended to show how wildlife adventures can be respectful of the environment and the animals because many people view "eco-travel" with mixed feelings. Although tourists may draw attention to problem areas and contribute resources that directly or indirectly help underwrite conservation efforts, they may also be disturbing the natural settings that conservationists are trying so hard to preserve. This book pays particular attention to those sites that promote the least environmental impact while providing a thrilling educational and emotional experience. In fact, many of the sites featured in this book have been specifically established to study and to reintroduce species that have been threatened and to restore their decimated habitats.

The earth's animals are in a critical state due to encroachment by humans, poaching, the illegal pet trade, and habitat destruction. While heroic efforts are being taken on a global scale to save and preserve these animals and their environments for future generations, it is our hope that this book will contribute to the general awareness of such conditions everywhere and to encourage people to contribute by word and deed to the many conservation efforts already under way.

Destination Wildlife has been very much a collaborative effort with contributions from fellow travelers, naturalists from the National Wildlife Federation, and a host of others who have committed their time and talent to creating opportunities for anyone to experience the wild in a way never before possible— and perhaps never possible again.

The natural world has an undeniable appeal beyond the thrill of adventure. There is an indefinable something that touches one's soul. Its unpredictability and its grandeur have captured our collective imaginations, inspiring great works of art through the ages. Even for the amateur, to photograph a pride of lions on the African savanna, to try to capture the essence of a scarlet macaw in flight with the flick of a paintbrush, or to record one's deepest responses to encounters with nature in a travel journal—all come from the same place: our innate and enduring bond with wild things.

THINGS YOU SHOULD KNOW

Destination Wildlife is arranged generally by continent. In some instances—for example, South America—we have included territories that, while not technically part of that continent, fit quite naturally into the geography. The listings for each continent are then arranged alphabetically by site name or, as in larger territories such as the United States, arranged first alphabetically by state and second by site name. In addition to the description and highlights of the site, each listing contains information on location, hours of operation, contact information, cost, on-site amenities, best times, and field notes.

LOCATION: In most instances provides the distance from the nearest major city or common access point of the destination to the main entry point of the site. For some of the more obscure places, further details are provided or you will be referred to the best source for directions, which is often a website.

HOURS OF OPERATION: Provides information on when the site is open for visitation. Because times and dates are subject to change—and in some cases, subject to conditions beyond anyone's control—we suggest that you always verify by contacting the site before travel.

CONTACT: Gives direct or indirect contact information—address, telephone numbers, website, and/or email addresses. Sometimes the best contact information is a commercial website, such as a tour company. Many sites can be visited only via an authorized tour company. This information is usually identified as such.

COST: Provides an approximate estimate of what it would cost to visit the site and, in some instances, attendant costs such as transportation and accommodation. The prices contained herein were converted and rounded to the nearest US dollar at press time. Prices and currency exchanges fluctuate, so it is important to verify before travel.

ON-SITE AMENITIES: Provides information on what the site has to offer to its visitors—for example, tours, eateries, restrooms, lodging, and visitors centers. If the site offers or facilitates other activities, such as organized tours and guides, the information will be listed in this section.

BEST TIMES: Provides the best time of year to visit each site for optimal wildlife viewing. In some instances, there are times that you may want to stay away from the site—for example, to avoid high-season crowds and inclement weather, such as excessive heat, monsoons, or heavy snowfalls.

FIELD NOTES: Provides insider tips from those who have already been to the site, things you will want to know as a first-time visitor: what to wear, what to carry, what to watch for, and what to watch out for! Also, this section includes any restrictions that the site may have, such as age limits and handicapped accessibility.

We welcome your comments and suggestions. Please visit our website at www.destinationwildlife.com.

A FEW NOTES FOR AMERICANS TRAVELING ABROAD

The US federal government encourages travelers to register with the Department of State. This is a precautionary measure taken in the event of an emergency in your homeland or in the country you are visiting so that you may be contacted should any such situation arise. Registration is a free service and is easily accomplished online at https://travelregistration.state.gov.

Many countries have restrictions on what may be imported. It is best to check with the embassies of your destination countries concerning their list of prohibited items. A listing of foreign embassies and consulates is available online at http://state.gov/s/cpr/rls/dpl/32122.htm.

General guidance on required entrance vaccinations and other health-related precautions in regard to visiting foreign countries can be found at the Centers for Disease Control and Prevention's website, wwwn.cdc.gov/travel/default.aspx.

All international travel now requires a passport. For information on applying for a US passport visit www.travel.state.gov/passport/passport_1738.html, or pick up an application form at your local post office or library.

NORTH AMERICA

United States, Canada, Mexico

ALASKA MARITIME NATIONAL WILDLIFE REFUGE

ALASKA, USA

The Alaska Maritime National Wildlife Refuge encompasses nearly 5 million acres of land in the Alaskan wilderness and is home to more than 40 million seabirds, whose nesting and mating habits are studied by scientists visiting from around the world. Visitors and scientists alike are often privy to the spectacular sight of "bird cities," where entire colonies of birds congregate for a time.

Among the many seabirds found in the refuge are horned and tufted puffins; fork-tailed storm petrels; and Aleutian cackling geese, a bird that is world famous because it was removed from the endangered species list only a few years ago.

Migrating birds such as the yellow bittern, the Chinese egret, the Siberian blue robin, and the Eurasian siskin have been spotted in the refuges of the Aleutian Islands.

The refuge actually comprises 12 distinct refuges with many dating back to some of the earliest conservation efforts in America. The diversity of landscapes covered by the immense refuge, from dormant volcanoes to forests of kelp, allow for an incredible array of wildlife that includes not only 55 species of birds but also an abundance of marine mammals such as sea lions, seals, walrus, and sea otters.

Fur seals and Arctic foxes can be spotted on the Pribilof Islands and brown bears make their home on Unimak Island. Walrus can be observed on St. Matthew Island, though viewing is

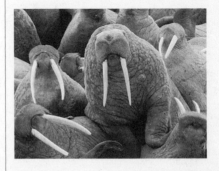

better in the area of Round Island, just off of the refuge grounds.

LOCATION: *Headquarters:* Homer, on the Kenai Peninsula.

HOURS OF OPERATION: Year-round, 24/7.

CONTACT: *Headquarters:* Tel: 907-2356546; Web: http://alaskamaritime.fws.gov. *Alaska Islands and Ocean visitors center:* 95 Sterling Hwy, Homer, AK 99603; Tel: 9072356961; Web: www.islandsandocean.org; email: info@islandsandocean.org.

COST: *Visitors center and refuge:* Free. Other costs vary, depending on type of lodging and tours.

ON-SITE AMENITIES: *Visitors center:* Overlooks Kachemak Bay; teaches visitors about the area's wildlife with a particular focus on the refuge's conservation efforts. *National refuge:* Numerous hiking trails; expert guides are available. Camping is permitted, although there are no specially designated campgrounds.

BEST TIMES: May through October.

FIELD NOTES: Everything that you would need to purchase can be found in the area, especially in the town of Homer. A first aid kit, water, and food supplies are recommended for those camping.

ALASKA PENINSULA NATIONAL WILDLIFE REFUGE

ALASKA, USA

The Alaska Peninsula National Wildlife Refuge provides for the conservation of many animals by protecting the area's water resources and offering a safe environment for shorebirds, raptors, and fish.

On a visit you may observe brown bears, moose, caribou, wolves, wolverines, foxes, river otters, and beavers, all of which are refuge residents. The refuge is also home to five species of salmon; the Arctic grayling; Dolly Varden char,

rainbow, and lake trout; northern pike; and burbot. More than 200 species of birds have been recorded in the refuge, including bald eagles, owls, falcons, ravens, ducks, geese, and swans plus many other seabirds, shorebirds, and passerines. Marine mammals such as sea lions, harbor seals, sea otters, and migratory whales use the shores and offshore waters.

The best way to start your trip to the Peninsula Refuge is to stop at the King Salmon visitors center. The center, located at the King Salmon Airport, is open all year. Staff at the center's information and trip planning desk will help you get the most out of your trip to the Alaska Peninsula. While at the visitors center, be sure to see the exhibits, engage in the interactive programs, and see the wildlife films. Because the center also hosts an adjunct of the Alaska Geographic store, it's a great place to find guidebooks, maps, and even souvenirs. Information on locating guides and charter services for flights, fishing, hunting, and more is also available.

LOCATION: *Refuge:* Alaska Peninsula. *Visitors center:* King Salmon Airport.

HOURS OF OPERATION: *Refuge:* Year-round, 24/7. *Visitors center:* Daily, May–Sept, 8 a.m. to 5 p.m.; Oct–Apr, closed Sun.

CONTACT: *Main office:* Alaska Peninsula National Wildlife Refuge, PO Box 277, MS 545, King Salmon, AK 99613; Tel: 9072463339; Web: http://alaska peninsula.fws.gov; email: akpeninsula @fws.gov.

COST: *Visitors center:* Free. Other costs vary, depending on type of lodging, tours, and other amenities.

ON-SITE AMENITIES: Expert guides, boating, numerous hiking trails, backpacking, flightseeing, camping, fishing, swimming, birding, wildlife photography.

BEST TIMES: May through September.

FIELD NOTES: A first aid kit, water, and food supplies are recommended for those camping. Binoculars, field books, comfortable walking shoes, and seasonal clothing are recommended. Refuge lands are remote and accessible only by small aircraft, boat, or rugged cross-country hiking. There are no roads or maintained trails.

ARCTIC NATIONAL WILDLIFE REFUGE

ALASKA, USA

The Arctic National Wildlife Refuge (ANWR) supports a greater variety of animal and plant life than any other refuge in the Arctic Circle. Because it encompasses distinctly different habitats within its borders, visitors traveling from one part of the refuge to the other have the opportunity to see a great variety of landscapes and animals.

The northern section of the refuge includes barrier islands, coastal lagoons, and river deltas, where migratory waterfowl, such as sea ducks, geese, swans, and shorebirds can be found as well as fish such as the Arctic cisco and the Dolly Varden. In summer, the coastal lands are used by caribou that come to

the ice fields to escape the stinging bites of insects. In winter, polar bears use the area's snow dens to give birth.

Stretching southward from the coast is the Arctic coastal plain. The rolling hills, rivers, and small lakes are covered in tundra vegetation—shrubs, sedges, and mosses—where caribou give birth to and raise their young during the early summer months. Migratory birds make their way here during the same time. In September, snow geese by the tens of thousands pass through before they migrate south.

To the south of the coastal plain, the peaks of the Brooks Range rise to almost 10,000 feet. This is the northern terminus of the Rocky Mountains, and elevation here creates its own unique habitat. Gyrfalcons, golden eagles, and peregrine falcons nest in the mountain regions, and the rivers here are temporary homes for harlequin ducks and red-breasted mergansers. Throughout the year, wolves, sheep, grizzly bears, and Arctic ground squirrels are found here.

The boreal forest of interior Alaska makes up the southern part of the refuge. The area starts with sporadic islands of spruce trees that meld into a progressively more dense forest. Migratory birds use the area for breeding in the spring and summer. Caribou travel here from the north and spend their summers in the forests. Animals that make their permanent home in the area include moose, lynx, martens, wolverines, and bears.

The ANWR is famous for the controversy surrounding land-use issues because the area is known for being rich in oil. Constant vigilance is required by local conservationists to ensure that human enterprise doesn't compromise the integrity of the refuge.

LOCATION: Arctic coast, Brooks Range, and Yukon Basin. Most of the refuge is accessible only by aircraft. Commercial air service from Fairbanks is available to Fort Yukon, Arctic Village, Deadhorse, or Kaktovik; from one of these towns, visitors can charter a bush plane into the refuge.

HOURS OF OPERATION: Year-round, 24/7.

CONTACT: *Main office:* Arctic National Wildlife Refuge, 101 12th Ave, Room 236, Fairbanks, AK 99701; Tel: 9074560250 or 8003624546 (toll-free); Web: http://arctic.fws.gov. *Air taxi information:* http://arctic.fws.gov/airtaxi.htm; email: arctic_refuge@fws.gov.

COST: Depends on recreational guide and tour package. Permits are required only for commercial endeavors.

ON-SITE AMENITIES: There are no amenities. Campsites are where you make them.

BEST TIMES: May through September.

FIELD NOTES: The best way to get to the refuge is by air taxi. The ANWR is one of the last undomesticated areas in the United States; thus guides—and taking extreme caution—are advised. In fact, guided tours could not be more highly recommended. (ANWR's website provides a list of authorized recreational guides.) Everything required for your trip must be purchased in advance. Remember that foot travel in the refuge is often slow-going over unstable terrain. Hiking a specific distance here may take two to four times as long as it would on groomed trails elsewhere. Plan to be completely self-sufficient. Cell phones do not have coverage across the refuge, and satellite phones may not work in mountainous terrain or in harsh weather conditions. Pack out all trash or burn it completely to powdery, white ash and pack out any remaining unburned pieces. Reduce the chances of dangerous animal encounters by not allowing food scraps or food odors to attract wildlife. Be prepared to handle any situation completely on your own. Topographic maps and emergency supplies are essential.

DENALI NATIONAL PARK AND PRESERVE

ALASKA, USA

If you visit Denali thinking that your trip is all about Mt. McKinley—albeit the highest and possibly the most impressive mountain in North America—you won't be disappointed. For the intrepid traveler, the view from Mt. McKinley is stunning, and the experience itself is amazing. Everything from learning about the mountain to taking gentle hikes to engaging in serious mountain climbing will make your trip worthwhile. What you may not anticipate is that Mt. McKinley is just one facet of Denali National Park and Preserve. The bird-watching is superb, and you are likely to see both caribou and grizzlies in one afternoon's drive.

Denali National Park and Preserve is Alaska's premier national park and offers visitors an array of activities and services. Wildlife enthusiasts will enjoy the opportunity to see the region's diverse indigenous animals. Sporting enthusiasts look forward to the outdoor activities available year-round at the park. Whether it is hiking, climbing, or dogsledding, there is enough to do at Denali to keep you busy every day

of your visit and still leave you eager to return.

Many visitors to Denali are there to view what has become known as the park's "Big Five": Dall sheep, moose, caribou, grizzlies, and wolves, which are common to the area and are seen regularly. Collared pikas, wolverines, red foxes, black bears, hoary marmots, Arctic ground squirrels, and snowshoe hares all take residence here as well. With proper care and forbearance, visitors can have unprecedented access to animals that would otherwise never be seen in their natural habitats by humans.

Aside from the wildlife, the very landscape of Denali is an attraction for visitors. From the famed Mt. McKinley (also locally known as Denali, which means "the high one" in the Athabaskan language and which is the name officially recognized by the state of Alaska), there are 6 million acres of beautiful wilderness that is almost begging to be explored. There are three shuttles that will take you to different points in the park and then there are three bus tours led by expert guides that go through the park itself. Once you are seriously in the park (after the 15-mile mark), the only way to continue to travel is by bus, bicycle, dogsled, or foot.

LOCATION: 240 miles north of Anchorage on Alaska Rte 3.

HOURS OF OPERATION: *Visitors centers:* May 15–Sept 18, 8 a.m. to 6 p.m. *Park:* Year-round. Tours leave at various times. *Main office:* Denali National Park, PO Box 9, Denali Park, AK 99755; Tel: 9076832294; Web: www.nps.gov/dena.

COST: *Entrance* (7-day pass): Individual, US$10; private vehicle US$20. *Camping:* US$12–$20.

ON-SITE AMENITIES: Visitor and wilderness centers, six campgrounds, guided tours, hiking excursions, nature walks, ranger programs, field seminars. Facilities for nature walks, mountaineering, backpacking, cycling, fishing, skiing, snowshoeing, and dogsledding. The park also has four remote wilderness lodges, located at mile 90 on the Denali Park Road, in the Kantishna area. For further information contact the park directly.

BEST TIMES: Mid May through mid September.

FIELD NOTES: Vehicle use in the park is limited. Reservations for campgrounds are recommended. Climbing equipment should be brought with you. Binoculars, cameras, comfortable walking shoes, and seasonal clothing are recommended. Denali is a true wilderness area. Before venturing into the park, read the safety information in the *Denali Alpenglow*, the park newspaper. Grizzly bears and moose are dangerous, and visitors are advised to keep their distance at all times. Crossing glacial rivers is treacherous, and the potential for hypothermia is always a factor in the subarctic. Pets must be leashed at all times when visiting Denali National Park and Preserve and are not allowed on trails, river bars, or in the backcountry.

GLACIER BAY NATIONAL PARK AND PRESERVE

ALASKA, USA

It has been said that people spoke about the magical, rugged beauty of this area long ago. The elders of the Tlingit Indians talked about an ice-covered ancestral homeland. Later, explorers to the region wrote about this astounding landscape. As recently as 1750, a single glacier, thousands of feet thick, filled what is now a 65-mile-long fjord. Today, visitors to Glacier Bay National Park and Preserve are still humbled beyond words at first sight of this majestic park.

The park comprises many ecosystems, from tidewater glaciers to snow-capped mountain ranges, ocean coastlines, deep fjords, and freshwater rivers and lakes. Although it is sometimes inhospitable, the area supports a vast array of marine and animal life.

Each summer humpback whales return to the bay from their wintering grounds near Hawaii to feed on the abundant small schooling fish. Minke and killer whales along with harbor and Dall porpoises feed in the park's productive near-shore waters, and Steller sea lions congregate on rocky islands to mate and rest. Thousands of harbor seals breed and nurture their pups on the floating ice in Johns Hopkins Inlet and among the rocky reefs of the Beardslee Islands. Sea otters are rapidly populating Glacier Bay, Icy Strait, and Cross Sound.

Visitors can also observe many kinds of land mammals. The mountain goat and brown bear were quick to repopulate after the last glaciers' retreat. Other animals have followed. The coyote, moose, and wolf have moved in more recently but are now established in the park. The big boys of the park—the black bears—prowl the forested portions of the lower bay, and glacier

bears, a rare silvery color phase of the black bear, are occasionally spotted. River otters are widespread as are marten, mink, and weasels; wolverines are scarcer and rarely sighted. The Alsek River Delta, in the preserve, is home to lynx, snowshoe hares, and beavers.

Many land animals take advantage of water for foraging and travel. Moose and bear, for example, are accomplished long-distance swimmers and are frequently seen dog-paddling their way across the bay. Bears work the beaches when the tide is low, turning over rocks looking for tasty barnacles, clams, and other food. Wolves and coyotes find the traveling easier along the edge of tall beach grasses than through the tangles of alder thickets. At times, even the most upland of animals, like marmots and mountain goats, are drawn to the water's edge to nibble seaweed or to lick salt spray. One thing is for certain, the ocean is truly the common element that bonds the wildlife of the park.

LOCATION: West of Juneau, Alaska. Can be reached only by plane or boat; the only road runs 10 miles from the small town of Gustavus and its airfield to park headquarters at Bartlett Cove. In the summer, Alaska Airlines has daily flights from Juneau to Gustavus; private air taxis and charters provide year-round service. Glacier Bay is also accessible via the water; visitors travel to the park on cruise ships, tour and charter boats, and privately owned vessels.

HOURS OF OPERATION: Daily, 24/7, late May–early Sept. *Exhibits:* 24/7. *Information desk and Alaska Geographic bookstore:* Daily, 11 a.m. to 9 p.m.

CONTACT: Glacier Bay National Park, PO Box 140, Gustavus, AK 99826-0140; Tel: 9076972230 (general information) or 9076972627 (permits); Web: www.nps.gov/glba.

COST: *Entrance:* Free. Reservations, and sometimes fees, are required for boating, camping, rafting, and many other services.

ON-SITE AMENITIES: Glacier Bay Lodge and Tours: Provide accommodations; call 8667616634, for reservations. *Camping:* A walk-in campground is located in the park at Bartlett Cove; maximum stay is 14 days. For backcountry camping there are unlimited opportunities; camping is free and no reservations are needed, but permits are required (available directly from the park).

BEST TIMES: Late April to late September.

FIELD NOTES: Foul-weather gear is important. Layers of clothing along with gloves, hats, sunglasses, and sunscreen are recommended; some activities require specific equipment or clothing. Be sure to check the park's website for all the gear you'll need for your trip.

KACHEMAK BAY STATE PARK AND STATE WILDERNESS PARK

ALASKA, USA

Kachemak Bay State Park occupies most of the southwestern part of Alaska's Kenai Peninsula. The park comprises three distinct topographies: glaciers, lagoons and lakes, and forests, each with its own unique appeal. The 13-mile-long glacial area is physically arresting, with almost limitless opportunities for hiking, climbing, and wildlife viewing. It's a photographer's paradise. The lagoons and lakes in the area are home to an array of aquatic life that is seldom found elsewhere. The diversity, quality, and quantity of fish available mean visitors can expect world-class fishing. Sea otters, seals,

porpoises, and whales all frequent the area and make ideal subjects for both amateur and professional wildlife photographers. The forests in Kachemak provide a habitat for wolves, black bears, coyotes, mountain goats, moose, and a variety of other wildlife.

Inaccessible by car and with more than 80 miles of hiking routes throughout its 400,000 acres, the park is a serious enthusiast's dream. Here you can experience nature in a pristine environment with well-protected wildlife.

LOCATION: Southwest Kenai Peninsula, Alaska.

HOURS OF OPERATION: 24/7, allowing for camping and extensive guided tours.

CONTACT: *Main office:* Kachemak Bay State Park, PO Box 1247, Soldotna, AK 99669; Tel: 9072625581; Web: www.dnr.state.ak.us/parks/units/kbay/kbay.htm.

COST: *Cabin rentals:* US$50–$65, depending on season. *Fishing and hunting permits:* Can be purchased in Homer.

Tours: Vary in price, depending on duration and style. Contact the park directly for specific information.

ON-SITE AMENITIES: 80 miles of hiking trails. Cabins in Halibut Cove Lagoon, Leisure Lake, Moose Valley, and Tutka Bay. Camping permitted in most areas; a number of sites contain fireplaces, tent platforms, picnic tables, and outhouses. Facilities for fishing and boating.

BEST TIMES: Late spring to early fall.

FIELD NOTES: Visitors arrive at the park via boat or airplane; there are no access roads. There are very few amenities available in the park. Homer, a nearby town, offers support to visitors of the area. Permits and transportation (air, water taxi, or boat rentals) can be obtained there. Reservations for cabins should be made as early as possible, as they book quickly. The cabins are charming, yet rustic in style. Visitors should be prepared for severe and unpredictable weather and should dress for cool, wet, and windy conditions. Extra clothing, rain gear, and waterproof packaging for your photographic equipment are all needed. Firewood can be brought in or collected on-site; however, only dead, downed wood can be used and is not always readily available. Carry some backup wood with you in any event.

KATMAI NATIONAL PARK AND PRESERVE

ALASKA, USA

Katmai National Park and Preserve began in 1918 as a national monument, formed to preserve and protect the Valley of Ten Thousand Smokes. The current national park includes this 40-square-mile, 100- to 700-foot-deep ash flow, deposited by Novarupta Volcano. Katmai is still known for its volcanoes, remote wilderness, incredible salmon runs, and potpourri of marine life and land animals, but it is no doubt most famous for its bear population.

There are two main types of bears in Katmai: grizzlies and brown bear. The brown bear is usually bigger, but

seal. Killer and gray whales can also be seen swimming along the rugged coast of the park.

LOCATION: On the Alaska Peninsula, across from Kodiak Island. Headquarters is in King Salmon, southwest of Anchorage by about 290 air miles. One popular site is Brooks Camp, along the Brooks River, which can be reached only by small float plane or boat.

because the size difference isn't great and their territories overlap, it is hard for most people to distinguish between the two. One of the many spectacular sights that attracts much attention is the bear fights, when males clash for mating rights and dominance. But all bear behavior is taken very seriously inside and outside of the park. Because each bear is an individual, no one can predict with 100% accuracy how a given bear will act in a given situation. Katmai's website provides a downloadable copy of "Bear Safety in Alaska's National Parklands," for visitors to use any time of the year.

HOURS OF OPERATION: Year-round, 24/7. *Brooks Camp:* Park concessioner services available June 1–Sept 17.

CONTACT: Katmai National Park and Preserve, 1 King Salmon Mall, PO Box 7, King Salmon, AK 99613; Tel: 9072463305; Web: www.nps.gov/katm.

COST: *Entrance:* Free. *Brooks Camp Campground* (per person, per night): US$8, June 1–Sept 17; visit www.recre ation.gov for reservations.

ON-SITE AMENITIES: Visitors center, guided tours, and hiking trails. Facilities in the campground include a food cache, gear cache, fuel storage locker, potable water, cooking shelters, outhouse, and electric fence. The campground facilities are available from June 1 to September 17; outside these dates, plan on providing all of your own equipment.

While bears are the stars of Katmai, there are some wonderful bit players at the park as well. Land animals include moose, caribou, red fox, wolf, lynx, wolverine, river otter, mink, marten, weasel, porcupine, snowshoe hare, red squirrel, and beaver. Park visitors can also see a variety of marine mammals, such as the sea lion, sea otter, and hair

BEST TIMES: Prime bear viewing months at Brooks Camp are July and September, although a few bears may be in the area at any time between late May and

December. Bear viewing along the coastal areas is possible from June through August. Backcountry activities are best during June through September.

FIELD NOTES: All food, beverages, garbage, and any other odorous items must be attended at all times and stored in a bear-resistant container (BRC), sometimes called a "bear barrel." A limited number of BRCs are available for temporary checkout, free of charge at Brooks Camp and at the King Salmon visitors center. The minimum recommended safe distance from any bear is 50 yards. Avoid actions that interfere with bear movement or foraging activities. If you are camping in the backcountry you may want to consider bringing an electric fence. Electric fences have been adapted for use in bear country and have been effective at minimizing intrusions into campsites. Visitors planning to use electric fences must bring their own equipment; the park does not provide electric fencing material.

KENAI FJORDS NATIONAL PARK

ALASKA, USA

In a testament to the conservation efforts of the inhabitants in the area, the same biodiversity found in the Kenai Peninsula before the arrival of Europeans can still be found in the Kenai Fjords National Park today. You'll be the privileged spectator to an array of wildlife that includes moose, mountain goat, and both the brown and black bear. Caribou, wolverines, coyotes, and wolves, all make their home in Kenai. The bald eagle is plentiful and easily spotted. The park's aquatic animals are just as varied; beavers, otters, orcas, beluga whales, porpoises, and sea lions can be observed. Exit Glacier is the only part of the park that is accessible by car, and only during the summer season. In the winter, access is by snowmobile, sled dog, and cross-country skis. Exit Glacier offers some of the most beautiful scenic hiking

trails in the world. Park rangers provide walks and tours that allow you close access to the glacier and expert lectures.

While hiking the trails is your best bet for sighting the many land mammals, boat tours provide optimal viewing of the park's aquatic life. Full- and half-day tours are available from numerous private companies. Most tours have a park ranger onboard, who will provide expert insight into all aspects of the area.

LOCATION: Kenai Peninsula, Alaska, approximately 126 miles from Anchorage, just outside of the town of Seward.

HOURS OF OPERATION: *Visitors center:* Daily; May 3–May 16, 9 a.m. to 5 p.m.; May 17–Sept 1, 8:30 a.m. to 7 p.m.; Sept 2–Sept 27, 9 a.m. to 5 p.m. *Exit Glacier Nature Center:* Daily; May 17–Sept 1, 9 a.m. to 8 p.m.; Sept 2–Sept 27, 9 a.m. to 5 p.m.

CONTACT: *Main office:* Kenai Fjords National Park, PO Box 1727, Seward, AK 99664; Tel: 9072247500; Web: www.nps.gov/kefj.

COST: *Entrance and camping:* Free. *Public-use cabins* (per night): US$35–$50.

ON-SITE AMENITIES: Amenities are few but include a visitors center, park ranger programs/services, and public-use cabins. Privately run activities, park-hosted events, and ranger-led programs include wildlife watching, boat tours, hiking, flightseeing, kayaking, fishing, and mountaineering. For a list of current tour operators, visit the **Seward Chamber of Commerce's** website (www.sewardak.org). Convenient and comfortable lodging can be found in the town of Seward; cabins directly on the shores of Resurrection Bay are available, allowing easy access to the boat tours of both the bay and the glaciers.

BEST TIMES: May through September.

FIELD NOTES: Warm clothing (in layers) is a must, even in the summer months. Reservations for cabins, boating tours, and other amenities are highly recommended in the high tourist season. *Cautionary notes:* This is the wilderness, so when visiting the park you might want to carry emergency supplies, like extra food and water, at all times—whether traveling independently or on a group tour. Remember, nature happens! Radical shifts in the weather, falling ice, avalanches, and earthquakes can occur in this territory. Always be on the lookout for bear (read up on precautions and ask the ranger/guides for advice); and should you encounter a moose along your travels, the key to safety is distance. Cow moose are very protective of their young—extreme caution should be taken not to come between the cow and the calf.

KODIAK NATIONAL WILDLIFE REFUGE

ALASKA, USA

In 1899, the writer and naturalist John Burroughs explored Alaska's Kodiak Island along with fellow naturalist John Muir and adventurer and soon-to-become president, Theodore Roosevelt. Burroughs was so stirred by the island's pristine natural beauty that he later wrote, "Bewitching Kodiak! The spell of thy summer freshness and placidity is still upon me." Today, Kodiak Island, part of Kodiak National Wildlife Refuge, is known as Alaska's Emerald Isle because of its spectacular Norwegian-like fjords and Irish-like lush green mountains.

Kodiak Island is home of the famous Kodiak bear. Isolated from the Alaskan mainland since the last ice age, some 10,000 years ago, the Kodiak bear is considered a subspecies of the Alaskan brown bear. The males equal the size of polar bears, weighing as much as 1,100 pounds, and standing 10–11 feet tall on their hind legs. To protect the bear as well as the habitat of the island's other inhabitants, the Kodiak National Wildlife Refuge was established in 1941. Today, approximately 2,300 Kodiaks live in the refuge, which covers the southern two-thirds of the island as well as a portion of neighboring Afognak Island and the islands of Uganik and Ban—a total area of 3,000 square miles.

In addition to the Kodiak bear, only five other species of land mammals are native to the refuge: red fox, river otter, ermine, tundra vole, and the little brown bat. A variety of nonnative mammal species were introduced during the mid 20th century to increase recreational hunting opportunities. Some of these managed to flourish, including the black-tailed deer, mountain goat, Roosevelt elk, and snowshoe hare. The refuge is also home for marine mammals, such as sea lions and five species of salmon. Bird-watchers will find more than 200 species of birds, including at least 600 nesting pairs of bald eagles.

Among the recreational activities available at the refuge are hiking, fishing, hunting, boating, canoeing, rafting, camping, wildlife observation, photography, and flightseeing. The refuge's headquarters and visitors center, located 5 miles south of downtown Kodiak, offers staff-led interpretive programs and outdoor classroom experiences, nature displays, video programs, trip planning information, and a bookstore. The refuge has seven public-use cabins, which are available on a reservation/lottery basis. Additional lodging is available outside the refuge. Authorized concessioners offer half-

day and full-day flightseeing trips—this is a spectacular way to view the refuge and possibly the best way to see and photograph Kodiak bears.

LOCATION: Kodiak, Alaska.

HOURS OF OPERATION: *Refuge:* Year-round, 24/7. *Visitors center:* Winter, weekdays, 8 a.m. to 7 p.m.; Memorial Day–Labor Day, weekdays, 8 a.m. to 7 p.m., weekends, 12 p.m. to 4 p.m.

CONTACT: *Headquarters:* Kodiak National Wildlife Refuge, 1390 Buskin River Rd, Kodiak, AK 99615; Tel: 9074872600 or 8884083514 (toll-free); Web: http://kodiak.fws.gov; email: kodiak@fws.gov.

COST: *Permits:* Required for crossing Native American–owned land and other areas of the refuge; most are free, but inquire at the visitors center for further information. *Public-use cabins* (per night): US$30; reservations available by lottery (download application from the refuge's website).

ON-SITE AMENITIES: Visitors center with bookstore and seven public-use cabins.

BEST TIMES: Memorial Day through Labor Day.

FIELD NOTES: The refuge is accessible only by boat or plane. Fly a commercial airline from Anchorage to Kodiak, where you can book an air charter to the refuge. Ferries are available through the **Alaska Marine Highway System**; for more information and reservations visit www.dot.state.ak.us/amhs.

YUKON DELTA NATIONAL WILDLIFE REFUGE

ALASKA, USA

The preservation of the Yukon Delta National Wildlife Refuge is of critical importance because the area supports one of the world's largest and most vital gathering spots for waterfowl. In addition to emperor geese and other birds that may live their entire lives in the refuge, millions of waterfowl descend on the refuge in the spring to nest.

More than 1.5 million ducks and geese breed in the refuge every year. It is not uncommon to find as much as a third of all the northern pintails on the continent within the confines of the refuge. The refuge provides spring nesting grounds to 40,000 loons, 40,000 grebes, 100,000 swans, and

30,000 cranes. The number of shorebirds that use the refuge for staging and breeding is staggering. The species diversity and density of the shorebirds found in the refuge makes it the premier nesting area in the nation and on par with the best areas in the world, of which there are a select few.

The refuge is also home to 19 recorded species of raptors. The Kisaralik River is one of the most important areas of the refuge for the nesting and conservation of golden eagles, bald eagles, and peregrine falcons.

Huge numbers of caribou once roamed the area that is now the Yukon Delta National Wildlife Refuge. After peaking in the 1860s, the number of caribou in the area plummeted over the following century. Due in part to conservation efforts by refuge officials in concert with local activists, the caribou population is climbing again; there are now more than 40,000 living in the refuge.

Numerous species of marine mammals are found in the region, including the threatened Steller sea lion. Visitors may also observe Pacific walruses, spotted seals, ringed seals, and Pacific bearded seals. The refuge's waters are home to roughly 40 species of fish. Salmon are found in the Yukon and Kuskokwim rivers, and freshwater fish include whitefish, sheefish, Alaska blackfish, burbot, northern pike, rainbow trout, and grayling. Pacific herring, halibut, tomcod, and starry flounder can be found in the near-shore ocean habitats of the refuge.

The refuge is accessible only by air. Commercial airlines fly into Bethel Airport, one of the most popular airports in the state and the perfect point of access for the refuge. The town offers visitors a warm welcome and numerous opportunities for lodging.

LOCATION: Bethel, Alaska.

HOURS OF OPERATION: Year-round, 24/7.

CONTACT: *Headquarters:* Yukon Delta National Wildlife Refuge, State Hwy, Box 346, Bethel, AK 99559; Tel: 9075433151; Web: http://yukondelta .fws.gov.

COST: *Entrance:* Free. *Guided tours:* Fees determined by the provider. *Permits:* Hunting, trapping, and fishing permits required by the state; fees vary.

ON-SITE AMENITIES: Amenities outside of the town of Bethel are extremely limited. Several Native American villages are in the refuge, but it is strongly recommended that you bring everything that you will need with you. The refuge headquarters houses a visitors center that offers information about the local wildlife and a historical perspective on the use of the refuge by the Yup'ik Eskimo population. A small sales outlet is available with educational and interpretive products. There are no interpretive facilities or exhibits on the refuge.

BEST TIMES: April through September.

FIELD NOTES: Fishing, hunting, trapping, boating, and photography are all world class in the refuge. All equipment must be purchased in advance. Contact the refuge for recommendations on tour providers.

CABEZA PRIETA NATIONAL WILDLIFE REFUGE

ARIZONA, USA

In 1540, 90 years before the Pilgrims landed at Plymouth Rock, Spaniards explored the desert area of what is now southwestern Arizona in search of the legendary city of Cibola, the city of gold. They named the area Cabeza Prieta, or "Dark Head," after the granite mountain with a gray lava peak that dominates the desert. More than 300 years later, would-be prospectors crossed Cabeza Prieta, thinking it was a shortcut to the California goldfields. With water virtually nonexistent and temperatures soaring above 100°F for days on end, many of them didn't make it. Travelers called the dusty and deadly footpath they followed *El Camino del Diablo*, "the Devil's Highway." An estimated 400 died along the road, and many of their grave mounds can still be seen today within the Cabeza Prieta National Wildlife Refuge.

In 1939, in an effort to save the remaining 150 bighorn sheep that lived in the desert's rocky hills, Cabeza Prieta was designated a wildlife refuge. Water holes were dug in the rugged mountains. The bighorn sheep popula-

tion rebounded, and today the bighorn is the refuge's official mascot.

Larger than the state of Rhode Island, the refuge is the third largest refuge in the lower 48 states, covering over 860,000 acres of rugged mountains and arid desert. It is home to more than 40 species of mammals. In addition to the bighorn, visitors may see pronghorn sheep, mule deer, coyotes, bobcats, mountain lions, kit and gray foxes, ringtail raccoons, badgers, spotted skunks, collared peccaries, cactus and canyon mice, white-throated wood and kangaroo rats, three species of jackrabbits, and a dozen species of bats.

The animals have developed a number of techniques to survive in the harsh desert environment. Some are very shy and venture only short distances out from their protective rocks or burrows. Some are nocturnal, while others have developed protective coloration. Some are extremely efficient in obtaining and conserving water. Others live solely on water extracted from plant life. As might be expected, the refuge is home to a number of reptiles, such as the collared lizard, Gila monster, desert banded gecko, chuckwalla, and red-backed whiptail. Bird-watchers might spot elf owls, Gila woodpeckers, red-tailed hawks, vermilion flycatchers, and Gambel's quails.

More than 400 different plant species have adapted to the arid desert conditions of Cabeza Prieta. Within the refuge are found creosote bush, bursage, mesquite, palo verde, and many species of cacti, including ocotillo, cholla, and the majestic saguaro. All play important roles in maintaining the delicate balance of the desert ecosystem.

LOCATION: *Visitors center:* Ajo, Arizona, about 110 miles southwest of Phoenix.

HOURS OF OPERATION: Vary seasonally; winter (between Nov and Mar), daily; summer, Mon–Fri. Subject to closure for breeding seasons; phone the visitors center for hours of operation and closures.

CONTACT: *Headquarters:* Cabeza Prieta National Wildlife Refuge, 1611 North Second Street, Ajo, AZ 85321; Tel: 5203876483; Web: www.fws.gov/south west/refuges/arizona/cabeza.html.

COST: *Entrance:* Free. *Permits:* Required to enter the refuge; available at the visitors center.

ON-SITE AMENITIES: The refuge's visitor center provides wildlife displays, a short refuge interpretive trail, entry permits to the refuge, and information about guided tours. Evening presentations featuring the history, flora, and fauna of the area are given between November and March. Local authorized concessioners give vehicle tours.

BEST TIMES: November through March when temperatures are relatively mild and wildlife is most active.

FIELD NOTES: The roads through the refuge are virtually unmaintained; it is mandatory for self-drivers to have 4-wheel-drive vehicles with high clearance. Bring your own water, food, and sunscreen. The area has been used as a military test ground: Do not touch unexploded ordinances (bombs).

GRAND CANYON NATIONAL PARK

ARIZONA, USA

Grand Canyon National Park lies on the Colorado plateau in northwestern Arizona and encompasses almost 1.25 million acres. This World Heritage Site is best known for its geologic significance and attracts research scientists from around the globe.

The canyon, created by the Colorado River, is one of the best examples of arid-land erosion in the world. The 277-mile-long canyon is an average of 4,000 feet deep. Grand Canyon National Park, however, offers more than just geology. It's also home to a stunning array of animal life.

Mountain lions (*Puma concolor*, also called cougars or pumas) are the region's only remaining large predator. This cat is quite shy and thus little is known about its behavior, range, and habits. A total of 34 mammal species are found along the Colorado River corridor, including 15 types of rodents and 8 kinds of bats. Unfortunately, the once-native river otters may have recently disappeared from the park, and it is now unlikely that you'll spot a muskrat. On the other hand, since the construc-

tion of the Glen Canyon Dam, the beaver population has increased in size and range. Antelope squirrels and pocket mice are common. Although the bats in the Grand Canyon typically roost in the desert uplands, you can observe them along the riverbank as they feed on the many insects found near the water.

Other animals that live in the park are coyotes, ringtails, and spotted skunks. Bird-watchers might see one of the many riparian predators feeding on invertebrates, rodents, and reptiles. Raccoons, weasels, bobcats, and gray foxes are harder to find. Mule deer and desert bighorn sheep are the ungulates that frequent the river corridor. Since the removal of 500 feral burros in the early

1980s, bighorn sheep numbers have rebounded. Visitors often see mule deer; the deer, however, are not usually permanent residents of the valley floor but travel down from the rim when food and water resources there become scarce.

Because the park contains several ecosystems—including five life zones and three desert types—visitors can expect to see an amazing range of wildlife. Two protected ecosystems found within the park are the boreal forest and desert riparian communities. According to the park's website, the Grand Canyon is home to more than 1,500 plant, 355 bird, 89 mammalian, 47 reptile, 9 amphibian, and 17 fish species. Several of these animal and plant species are found only at the park.

The park encompasses a semiarid environment and contains the raised plateaus and sculpted rock formations found throughout the US Southwest. Besides the expected cacti and scrubby vegetation, the park contains coniferous forests at its higher elevations.

The Grand Canyon reveals an astounding record of the past 2 billion years of the earth's geological history. A rich and diverse fossil record and a vast array of geologic features and rock types have been exposed in the layered walls of the canyon. The numerous caves found throughout the park contain extensive and significant remains for paleontological, archaeological, and biological research.

LOCATION: Grand Canyon, AZ; the northwest corner of Arizona, close to the borders of Utah and Nevada

HOURS OF OPERATION: *South Rim:* 24/7. *North Rim:* Mid May–mid Oct.

CONTACT: *Main office:* Grand Canyon National Park, PO Box 129, Grand Canyon, AZ 86023; Tel: 9286387888; Fax: 9286387797; Web: www.nps.gov/grca.

COST: *Entrance:* Noncommercial vehicle, US$25; individuals (foot, bicycle, motorcycle), US$12; children (under 15 years), free; annual pass, US$50. *Camping:* Individual, US$12–$18; group, US$30–$50. *Lodging:* US$52–$322.

ON-SITE AMENITIES: Restaurants, shops, coin-operated laundry, pet kennels, and post office. Free shuttle bus service (see website for schedule), mule and raft rentals. Camping reservations can be made through the National Recreation Reservation Service (call 8774446777 or visit www.recreation.gov). There are seven in-park lodges; for options and information visit www.grandcanyonlodges.com. **Grand Canyon Village** (South Rim): Call 3032972757 or 8882792757 (toll-free) or visit www.grandcanyonlodges.com. **Grand Canyon Lodge** (North Rim): Call 8773864383 or 4809981981 (outside of USA) or visit www.foreverlodging.com.

BEST TIMES: April through October.

FIELD NOTES: Carry water in your vehicle, particularly during summer months.

CHANNEL ISLANDS NATIONAL PARK

CALIFORNIA, USA

Off the coast of southern California, Channel Islands National Park is made up of five remote islands—Anacapa, Santa Cruz, Santa Rosa, San Miguel, and Santa Barbara—and is home to the world's largest breeding colonies of sea lions and seals. As isolated and virtually undeveloped today as they have been for thousands of years, the islands are accessible only by boat and camping is the only option for overnight accommodations. You'll see many types of ocean mammals on any of these islands, but a hike to the western edge of San Miguel will give you the opportunity of a lifetime if your visit coincides with the annual breeding time of the northern fur seal, harbor

seal, elephant seal, or California sea lion.

In addition to seals and sea lions, whales abound in the waters surrounding the islands and can be seen not only from boats but also from the islands' shores. Be prepared to be enchanted by the sights and sounds of many other sea creatures, including gray, humpback, and sperm whales; orcas, porpoises, and bottlenose dolphins.

These beautiful islands also host a variety of birds. Here's where visitors will find the only nesting population of brown pelicans on the US west coast. The park is also home to the world's largest population of Xantus's murrelets, and the island scrub jay, which is found only on the Channel Islands.

If you are lucky, you will also be treated to a sighting of the elusive and endangered island fox, which is found only in the park.

LOCATION: Approximately 20 miles off the coast of southern California. The nearest mainland city is Ventura.

HOURS OF OPERATION: Year-round, 24/7. Call ahead for transportation to the islands.

CONTACT: *Main office:* Channel Islands National Park, 1901 Spinnaker Drive, Ventura, CA 93001; Tel: 8056585730; Fax: 8056585799; Web: www.nps.gov/chis.

COST: *Entrance:* Free. *Camping* (per night): US$15.

ON-SITE AMENITIES: Visitors centers on the mainland are located in Ventura and Santa Barbara. Visitor contact stations are on Santa Barbara and Anacapa Islands. There is one campground on each island; for reservations, call 8774446777 or visit the National Recreation Reservation Service at www.recreation.gov.

BEST TIMES: Winter through summer are the best times for wildlife sightings.

FIELD NOTES: Dress in layers for all-day comfort. Wear comfortable walking or hiking shoes. Remember to pack enough food and water for your trip. The park has a number of rules and regulations for the protection of the environment; be sure to check out the Laws and Policies section on the park's website, where you can also find good guidelines for preparing for an overnight stay.

DEATH VALLEY NATIONAL PARK

CALIFORNIA, USA

Death Valley National Park is a land of extremes. The elevation at Furnace Creek in the heart of Death Valley is 214 feet below sea level. Badwater Basin's elevation is 282 feet below sea level, the lowest place in North America and one of the lowest in the world. And Death Valley is hot! In 1917, there were 43 consecutive days when the temperature soared to 120°F or higher. In 1996, there were 40 such days. On July 15, 1972, the ground temperature at the aptly named Furnace Creek reached an astounding 201°F! It doesn't rain much either. In 1929, there was no precipitation at all, and between 1931 and 1934 it rained a total of only 0.64 inch in 40 months! Lowest, hottest, and driest—no

horses, bobcats, mountain lions, foxes, coyotes, badgers, jackrabbits, or porcupines, not to mention a variety of other small mammal species. Among the many reptiles that have adapted well to the park's harsh, hot, and dry environment are the desert tortoise, desert banded gecko, iguana, chuckwalla, and many types of lizards. Even fish are found in Death Valley: Pupfish and mosquito fish live in the watering holes, springtime marsh lands, creeks, and manmade irrigation ditches.

wonder early pioneers named it Death Valley.

Although it may be hard to believe, Death Valley is home to more than 1,000 species of plants, more than 50 of which are found nowhere else in the world. During the month of April, desert annuals, called ephemerals (short lived), turn the valley floor into a showy carpet of white, purple, blue, yellow, red, and brilliant magenta wildflowers. By mid May the wildflowers are gone, exposing brown desert sand and white salt flats. In the areas above 400 feet in elevation, a variety of cacti grow, including barrel, hedgehog, prickly pear, and cholla cacti, as well as a number of succulents, such as pickleweed, dead man's fingers, and Panamint live-forever. Joshua and Mojave yucca trees grow in the park at higher elevations.

The park is home to many mammal species. Visitors may spot desert bighorn sheep, mule deer, burros, wild

Death Valley offers a variety of activities for visitors. Short or long wilderness walks along the salt flats and among the wildflowers are very enjoyable, and the park includes nine campgrounds. Visitors can take living history guided tours of Scotty's Castle, built during the late 1920s by eccentric Chicago millionaire Albert Johnson and his colorful prospector and con-man friend Frank "Scotty" Harris. The park has a borax mine and museum and ghost towns to explore, with names like Chloride City, Rhyolite, and Panamint City. There are two resort hotels in the park: Furnace Creek Inn and Furnace Creek Ranch. Golfers can tee off on the world's lowest (in elevation) 18-hole course in the world.

LOCATION: Furnace Creek (main point of entry) is 220 miles west of Las Vegas, Nevada, and 240 miles north of Baker, California.

HOURS OF OPERATION: Year-round, 24/7. *Scotty's Castle visitors center and museum:* Daily; winter, 8:30 a.m. to 5 p.m.; summer, 9 a.m. to 4:30 p.m. **Borax Museum** (in Furnace Creek): Daily; winter, 9 a.m. to 5 p.m.; summer, 10 a.m. to 4 p.m. **Furnace Creek Ranch:** Year-round. **Furnace Creek Lodge:** Mid Oct–mid May.

CONTACT: *Headquarters:* Death Valley National Park, PO Box 579, Death Valley, CA 92328; Tel: 7607863241; Web: www.nps.gov/deva.

COST: *Entrance* (7-day pass): Private vehicle, US$20; individual (foot, motorcycle, or bicycle): US$10. *Scotty's Castle:* Living history tour (adults), US$11; underground mysteries tour (adults): US$11.

ON-SITE AMENITIES: Visitors center and museum at Furnace Creek, Scotty's Castle, campgrounds, two hotels, restaurant and cafeteria, golf course.

BEST TIMES: Open year-round, but the best time is spring, when the wildflowers are in bloom. Summer is the off-season at Death Valley.

FIELD NOTES: Death Valley is usually sunny, dry, and clear year-round. Wear comfortable clothing, sturdy shoes, sunglasses, and sunblock. In the summer, don't forget a wide-brimmed hat and plenty of water.

DON EDWARDS SAN FRANCISCO BAY NATIONAL WILDLIFE REFUGE

CALIFORNIA, USA

Encompassing 30,000 acres of wetlands, mudflats, salt ponds, tidelands, vernal pools, and bay water, the Don Edwards San Francisco Bay National Wildlife Refuge was the first urban wildlife refuge in the United States. Established in 1974, the refuge, located along the southeastern shores of the heavily populated San Francisco Bay area, provides sanctuary for 280

species of shorebirds and migratory waterfowl. Millions of birds rest in the refuge every year during their spring and fall migrations. In addition, the refuge provides a year-round safe habitat for the endangered California clapper, a rail with a downward curving beak, and the salt marsh harvest mouse.

Spring brings spectacular wildflower displays to the refuge. It is also nesting time for more than 80 species of birds, including the marsh wren, salt marsh song sparrow, and the snowy plover. During the summer, the refuge becomes a nursery for many small mammals. The gray fox gives birth to her pups as does the harbor seal. In August, migratory birds from Canada, Alaska, and the Arctic begin to arrive by the hundreds of thousands. In October, migratory waterfowl arrive, as does the golden-crowned sparrow and yellow-rumped warbler. During the winter, thousands of waterfowl and shorebirds can be seen in the refuge; among them are the surf scoter, ruddy duck, bufflehead, and eared grebe; golden eagles are also occasionally seen.

LOCATION: *Visitors center:* Fremont, California, near the Dumbarton Bridge toll plaza.

HOURS OF OPERATION: *Visitors center:* Tues–Sun, 10 a.m. to 5 p.m.; closed on federal holidays. *Refuge trails:* Nov 1–Mar 31, 7 a.m. to 6 p.m.; Apr 1–Oct 31, 7 a.m. to 8 p.m.

CONTACT: *Visitors center:* Don Edwards San Francisco Bay National Wildlife Refuge, 1 Marshlands Rd, Fremont, CA 94536. *Park:* Tel: 5107920222; Web: www .fws.gov/desfbay; email: sfbaynwrc@ fws.gov.

COST: Free.

ON-SITE AMENITIES: The visitors center provides wildlife exhibits, educational programs (including information for school groups), an observation deck, trail maps, and a bookstore. About 30 miles of marked trails for self-guided tours run through the refuge.

BEST TIMES: Year-round; however, portions of the refuge are closed periodically for wildlife protection. Contact the visitors center for updates.

FIELD NOTES: Stay on marked trails at all times. Pick up a bird or plant brochure from the visitors center. Although binoculars can be borrowed from the visitors center, bring your own just to make sure you don't miss out. Dogs are allowed but must stay on a leash no longer than 6 feet. Fires, swimming, camping, and skateboarding as well as plant, animal, and mineral collection are prohibited.

LAVA BEDS NATIONAL MONUMENT

CALIFORNIA, USA

The area within the Lava Beds National Monument was created by numerous volcanic eruptions occurring over the course of a half million years; the most recent was a mere 1,000 years ago. The park's incredibly rugged, alien-looking terrain of lava flows, cinder cones, pit craters, and lava tube caves are the work of the Medicine Lake shield volcano. Most people think of volcanoes as having steep sides with a deep crater at the peak; a shield volcano, however, has gradually sloping sides that were built up over time as layers of lava flows solidified on top of each other. The profile of these volcanoes resemble a warrior's shield lying on the ground. Occasionally, hot lava flows beneath the cooled surface crust; these underground rivers of lava create

tubes or caves. There are more than 200 such caves in Lava Beds National Monument.

It takes a long time for lava fields to break down enough to form soil. Once this happens, plants are able to take hold; they in turn provide food and shelter for a variety of animals. Today, more than 50 species of mammals live in the monument area. The northern grasslands is home for jackrabbits, ground squirrels, kangaroo rats, marmots, quail, meadowlarks, sage grouse, hawks, and bald eagles. During the winter, mule deer come to feed in the area. Coyotes inhabit the park, as do foxes, bobcats, and black bears. The monument is also home to two species of frogs; several species of lizards and snakes, including rattlesnakes; and a few types of crustaceans and other invertebrates. Owing to the many caves, visitors can find at least 14 bat species living in the park.

The monument has miles of well-marked and maintained trails. Trail maps are available at the visitors center. While at the center be sure to see the natural history museum and take in the spectacular views of the surrounding valley from the observation deck. Cave exploration is a very popular activity at Lava Beds. Ladders and handrails have been installed in some caves, but only Mushpot Cave, located near the visitors center, has a lighting system. About a half mile from the center is the campground, which has 43 campsites for tents, pickup campers, and small trailers.

LOCATION: Approximately 20 miles south of the California–Oregon border, a 2-hour drive from Klamath Falls, Oregon, the closest city with a commercial airport.

HOURS OF OPERATION: *Monument:* Year-round, 24/7. *Visitors center:* winter, 8 a.m. to 5 p.m.; summer, 8 a.m. to 6 p.m. *Public toilets:* 24/7.

CONTACT: *Headquarters:* Lava Beds National Monument, 1 Indian Well, Tulelake, CA 96134. *Visitors center:* Tel: 5306678104; Web: www.nps.gov/labe.

COST: *Entrance* (7-day pass): Private vehicle, US$10; individual (on foot, motorcycle, or bicycle), US$5. *Campsite:* US$10. *Self-guided cave tours:* free.

ON-SITE AMENITIES: Visitors center, Lava Beds Natural History Museum, cave exploration, observation deck, campgrounds, toilet facilities, and bookstore. *Indian Well Campground:* 43 sites; features an amphitheater, two restrooms, and fresh drinking water.

BEST TIMES: April through October. The park is open year-round, but during the winter some roads may be closed due to snow. The park tries to keep the road to the visitors center plowed throughout the winter.

FIELD NOTES: Wear sturdy shoes and bring a flashlight for exploring the caves. Pets are permitted in the campgrounds but must stay on a leash; they are not permitted on trails or in the caves. There are no restaurants located in the park. The bookstore in the visitors center provides snack food, ice, flashlights (for loan or purchase), caving helmets, film, batteries, books, and souvenirs. Campsites are available year-round, as are water and restrooms. Note that the park may close portions of the campground for seasonal maintenance or energy efficiency in winter when campers are scarce. The visitors center, restrooms, and one campsite are handicapped accessible. Caves are inaccessible to anyone unable to navigate steep stairs and rocky trails; some caves have very low ceilings.

REDWOOD NATIONAL AND STATE PARKS

CALIFORNIA, USA

Looking out the window of a 30-story skyscraper to the street below gives one an appreciation of the towering height of the California coastal redwood tree. Growing as tall as 360 feet and with a diameter as much as 17 feet, coastal redwoods live 600 to 1,200 years and sometimes as long as 2,000 years! No wonder its scientific name is *Sequoia sempervirens*, Latin for "ever living." During the warmer Paleozoic Era over 160 million years ago, redwoods thrived in Europe, Asia, and North America. Today, only three genera still exist: the dawn redwood of central China, the giant sequoia of the southern Sierra Nevada mountain range in California, and the coastal redwood. The coastal redwood is found only along a 50-mile-wide band of the Pacific coast from southern Oregon to central California; the trees draw one quarter of their water needs from coastal fog.

In 1980, the Redwood National and State Park (RNSP) was created to protect the coastal redwood. Almost half of the world's remaining coastal redwoods live within the 131,983-acre park. The park includes 38,932 acres of

old-growth or never-cut, virgin forest. Besides the redwoods the park protects other indigenous flora and a variety of birds, reptiles, amphibians, and mammals: Steller's jays, chickadees, wrens, lizards, tree frogs, giant salamanders, elk, black bears, raccoons, and mountain lions can be seen in the park. The park includes some California coastline, offering protection for coastal beach, dune, and tidepool wildlife, such as the osprey, anemone, crab, and sea star. The RNSP is also home to many endangered and threatened species; visitors may see bald eagles, brown pelicans, northern spotted owls, snowy plovers, Chinook salmon, steelhead trout, marbled murrelet, and tidewater goby.

Walking among the redwoods is an incredible experience, and the RNSP has dozens of trails from which to enjoy the thrill. Visitors can take the Stout Grove Trail, a quarter-mile stroll through colossal redwoods or hike along the strenuous 10-mile round-trip Little Bald Hills Trail. Try one of the many other paths through the redwoods, along the coast, or among the tidepools; the park maintains more than 70 miles of trails. Campers can choose from four campgrounds, three among the redwoods and one along the coast.

LOCATION: The main park headquarters and information center is located in Crescent City, California. The north

end access of the park is approximately 10 miles south of Crescent City.

HOURS OF OPERATION: *Headquarters and information center:* Year-round; Mar–Oct, 9 a.m. to 5 p.m.; Nov–Feb, 9 a.m. to 4 p.m. *Ranger station:* Generally 8 a.m. to 4:30 p.m.

CONTACT: *Headquarters:* Redwood National and State Parks, 1111 Second St, Crescent City, CA 95531; Tel: 707-4657306; Web: www.nps.gov/redw.

COST: *Entrance:* Free. *Campgrounds:* Fees for day use, camping, and extra vehicle parking; call 8004447275 for information and reservations.

ON-SITE AMENITIES: Four campgrounds and four visitors/information centers are located in the park: Hiouchi information center and Jedediah Smith, Prairie Creek, and Kuchel visitors centers. Contact park headquarters for locations, directions, and hours of operation. Toilet and shower facilities are at the campgrounds, but no trailer hookups.

BEST TIMES: Open year-round, but during the winter some roads and trails may be closed. The Hiouchi information center is closed during the winter. Contact park headquarters for closure information.

FIELD NOTES: Wear layered clothing, hat, and sturdy hiking shoes. Bring insect repellant, food, and water. Dogs are allowed in the campgrounds but must stay on a 6-foot leash and must sleep in a tent or camper.

SHASTA-TRINITY NATIONAL FOREST

CALIFORNIA, USA

With an area of more than 3,450 square miles, Shasta-Trinity National Forest is the largest national forest in California. Varying in elevation from 1,000 to 14,162 feet above sea level, it includes five wilderness areas; forestland; 6,278 miles of rivers and streams; hundreds of mountain lakes; the largest manmade lake in California, Lake Shasta; and majestic Mount Shasta.

Dozens of tree species grow within the Shasta-Trinity National Forest, including a wide variety of conifers such as the sugar, ponderosa, foxtail, lodgepole, and western white pine; Douglas, California, and white fir; cedar; hemlock; and spruce. Hardwood trees such as black, tan, blue, and live oak thrive in the national forest as do maple, cottonwood, aspen, dogwood, and madrone. There are more than 300 species of wildflowers, including tiger lily, pitcher plant, yellow monkey, aster, and cycladenia.

This forest supports a diverse animal population, and bird-watchers might spot blue jays, ravens, warblers, hawks, falcons, and golden eagles. On the ground, black bears roam the mountainous areas, eating berries, grubs, and fish. Blacktail deer and a few small herds of elk inhabit the forest's lowlands and alpine meadows. Shasta-Trinity is also home to mountain lions, bobcats, coyotes, and red and gray foxes. Nocturnal animals such as raccoons, skunks, and the rarely seen ringtail cat quietly forage in the forest. Smaller mammals such as squirrels, chipmunks, bushy-tailed wood rats, jackrabbits, and martens can be seen throughout the forest.

Hiking, camping, auto-touring, wildlife photography, motor boating, house boating, windsailing, fishing, horseback riding, and hunting are popular recreational activities here. There are dozens of miles of well-marked trails and more than 300 miles of beach and shoreline along the many fingers of Lake Shasta. There are numerous designated public campgrounds, but visitors are free to camp just about everywhere in the forest, with few restrictions.

LOCATION: Main headquarters is located in Redding, California.

HOURS OF OPERATION: *Main headquarters and ranger station:* Generally 8 a.m. to 4:30 p.m.

CONTACT: *USDA Service Center:* 3644 Avtech Pkwy., Redding, CA 96002. *Headquarters:* Tel: 5302262500; Web: www.fs.fed.us/r5/shastatrinity.

COST: *Forest entrance:* Free. *Mount Shasta Wilderness Area entrance:* Free wilderness permit required. *Hiking:* Summit pass required for hikers going above 10,000 feet in elevation: US$15

for 3 days. *Campfires:* Free permit required for all wilderness areas; available at any ranger station. *Woodcutting:* Permits are US$5 per cord; may not be available during fire season. Permits and passes are available from the Mount Shasta or McCloud ranger station.

ON-SITE AMENITIES: Nine ranger stations/visitors centers are scattered throughout the national forest (contact main headquarters for locations). Toilet and shower facilities are at campgrounds. Boat docks, ramps, and boat rental concessioners are located at Shasta Lake.

BEST TIMES: May through October.

FIELD NOTES: Maps may be purchased in person or by mail from the National Forest Service. Most of the campsites are run on a first-come, first-served basis and fill quickly. Reservations can be made 180 days in advance for a few select sites by contacting the main headquarters reservations office.

YOSEMITE NATIONAL PARK

CALIFORNIA, USA

Yosemite National Park offers discovery after discovery as you explore the giant sequoias, granite cliffs, waterfalls, and other natural wonders, which are home to more than 400 species of vertebrates as well as 20% of California's flora. The natural duality between the meadows and the forests provides the perfect habitat for animals such as the great gray owl, willow flycatcher, Yosemite toad, and mountain beaver. As part of the Sierra Nevada mountain range, the varied elevation found in the park fosters the growth of populations of otherwise rare animals such as the pika, yellow-bellied marmot, white-tailed jackrabbit, Clark's nutcracker, and rosy finch. And the treeless alpine habitats are the areas favored by Sierra Nevada bighorn sheep.

A total of 37 animal species at Yosemite National Park currently have special status under either California or federal endangered species legislation. The park has instituted several programs to preserve the integrity of the natural ecosystems and to foster the preservation of the wildlife found there. The success of the black bear is an excellent example of how the park's evolving and comprehensive program supports and preserves the natural habitats in the Sierra Nevada. The park has implemented a variety of programs and policies designed to limit human–bear interaction while allowing visitors to observe and learn about these amazing creatures.

LOCATION: Sierra Nevada region of northeastern California, near the town of Mariposa.

HOURS OF OPERATION: Year-round, 24/7.

CONTACT: *Main office:* Yosemite National Park, PO Box 577, Yosemite, CA

95389; Tel: 2093720200; Web: www.nps .gov/yose.

COST: *Entrance:* Passenger vehicle, US$20. *Lodging* (per night): US$74–$482, depending on style and location.

ON-SITE AMENITIES: Campsites (most need advance reservations), picnic grounds, and lodging (from unheated tent camps to luxury hotels). Free shuttle buses, visitors centers, park rangers, and tours (including open-air trams led by park guides). The park also facilitates hiking and climbing; the Half-Dome day hike is one of the more popular yet arduous adventures.

BEST TIMES: Early spring to mid fall.

FIELD NOTES: Yosemite is a year-round park, but the winter months are often snow laden with limited activities for visitors. Popular destinations include the famous Mariposa Grove of giant sequoias, Tioga Road (a 30-mile scenic drive between Crane Flat and Tuolumne Meadows), and Glacier Point. Reservations for lodging and campgrounds are accepted up to 366 days in advance and are highly recommended; visit the park's website for more information. Parking remotely and using the free shuttle bus is advised.

ARAPAHO NATIONAL WILDLIFE REFUGE

COLORADO, USA

Located in north-central Colorado, the Arapaho National Wildlife Refuge lies in a glacial basin approximately 30 miles in diameter. Slow-running streams wind through the basin floor, creating lush meadows, ponds, and wetlands. Eventually, the streams merge to form the North Platte River. The basin's first visitors, the nomadic Ute Native Americans, came to the area during the summer to hunt buffalo. Rimmed by the Rabbit Ears, Never-Summer, and Medicine Bow mountain ranges, the natural corral was called the "Bull Pen" by the Utes.

Today, the refuge provides a protected place for migratory waterfowl to nest and rear their young. Founded in 1967, the 24,800-acre refuge is visited by tens of thousands of waterfowl a

year. They begin arriving in late April after the ice melts, and by late May, thousands of ducks and geese are nesting there. By the end of June, there are nearly 10,000 ducklings and goslings paddling about in the basin's many ponds. Visitors to the refuge can see mallard, pintail, gadwall, and American wigeon ducks. In the deeper ponds, there are diving ducks, like the redhead and lesser scaup. The refuge is also visited by a variety of marsh and shore-birds, including rails, willets, sandpipers, yellowlegs, dowitchers, herons, and grebes. Many of the waterfowl stay all summer, as their young grow and perfect their swimming, diving, and flying skills. With autumn comes additional migratory waterfowl. Winter arrives early at 8,800 feet, so by late October most migrating species have left.

The refuge has a variety of full-time residents as well. In the drier regions visitors will find sage grouse, prairie falcons, several species of hawks, and golden eagles. There are a variety of mammals too: beaver, muskrat, badger, pronghorn antelope, red fox, mink, weasel, and porcupine. Mule deer, elk, and moose also winter in the refuge.

LOCATION: The refuge headquarters are in Walden Colorado.

HOURS OF OPERATION: Year-round for day use. Only the main road to the headquarters building is kept open and plowed during winter.

CONTACT: *Headquarters:* Arapaho National Wildlife Refuge, 953 JC Rd 32, Walden, CO 80480; Tel: 9707238202; Web: www.fws.gov/Arapaho; email: arapaho@fws.gov.

COST: *Entrance:* Free. *Permits:* Required for fishing and hunting; contact the refuge headquarters for information and fees.

ON-SITE AMENITIES: Headquarters/visitors center and toilet facilities. The refuge maintains a self-guided 6-mile auto tour with numerous designated parking areas to stop and observe wildlife. There are also walking nature trails, built and maintained by Wildlands Restoration Volunteers.

BEST TIMES: May through early October. If planning to visit December through April call ahead to find out about weather, road conditions, and closures.

FIELD NOTES: Overnight camping is not allowed. Bring your own food, water, binoculars, and camera. Fires are not allowed. The refuge is closed to fishing from June 1 through July 31 to reduce disturbance to nesting birds.

ROCKY MOUNTAIN NATIONAL PARK

COLORADO, USA

There's a reason that nature lovers and biologists alike flock to Rocky Mountain National Park—to play, dream, experience, and study. The magnificence of the park cannot be exaggerated. From the wet, grassy valleys (at 8,000 feet in elevation) to the rugged mountaintops (Longs Peak rises 14,259 feet), visitors experience an amazing range of natural beauty.

The park is so vast and varied that visitors should be prepared for dramatic climate changes as they travel throughout the park and change elevations. Cool, clear summer mornings often give way to afternoon thundershowers; and the winter landscape can take on a lunar appearance with blinding snow and ripping wind.

Much of the park's abundant plant and animal life thrive around the 150 lakes and 450 miles of streams that make up the wetlands. However, the drier pine forests and grassy hillsides are home to many small tree-living and ground-dwelling critters.

Although the large mammals draw many visitors to the area, don't forget to look for some of the other 66 native mammal species in the park. Unfortunately, three native mammals are locally extinct—grizzly bear, gray wolf, and bison—and two others—lynx and wolverine—are quite rare. In fact, little is known about population trends in the park for most of the mammals, although elk, mule deer, and bighorn sheep have been monitored by park staff and researchers.

Rocky Mountain National Park is committed to protecting its animal population from the large elk to the small boreal toads. Visitors can readily spot and photograph at least some of the park's 1,000 elk. To observe the rare moose, travel to the Kawaneeche

Valley; and watch bighorn sheep at the mineral licks of Horseshoe Park. The sheep and mountain goats are usually found at higher elevations. Although secretive and rarely seen, mountain lions and bobcats are actually fairly common in the park. Bear lovers might see black bears in the park's lower forested areas.

In the winter, both snowshoe hares and ermine become white to blend in with the snow. Marmots and ground squirrels hibernate through the cold months, but should be easy to observe in the summer.

LOCATION: Estes Park, Colorado.

HOURS OF OPERATION: Year-round, 24/7. *Visitors center:* Daily, weather permitting, May 23–Oct 8, 10:30 a.m. to 4:30 p.m.

CONTACT: *Headquarters:* Rocky Mountain National Park, 1000 Hwy 36, Estes Park, CO 80517; Tel: 9705861206; Web: www.nps.gov/romo/index.htm.

COST: *Entrance* (7-day pass): Private vehicle, US$20; individuals (on foot, bicycle, motorcycle, and moped), US$10. Passes are available at all Rocky Mountain National Park entrance stations.

ON-SITE AMENITIES: Visitors center, restrooms, and trails. A free shuttle bus system runs throughout the park, providing terrific scenic tours. Other activities, such as bicycle, fishing, and horseback tours can be arranged through private contractors working in

the park. (Details available at the park's website.) *Camping:* The park has five drive-in campgrounds and one drive-in group camping area. Moraine Park and Glacier Basin campgrounds take reservations, as does the group camping area. Other campgrounds are first-come, first-served and fill on most summer days. No electric, water, or sewer hookups at any campsite.

BEST TIMES: Late April to late September.

FIELD NOTES: To keep you out of harm's way and to keep both bears and mountain lions at a safe and enjoyable distance practice the following rules: In campgrounds and picnic areas, if there is a food storage locker provided, use it. Avoid storing food and coolers in your vehicle; if you must, store food in airtight containers in the trunk or out of sight. Close vehicle windows completely. Do not store food in tents or popup campers in campgrounds or in vehicles at trailheads. Food, coolers, and dirty cookware left unattended, even for a short time, are subject to confiscation by park rangers. Dispose of garbage in bear-resistant dumping containers and trash cans. In the backcountry, store food, scented items, and garbage in commercially available bear-resistant portable canisters or carefully hang food 10 feet up and 4 feet out from a tree trunk. Pack out all garbage. Never try to retrieve anything from a bear. Report all bear incidents to a park ranger. Do not leave pets or pet food outside and unattended, especially at dawn and dusk. Pets can attract animals into developed areas. (Pets are permitted in the park but not on the trails or in the backcountry and must be kept on a leash at all times.) Avoid walking alone. Watch children closely and never let them run ahead or lag behind on the trail. Talk to children about lions and bears and teach them what to do if they meet one.

ZAPATA RANCH

SAN LUIS VALLEY, COLORADO, USA

Whether it's for relaxation, spectacular vistas, a taste of ranching with real cowboys and cowgirls riding herd, or hiking with an eye for wildlife and flora in the wholesome Colorado air, the Zapata Ranch has the best of the American West: a rich wealth of land and nature with the people working it taking nothing more than what they need.

Zapata, owned by the Nature Conservancy, is a working ranch at the base of the 14,000-foot Sangre de Christo Mountains and bordering the Great Sand Dunes National Park. At the ranch, traditional ranching is combined with progressive techniques in a bold experiment in modern land stewardship.

The 150,000-acre Great Sand Dunes National Park is named for its 700-foot-high sand dunes, considered to be the largest in North America. The park is located in a massive basin at an elevation of 7,500 feet, nestled between the San Juan and Sangre de Christo Mountains, about 4 hours away from either Boulder or Denver. The ranch lands are of tremendous biological significance, providing habitat for a number of rare animal and plant species, including the white-faced ibis and native insects. The ranch hosts one of the world's largest populations of slender spiderflowers.

In addition to the majestic sand dunes, the landscape also features thousands of acres of meadows, wetlands, and cottonwood groves populated with plenty of elk, deer, bison, coyotes, ferruginous hawks, and sage sparrows; the sandhill crane stops over when migrating.

Zapata Ranch dates back to the 1800s, but archaeological evidence reveals that Native Americans used the area for camps and for bison kills. It seems as though humankind has had an intimate relationship with this land and its animals for thousands of years.

The staff is well versed in scientific research and conservation, conducting workshops and guided tours as well as managing the cattle and bison ranch. Active and hardy visitors are invited to take part in the actual operation of the ranch, but feel free to just kick back and absorb the magic and wonder of the valley. Either way, the staff is happy to answer any and all questions in the truest tradition of western hospitality.

LOCATION: Mosca in the San Luis Valley region of southeast Colorado.

HOURS OF OPERATION: Year-round, except from Christmas through New Year's. *Park trail:* Mar–Oct, dawn to dusk.

CONTACT: Zapata Ranch, 5303 State Hwy 150, Mosca, CO 81146; Tel: 7193782356 or 8885ZAPATA (toll-free); Web: www.zranch.org; email: cowboy@zranch.org.

COST: *Ranch stay:* US$1,700 per week, all inclusive. *Pack trips:* US$2,500, including wilderness camping. Call for information on workshops and retreats. *Day trips:* Ranch visits, horseback riding on trails, bison tours by vehicle.

ON-SITE AMENITIES: Accommodations in restored traditional buildings, hot tub facilities, separate laundry.

BEST TIMES: March to October, when the scenic trails are open.

FIELD NOTES: Bring everything you need for warm days and cool evenings. Weather in the mountains is changeable, so pack sunscreen, hats, glasses, layers of clothes, and boots.

EVERGLADES NATIONAL PARK

FLORIDA, USA

Known for its stunning displays of wildlife, Everglades National Park, at the southern tip of Florida, is the largest subtropical wilderness in the United States. More than 40 species of mammals, many of which are endangered, live in the park. Everglades National Park is a wilderness area where the American alligator roams at will in the freshwater lakes, rivers, and swamps—and is often seen walking the park grounds. Besides alligators, you may spot American crocodiles, deer apple snails, and muskrats, all of which use the park's habitat for their survival.

Many of the few remaining Florida panther, which have been listed as endangered for more than 40 years, live in or near the park. West Indian manatees, another endangered animal, can be seen in groups resting just below the water's surface. (Boaters are asked to be particularly cautious so as not to hurt them.) Other endangered species that live in the park include the Atlantic ridley, hawksbill, and leatherback turtles. More than 366 species of birds

are found in the Everglades; look for the wood stork, the only species of stork found in North America, and the federally endangered red-cockaded woodpecker. Red fox, black bear, bobcat, river otter, and Everglades mink are among the mammals you may encounter.

Although not native to the park, pythons, boa constrictors, parakeets, and parrots have been spotted. And white-tailed deer are often seen wading through the sawgrass prairies, along with the wild hogs, which can be found roaming freely.

The park's many miles of walking trails and canoeing and kayaking routes provide plenty of opportunity for wildlife viewing and adventure. The Everglades 47 campsites range from chickees (elevated wooden platforms rising out of the water) to ground sites situated along the interior bays to beach sites along the coast.

LOCATION: Homestead, in south Florida. The park is accessible from various entrance gates: the main park entrance, Gulf Coast entrance, and Shark Valley.

HOURS OF OPERATION: Year-round, 24/7. *Main park and Gulf Coast entrances:* 24/7. *Shark Valley entrance:* Daily, 8:30 a.m. to 6 p.m.

CONTACT: *Headquarters:* Everglades National Park, 40001 State Rd, Homestead, FL 33034-6733; Tel: 3052427700; Fax: 3052427711; Web: www.nps.gov/ever.

COST: *Entrance:* Private vehicle, US$10; pedestrian/cyclist, US$5, children (16 years or younger), free; annual pass, US$25. *Camping* (per night): US$16.

ON-SITE AMENITIES: Visitors centers, campsites, picnic areas, ranger-led activities, lodging, camping, interpretive trails, marina, restaurants, walking trails (board trails are wheelchair accessible), and opportunities to canoe or kayak. Boat rentals and tours. For more information on tours, accommodations, and booking visit the park's website.

BEST TIMES: During the dry season (December to April), most facilities are open and a full range of tours and programs are available. During summer, expect rains and hurricanes; weather conditions can change dramatically and quickly.

FIELD NOTES: Biting insects are abundant during summer months. For summer camping, come prepared with all the necessities to do battle. Insect repellent alone may not be enough.

FLORIDA PANTHER NATIONAL WILDLIFE REFUGE

FLORIDA, USA

Weighing in at up to 150 pounds and measuring between 5 and 8 feet in length, the Florida panther is listed as a critically endangered member of the cougar family. There are only 80–100 of these amazing creatures left, which makes the mission of the Florida Panther National Wildlife Refuge vital.

Panthers need extensive areas for themselves and their mates. A breeding unit can require up to 200 square miles of territory and consists of one male and up to five females. For decades, the Florida panther's natural habitat has been sacrificed for human convenience, resulting in a decimation of the cat population. The Panther Refuge and two other contiguous parks provide the panthers with the area needed to roam and breed.

Besides the panther, many other species of mammals, birds, and reptiles can be found in the refuge, many listed as state or federally threatened, endangered, or of special concern. The Florida black bear, alligator, wood storks, limp-

kins, swallow-tailed kites, indigo snakes, Everglades minks, and big cypress fox squirrels are a few examples. Other residents of the refuge are white-tailed deer and feral hogs, which happen to be prey for the panthers. Wild turkeys and bobwhite quail can also be found on the grounds.

The Florida Panther National Wildlife Refuge offers the visitor two looped paths for wildlife observation. The first is handicap accessible, with a boardwalk and an overlook; it is roughly a third of a mile long. The second, less manicured path is just over 1 mile long

and is not handicap accessible. It offers a more tactile experience because the vegetation grows along and often in the path.

The best time for wildlife observation is in the early morning or late afternoon. Birds seen along the trails include the red-shoulder hawk, swallow-tailed kite, and osprey. The trails wind through hardwood hammocks, pine flatwoods, and wet prairies.

LOCATION: 20 miles east of Naples, Florida.

HOURS OF OPERATION: Year-round, dawn to dusk.

CONTACT: *Main office:* Florida Panther National Wildlife Refuge, 3860 Tollgate Blvd, Suite 300, Naples, FL 34114; Tel: 2393538442; Web: www.fws.gov/floridapanther; email: floridapanther@fws.gov.

COST: Free.

ON-SITE AMENITIES: Two main hiking trails, one of which is handicap accessible, various activities, guided tours, and special events through the year.

BEST TIMES: March through June.

FIELD NOTES: Water, insect repellent, and sunscreen are recommended. Visitors will need to allow themselves enough time to leave the refuge and return to their vehicles before the gates are locked at sunset. It is advised that you call the main office to check trail conditions before heading out. *Special note:* Due to the possibility of an encounter with a Florida panther it is advised that visitors hike in pairs or groups. Keep small children under very close observation. Should a panther approach hold your child as close to your body as possible, in an effort to appear larger. Do not crouch down or run; maintain eye contact with the panther as you back away slowly. If the panther should continue toward you it is recommended that you yell, shout, wave your arms, and/or throw sticks at the animal until it recedes.

TEN THOUSAND ISLANDS NATIONAL WILDLIFE REFUGE

FLORIDA, USA

Established in 1996, under the provisions of the Arizona-Florida Land Exchange, Ten Thousand Islands National Wildlife Refuge is part of the extensive Ten Thousand Islands estuary. The islands form a unique coastal system made up of barrier and back-bay islands, extending from Naples, Florida, through the Everglades National Park and Florida Bay.

Ten Thousand Islands National Wildlife Refuge, part of the largest mangrove forest in North America and covering more than 35,000 acres, is

home to an amazing array of wildlife: avian, aquatic, and mammal. But don't forget the reptiles; alligators in this area are plentiful and can be easily viewed and photographed from a comfortable distance.

Shorebirds, bald eagles, ospreys, loggerhead sea turtles (who drag themselves onto the beaches to nest), Indian manatees, river otters, and the bottlenosed dolphins call these islands home. In particular, wildlife enthusiasts can marvel at the settlement of some 10,000 wading birds during the summer months on a small island in Pumpkin Bay.

Wildlife viewing can be done by boat or on foot. Fishing is allowed inside the refuge. Anglers seek redfish, spotted sea trout, snook, and snapper. Boat launching facilities are available in Goodland and Port-of-the-Islands.

Marco Island, near the northern tip of the refuge, is an excellent departure point for your activities in the area.

Marco has hotels, boat charters, restaurants, and tour services. Remember that the majority of the islands offer few, if any, amenities.

LOCATION: 20 miles southeast of Naples, Florida, between Marco Island and Everglades City. The refuge is best accessed by boat. Launching points are found in Goodland and Port-of-the-Islands.

HOURS OF OPERATION: Year-round, 24/7.

CONTACT: *Headquarters:* Ten Thousand Islands National Wildlife Refuge, 3860 Tollgate Blvd, Naples, FL 34114; Tel: 2393538442; Web: www.fws.gov/south east/tenthousandisland.

COST: *Entrance:* Free. *Accommodations, tours, and activities:* Vary.

ON-SITE AMENITIES: The refuge hosts bird walks, canoe trips, and special events throughout the year. Check the website for current schedules. Accommodations can be found on Marco Island. For more information, visit http:// tenthousandislandsflorida.com.

BEST TIMES: Year-round.

FIELD NOTES: Activities include fishing, hunting, boating, photography, swimming, wildlife viewing, and camping. Backcountry camping on the islands is free but requires a permit. Camping is allowed only on the outer barrier islands of the refuge for the purposes of fishing and wildlife observation. There are no facilities on the islands. Campfires can be made only from dead branches found on the ground; no cutting of live trees or plants is permitted. In the winter, manatees gather at Port-of-the-Islands, north and south of the US 41 Bridge. Between 100 and 200 manatees can be seen here at any given time. Mosquitoes are abundant so take appropriate precautions.

BLACKBEARD ISLAND NATIONAL WILDLIFE REFUGE

GEORGIA, USA

Blackbeard Island National Wildlife Refuge, one of the oldest wildlife refuges in the United States, is named after the infamous pirate Edward Teach (1680–1718), aka Blackbeard. Legend has it that he made frequent trips to this island bank off the coast of Georgia to bury plundered treasure, although none of it has ever been found. In 1800 the US Navy bought the island and used its oak forests for shipbuilding. Between 1880 and 1910, the island was used to quarantine yellow fever victims.

The Bureau of Biological Survey began to manage the 5,600-acre island in 1924, turning it into a sanctuary for native wildlife and migratory birds. In 1940, President Roosevelt proclaimed it a National Wildlife Refuge. Currently, it is one of seven refuges totaling 56,000 acres managed by the Savannah Coastal Refuges Complex, in Savannah, Georgia.

Accessible only by boat, the island features pine and oak forest, interconnected sand dunes heavily covered by

oak and palmettos, freshwater and saltwater wetlands, and sandy beach. More than 11,000 visitors come here each year to observe and photograph the island's wildlife and natural wilderness beauty. They also come to participate in a variety of recreational activities, including hiking, biking, archery, hunting, fishing, crabbing, sea kayaking, swimming, and relaxing on the beach.

The refuge provides a safe haven for a variety of threatened and endangered species; among them are loggerhead and leatherback sea turtles, American bald eagles, American alligators, piping plovers, and wood storks. In addition, the refuge provides a temporary winter home for many migratory waterfowl. Blackbeard is also the home of many wading birds, shorebirds, songbirds, hawks, and falcons. The island has a population of deer and feral hogs, which can be hunted by permit during specific, designated times.

LOCATION: Eulonia, Georgia, in McIntosh County. The island is 18 miles southeast by boat.

HOURS OF OPERATION: Year-round, for day use.

CONTACT: Savannah Coastal Refuges, Parkway Business Center, 1000 Business Center Dr, Suite 120, Savannah, GA 31405; Tel: 9128324608; Web: www.fws.gov/blackbeardisland/index.htm; email: savannahcoastal@fws.gov.

COST: *Entrance:* Free. *Boat to the island:* Commercial transportation only; costs vary. *Permits:* Required for hunting; obtain through the Savannah Coastal Refuges.

ON-SITE AMENITIES: There is no headquarters or visitors center on the island. Public toilet facilities are available. The refuge offers environmental education and interpretive programs conducted by private commercial and nonprofit organizations. For a list of current tours operators click "Recreation Opportunities" on the refuge's website.

BEST TIMES: December through April is best for viewing migratory waterfowl that winter on the island. Other wildlife can be observed year-round.

FIELD NOTES: Overnight camping and fires are not allowed. Bring your own food and water.

HAWAIIAN ISLANDS HUMPBACK WHALE NATIONAL MARINE SANCTUARY

HAWAII, USA

Every year, 4,000–5,000 north Pacific humpback whales take a 3,000-mile-long swim from their cold-water feeding grounds off the coast of Alaska to the warm waters of the Hawaiian Islands. They begin arriving in December and stay through April. They've been making the trek every year since at least 1840, when 19th-century whalers first documented the humpback's amazing journey. While enjoying the warm waters and living off fat reserves (they eat only in Alaska's cooler waters), the humpbacks perfect their singing and acrobatic skills, attract mates, breed, calve, nurse, and begin raising their young within the Hawaiian Islands Humpback Whale National Marine Sanctuary.

Once plentiful, the 50-foot-long, 40-ton gentle giants were hunted to near extinction. Although estimates vary considerably, by the mid 20th century,

there may have been as few as 15,000 worldwide, down from a prewhaling population of 200,000. In 1966, the International Whaling Commission ordered the protection of the humpback. In 1973, the United States passed the US Endangered Species Act and immediately placed this whale on the

endangered list. To protect the whales' winter breeding ground, the National Oceanic and Atmospheric Administration (NOAA) began a campaign to protect the area around the Hawaiian Islands. In 1992, the US Congress passed the Hawaiian Islands National Marine Sanctuary Act, and in 1997 an area of 1,400 square miles near Hawaii was established as a whale habitat sanctuary, the only US sanctuary of its kind. Today, the humpback population is rebounding, thanks to the sanctuary's habitat protection and public awareness programs as well as the efforts of other like-minded organizations.

In addition to its mission of habitat protection and scientific research and study of the humpback whale, the sanctuary runs a public education and visitors center located in Kihei on the island of Maui. The center includes a whale museum, elevated whale-watching platforms, and a variety of public educational and outreach programs.

There are a number of whale-watching locations along the shores of the sanctuary, such as the Lanai Lookout on the east side of Oahu. The colossal creature's acrobatic skills, breeching, and spouting can be seen from miles away; their songs can be heard 800 feet away. For those who'd like a closer look, there are whale-watching tour boat operators located on the islands of Maui, Hawaii, Oahu, and Kauai. Tours typically last 2–3 hours and operate daily from late December through April. In addition to the migratory humpback whale, the sanctuary is also the year-round home of sperm whales, pilot whales, pygmy killer whales, melon-headed whales, and beaked whales.

LOCATION: The sanctuary education center is on Maui.

HOURS OF OPERATION: Mon–Fri, 10 a.m. to 3 p.m.

CONTACT: *Education center:* Hawaiian Islands Humpback Whale National Marine Sanctuary, 726 S. Kihei Rd, Kihei, HI 96753; Tel: 8088792818 or 8008314888 (toll-free); Web: http://hawaiihumpbackwhale.noaa.gov.

COST: *Education center:* Free.

ON-SITE AMENITIES: Museum, elevated whale-watching platform, gift shop/bookstore.

BEST TIMES: Late December through April.

FIELD NOTES: Want to get some real hands-on experience? Each year the sanctuary hosts an ocean count program, in which residents and visitors to the islands can take part in a volunteer whale count. The program allows visitors to observe humpback whales in their breeding grounds by taking part in the shore-based census taken during the peak breeding season. Registration for the Sanctuary Ocean Count program starts each December (for more information and to register, contact the island coordinator: Hawaii and Oahu, 88855WHALE, ext. 253; Kauai, 8082462860). Some sites fill up quickly, so it is recommended that you register as early as possible.

CAMAS NATIONAL WILDLIFE REFUGE

IDAHO, USA

Established in 1937, Camas National Wildlife Refuge provides a valuable nesting and breeding grounds for thousands of migratory waterfowl. The refuge encompasses about 10,500 acres, of which about half is lake, pond, marshland, or mudflat. In the spring and fall, thousands of migratory waterfowl descend on the refuge. Visitors may see as many as 50,000 birds, including tundra and trumpeter swans; mallard, redhead, and ruddy ducks; gadwall, shoveler, and scaup ducks; and Canada goose. Many birds stay long enough to nest and breed, leaving the ponds and lakes teeming with ducklings and goslings during the late spring and summer.

Songbirds visit the refuge too, albeit on a different schedule than the water-fowl. During spring migration (May to June), the number of songbirds peaks. After resting, feeding, and regaining their energy, the birds continue on their northerly flights. Activity peaks again in August through September, when the songbirds are heading south for the winter. Bird-watchers can expect to see larks, swallows, kinglets, bluebirds, thrushes, robins, mockingbirds, starlings, and warblers.

The refuge's marshes and mudflats make great temporary homes for various species of egrets, herons, sandpipers, ibis, and cranes. The drier areas and grasslands provide year-round homes for pheasants, grouse, owls, hawks, falcons, turkey vultures, and bald eagles.

Mammal lovers will find plenty of species to keep them interested. The refuge is home to voles, ground squirrels, and deer mice as well as muskrats, beavers, cottontail rabbits, weasels, badgers, red foxes, and coyotes. The white-tailed deer is the most common large mammal, but mule deer, pronghorn antelope, elk, and moose are also present year-round.

LOCATION: Refuge headquarters are in Hamer, Idaho, 36 miles north of Idaho Falls.

HOURS OF OPERATION: Year-round, daylight hours. *Headquarters:* Mon–Fri, 7 a.m. to 4:40 p.m.

CONTACT: *Headquarters:* Camas National Wildlife Refuge, 2150 E. 2350 N, Hamer, ID 83425; Tel: 2086625423; Web: www.stateparks.com/camas.html.

COST: *Entrance:* Free. *Permits:* Required for hunting (contact headquarters for hours and bag limits).

ON-SITE AMENITIES: Headquarters office, toilet facilities, hiking trails.

BEST TIMES: Spring and fall are best for observing migrating birds.

FIELD NOTES: With a permit, ducks, geese, coots, snipe, pheasant, and sage grouse may be hunted. No other species may be killed. Temporary blinds may be constructed and taken down at the end of each day; permanent blinds are not permitted. Wear comfortable walking shoes. Bring camera and binoculars. There are no food concessions, picnic tables, or campgrounds. Hunters must use nontoxic shot. No fishing or boating is allowed.

NEAL SMITH NATIONAL WILDLIFE REFUGE

IOWA, USA

A visit to the Neal Smith National Wildlife Refuge will provide you with an experience much like that of yesteryear. The midwestern United States used to be a vast tallgrass prairie land extending for hundreds of miles across what is now 14 states and into Canada. Interspersed among the grasslands were savannas, or pockets of park-like areas of bur oak, walnut, and hickory trees. Estimates vary, but as recently as two centuries ago perhaps as many as 75 million buffalo roamed the midwestern prairie. In 1806 Lewis and Clark wrote about them, saying that the moving herds "darkened the whole plains." By 1900, there were only 300 buffalo left in the United States. The animals had been hunted almost to extinction, their native lands had been plowed, converted into farmland, and built on to create cities and towns.

In recognition of Iowa's lost prairie, US Congressman Neal Smith championed the creation of a refuge to protect and restore Iowa's natural grasslands and savannas. In 1990 Congress approved the creation of the refuge, and in 1991 the first parcel of land was purchased by the federal government. Originally named Walnut Creek National Wildlife Refuge, the area was later renamed after the congressman who advocated for its creation. Today, the refuge protects 5,000 acres and is again home for growing herds of buffalo and elk. In addition, the protected tallgrass and savannas hold a diversity of wildlife. There are hundreds of plant species and more than 350 species of birds. Among the nearly 100 species of mammals are white-tailed deer, beavers, badgers, weasels, and plains pocket gophers. The federally endangered Indiana bat has been recorded in the refuge.

A recent moth survey revealed more than 530 species, including one new to science. The refuge's ongoing effort to develop the habitat of and reintroduce the regal fritillary, a rare prairie butterfly, has resulted in a resident population. The refuge is also home to dozens of amphibians, reptiles, and fish.

Paved trails radiate out from the visitors center. There is a 740-acre bison and elk enclosure that can be toured via private automobile along a 4.5-mile paved road. Portions of the refuge are open for hunting deer and game birds.

LOCATION: 20 miles east of Des Moines, Iowa, on state Rte 163 (E. University Ave).

HOURS OF OPERATION: *Visitors center:* Year-round, daily; Mon–Sat, 9 a.m. to 4 p.m.; Sun, 12 p.m. to 5 p.m. Closed Thanksgiving, Christmas, and New Year's Day. *Wildlife drive/nature trails:* Year-round, daily, sunrise to sunset.

CONTACT: Neal Smith National Wildlife Refuge, PO Box 399, Prairie City, IA 50228; Tel: 5159943459; Web: www .fws.gov/midwest/nealsmith; email: nealsmith@fws.gov.

COST: *Entrance:* Free.

ON-SITE AMENITIES: Visitors center, bookstore, theater, educational classrooms, restroom facilities, walking trails, and scenic drives. *Hunting:* Permits required; contact visitors center for rules and regulations.

BEST TIMES: Winters can be harsh. Spring is the best time for blooming wildflowers.

FIELD NOTES: Bring a camera and good walking shoes. Some of the trails are paved with gravel and others with wood chips. For safety reasons, stay in the car when driving through the buffalo and elk enclosure.

ACADIA NATIONAL PARK

MAINE, USA

Located in Hancock County, Maine, Acadia National Park encompasses a number of islands and some inlet areas but is best known for Mount Desert Island, which is surpassed in size in the northeast only by New York's Long Island. The island is also known for Cadillac Mountain, rustic enclaves,

businesses offer both land- and sea-based tours of the area.

The lodging is as diverse as the landscape. For those interested in roughing it, many campgrounds are available. If you are looking for a step up, a B&B or a cabin rental may be in order. Going to the other extreme, five-star hotels overlooking the water are only minutes away.

and incredible fishing; it's the epitome of the quaint charm of New England.

For wildlife enthusiasts, the heights of the Cadillac Mountain area combined with the beautiful Atlantic coast provides an array of distinct ecosystems within hours of each other. More than 270 species of birds are found in Acadia; many of them use the area for breeding. Here you can see the endangered peregrine falcon and the bald eagle. And among the many mammals that inhabit the park are coyotes, white-tailed deer, red foxes, snowshoe hares, beavers, and harbor seals. Whale watching is another favorite activity at Acadia.

There are more than 120 miles of trails in the park, ranging from the short and brief to the aptly titled Precipice Trail; many of them interlock, allowing hikers to climb several peaks in a single day. Park rangers are available to offer advice and sometimes guide a tour. In addition, numerous private

LOCATION: Hancock County, Maine. The winter visitors center is on Rte 233 (Eagle Lake Rd), 2 miles west of Bar Harbor; Hulls Cove. The main visitors center is on Rte 3 north of Bar Harbor; the Thompson Island information center is on Rte 3, just over the bridge from the mainland.

HOURS OF OPERATION: *Headquarters:* Year-round; closed Thanksgiving Day, Dec 24–25, and Jan 1. *Hulls Cove:* Apr 15–Oct 31. *Thompson Island:* Mid May–mid Oct. Hours vary; see the park's website for more information.

CONTACT: *Main office:* Acadia National Park, PO Box 177, Bar Harbor, ME 04609; Tel: 2072883338; Web: www.nps.gov/acad.

COST: *Entrance* (7 days): Personal vehicle, June 23 to early October, US$20, May 1 to June 22, US$10; individual (on foot, motorcycle, or bicycle), US$5. Annual passes are available. Some ranger-led programs require a fee, though most are free. *Camping and other activities:* Check the park's website for fees and requirements, which depend on the site and season.

ON-SITE AMENITIES: Museums, campgrounds, visitors centers, biking, boating, climbing, fishing, picnicking, scenic drives, tide pooling, horseback riding, and swimming. Expert guides, senior and junior ranger programs. **Jordan Pond House Restaurant:** This is the only dining facility in the park; they serve lunch, tea, and dinner from mid May through late October.

BEST TIMES: May through October.

FIELD NOTES: Everything that you would need to purchase can be found in the park. A first aid kit, water, and food are recommended for campers. Binoculars, field books, comfortable walking shoes, and seasonal clothing are recommended. Some ranger-led programs require reservations made no more than 3 business days in advance. Firewood may not be brought in from other areas because it could contain nonnative insect species, which could pose a serious threat to the park's resources; quarantines have been issued for some areas. Firewood is available and can be purchased locally near both Blackwoods Campground and Seawall Campground in the park.

MOOSEHORN NATIONAL WILDLIFE REFUGE

MAINE, USA

Designated as one of the oldest national wildlife refuges and part of the early conservation movement in America, Moosehorn National Wildlife Refuge is home to an amazing array of wildlife, including migrating waterfowl, wading birds, shorebirds, upland game birds, songbirds, and birds of prey.

The refuge is made up of two parts: the Baring Division is larger at 17,200 acres, and is located southwest of Calais. The Edmunds Division is 7,200 acres and is located between Dennysville and Whiting; it borders the tidal waters of Cobscook Bay. Within each division is a national wilderness area, which is home to moose, beavers, black bears, deer,

foxes, porcupines, red squirrels, painted turtles, snapping turtles, and many salamanders and frogs.

The refuge is situated in the Atlantic flyway, so bird-watchers can expect to spot Canada geese, American black ducks, common golden eyes, ruffed grouse, American woodcocks, herring gulls, northern flickers, tree and barn swallows, American robins, and ovenbirds. Other birds in the refuge are red-winged blackbirds, least sandpipers, and Bonaparte gulls, ospreys, common loons, American kestrels, various owls, and bald eagles.

LOCATION: Southwest of Calais, Maine.

HOURS OF OPERATION: Year-round, from a half hour before sunrise to a half hour after sunset. Access to the refuge in the evenings and at night by special-use permit. *Headquarters:* Mon–Fri, 8 a.m. to 4 p.m., except holidays. An information booth provides after-hours visitors with brochures and maps.

CONTACT: Moosehorn National Wildlife Refuge, RR 1 Box 202, Suite 1, Charlotte Rd, Baring, ME 04694; Tel: 2074547161; Fax: 2074542550; Web: www.fws.gov/northeast/moosehorn; email: fw5rw_mhnwr@fws.gov.

COST: *Entrance:* Free.

ON-SITE AMENITIES: Headquarters office, after-hours information booth; two observation decks, more than 50 miles of trails; educational programs and special events. Visitors who call ahead are invited to accompany wildlife biologists on woodcock- and waterfowl-branding operations.

BEST TIMES: March through May. Dawn and dusk are ideal for wildlife viewing.

FIELD NOTES: Excellent brook trout, smallmouth bass, and pickerel waters are found throughout the refuge. Visitors should check state and federal regulations for rules and regulations. The refuge hosts a children's fishing derby in June. Other activities include biking and skiing.

ASSATEAGUE ISLAND NATIONAL SEASHORE AND WILDLIFE REFUGE

MARYLAND, USA

Wild ponies have lived on Assateague Island since the 1600s. No one is certain how the ponies—horses, really—got there, but early colonial settlers may have used the narrow, 37-mile-long, 48,000-acre island as a natural corral for grazing horses. Or perhaps a Spanish galleon with a cargo of horses sank offshore. Recently, a Spanish shipwreck was discovered on the ocean floor just off the island, lending credence to the Spanish galleon theory. Regardless, the horses became well adapted to a predator-free life on the island, living off cordgrass, dune grasses, bayberry twigs, and persimmons. Today, the island supports over 300 wild horses, divided into two herds of approximately equal number, separated by a fence along the Maryland–Virginia state line.

Established in 1962, the Assateague Island National Seashore and Wildlife Refuge provides a protected, year-round habitat for plant and animal wildlife as well as a safe resting and feeding area for migratory birds. The refuge also provides a number of recreational activities for visitors, including sightseeing, hiking, crabbing, bird-watching, wild pony tours, fishing, hunting, biking, swimming, and beachcombing along some of the best beaches on the east coast. The 142-foot-tall Assateague Lighthouse, constructed in 1833, is on the National Register of Historic Places and, with its alternating red and white bands, is one of the most recognizable lighthouses in the nation. Visitors can tour the working lighthouse.

During the spring, large numbers of migratory birds descend on the island.

Visitors can see herons, terns, rails, pelicans, ducks, and snow geese. Bald eagles, peregrine falcons, and great horned owls are among the refuge's full-time bird residents. More than 300 species of migrating and resident birds frequent the island. In addition to the wild ponies, the island is home to a variety of other mammals, including sika and white-tailed deer, red foxes, river otters, Virginia possums, raccoons, eastern cottontail rabbits, and a variety of bats.

LOCATION: About 9 miles south of Ocean City, Maryland. The Maryland–Virginia state line divides Assateague Island in half. The Maryland visitors center/park headquarters is in Berlin; the Virginia visitors center is in Chincoteague Island.

HOURS OF OPERATION: Year-round; Maryland—24/7; Virginia—hours vary, contact the visitors centers for more information.

CONTACT: *Maryland headquarters/visitors center:* 7206 National Seashore Ln, Berlin, MD 21811; Tel: 4106411443; Web: www.assateagueisland.com and www.nps.gov/asis. *Barrier Island visitors center:* Tel: 4106411441. *Sinepuxent District Rangers Station/campground office:* Tel: 4106413030. *Toms Cove visitors center:* 8231 Beach Rd, Chincoteague Island, VA 23336; Tel: 7573366577.

COST: *Entrance* (7-day pass): Private vehicle, US$10; individual (on foot, motorcycle, or bicycle), US$3; passes are good for both Maryland and Virginia sides of the island. *Permits:* Required for over-sand vehicles, overnight camping, fishing, and campfires; contact the park headquarters for more information.

ON-SITE AMENITIES: Island marine ecotours, nature trails, swimming, birdwatching, crabbing, fishing, sightseeing, and more than 37 miles of beaches. The refuge has two visitors centers: Toms Cove and Barrier Island. Toms Cove features wildlife exhibits, a hands-on tide pool touch tank, bookstore, and gift shop.

BEST TIMES: May through October.

FIELD NOTES: At the end of every July on the Virginia side (the exact time is not announced until the day before), there is a wild pony swim across tidal marshlands to the mainland, where the horses are sold at auction. Some 150 ponies are rounded up to make the swim, while as many as 40,000 visitors watch from along the shoreline. Depending on personal preference, you might want to join or avoid the ponyswim crowd. *Camping:* Campsites are available on the Maryland side in both the state and national parks. Campers can choose from either oceanside or bayside sites, each with its own advantages and disadvantages. Camping oceanside in the state park allows for hot showers, but coastal windy conditions prevail. Camping on the bayside means cold showers; however, it is best for experiencing the wild horses. Each day at dawn and dusk, herds of eight or more of these grand beings travel to each and every campsite looking for handouts. *Remember:* It is illegal to feed or pet the horses. All food supplies should be kept in your vehicle at all times, even when you are on-site. Mosquitoes are abundant here; insect repellent should always be kept on hand. You need to bring your own firewood or purchase it from nearby vendors. There are some great crabbing sites in the area, one of the best being just before the bridge leading you to the island. Take a steaming pot with you for an unforgettable fresh crab lunch. Assateague Island is a great spot for families; kids love it. Camping sites book fast so you'll want to make your reservations as early as possible.

BLACKWATER NATIONAL WILDLIFE REFUGE

MARYLAND, USA

It is not only the ducks and geese that make this refuge special. The Blackwater National Wildlife Refuge is also home to the largest breeding population of bald eagles on the east coast, the endangered Delmarva fox squirrel, and the migrant peregrine falcon.

Located on the eastern shore of Maryland, and approximately 12 miles south of Cambridge, the refuge, consisting of 27,000 acres, was originally established in 1933 to protect ducks and geese that were migrating along the Atlantic flyway. Today the refuge hosts more than 35,000 geese and 15,000 ducks, during the November migration.

A trip to Blackwater offers visitors a variety of activities. A scenic trip down Wildlife Drive provides outstanding views of waterfowl, shorebirds, turtles, bald eagles, osprey, and the Delmarva fox squirrel. It's the visitor's choice here: walk, drive, or bike the scenic 4-mile-long route. There are several osprey platforms located along the drive, which allow bird-watchers the opportunity to get up close and personal.

Perhaps butterflies are more your thing. In 2002, Blackwater officially

opened their butterfly garden located behind the visitors center. The garden features a variety of butterfly-attracting plants; thus a brilliant collection of butterflies frequent the grounds.

If you're a hiker, the refuge has four scenic land trails: the Marsh Edge Trail, which runs along the Little Blackwater River and the Blackwater River for about a third of a mile, is the most popular. The trail provides hikers with a covered picnic area, benches, and an observation boardwalk that extends out into the river. The half-mile-long Woods Trail offers visitors a chance to spot the Delmarva fox squirrel. The Key Wallace Hiking Trail and Demonstration Forest is the longest land trail in Blackwater at 2.7 miles. The Tubman Trail (named after Harriet Tubman, who was born in the area) leads visitors through mixed pine and hardwood forests; at just under 2 miles, it takes 1.5 hours to complete.

Blackwater has three marked water trails for canoes and kayaks, which can be used to explore the tidal marshes and brackish ponds for an up-close look at the refuge's residents and visiting wildlife. Cyclists will find several routes to choose from. Even fishing and crabbing are allowed in the refuge in season—but by boat only and not from shore.

LOCATION: Cambridge, Maryland.

HOURS OF OPERATION: *Wildlife Drive and associated trails:* Daily, dawn to dusk. *Visitors center:* Daily, Mon–Fri, 8 a.m. to 4 p.m.; Sat–Sun, 9 a.m. to 5 p.m. Closed Thanksgiving Day and Christmas Day.

CONTACT: *Headquarters:* Blackwater National Wildlife Refuge, 2145 Key Wallace Dr, Cambridge, MD 21613; Tel: 4102282677 or 8007352258 (TDD); Web: www.fws.gov/blackwater; email: fw5rw_bwnwr@fws.gov.

COST: *Permits:* Daily permit required for all visitors to Wildlife Drive; permit fees waived for those with an annual pass, lifetime passport, or current duck stamp. *Permit fees:* Private vehicle, US$3; individual (pedestrian or bicyclist), US$1; commercial van or bus, depends on number of passengers (contact headquarters for more information). Passes are available at the visitors center; information about duck stamps and passes can be found on the refuge's website.

ON-SITE AMENITIES: The visitors center features wildlife exhibits, an authentic eagle's nest, Eagle Cam and Osprey Cam monitors, book and gift shop, butterfly garden, restrooms, maps and brochures, and an informational kiosk. It also houses a nature observatory, which features bird exhibits and spotting scopes for viewing the Blackwater River, the marsh, and the Osprey Cam platform. There is also a library where visitors can browse the refuge book collection to learn more about the local wildlife and birding.

BEST TIMES: October through December for the largest concentration of wildlife.

FIELD NOTES: Pets are not allowed out of vehicles on the Wildlife Drive or on the trails, even if on a leash. This policy is to protect the endangered ground-feeding Delmarva fox squirrel. Pets can be walked in the parking lot around the visitors center.

ISLE ROYALE NATIONAL PARK

MICHIGAN, USA

Located on the northwestern corner of majestic Lake Superior, Isle Royale National Park is made up of a unique and remote island archipelago. Historically, its physical isolation and primitive wilderness was a hindrance to human habitation; ironically, today that wildness is precisely one of the island's main attractions. Accessible only by boat or seaplane, visitors enjoy this island park by hiking its trails, exploring its rugged coast, paddling its inland waterways, or venturing into deeper waters to view its shipwrecks.

This rugged northwood's wilderness, encompassing one large island and almost 400 smaller islands, is a roadless backcountry that's home to wild creatures, secondary growth forests, refreshing lakes, and rugged shores. Its 850 square miles include submerged land, which extends 4.5 miles out into the largest freshwater lake in the world.

One of the biggest draws for visitors to this park is its large mammal population. The ecological study of wolves on Isle Royale, now in its 46th year, is the longest-running, large-mammal predator–prey study on earth. Research has shown that all members of the Isle Royale wolf population have descended from a single female, which arrived during the late 1940s. This intense level of inbreeding has led to a 50% loss of genetic variability within the population today. Genetic information suggests that the island's moose population is most closely related to moose in northwestern Minnesota—perhaps challenging the long-held idea that moose swam across the lake to reach Isle Royale and instead suggesting that humans may have transported them there.

Other mammals found in the park include beavers, coyotes, red foxes, lynx, skunks, and squirrels. Visitors may see loons, herons, snow and Canada geese, ducks, and birds of prey such as hawks and falcons.

LOCATION: Isle Royale National Park is located in the northwest corner of Lake Superior. The transportation services depart from Houghton and Copper Harbor, Michigan, and Grand Portage, Minnesota.

HOURS OF OPERATION: *Rock Harbor visitors center* (northeast corner of park): Daily, July–Aug, 8 a.m. to 6 p.m.; May–June, Sept, reduced schedule. *Windigo visitors center* (southwest corner of park): Daily, July–Aug, 8 a.m. to 4:30 p.m.; May–June, Sept, reduced schedule. *Houghton visitors center:* June–July, Mon–Fri, 8 a.m. to 6 p.m., Sat, 11 a.m. to 6 p.m.; Aug–mid Sept, reduced hours. Call 9064820984, to check hours of all visitors centers. The park is closed Nov 1–Apr 16.

CONTACT: *Administrative offices:* Isle Royale National Park, 800 E. Lakeshore Dr, Houghton, MI 49931-1896; Tel: 9064820984; Fax: 9064828753; Web: www.nps.gov/isro.

COST: *Entrance* (per day): US$4. *Season passes:* Individual, US$50; boat rider, US$150.

ON-SITE AMENITIES: Visitor centers, hiking trails, interpretive programs, campsites, and guided tours.

BEST TIMES: April through October.

FIELD NOTES: If you only have a day at Isle Royale, several short hikes will get you into the backcountry for solitude and exploration. Pick the 1-mile trip near Windigo or the 4-mile loop to Scovill Point. One option is to take a ranger-led walk. Hikers should carry water, snacks, rain gear, and a first aid kit. Wear broken-in sturdy boots or walking shoes. Mosquitoes and black flies are abundant in late June and early July so bring repellent.

GLACIER NATIONAL PARK

MONTANA, USA

Around 20,000 years ago a thick blanket of ice covered everything in northwest Montana except for the tallest peaks of the Rocky Mountains. When the ice receded, it left behind its artistry: sculpted cliffs, carved canyons and valleys, streams, lakes, waterfalls, and glaciers, with a towering ridge of mountains forming part of the continental divide. Montana's early inhabitants, the Blackfeet, aptly called the mountains *Miistakis*, or the "Backbone of the World." Today, nearly 1,600 square miles of this still-pristine ecosystem forms Glacier National Park.

Glacier National Park, founded in 1910, is so named because of its many glaciers. In the late 19th century, explorers reported approximately 150 glaciers;

today there are 27. More than 1,100 species of plants flourish within the park, including bear grass, monkey flower, glacier lily, Indian paintbrush, red cedar, hemlock, limber pine, western larch, Engelmann spruce, and Douglas fir. Some 30 species of these plants are found nowhere else. Wildlife abounds throughout the park and may be seen at any time. There are 260 species of birds, including the peregrine falcon, great horned owl, the gold and bald eagles, and several species of hawks. Among the more than 60 species of mammals, visitors may observe mountain goats (the park's official symbol), bighorn sheep, moose, elk, several species of deer, coyotes, wolves, badgers, wolverines, otters, and black bears. The park is also home for two threatened species: the grizzly bear and Canada lynx. Fish abound in the park's numerous streams, and more than 700 lakes (less than half of these are named). Among the 23 species found are cutthroat trout, northern pike, kokanee salmon, mountain whitefish, and the endangered bull trout.

Although the park is in a sparsely populated part of the country, nearly 2 million people visit it each year. It offers numerous recreational activities, including short nature and wildlife walks, hiking, backpacking, fishing, biking, camping, boating, horseback riding, vehicle touring, and cross-country skiing. There are more than 700 miles of well-marked trails winding throughout the park, varying in length and difficulty from short nature walks to day-long hikes, to overnight backpacking adventures. Sightseers shouldn't miss driving the 53-mile-long Going-to-the-Sun Road, which bisects the park and crosses the continental divide at Logan Pass at an elevation of 6,646 feet. Completed in 1932, the Going-to-the-Sun Road is the only American roadway listed as both a National Historic Landmark and a Historic Civil Engineering Landmark.

The park, along with its authorized concessioners, offers a variety of hiking, boating, horseback, and bus and van tours. Educational tours that focus on the wildlife, geology, history, and culture of the park are available. For example, the Blackfeet Nation offers a day-long bus tour through the park along the Going-to-the-Sun-Road that offers a Native American spiritual and philosophical perspective of the scenic parklands.

LOCATION: Northwestern Montana, 25 miles east of Kalispell.

HOURS OF OPERATION: Year-round, 24/7; not all areas are open or accessible during the winter. Most facilities are open late May–early Sept.

CONTACT: *Headquarters:* Glacier National Park, PO Box 128, West Glacier, MT 59936; Tel: 4068887800; Web: www .nps.gov/glac.

COST: *Entrance* (7-day pass; May 1–Oct 31): Individual, US$12; noncommercial car with passengers, US$25.

ON-SITE AMENITIES: Many Glaciers Hotel: Located along the shores of Swiftcurrent Lake, US$135–$255. Many food concessioners, bars, and gift shops; facilities for backcountry camping, bicycling, and boating are found within the park. Boat tours and rentals, bus tours, fishing, guided hiking, and horseback riding are available. Campgrounds are run on a first-come, first-served basis with the exception of Fish Creek and St. Mary, which may be reserved in advance by contacting the Park Recreation and Reservation Service.

BEST TIMES: Late May through early September. Autumn is less crowded, and the colors are spectacular in late September and early October, but not all facilities are open.

FIELD NOTES: Campground reservations are advisable; permits are required for fishing and overnight backpacking. Dogs are not allowed on the hiking paths.

FORT NIOBRARA NATIONAL WILDLIFE REFUGE

NEBRASKA, USA

For thousands of years the water and lands of Fort Niobrara National Wildlife Refuge have been residence to a diverse array of wildlife. Fossils found throughout the refuge grounds confirm that the area was once home to more than 20 now-extinct species, including the long-jawed mastodon, giant bison, and the three-toed horse. In more modern times, large herds of bison and elk were once plentiful in the area, but overhunting and habitat loss have led to their decline.

Fort Niobrara Military Reserve was established in 1879 as part of the effort to moderate relations between settlers and the Sioux Indians. Once it was no longer needed as a military base, the area was designated to be a preserve and breeding ground for native birds. In 1912, the mission was expanded to include the conservation of bison and elk, which once foraged in the grasslands of the Great Plains.

Visitors to the refuge can observe some of the 350 bison and 100 elk that live within the grounds. Each fall, about 120 bison are auctioned off; this helps maintain the herd numbers and preserve the habitat for future generations. The auction is open to the public.

Fort Niobrara is home to more than 48 types of mammals, including prairie dogs and white-tailed and mule deer. Bird lovers will find more than 230 varieties and may spot a burrowing owl, sharp-tailed grouse, or prairie chicken. Many reptile, amphibian, and fish species also live within the refuge boundaries.

LOCATION: About 5 miles east of Valentine, Nebraska, on US Hwy 12. The visitors center is about 1 mile from the refuge entrance.

HOURS OF OPERATION: *Visitors center:* Daily, Memorial Day–Labor Day, 8 a.m. to 4:30 p.m.; winter, Mon–Fri. Closed on federal holidays.

CONTACT: Refuge Manager, Fort Niobrara National Wildlife Refuge, Hidden Timber Rte, HC 14, Box 67, Valentine, NE 69201; Tel: 4023763789; Web: www .fws.gov/fortniobrara; email: fortnio brara@fws.gov.

COST: *Entrance:* Free. *Watercraft launching:* Small fee.

ON-SITE AMENITIES: Fishing, visitors center, exhibits, bookstore, auto touring, observation deck, nature trails, float trips, canoeing, tubing, annual bison roundup and auction, and junior ranger program.

BEST TIMES: Animals can be viewed year-round. The annual bison roundup takes place in the fall. Contact the refuge staff for special event dates.

FIELD NOTES: The area can be explored by foot or by floating the Niobrara River. Allow 2–4 hours for a float trip. Private outfitters in the area rent watercraft and provide shuttle services.

ADIRONDACK PARK

NEW YORK, USA

Situated in north-central New York State, Adirondack Park occupies more than 6 million acres of land, which makes it one of the largest contiguous parks in the continental United States. There are 30,000 miles of rivers and streams that feed into more than 3,000 lakes and ponds in the park. Slightly less than half of the park is owned by the state of New York, but that percentage increases every year as the state buys more of the land and receives land as a donation.

The park was created in 1892 owing to the writings of surveyor Verplanck Colvin, who was an advocate for protection against deforestation and the impact it would have on the Erie Canal and the Hudson Valley. Today, the park exists to protect not only the forests but

LOCATION: North-central New York State.

HOURS OF OPERATION: Year-round, 24/7.

CONTACT: New York State Adirondack Park Agency, PO Box 99, 1133 NYS Rte 86, Ray Brook, NY 12977; Tel: 5188914050; Fax: 5188913938; Web: www.apa.state.ny.us/About_Park/index.html. *Paul Smiths visitors center:* Tel: 5183273000. *Newcomb visitors center:* Tel: 5185822000.

COST: *Entrance and camping:* Free. *Permits:* Costs vary.

also the wildlife found in mountains, highlands, rivers, and lakes within the park. Conservation efforts include the reintroduction of the American beaver, fisher, American marten, moose, Canada lynx, and osprey, all of which can now be found throughout the park.

The Adirondacks are considered an adventurer's playground. The region contains nearly 2,000 miles of hiking trails, with destinations ranging from mountain summits to remote waterfalls. Visitors can enjoy a variety of outdoor activities such as canoeing, kayaking, hiking, and swimming. With more than 100 campgrounds and unlimited lodging selections, travelers will have no trouble finding something that suits their needs and budget.

ON-SITE AMENITIES: Campgrounds, lodging, visitor centers. Unlike most parks, the Adirondacks encompasses villages, small towns, and hamlets. Visitors to the area can easily find a wide range of accommodations from bed and breakfast rooms to chain hotels.

BEST TIMES: May through October.

FIELD NOTES: Bring food, water, and supplies if camping, hunting, or fishing. Permits are required for hunting and fishing and can be obtained in most state offices. Canoeing is fantastic along the parks many waterways and often allows for up-close wildlife viewing. For canoe routes and maps visit www.adirondacks.com.

ALLIGATOR RIVER NATIONAL WILDLIFE REFUGE

NORTH CAROLINA, USA

The Alligator River National Wildlife Refuge is dedicated to the preservation of the various ecosystems found within this strip of park. Refuge staff and volunteers have focused efforts on finding and reversing man-made drainage systems that have diminished water levels within the 13-mile-long by 15-mile-wide preserve. As a result of this work, natural habitats and the wildlife that live in them are making a comeback.

The species diversification in the Alligator River Refuge offers the visitor a rare opportunity to spend time with animals both rare and endangered; red wolves, red-cockaded woodpeckers, and American alligators make their home in the area. The red wolf is one of the world's most endangered wild canids. Although once common in the southeastern United States, the red wolf became virtually extinct by the 1980s as a result of predator control programs and loss of habitat. Biologists eventually captured 17 animals, 14 of which became the founders of a successful captive breeding program. By 1987, enough red wolves had been bred in captivity to begin a reestablishment program at Alligator River.

Within the refuge, black bears and white-tailed deer are thriving. In fact, Alligator River is home to eastern North Carolina's largest population of black bears and one of the largest in the eastern United States. Many migratory birds find respite here during their semi-yearly sojourns.

Active visitors will find two short hiking trails that provide access to an excellent cross-section of the refuge's

habitats. The Creef Cut trail begins at the information kiosk and has an extensive boardwalk and fishing platform to compliment the wildlife viewing. The Sandy Ridge trail is an earthen path that leads to a wooden boardwalk that meanders through a cypress swamp. Refuge employees lead tours and events throughout the year. Many events are run on a regular schedule and do not require reservations, although they are mostly recommended.

LOCATION: Mainland portions of Dare and Hyde Counties, North Carolina.

HOURS OF OPERATION: Year-round.

CONTACT: *Main office:* Alligator River National Widlife Refuge, PO Box 1969, Manteo, NC 27954; Tel: 2524731131; Web: www.fws.gov/alligatorriver; email: alligatorriver@fws.gov.

COST: *Entrance:* Free. *Guided programs and events:* Fees vary. *Red Wolf Howling Safaris:* US$5. *Alligator River and Pea Island canoe tours:* Adults, US$35; children under 12 years, US$20.

ON-SITE AMENITIES: Restroom facilities. Expert guides, boating, numerous hiking trails, paddling trails, bike trail, fishing, swimming, kayaking, birding, hunting, wildlife photography. Special events and programs run by the refuge include red wolf tracking, Red Wolf Howling Safaris, Alligator River and Pea Island canoe tours, and bird walks. For more information, tours, and reservations visit the refuge online.

BEST TIMES: October through May. Insects are less active during times of cooler temperatures.

FIELD NOTES: Hats, wading shoes, insect repellent, sunscreen, cameras, and fishing/hunting permits. Carry snacks and drinking water because none is available on-site. Early registration is required for the Red Wolf Howling Safari; call 2527965600 or register online at www.redwolves.com.

GREAT SMOKY MOUNTAINS NATIONAL PARK

NORTH CAROLINA, USA

The Cherokee called the mountain range they inhabited "Shaconage," or "Place of Blue Smoke." Today, the same range is called the Great Smoky Mountains due to the blue-gray mist that frequently shrouds its tall peaks. In the Great Smoky Mountains National Park, 16 peaks rise to a height of over 6,000 feet, and mountains receive as much as 85 inches of rain a year. The precipitation and evaporation create the characteristic wispy smoke-like fog found throughout the region.

In the early 20th century, large-scale logging operations nearly clearcut the

Great Smoky forests to extinction. Citizens groups and the park raised enough money to purchase the mountain range, and in 1934 the Great Smoky Mountains National Park was created. Today, the park contains abandoned mills and other relics from the bygone logging era within the largest wilderness area in the eastern United States. The park is home to 66 species of mammals, 240 species of birds, 50 species of native fish, and 80 species of reptiles and amphibians.

The park's official symbol is the American black bear, and officials estimate that approximately 1,500 bears live in the park. White-tailed deer, elk, bobcats, red and gray foxes, coyotes, opossums, beavers, woodchucks, and groundhogs inhabit the park, and 11 species of bats hunt the evening skies. Raccoons and skunks rummage through park campsites looking for food, competing with myriad other small mammals and rodents.

The Great Smoky Mountains is also a haven for bird-watchers. Nearly half the park's bird population breeds within the park boundaries. The park's southern lowlands are home to the most birds, including downy woodpeckers, eastern screech owls, belted kingfishers, sparrows, goldfinches, yellow-billed cuckoos, and wood thrushes. Within the park's spruce forests, along the higher ridges, live golden-crowned kinglets, northern saw-whet owls, warblers, wrens, and chickadees. In the park's northern hardwood forests, birdwatchers can spot blue-headed vireos, rose-breasted grosbeaks, black-throated warblers, and northern cardinals.

Visitors to the park can take scenic auto tours, hike on the park's 650 miles of trails, bike, camp, and picnic. There are three visitors centers in the park that offer a variety of ranger-led wildlife, historical, and cultural programs.

LOCATION: The park has three entrances. *Tennessee:* Gatlinburg on US Rte 441 and Townsend on State Rte 73. *North Carolina:* Cherokee on US Rte 441. The nearest commercial airport is McGhee-Tyson, south of Knoxville, Tennessee, approximately 45 miles west of the Gatlinburg entrance.

HOURS OF OPERATION: 24/7. Some roads, campsites, and visitor facilities are closed during the winter. *Visitors centers:* Daily, except Christmas, generally 9 a.m. to 4:30 p.m.; hours vary seasonally, so contact the park for more specific information.

CONTACT: *Headquarters:* Great Smoky Mountains National Park, 107 Park Headquarters Rd, Gatlinburg, TN 377738; Tel: 8654361200; Web: www.nps.gov/grsm.

COST: *Entrance:* Free. *Picnic pavilions rental:* Small fee. *Camping* (per night): US$14–$23; reservations are recommended. *In-park accommodations:* **Le Conte Lodge:** Cabins (per person, per night): from US$64; lodges (up to 12 people, per night): US$512–$768; meals are extra for all lodging; call 8654295704 or visit www.lecontelodge.com.

ON-SITE AMENITIES: Three visitors centers and two welcome centers. **Le Conte Lodge:** The only lodging inside the park. Picnic facilities, campsites, two historic gristmills, toilet facilities, and bookstore as well as 650 miles of marked trails.

BEST TIMES: Although open year-round; some areas may be inaccessible during winter.

FIELD NOTES: Dogs are allowed in the park if kept on a 6-foot leash; however, they are not allowed on park trails. Willfully coming within 150 feet of any bear is considered a violation of federal regulations and can result in fines and arrest. Keep your distance from all wildlife and never feed them. Le Conte Lodge is accessible only by foot; there are five trails leading to the lodge, which require a certain degree of physical fitness. Mondays, Wednesdays, and Fridays, you can hike to the lodge alongside the llama pack train, the lodge's only means of supply delivery. Snow and ice may be present on the trails as late as May and as early as October; appropriate precautions should be taken.

WICHITA MOUNTAINS WILDLIFE REFUGE

OKLAHOMA, USA

The romance of the old west is nestled in the pristine 60,000 acres of Wichita Mountains Wildlife Refuge. Visitors feel as if they had stepped back in history as they watch large herds of bison, elk, and deer roaming the prairie. The animals here are protected and have plenty of room to graze.

The refuge is also home to Texas longhorn cattle. Within the prairie grasslands, rocky outcrops, wetlands, and oak forests visitors can watch prairie dogs, river otters, burrowing owls, squirrels, fish, reptiles, and birds. The refuge includes a well-maintained mountain bike trail from which the beauty of the plains can be enjoyed.

Hiking is permitted during daylight hours. The refuge offers 15 miles of hiking trails and a well-maintained bike trail. In addition to watching and pho-

tographing the animals in the refuge, visitors can also enjoy camping (summer and winter), hiking, backpacking, rock climbing, and freshwater fishing. The refuge maintains wheelchair-accessible trails and ramps. Don't forget to stop in the visitors center and learn about children's activities, scenic drives, picnicking, bird-watching, nature viewing, and historic sites.

LOCATION: Indiahoma, Oklahoma. To reach the refuge gate: from I-44 take Hwy 49 (exit 45); from Hwy 62, take Hwy 115 (Cache exit).

HOURS OF OPERATION: Daily, 7 a.m. to 6 p.m.

CONTACT: *Headquarters:* Wichita Mountains Wildlife Refuge, 32 Refuge Headquarters, Indiahoma, OK 73552; Tel: 5804293222; Web: www.fws.gov/south west/refuges/oklahoma/wichitamoun tains. *Visitors center:* Tel: 5804293222. *Tour reservations:* Tel: 5804292151.

COST: *Entrance:* Free. *Camping* (per night): US$8, without electricity; US$16, with electricity; semi-primitive walk-in tent sites (no vehicle access), US$6. *Backcountry camping permit* (per person): US$2. *Guided specialty tours:* US$5.

ON-SITE AMENITIES: Visitors center; guided specialty tours (see website for details). Doris Campground offers both individual and group sites with tables, fire rings, and fire grates. There is a centrally positioned restroom/shower complex, which is open all year, except during winter months.

BEST TIMES: June through October.

FIELD NOTES: Children must be at least 8 years old to attend guided tours. The tours vary, depending on wildlife activity and weather conditions.

HAWK MOUNTAIN

PENNSYLVANIA, USA

Hawk Mountain, a leader in worldwide conservation and preservation efforts of migratory birds of prey, is a model research, educational, and observation facility that works with and influences other preserves and facilities worldwide. The efforts at Hawk Mountain are led by a staff of 16 full-time employees and approximately 200 volunteers. Be sure to check out the visitors center and the Acopian Center for Conservation Learning.

Adjoining the Appalachian Trail, the sanctuary encompasses more than 2,600 acres. Although the marvelous trails through the refuge will bring you into

HOURS OF OPERATION: Year-round, dawn to dusk.

CONTACT: *Administrative offices and visitor center:* Hawk Mountain, 1700 Hawk Mountain Road, Kempton, PA 19529; Tel: 6107566961; Web: www .hawkmountain.org; email: info@hawk mountain.org.

COST: *Trail fee:* US$3–$7, depending on age and time of visit; free to members.

ON-SITE AMENITIES: The visitors center includes a gift store and sells snacks and drinks. Guides, marked trails for self-guided hikes of 1–4 hours, native plant garden, art gallery, and picnic areas.

close contact with the flora and fauna of Hawk Mountain, you will be able to start your bird-watching as soon as you arrive because there is an observation area less than 100 yards from the parking lot from which you can see various species of vultures, hawks, eagles, and falcons.

The dedication to furthering education about birds of prey at the Hawk Mountain Sanctuary is unparalleled, and the sanctuary's mission of education extends to the visitors who are welcomed every day. The expert staff is always willing to help visitors get the most out of the sanctuary's site and facilities.

LOCATION: Kempton, Pennsylvania, 1.5 hours from Scranton.

BEST TIMES: August through December, during the migration season.

FIELD NOTES: During spring and autumn weekends, staff volunteers are situated at lookout points to assist in bird identification. Because bird-watching requires a good amount of sitting and the area is mountainous, you will want to bring a comfy blanket or mat. The staff at the visitors center will direct you to the best trails, taking into account your abilities and desires. A free map of the area trails can be downloaded by visiting the website.

BADLANDS NATIONAL PARK

SOUTH DAKOTA, USA

Badlands National Park, an area of more than 244,000 acres, is home to the most endangered land mammal in North America: the black-footed ferret, which was thought to be extinct until 1981 when about 130 animals were found in Wyoming and were reintroduced onto sites in the plains and western states. Three other endangered prairie dwellers—the bighorn sheep, bison, and swift fox—also have been successfully reintroduced to this habitat and can be seen roaming the park.

At Badlands, visitors can explore this remarkable ecosystem of mixed- and short-grass prairie, view fossil beds up to 37 million years old, and climb on the rock formations. During the summer season a variety of range-led programs will appeal to those with varying interests and abilities, from walks and talks to countless outdoor adventures.

LOCATION: 80 miles from Rapid City, South Dakota.

HOURS OF OPERATION: Year-round, 24/7. *Ben Reifel visitors center:* Daily, except Thanksgiving Day, Christmas Day, and New Year's Day. *White River visitors center:* Daily, June 1–Sept 15. Call for hours.

CONTACT: *Headquarters:* Badlands National Park, PO Box 6, 25216 Ben Reifel Rd, Interior, SD 57750-0006; Tel/TDD: 6054335361; Fax: 6054335404; Web: www.nps.gov/badl/contacts.htm.

COST: *Entrance* (7-day pass): Private, noncommercial vehicle, US$15; motorcycle, US$10; bicycle or foot, US$7. Various annual passes are honored. *Camping* (14-day limit): Sites are available on a first-come, first-served basis; Cedar Pass Campground, US$10 per night; Sage Creek Campground, free; see website for facilities and restrictions.

ON-SITE AMENITIES: The visitors centers have restrooms and information and exhibits about the park. **Cedar Pass Lodge:** Open April through October, the lodge has rental cabins, a gift shop, and a full-service restaurant; call 6054335460 for reservations. Campgrounds, hiking trails, and self-directed auto touring. Ranger-guided geology walks, prairie walks, and fossil discussions. Junior ranger program, in which parents are welcome to participate.

BEST TIMES: Spring or fall do not have the temperature or weather extremes of the summer and winter, but dramatic climatic changes within a brief period of time are always possible.

Temperatures range from −46°F to 116°F throughout the year, and high winds are common. Summers are hot and dry, and violent thunderstorms have been known to pop up. Winters are generally cold, with 12–24 inches of total snowfall for the season. Many informative ranger-guided programs take place during the summer, so keep that in mind when planning your visit.

FIELD NOTES: Visitors should dress in layers because of fluctuating temperatures. Wear a hat and sunglasses, sunscreen, and carry plenty of water while hiking. The Sage Creek Rim Road is surfaced with gravel and can become impassable after heavy rains or snows.

BIG BEND NATIONAL PARK

TEXAS, USA

Often called one of the last remaining wild corners of the United States, Big Bend National Park is known as a land of strong beauty for its savage and always imposing rugged terrain. Here you can experience unmatched sights, sounds, and solitude. The park is home to more varieties of birds, bats, and cacti than any other national park in the country. It is the only place to find the endangered Mexican long-nosed bat in the entire United States.

Larger mammals such as white-tailed and mule deer, coyotes, mountain lions, and black bears also inhabit the park. Some visitors have reported hearing scratching and commotion around their campsites at night, and wildlife

rainfall, many of the 75 species of mammals found in the park take on extremely cautious lifestyles. Many leave their burrows only under cover of night, and others may forage during the cool of the early morning. Thus animal spotting can't be absolutely guaranteed.

experts believe such activity is caused by gray foxes or bands of javelinas or peccaries (not to be confused with wild pigs).

The greatest success story in Big Bend, however, is the return of the Mexican black bear. Rarely spotted in the park from the 1940s to the late 1970s, it was feared that this black bear was forever gone from the area. In the early 1980s, however, a female black bear from the Sierra del Carmen in northern Mexico wandered through diverse terrain and swam rivers to arrive in the Chisos Mountains of Big Bend National Park. She may have brought her young with her and likely encountered a wandering male already within the park. How and why the bears came remain mysteries, but their return is a remarkable event.

Big Bend National Park contains three distinct environments: mountain, desert, and river. Within an hour, visitors can drive from the banks of the Rio Grande into the mountains to an elevation of nearly a mile above sea level. This incredible range of climates and ecosystems allows visitors to experience a great variety of wildlife and scenery. Because of the high temperatures and low

LOCATION: Southwest Texas. Big Bend is hundreds of miles from the nearest large city; see the website for directions and preparation tips.

HOURS OF OPERATION: Year-round, 24/7. *Panther Junction visitors center:* Daily, 8 a.m. to 6 p.m.; may be closed Christmas Day. Contact headquarters for hours of entrance stations and other visitor centers.

CONTACT: *Headquarters:* Big Bend National Park, PO Box 129, Big Bend National Park, TX 79834; Tel: 4324772251; Web: www.nps.gov/bibe. *Weather information hotline:* Tel: 4324771183.

ON-SITE AMENITIES: Visitor centers, several developed frontcountry and primitive backcountry campsites (reservations are recommended for busy seasons). **Chisos Lodge:** This is the only lodging available in the park; call 4324772291.

BEST TIMES: March through June.

FIELD NOTES: Before camping in the park, consult with a park ranger so you are prepared in every way. Having enough food, water, and other essential supplies is important in this formidable area.

LAGUNA ATASCOSA NATIONAL WILDLIFE REFUGE

TEXAS, USA

Laguna Atascosa National Wildlife Refuge abuts the Adolph Thomas County Park in Rio Hondo, Texas. The reserve is close to the Mexican–US border and belongs to the Western Hemisphere Shorebird Reserve Network. Although most famous for its harboring and supporting of migratory waterfowl, the reserve is also dedicated to the preservation of big cats such as the endangered ocelot and Gulf Coast jaguarundi. The refuge supports one of only two known breeding populations of ocelots in Texas.

Although the redhead duck is the bird most associated with the refuge, the area actually hosts a spectacularly diverse array of birds that either visit or make their home there. More than 400 species of birds have been spotted at Laguna, more than any other refuge in the United States. And many of these birds cannot be seen outside the Rio Grande area. Visitors to Laguna Atascosa may also spot white-tailed deer, green jays, javelinas, coyotes, bobcats, alligators, armadillos, and the hawksbill and Kemp's ridley sea turtles.

Cattle ranchers moved to the area in the 1800s, and farmers put down roots in the next century. As a result, most of the native vegetation in the Rio Grande Valley has disappeared. The Laguna Atascosa National Wildlife Refuge is active in restoring the plants and thorn forests that provide a home and food for the local wildlife.

The refuge's 45,000 acres are adjacent to the Adolph Thomas County Park, which provides an excellent base camp for those exploring the miles of trails that wind through Laguna. The park offers camping, fishing, hiking, boating, and other leisure activities.

LOCATION: Rio Hondo, Texas, 25 miles east of Harlingen.

HOURS OF OPERATION: *Visitors center:* Daily, 8 a.m. to 4 p.m.; closed Thanksgiving Day, Christmas Day, and New Year's Day.

CONTACT: *Main office:* Laguna Atascosa National Wildlife Refuge, PO Box 450, Rio Hondo, TX 79834; Tel: 9567483607; Web: www.stateparks .com/laguna_atascosa.html; email: r2rw_la@fws.gov.

COST: *Entrance:* Free on the first Sunday of each month; private vehicle, US$3; bicycle/foot entry per family, US$3; group rates, school rates, and annual passes are also available.

ON-SITE AMENITIES: The refuge has areas open to public access for wildlife-oriented recreational activities, including wildlife observation, photography, hiking, biking, fishing, and hunting. There are two designated self-guided auto tour routes, a system of walking/ biking trails, a photo/observation blind, and a visitors center. Overnight camping and a boat ramp are available in the Adolph Thomas County Park, located near Arroyo City.

BEST TIMES: October through April.

FIELD NOTES: Bring appropriate food, and camping supplies if you are planning on staying. No feeding of the wildlife is permitted; doing so may harm the animals of the refuge. Recorded calls and calling devices to lure wildlife are not allowed on refuge grounds. Mosquitoes, chiggers, wasps, scorpions, and other biting insects are found within the park; wear insect repellent and stay alert.

BRYCE CANYON NATIONAL PARK

UTAH, USA

Geologically speaking, Bryce (pronounced *brais*) Canyon National Park is not technically a canyon. It is, rather, an enormous deep bowl filled with fascinating horseshoe-shaped amphitheaters and spires that resemble reddish windowless skyscrapers worn down by the weather.

Amid its unique rock formations, there are mammals galore, including the mountain lion, one of the largest members of the cat family. While many animals go into their dens for the winter, it is actually the best time to see the mountain lion. Spotting this cat is quite rare, however.

On the opposite end of the size spectrum is the prairie dog, a cute little creature that lives in burrows under the ground. Being a small rodent, the prairie dog is tasty prey and must constantly be on guard to ward off becoming some predator's next meal; their enemies include hawks from above and rattlesnakes from below. For protection, prairie dogs live in colonies and actually post guards to alert the others when danger looms. Unlike the elusive mountain lion, the Utah prairie dog (there are five species in all) can regularly be seen in the meadows that border the roads in the northern portion of the park.

Visitors are treated to some 175 species of birds, including the condor. These large birds of prey soar above Bryce National Canyon, a sight that is, as it were, uplifting in itself.

LOCATION: Bryce Canyon, Utah, approximately 80 miles from Cedar City.

HOURS OF OPERATION: Daily, May–Sept, 8 a.m. to 8 p.m.; Oct, 8 a.m. to 6 p.m.; Nov–Mar, 8 a.m. to 4:30 p.m.; Apr, 8 a.m. to 6 p.m.

CONTACT: Bryce Canyon National Park, PO Box 640201, Bryce, UT 84764-0201. Tel: 4358345322; Web: www.nps.gov/ brca; email: via website.

COST: *Entrance* (7-day pass): Private vehicle, US$25; individual (on foot, bicycle, or motorcycle or in a noncommercial group): US$12; fee includes unlimited use of the shuttle during operating season. *Backcountry permits:* US$5–$15; required for overnight hiking; obtain at the visitors center.

ON-SITE AMENITIES: Visitor center (about 4.5 miles south of the intersection of Hwy 12 and Hwy 63; 1.5 miles inside Bryce Canyon National Park's northern boundary), shuttle bus throughout the park, ranger programs, geology talks and hikes, winter snowshoe hikes, and canyon trail rides by horse or mule (operated by an independent concessioner within the park), and other activities. **Bryce Canyon Lodge:** This independently operated lodge has 114 rooms, including lodge suites, motel rooms, and cabins; open April 1 through October 31; dining room open for breakfast, lunch, and dinner (reservations required for dinner); gift shop; contact Xanterra Parks and Resorts, 6312 S. Fiddlers Green Circle 600 N., Greenwood Village, CO 80111; for information call 8882972757 or 3032972757 (outside USA). Additional lodging is available in the local area. *Campgrounds:* Two campgrounds within the park are North and Sunset; for reservations (May 15 to September 30), call 8774446777.

BEST TIMES: Late April through late October.

FIELD NOTES: There are 15 lookout points along Bryce Canyon's 18-mile scenic drive. The most famous are found in the amphitheater: Sunrise, Sunset, Inspiration, and Bryce Points. The park offers downloadable maps, brochures, newspapers, motel and restaurant guides, and backcountry guides from its website. These resources help visitors familiarize themselves with the area and available activities. Bryce Canyon has two trails designated for overnight hiking; backcountry camping is by permit only, on a first-come, first-served basis.

LEWIS AND CLARK NATIONAL WILDLIFE REFUGE

WASHINGTON, USA

Near the mouth of the Columbia River, accessible only by boat, the Lewis and Clark National Wildlife Refuge encompasses more than 35,000 acres and includes 20 islands along with sandbars, mudflats, and tidal marshes. Roughly a third of the Columbia River estuary is located in the refuge.

The variety of aquatic life in the area is second to none and includes coho, chum, and chinook salmon and steelhead and cutthroat trout. Other fish are white sturgeon, American shad, smelt, perch, starry flounder, bass, catfish, and Pacific lamprey—in short, it's a fisherman's paradise.

Although the fishing in the area is much vaunted by sportsmen, the true attraction for wildlife enthusiasts is the migratory bird population. The refuge is the winter home for many Canadian and Alaskan birds. Mallards, pintails, American wigeons, canvasbacks, and lesser scaups are some of the 30,000 ducks found here. Birdwatchers will also find 5,000 Canada geese and more than 1,000 tundra swans. These migratory birds visit comfortably with their winged cousins who stay year-round, such as the bald eagle, great blue heron, and various gulls.

LOCATION: Lewis and Clark Refuge is administered from the Julia Butler Hansen Refuge office in Cathlamet, Washington.

HOURS OF OPERATION: Year-round, generally during daylight hours.

CONTACT: *Refuge office:* Lewis and Clark National Wildlife Refuge, 46 Steamboat Slough Rd, Cathlamet, WA

98612; Tel: 3607953915; Web: www.fws .gov/pacific/refuges/field/wa_L&C .htm.

COST: *Entrance:* Free. *Permits:* Required for hunting and fishing and other activities. *Camping:* Contact the refuge office for fees.

ON-SITE AMENITIES: Camping is offered nearby. Boat launch facilities are located at various points in Washington and Oregon along the lower Columbia River, including Skamokawa in Washington and John Day Point and Aldrich Point in Oregon.

BEST TIMES: October through April. February through March for optimum bird viewing.

FIELD NOTES: The islands of the Columbia River estuary are accessible only by boat. Tidal flows and fluctuations, strong winds, and wakes from ships in the navigation channel can make boating difficult and sometimes dangerous. Deep channels separate most of the islands at high tide, but tide tables and navigation charts should be consulted to avoid grounding and sandbars.

MOUNT RAINIER NATIONAL PARK

WASHINGTON, USA

Only an hour's drive southeast of the Seattle/Tacoma metropolitan area lies a vast pristine wilderness. Mount Rainier National Park was named after the highest peak in the Cascade Mountains—a snowcapped Goliath that inspires awe with its breathtaking beauty and dwarfs everything around it. At 14,410 feet, Mount Rainier stands almost 3 miles higher than the land to the west and about 1.5 miles higher than

the closest mountains. It is an active volcano that last erupted about 150 years ago, which is pretty recent in geological time. The park's raw beauty and natural wilderness makes it a popular area, drawing nearly 2 million people a year. Nonetheless, the park remains unspoiled. Approximately 97% of the park is undisturbed wilderness; the remaining area is part of a National Historic Landmark district.

Within the park's 235,625 acres, visitors can find at least 56 species of mammals, 11 species of amphibians, 5 species of reptiles, and more than 229 species of birds. The parklands include about 380 lakes and 470 rivers, in which 18 native fish species thrive. Some of the more popular mammals are elk and black bear. Mountain goats typically stay high in the mountains and thus are less often spotted. Visitors can also expect to see Columbian black-tailed deer and Douglas squirrels. For bird-watchers, the park is home to noisy Steller's jays, common ravens, owls, bald eagles, peregrine falcons, and ducks and other waterfowl. Four species that are known to have once lived in the park are the gray wolf, grizzly bear, Canada lynx, and chinook salmon; but these animals may now be gone from the area.

LOCATION: Year-round access to the park is via Washington State Rte 706 to the Nisqually entrance in the southwest corner of the park. Limited winter access is available via Hwy 123 in the southeast corner of the park. The Carbon River/Mowich Lake area, in the northwest corner of the park, is accessed via state Rte 165 through Wilkeson. In summer only, the north and east sides of the park can be accessed via Hwy 410.

HOURS OF OPERATION: Year-round, although some areas may be closed or difficult to access owing to rain or snow.

CONTACT: *Main office:* Mount Rainier National Park, 55210 238th Ave East, Ashford, WA 98304; Tel: 3605692211; Web: www.nps.gov/mora.

COST: *Entrance* (7-day pass): Private vehicle, US$15; individuals over 16 years old (on motorcycle, bicycle, horseback, or foot or in noncommercial groups), US$5.

ON-SITE AMENITIES: Visitors centers, wilderness information centers, ranger station, museum, lodging, several campgrounds, picnic areas, two restaurants, two snack bars, and gift shops. **National Park Inn:** Located in the Longmire Historic District at an elevation of 2,700 feet; open year-round; 25 guest rooms, full-service restaurant, gift shop, and post office; call 3605692275. **Paradise Inn:** Built in 1916, generally open May through September; located at Paradise at an elevation of 5,420 feet; 117 guest rooms, gift shop, post office, full-service restaurant, snack bar, lounge; call 3605692275.

BEST TIMES: May through September.

FIELD NOTES: Geological studies and monitoring show that Mount Rainier is an active volcano. Although visitors can expect days or weeks of advance warning of an impending eruption, other hazards (falling rocks, avalanches), can occur with little warning. Pets are permitted in parking lots, campgrounds, and on paved roads. Pets must, at all times, be leashed or crated and with their owners. Preserve the natural features of the park, do not drive nails into trees or create ditches around your tent, do not feed any wildlife (including birds), and do not pick, cut, gather, or dig any plant or tree. Bring the following essentials: a map (can be purchased in the park), compass, flashlight, food (if camping), layers of clothing to accommodate changeable weather, pocketknife, matches, candles, and first aid kit, sunglasses, and sunscreen.

OLYMPIC NATIONAL PARK

WASHINGTON, USA

Olympic National Park is located on a peninsula jutting into the Pacific Ocean off the Washington State coast. The park, a World Heritage Site, was founded in 1909 by President Theodore Roosevelt. Later named an International Biosphere Reserve, the park was recently designated as the Olympic Wilderness; which helps further ensure the protection of the land and its flora and fauna.

The park runs 73 miles along the Pacific coast and is bordered by the Olympic Mountains and rain forest. The park comprises distinct and diverse habitats for a wide range of wildlife, including the coyote, wolf, red fox, black bear, raccoon, fisher, short- and long-tailed weasel, mink, porcupine, spotted and striped skunk, cougar, bobcat, Roosevelt elk, and mountain goat.

On any given trip to the coastal areas of Mora and Rialto Beach, Kalaloch, or Lake Ozette (a popular coastal access point), you will be the privileged spectator of a variety of marine life

including sea and river otters; harbor, northern fur, and northern elephant seals, Steller and California sea lions; gray, minke, and humpback whales; harbor and Dall porpoises; orcas; and Pacific white-sided dolphins.

The park offers a wide array of recreational opportunities as well as naturalist excursions available year-round.

LOCATION: Washington State coastline, Pacific northwest.

HOURS OF OPERATION: Year-round, 24/7.

CONTACT: *Main office:* Olympic National Park, 600 E. Park Ave, Port Angeles, WA 98362; Tel: 3605653130; Fax: 3605653015; Web: www.nps.gov/olym. *Road and weather information:* Tel: 3605653131.

COST: *Entrance:* Private vehicle, US$15, individual (on foot, bicycle, motorcycle), US$5. *Camping:* US$10–$18. Other fees may apply, depending on your choice of activities.

ON-SITE AMENITIES: Visitors centers, wildlife tours, ranger-guided tours, hiking, and boardwalk trails. *Camping:* The park has 16 campgrounds with more than 900 sites, handicap-accessible toilets, can accommodate RVs and trailers up to 21 feet; picnic tables and fire pits.

BEST TIMES: Depends on your choice of activities.

FIELD NOTES: Before heading out be sure to check with the ranger station for any road or campground closings. When visiting the coastal area it is a good idea to have a tide table with you; if you don't know how to use one, ask a ranger. Although there is much to see in a 1-day visit, to see all that the park has to offer, plan for a 2- to 4-day stay. Activities to enjoy here include fishing, kayaking, skiing, snowboarding, backpacking, and hiking.

GOOSEWING RANCH

WYOMING, USA

Nestled in a valley 7,000 feet above sea level, Goosewing Ranch wraps a true ranching lifestyle experience in the spectacular Wyoming wilderness with lots of modern amenities for even the most hardened city slicker. Goosewing Ranch is host to a variety of classic North American game: elk, moose, mountain sheep, antelope, bears, eagles, geese, cranes, and much more. The Gros Ventre River, which winds throughout the ranch's land, is home to native cutthroat trout. This working ranch is located in the Gros Ventre River Valley, in the heart of some of the West's wildest country.

In addition to the animals and fantastic scenery, activities for human-

folk abound. From target shooting, archery, roping, and arts and crafts to line dancing, campfires, and cookouts, the ranch staff offers much for the active visitor.

In the summer and fall, horseback riding is the main focus. No matter your level of ability or experience, the ranch has the perfect horse for you. Fly-fishing is excellent in the area, and guides are on hand twice a week for instruction. Guests can also go on day hikes or just relax and enjoy the scenery.

Winters at Goosewing Ranch feature deep snow, and the pristine backcountry is picture-postcard beautiful. Goosewing Ranch is accessible only by snowmobile at this time and no lodging is available. The ranch offers snowmobile tours and snowcoach rides to Yellowstone National Park or into the fabulous Wyoming backcountry.

LOCATION: About 40 miles northeast of Jackson, Wyoming, and about an hour drive through the Teton Wilderness; the final 15 miles are dirt road. The ranch is about 90 miles from the south entrance of Yellowstone National Park, about a 2-hour drive.

HOURS OF OPERATION: June 1– Sept 28.

CONTACT: Goosewing Ranch, PO Box 4084, Jackson Hole, WY 83001; Tel: 8887335251 (toll-free) or 3077335251 (outside USA); Fax: 3077331405; Web: www.goosewingranch.com.

COST: *Adult single occupancy:* Ranges from 3 nights at US$758 to 14 nights at US$3,032.

ON-SITE AMENITIES: Eight one-bedroom cabins that offer casual western comfort with various sleeping arrangements, full bath, fireplace, and porch. A five-bedroom guesthouse is available for larger groups.

BEST TIMES: June through September. Warm, dry days are the norm during summer; evenings and nights can be quite chilly.

FIELD NOTES: Bring warm clothes (temperatures drop during the evening even during the summer), boots, sunglasses, gloves, jackets, hats, and sunscreen. For winter snowmobile tours, a complete snowmobile outfit is provided (one-piece suit, boots, helmet, mittens, balaclava, and hand warmers); layering is advised for comfort. Fleece or sweatshirts, thermals, winter hat, and gloves are important. For overnight tours guests are asked to pack lightly; a small duffle bag per person is recommended.

GRAND TETON NATIONAL PARK

WYOMING, USA

This park is wild America at its finest. Grand Teton National Park encompasses a dramatic variety of environments from majestic mountains to pristine lakes to sage-covered valleys, all of which is home to an extraordinary amount of wildlife. Nearly 4 million visitors come to the park each year.

The dominant feature of the park is the Teton Range, which reaches an elevation of almost 14,000 feet. The valley, at 6,400 feet, is home to summer wildflowers; clear, cold lakes; and abundant wildlife. The forested mountains are crosscut by countless swift-flowing streams that cascade down

prey dive into the water to pluck out a cutthroat trout.

Most visitors come to the Tetons to see large mammals. Some species can be seen from observation points located along the roads; look out for moose, elk, mule deer, bison, and pronghorn sheep. If you want to see the more elusive grizzly and black bears, wolves, and mountain lions, you'll have to walk along a park trail. Some of the small mammals, such as uinta ground and red squirrels and least chipmunks, can be seen almost everywhere in the park, but only careful observers and adventurous visitors will spot the badgers, pine martens, long-tailed weasels, and wolverines that live in the park. Pikas, yellow-bellied marmots, and golden mantled ground squirrels live in rocky areas, and muskrats, beavers, and river otters are found in the wetlands.

The trumpeter swan, which is the largest waterfowl in North America, makes its home in the park. The most likely places to observe these birds are Swan Lake and Flat Creek. Bird lovers can see osprey and bald eagles throughout the park, especially near water, where the birds hunt and nest. One way to tell ospreys from bald eagles is to note the manner in which they carry a fish in their talons. Ospreys carry their prey parallel to their body. This is one park that is truly a treat, encompassing everything beautiful and remarkable

rocky canyons to fill large lakes below. The Snake River winds its way south through this awesome wilderness.

The unforgiving long, snowy, and bitterly cold winters play an important role in the ecology of this area. The snows often begin in early November and last through April. The relatively brief summers provide a respite from the rigors of winter and are a time of renewal and rebirth. The flora and fauna of the Grand Teton area have learned to adapt to the dramatic changes in both weather and elevation.

Visitors are rarely far from wildlife in Grand Teton. Mountain hikers are able to hear yellow-bellied marmots whistle warning calls as golden eagles circle above looking for prey or may catch a glimpse of black bears foraging for insect larvae in rotten logs. Bison, moose, and coyotes are frequently seen in the valley meadows. The lakes and river are home to a variety of fish, and birdwatchers may be able to watch as os-

about the American western wilderness.

LOCATION: Wyoming, approximately 275 miles from Salt Lake City, Utah (a 5- to 6-hour drive).

HOURS OF OPERATION: *Ranger station, visitors center, and information centers:* Hours vary by season, see the website for specific information.

CONTACT: Tel: 3077393343; Web: www.nps.gov/grte.

COST: *Entrance* (7-day pass to both Grand Teton and Yellowstone National Parks): Passenger vehicle, US$25; motorcycle, US$20; individual (on foot or bicycle), US$12.

ON-SITE AMENITIES: Visitors centers and ranger stations. Camping, biking (no formal bike trails; no bikes on hiking trails), scenic drives, and guided tours. *Climbing:* See www.tetonclimbing.blogspot.com for information on climbing in the park. Other activities available in the park include boating, fishing, hiking, and horseback riding. **American Alpine Club Climber's Ranch:** Not just for climbers; call 3077337271 or visit www.americanalpineclub.org. **Grand Teton Lodge Company:** Authorized concessioner with four lodges; call 8006289988 or visit www.gtlc.com.

BEST TIMES: May through October.

FIELD NOTES: Carry water, sunglasses, sunscreen, and bug repellent; pack a hat, rain gear, layers of clothes, and sturdy waterproof hiking boots. Other equipment and clothing depend on your chosen activities.

NATIONAL ELK REFUGE

WYOMING, USA

The National Elk Refuge is home to the largest herd of elk in North America. The elk are most active during fall, when their mating calls can be heard from miles around, but in the winter the US Fish and Wildlife Service offers unique observation tours, provided by a local contractor. Imagine riding a horse-drawn sleigh through a snowy wilderness to see an immense herd of elk.

The National Elk Refuge, which includes more than 25,000 acres of lakes,

rivers, and lands, is dedicated to preserving a habitat in which native elk can thrive. Although the survival and promulgation of the elk were the primary motives for the creation of the refuge, the area is also home to 47 mammal species and 147 bird species. During the winter, visitors can expect to see bighorn sheep, moose, bison, and mule deer. Springtime brings a variety of waterfowl such as northern pintails, mallards, gadwalls, and buffleheads.

The Jackson Hole and Greater Yellowstone visitors center provides information on tours, the refuge, and native wildlife. In addition the center offers excursions and lectures by noted experts.

LOCATION: Northeast of Jackson, Wyoming; south of Grand Teton National Park.

HOURS OF OPERATION: Year-round, 24/7; closed December 25. *Visitors center:* Daily, 9 a.m. to 5 p.m.; extended summer hours and closed Thanksgiving Day and Christmas Day.

CONTACT: National Elk Refuge, PO Box 510, Jackson, WY 83002; Tel: 3077339212; Web: www.fws.gov/na tionalelkrefuge; email: nationalelkref uge@fws.gov.

COST: *Entrance:* Adults, US$16; children 5–12 years old, US$12; children under 5 years old: free. *Private sleighs:* US$300 (maximum of 16–18 persons).

ON-SITE AMENITIES: Visitors center, guided wildlife tours, sleigh rides, and hiking excursions. The refuge hosts special events and lectures throughout the year; see the website for schedule. Permits for hunting and fishing can be obtained at the visitors center, which also provides information on lodging and other services.

BEST TIMES: October through March.

FIELD NOTES: Sleigh rides are available on a first-come, first-served basis and are handicapped accessible. Reservations are required for private tours and groups of 20 people or more and can be booked through the website. Smaller groups may make reservations, but advance booking is not necessary. Tickets are purchased at the visitors center, and a shuttle bus transports visitors to the boarding area.

PRYOR MOUNTAIN WILD MUSTANG CENTER

WYOMING, USA

The romantic frontier of the untamed west is alive on the plains of Wyoming where wild horses still roam free in the Pryor Mountain Wild Mustang Center. The 180 animals that make up this herd are descendants of horses brought over from Portugal and Spain by the early explorers. These tough horses have lived in this rugged area for nearly 200 years and have become genetically unique. Because of this, the herd is being carefully protected. The Pryor Mountain Wild Mustang Center, the first public wild horse range in America, is a not-for-profit educational institution. It is dedicated to preserving the Pryor Mountain mustangs and offering an opportunity for biologists to study the horses' evolution, habitat needs, and historical significance.

Visitors to the area should check in at the center before venturing out into the reserve. The center provides maps, and staff can direct you to the best areas for viewing the horses, based on current conditions and up-to-date tracking records. The center can also provide further information on individual wild horses, so be sure to ask.

One area in which wild horses can be seen is the desert lowlands, accessible via Hwy 37, a paved road that runs through the Bighorn Canyon National Recreation Area. Horses can be elusive here, but visitors to this part of the range can also see bighorn sheep, mule deer, and coyotes.

The most likely place to see the wild horses is East Pryor Mountain. This area is also home to black bears, mule deer, and even mountain lions. Access to this area requires 4-wheel drive with a low range and good tires.

LOCATION: Hwy 14A, Lovell, Wyoming, east of the Bighorn Canyon National Recreation Area.

HOURS OF OPERATION: Mon–Fri, 11 a.m. to 5 p.m., with extended summer hours.

CONTACT: Pryor Mountain Wild Mustang Center, PO Box 385, Lovell, WY 82431; Tel: 3075489453; Web: www.pryormustangs.org.

COST: *Entrance:* Free; donations for the center are gladly accepted.

ON-SITE AMENITIES: Gift shop, barn, and educational center.

BEST TIMES: Year-round.

FIELD NOTES: Proper respect of the wild horses is to be given at all times. Visitors are asked to remain at least 100 feet from the animals.

YELLOWSTONE NATIONAL PARK

WYOMING, MONTANA, AND IDAHO, USA

Yellowstone National Park was the first national park in the United States—and the world—and remains first in the hearts of the people. Straddling three states, the park was founded in 1872.

When you visit Yellowstone National Park you can easily envision what this land looked like hundreds or even thousands of years ago because much of this tremendous park is still wilderness and home to a large array of wildlife. Of course, the natural features and geysers, including Old Faithful, create a unique and wondrous landscape. In fact, more than half of the world's geothermal features are located in the park.

Yellowstone's wildlife includes an amazing array of amphibious, mammalian, and reptilian animals. Visitors

may catch sight of gray wolves, foxes, bobcats, cougars, lynx, badgers, river otters, long and short tailed weasels, and wolverines. Of course, the big guys—elk, bear, moose, bison, bighorn sheep, mountain goat, and pronghorn—capture the attention and interest of most visitors.

The park has numerous options for lodging: everything from tents to cabins to luxury suites. First-time visitors to Yellowstone National Park cannot expect to see everything; the park is large and offers abundant opportunities for wildlife observation and many activities, such as hiking, boating, bicycling, fishing, and horseback riding.

LOCATION: Encompasses parts of Wyoming, Montana, and Idaho.

HOURS OF OPERATION: Year-round, 24/7. Selected park areas, roads, and entrances may be closed at various times of year due to inclement weather. Be sure to check in advance.

CONTACT: *Visitor services:* Yellowstone National Park, PO Box 168, Yellowstone National Park, WY 82190; Tel: 3073442263; Web: www.nps.gov/yell.

COST: *Entrance:* Private vehicle, US$25; snowmobile or motorcycle, US$20; various passes are available. *Camping permits:* From US$12. *Accommodations:* Depends on the type.

ON-SITE AMENITIES: Visitors centers, stores, dining, lodging, campsites, and cabins; visit www.travelyellowstone.com for information and options. A range of summer and winter tours with expert guides is available.

BEST TIMES: April to September.

FIELD NOTES: An incredible array of activities are available. Plan your itinerary based on your tastes, but leave free time for extemporaneous exploration. Although rental equipment is available, you may want to consider packing your own fishing gear, bicycles, and other sporting equipment. **Xanterra Parks and Resorts:** Provides summer bus tours and winter snowcoach tours within the park, with loop tours departing from various locations; call 3073447311 for information or reservations. *Food:* Dining facilities are available throughout the park, ranging from fine dining (reservations required) to snack bars; for more information ask at any lodging front desk or dining room. *Camping:* Available on first-come, first-served basis; campgrounds are often filled by 11 a.m., so arrive early to obtain a site; camping of any type (tent, vehicle, or RV) outside designated campgrounds is not permitted.

BANFF NATIONAL PARK

ALBERTA, CANADA

Nestled in the Canadian Rockies, Banff National Park is the oldest and most famous park in the country. The 2,564-square-mile park is filled with scrumptious scenery, thanks to its countless valleys, mountains, glaciers, forests, meadows, and rivers. With close to 4 million visitors annually, park management has had to walk a fine line between tourism and the need to look out for the interests of the park's animals and plants. The town of Banff, which is located within the park, has been capped at 10,000 residents, and the expansion of ski resorts and golf courses has been halted. There also have been great efforts to protect the endangered Banff Springs snail, which is found only in thermal springs on the park grounds.

There are three ecosystems within the boundaries of Banff National Park. The montane contains forests of Douglas fir, trembling aspen, and lodgepole pine. The subalpine region has lush forests of lodgepole pine, Englemann spruce, and subalpine fir. The alpine region has sparse vegetation and is primarily made up of rock, talus, moraines, snow, ice, and water.

The park offers many opportunities to observe wildlife along its 1,000 miles of trails. Among the 53 types of mammals that live in the park are elk, mountain goats, bighorn sheep, northern river otter, and moose. Of particular note is the woodland caribou, which is considered a threatened species. Birdwatchers should look for bald and golden eagles, falcons, ospreys, three-toed woodpeckers, and mountain chickadees; some 280 bird species have been recorded at Banff.

Visitors to the park can take part in a variety of other activities, including canoeing, kayaking, backpacking, climbing, fishing, caving, and horseback riding. The more adventurous can try heli-hiking, and ice exploring. And don't forget to take advantage of the park's

world-famous thermal mineral springs. Whether you suffer from arthritis, rheumatism, or muscle soreness or have simply spent a long, hard day hiking, take the time to "take to the waters."

LOCATION: 80 miles northwest of Calgary, Alberta.

HOURS OF OPERATION: Year-round, 24/7. *Visitors center:* Closed December 25.

CONTACT: Banff National Park, Box 9, Banff, AB, Canada T1L 1K2; Tel: 4037621550; Fax: 4037623380; Web: www.pc.gc.ca/Banff.

COST: *Entrance* (per day): adult, US$10; senior (65 years and older), US$8.50; youth (6–16 years), US$5; family/group (up to 7 people), US$20. Additional fees for use of backcountry facilities.

ON-SITE AMENITIES: Information centers, restrooms, and gift shops. Both Banff information center and Lake Louise visitors center host exhibits and events. *Camping:* 13 campgrounds in the park; reservations must be made in advance. Both the town of Banff and the village of Lake Louise are located within the park's boundaries and offer a variety of services, including accommodations, restaurants, shops, and attractions; for more information, visit www.bannflakelouise.com.

BEST TIMES: May through October.

FIELD NOTES: Up-to-date travel and weather information is a must because the parklands are subject to heavy snow and/or avalanches. Early spring is the most likely time for an avalanche in the backcountry. Parks Canada warns that visitors are responsible for their own safety when driving, skiing, or hiking in such areas. Contact the weather office in Banff (call 4037622088) or a park visitors center.

JASPER NATIONAL PARK

ALBERTA, CANADA

An impressive array of wildlife makes its home in the Canadian Rockies. And Jasper National Park alone is home to 69 species of mammals, 277 types of birds, 40 types of fish, 16 species of amphibians and reptiles, and 1,300 species of plants. The park, situated on the eastern slopes of the Rocky Mountains in west-central Alberta, encompasses three ecosystems. The montane is warm

and dry and is where the town of Jasper is located. Bears, wolves, eagles, osprey, and mountain white fish are just some of the wildlife that you might encounter here. The subalpine is a huge forest lush with vegetation and an abundance of spruce trees. Here you'll find oddly stunted trees called krumholtz. Wolverines, lynx, caribou, and a species of large weasel that resembles a cat roam the area. In winter, this ecosystem is home to wrens, boreal chickadees, and the yellow-rumped warbler. The alpine is the most delicate of the ecosystems, and here visitors will find whistling marmots and pikas as well as the ptarmigan, a bird that thrives in cold, snowy conditions.

The Athabasca Glacier and the Columbia Icefield are located within the borders of the park. These large areas of ice are impressive to see, but visitors are warned to stay behind the safety barriers because crevasses often form by the glacier's edges. Tour-

ists have been known to die from hypothermia after falling into one of these cracks.

Backpacking, boating, mountaineering, horseback riding, and fishing are a few favorite summertime pursuits at Jasper National Park. In winter, visitors engage in cross-country skiing, snowshoeing, snowboarding, and ice skating.

LOCATION: 192 miles west of Edmonton, Hwy 16 (also called the Yellowhead Highway) runs through the park and is the main artery to and from Jasper. Trains and buses also service Jasper from Edmonton and Vancouver.

HOURS OF OPERATION: Year-round. *Icefield information center:* May 1–mid Oct.

CONTACT: Jasper National Park, Box 10, Jasper, AB, Canada, T0E 1E0; Tel: 7808526176; Fax: 7808526152; Web: www.pc.gc.ca/jasper. *Backcountry trail reservations:* Tel: 7808526177.

COST: *Entrance* (per day): Adult, US$10; senior (65 years and older), US$8; youth (6–16 years), US$5; family/group (up to 7 people), US$20. Additional fees may be required for camping, fishing, and special programs.

ON-SITE AMENITIES: Information centers, restrooms, and gift shops. *Camping:* Pocahontas, Whistlers, Wapiti, and Wabasso campgrounds take reservations (visit www.pccamping.ca or call

8777373783); all other campsites operate on a first-come, first-served basis. *Accommodations:* A wide variety of lodging is available, from hotels and motels to private villas; visit www .jasper.nps.lodging.com or www.jas percanadianrockies.com. Icefield information center offers accommodations and restaurants.

BEST TIMES: Peak season is July and August, so keep that in mind if you dislike crowds. If climate is a consideration, note that this area has long, cold winters and short, hot summers.

FIELD NOTES: Do not approach or feed wildlife; bears that become too dependent on treats from tourists have to be put down. Take special care when exploring the alpine areas of the park because its plants are especially fragile. Because the park maintains hundreds of miles of mountain bike trails and numerous road riding options, biking is an excellent way to explore this extraordinary place.

GWAII HAANAS NATIONAL PARK RESERVE

BRITISH COLUMBIA, CANADA

Frazzled souls who need to get away from it all can do just that at British Columbia's Gwaii Haanas National Park Reserve. This archipelago of 138 islands, named the Queen Charlotte Islands, is accessible only by boat, sea kayak, or chartered float plane, and lacks just about every creature comfort. What it does offer is spectacular scenery, fascinating native artifacts, lots of wildlife watching—and peace.

The reserve was created in 1988 through the joint efforts of the Haida Nation and the Canadian government. Many signs of the lives of the Haida people dot the islands; for example, visitors can see traditional upright carved poles at SG̱ang Gwaay on Anthony Island.

Migrating birds stop at the reserve every spring and fall to rest before they continue their journeys. It is also a major breeding location for peregrine

falcons. Saw-whet owls, Steller's jays, and hairy woodpeckers also live in the preserve's forests.

Sea mammals like gray and killer whales, dolphins, porpoises, and harbor seals can be spotted here. A rare bat, Keen's myotis, lives in a thermally heated cove on Hotsprings Island. The largest type of black bear in Canada, and a species with particularly strong paws, roams the reserve; and visitors will note that the bears, pine martens, and deer mice that live here are larger than their cousins on the mainland.

Sea creatures are abundant in the surrounding waters, thanks to kelp forests that provide a perfect home. Red turban and moon snails, limpets, periwinkles, and clams all can be found. Sea urchins are extremely common—too common, because these animals are a threat to the kelp forests. Their

population has exploded since their main predator, the sea otter, disappeared from the area.

Haide Gwaii, the original name for the Queen Charlotte Islands, means "place of wonder." Visitors can enjoy the scenery of San Christoval Mountains as well as the islands' rocky coastlines and cliffs. After a day of wildlife observation, relax in a thermal pool overlooking Juan Perez Sound on Hotsprings Island.

Because travel in Gwaii Haanas is by boat or float plane only, most visitors join a tour group. Tour operators operate from May through September and offer guided tours, charter vessel services, and passenger and cargo transport between points. Prices, services offered, and other amenities vary greatly; furthermore, tours fill up quickly, so it is advisable to make reservations well in advance. For a listing of current tour operators visit the park's website.

LOCATION: 400 miles north of Vancouver, 80 miles off the coast.

HOURS OF OPERATION: *Reserve:* Year-round, 24/7. *Park office:* Mon–Fri, 8 a.m. to noon and 1 p.m. to 4:30 p.m.

CONTACT: Gwaii Haanas National Park, Reserve and Haida Heritage Site, 60 Second Beach Rd, Skidegate (Haida Heritage Centre), PO Box 37, Queen Charlotte, BC V0T 1S0; Tel: 2505598818; Fax: 2505598366; Web: www.pc.gc.ca/pn-np/bc/gwaiihaanas; email: gwaii.haanas@pc.gc.ca.

COST: *Entrance* (per day): Adults, US$20; seniors, US$17; youths (6–16 years), US$10; children (5 and under), free; family group (up to 7 people), US$50.

ON-SITE AMENITIES: Watchmen sites have been developed to provide site security and protection of the cultural features and to offer visitors the opportunity to learn firsthand about the living Haida culture. Composting toilets are available at Watchmen sites.

BEST TIMES: July is the peak month for tourism. Keep in mind that a maximum of 300 visitors are allowed in the reserve at any given time, and only 3,000 visitors are allowed per year.

FIELD NOTES: Individual tourists must make reservations for visits between May 1 and September 30 and must take an orientation class that provides safety information and background information about the Haidi people. Be prepared to be flexible because severe weather conditions can significantly alter access to the islands. Bring enough food, water, clothing, equipment, and fuel to be comfortable for an extended stay.

KNIGHT INLET LODGE

BRITISH COLUMBIA, CANADA

For those looking for a wildlife experience that includes spotting grizzly bears, orcas, and eagles, the Knight Inlet Lodge may be the ultimate destination. Located on Minstrel Island and known for its extensive wildlife, the inlet and the area around the lodge play host to black bears, killer whales, eagles, sea lions, timber wolves, and many more animals.

You can observe sea lions at play and orca families interacting with one another from only a few feet away. The whales sometimes appear to be "playful" as they swim right alongside the tour boats. What's more, they've been known on occasion to converse with the guests. The lodge provides its visitors with all the means necessary for optimal interaction with the whales.

The lodge boasts exquisite dining, providing gourmet food, such as fresh local prawns, salmon, and Dungeness crab. Picnic lunches are available for those who want to spend the day touring, hiking, or fishing.

LOCATION: North of Vancouver Island, 180 miles from Vancouver, British Columbia. Accessible only by float plane.

HOURS OF OPERATION: Year-round, 24/7.

CONTACT: Knight Inlet Lodge, 10 3100 Kensington Cres., Courtenay, BC V9N 8Z9; Tel: 2503348858 or 8777644286 (toll-free); Fax: 2503348858; Web: www .knightinletlodge.com.

COST: *Rates* (3 days, 3 nights): From US$1,360 (including float plane). Fishing licenses are extra.

ON-SITE AMENITIES: The lodge offers specially designed wildlife tours, fishing, and gourmet dining. Rain gear and cooler boxes are available; check the website for available fishing equipment to arrange special trips.

BEST TIMES: June through October.

FIELD NOTES: Camera with a zoom lens is highly recommended; be sure to bring lots of film or memory cards. Waterproof protection for your photography or filming equipment is a must. Layered clothing is suggested; it can be chilly on the water and quite cool at night.

KOOTENAY NATIONAL PARK

BRITISH COLUMBIA, CANADA

Established in 1920, Kootenay National Park is one of a string of many parks in the Canadian Rockies. Once used as a meeting place for plains and mountain First Nations people and visited by fur traders and explorers, the park offers a wide array of scenic attractions.

The variety of ecosystems in Kootenay's 543 square miles include everything from the semiarid southwest corner to glacier-covered mountaintops. The dry parts of the park are home to a rare combination of Douglas fir, ponderosa pine, and wheatgrass. Even prickly pear cacti grow here. Whitebark pine, which is found in the mountainous regions, is the subject of a major conservation effort due to recent infestations of Asian blister rust.

The mountain goat, Kootenay's symbol, is abundant in the park. Visitors may spot grizzly and black bears, Rocky Mountain bighorn sheep, elk, moose, wolverines, marmots, white-tailed and mule deer, coyotes, and wolves while hiking or driving. Badgers are a less-common sight because there are only about 200 living within the park boundaries. Look for them along the valley bottom, which is an excellent place for wildlife watching in general, especially in winter.

The rubber boa is one of the special species in the park; they can be found around the thermal pools at Radium Hot Springs. This snake, which is the boa species living farthest north, has been called "two headed" because of its

identical head and tail. It is relatively docile and slow.

Those who wish to rough it can stay at one of the 431 campsites open during the summer months. These sites have restrooms, and Redstreak Campground has electricity hookups. Reservations must be made in advance.

LOCATION: Near Radium Hot Springs, British Columbia, approximately 552 miles from Vancouver and 106 miles from Calgary, Alberta. Flight connections may be made from Calgary or Vancouver to Cranbrook, where a car can be rented for the remainder of the journey. Calgary and Vancouver also have regular bus service to Radium Hot Springs.

HOURS OF OPERATION: Year-round. *Campgrounds:* Early May–late Sept; Dolly Varden campground, early Oct for the winter.

CONTACT: Kootenay National Park, PO Box 220, Radium Hot Springs, BC V0A 1M0; Tel: 2503479505; Fax: 2503479980; Web: www.pc.gc.ca/Kootenay; email: kootenay.info@pc.gc.ca.

COST: *Entrance:* Adult, US$10; senior (65 years and older), US$8; youth (6–16 years), US$5; family group (up to 7 people), US$20. *Campsites:* US$16–$38. Additional fees for use of backcountry facilities may apply.

ON-SITE AMENITIES: Campgrounds, 11 picnic sites, two information centers, restrooms, gift shop. Showers are available at Redstreak Campground only.

Radium Hot Springs Lodge: Recommended lodging overlooking the hot springs; 66 rooms, all with queen-size beds and breathtaking views; a herd of bighorn sheep regularly graze on the grounds; call 2503479341 or 8882229341 (toll-free) or visit www.radiumhot springslodge.com.

BEST TIMES: July and August are the most popular months for tourists, so keep that in mind if you want to avoid crowds.

FIELD NOTES: Summers are short and cool; winters are long and snowy. Dress in layers and always wear sunscreen and sunglasses, even during the snowy season. Remember to check weather forecasts and avalanche warnings (during winter and early spring) before your visit. Do keep a respectful distance from wild animals and look out for them while driving along Hwy 93, especially at night. This is bear country, and appropriate precautions should be taken, including storing all food and cooler items inside your vehicle or storage locker and removing rubbish from your campsite daily.

PACIFIC RIM NATIONAL PARK RESERVE

BRITISH COLUMBIA, CANADA

The Pacific Rim National Park Reserve (PRNPR) offers an astonishing array of habitats; here you can explore sandy beaches, mudflats, small wave-swept islands, rocky shorelines, dense coniferous rain forests, bogs, meadows, rivers, and streams. The three units of the reserve are Long Beach, West Coast Trail, and Broken Group Islands.

Long Beach is on Wickaninnish Bay, located on the west coast of Vancouver Island between the villages of Ucluelet and Tofino. This section has one campground, Green Point, with 105 campsites and walking trails, some leading down to the ocean.

The West Coast Trail is located along Barkley Sound between the villages of Bamfield and Port Renfrew. This section features a 47-mile backpacking trail with one eye-catching sight after another. Hikers come across sandstone

cliffs, caves, sea arches, sea stacks, waterfalls, and beaches. Along the way you might spot a cougar, bear, wolf, fox, or deer, and when you get to the sea, look out for whales, sea lions, and seals. One backpacker who hiked the trail said, "It's nature's eye candy."

The well-named Broken Group Islands consist of some 100 islands and rock formations in Barkley Sound. It's a bold and beautiful area, accessible only by boat and offers the opportunity for adventurous visitors to explore dozens of different sheltered coves and bays.

Throughout the reserve, visitors can engage in camping, hiking, canoeing, kayaking, scuba diving, fishing, and wildlife viewing. The reserve also provides interpretive programs. If you're a bird-watcher, there are birds galore: Some 330 species have been recorded, and of these, 96 species are known to breed within the reserve's boundaries. Look for bald eagles, common ravens, Steller's jays, chestnut-backed chickadees, black oystercatchers, great blue herons, belted kingfishers, winter wrens, common loons, pelagic cormorants, pleated woodpeckers, killdeer, and golden-crowned kinglets. During the spring and fall migration times, visitors may be treated to trumpeter swans, harlequin ducks, and snowy owls.

LOCATION: West coast of Vancouver Island.

HOURS OF OPERATION: Year-round, 24/7. *Visitors centers:* Dates and hours of operation vary; see the reserve's website.

CONTACT: Pacific Rim National Park Reserve, 2185 Ocean Terrace Rd, PO Box 280 Ucluelet, BC, V0R 3A0; Tel: 2507267721; Fax: 2507264720; Web: www.pc.gc.ca/pn-np/bc/pacificrim/index_E.asp; email: pacrim.info@pc.gc.ca.

COST: *Entrance:* Adults, US$8; seniors, US$7; youths, US$4; family groups, US$20; commercial groups (per person), US$6; school groups (per student), US$3. *Camping* (per night): From US$18.

ON-SITE AMENITIES: Campgrounds, firewood, gift shop, bathrooms, education center, visitors center, whale watching, picnic areas, walking and hiking trails, guided tours, and interpretive programs.

BEST TIMES: Mid March to mid October when most park facilities are open. During the rest of the year, most facilities are closed.

FIELD NOTES: Compass, water, sunglasses, first aid kit, sunblock, bug repellent, boots, hiking shoes, etc. When birding and hiking, it's imperative to be aware of your surroundings. The reserve is home to bears and cougars; keep an eye out for who is watching whom.

PRINCESS ROYAL ISLAND

BRITISH COLUMBIA, CANADA

If you are a hearty soul with a yen for the truly unusual, you could do a lot worse than visiting the Great Bear Rainforest, located on Princess Royal Island off what is called Canada's "Forgotten Coast," an extremely remote area of British Columbia. Access to the island is by boat or float plane only, and once you are there you will immediately sense that one thing is missing: other people. Aside from the Tsimshiam, a Native American people who once lived along the coast, almost no people have journeyed to the island's inland rain forest.

One of the great attractions that brings people to the island every year is an unusual bear. The white (or light) Kermode bear—named in honor of Francis Kermode, the zoologist who first studied the mammal—is actually a standard black bear with unusual coloring; it is not a polar bear. First Na-

tion peoples call this bear the White Spirit and say that Raven created the white bear as a reminder of the last ice age and decreed that the animals would live in peace and harmony forever.

The Kermode bear is found nowhere else on the planet. Although these are wild bears in every sense, their long isolation from humans has made them unafraid of people. Other bears and wildlife live on the island, including grizzly and black bears, foxes, deer, wolves, and golden and bald eagles. Bird-watchers may catch a glimpse of the endangered marbled murrelet. The sea around the island is home to a bevy of beauties, including killer whales (orcas), porpoises, salmon, and elephant seals.

Princess Royal Island is a place of many wonders. It encompasses a diverse habitat, ranging from sandy beaches, lowland old-growth rain forests, subalpine parklands, to alpine tundra, and visitors can also explore fjords, estuaries, and lakes. In the island's rain forests, visitors will be able to walk among some of the largest and oldest trees on earth, including Sitka spruce, red cedar, western hemlock, and Douglas fir. Some of these trees reach 300 feet and live more than 1,500 years.

It is also heaven on earth (or water) for paddlers who can wend their way through fjords and inlets along the coast. Once in a while, a Kermode bear can be spotted from the water. A caution, though: These waters are known for their strong currents and sea fog; only experienced paddlers should explore this coast. For the rest of us, local commercial vendors offer sightseeing trips that guarantee wildlife sightings— and a safe return to shore.

LOCATION: Located 260 miles north of Vancouver and 100 miles south of Prince Rupert; accessible only by boat or air. Scheduled commercial air service from Vancouver International Airport. Float plane, helicopter, ferry, and water taxi services are available from Prince Rupert and connect to most of the smaller communities throughout the region.

HOURS OF OPERATION: Year-round, 24/7. Tour dates vary.

CONTACT: Spirit Bear Adventures: 4- and 7-day tour packages; Tel: 250839-2346 or 8776442346 (toll-free); Fax: 2508391256; Web: www.klemtutourism .com. **Eco Summer Expeditions:** 8-day tour packages starting at US$3,300 per person; Tel: 2506740102 or 8004658884 (toll-free); Fax: 2506742197; Web: www .ecosummer.com. *Other packages:* Web: www.britishcolumbia.com.

COST: Depends on tour company.

ON-SITE AMENITIES: *Paddlers:* Take BC Ferries to Klemtu on Swindle Island; from there, Princess Royal Island is 4.6 miles north by boat. *Sightseeing trips:* Available from Bella Bella and Shearwater, which are accessible by ferry or air. **King Pacific Lodge:** This is the only lodging on the island; a stunning eco-lodge located on Barnyard Harbour; visit www.kingpacific lodge.com. *Camping:* A few campsites are available for paddlers; high tides can make camping difficult, so it is advised that you travel between full moons.

BEST TIMES: June through September.

FIELD NOTES: It is very important to bring cold- and wet-weather gear, including rubber boots. Carry a first aid kit, matches, flares, compass, knife, and sunscreen. Kayaking tours accept children on a limited basis; contact individual tour companies for specific information.

GROS MORNE NATIONAL PARK

NEWFOUNDLAND, CANADA

Appointed as a World Heritage Site and boasting a vast variety of great scenery and wildlife, Gros Morne National Park has something for everyone. Here visitors can engage in challenging hikes through the wild, swimming along the waterfalls and sandy beaches in summer, and cross-country skiing and snowmobiling in winter. But for those who are most interested in observing wildlife, this park will not disappoint.

Rare animals such as arctic hares, wolves, and marten weasels all find refuge within the park's borders. More commonly found mammals such as bats, American beavers, and black bears are native inhabitants. The Newfoundland marten was once common to the area, but now only a few hundred survive because much of its natural habitat has been lost. Unfortunately, martens are often caught in snares set for snowshoe hares. Visitors who want to see this animal should try the old-growth forest of Main River, in the northeastern part of the park. Should you be so lucky as to observe one you will want to have your camera on hand.

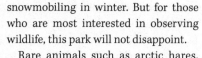

Because about 240 species of birds have been spotted in the park, birdwatchers can expect to add many to their lifetime checklists. In summer, Swainson hawks; hermit thrushes; ruby-crowned kinglets; yellow-bellied flycatchers; winter wrens; magnolia, black-throated green, and black-and-white warblers; restarts, and ovenbirds are seen in the park. Visitors who travel to the area between Sally's Cove and Western Brook will find American bitterns, northern harriers, greater yellowlegs, common snipes, Canada geese, northern ravens, black-backed woodpeckers, olive-sided flycatchers, Canada jays, spruce grouses, Wilson's warblers, and swamp sparrows.

LOCATION: West coast of Newfoundland.

HOURS OF OPERATION: Apr–Oct.

CONTACT: *Headquarters:* Gros Morne National Park, 130 Rocky Harbour, NL A0K 4N0; Tel: 7094582417; Fax: 7094582059; Web: www.grosmorne .com.

COST: *Entrance:* Adults, US$10; seniors, US$8; youth, US$5; family or group, US$20.

ON-SITE AMENITIES: Boating, guided tours, fishing, kayaking, swimming, hiking, and picnicking. Many interpretational and educational programs are free. Various campground facilities, B&Bs, inns, and cottages are available in the area.

BEST TIMES: May through August.

FIELD NOTES: Interpretive and educational programs run regularly from late June through September. Interpreters for guided events or talks are available for groups; call 7094582066 at least 2 weeks in advance.

WOOD BUFFALO NATIONAL PARK

NORTHWEST TERRITORIES AND ALBERTA,

CANADA

Wood Buffalo National Park is the result of a dramatic, last-minute effort to save one of the most enduring symbols of western North America: the bison. The year was 1922 and the plan was to protect the habitat of a small herd of wood bison whose population had dropped to less than 1,000 individuals. Today, these 22,400 square miles of northern boreal interior plains make up a UNESCO World Heritage Site and Canada's largest national park, encompassing the largest free-roaming and self-regulated bison herd in the world. The parklands are also home to Native American peoples, some of whom continue to live, hunt, trap, and fish according to longstanding tradition.

The geography of the park is spectacular and can be divided into four basic areas. The Caribou and Birch Uplands, home to spruce forests and lichen tundra, rise over 1,600 feet. Many fossils can be found within the eroding slopes of this rocky area. The Alberta plateau is the largest section of the park. Visitors to this wet area will be able to explore bogs, muskegs, streams, and rivers. Caves and sinkholes, known as karstland, dot landscape, dramatically demonstrating the effects of groundwater on the soluble gypsum bedrock. Bowl-shaped sinkholes are created when the caves collapse.

The delta area of the park encompasses more than 2,400 square miles. This part of the park features shallow lakes, marshes, grasslands, and forests and is home to many waterfowl and fish. Bird lovers are also in for a treat at the park. A trip to the salt plains offers the opportunity to observe the endangered whooping crane feeding far from its breeding grounds. This is the tallest

North American bird (about 4 feet); it has a pure white body with black markings on its face and a red crown.

During migration seasons, the delta becomes a resting area for millions of waterfowl. Sandhill cranes, geese, swans, and ducks all make temporary homes in the park. The northernmost colony of white pelicans as well as bald eagles and the endangered peregrine falcon can be seen in the Slave River area.

Mammals and reptiles can also be spotted in the delta. Visitors should look for muskrats, coyotes, red foxes, bears, caribou, beavers, wolves, and moose. The protected red-sided garter snake emerges in April to spend the summer in the bogs.

LOCATION: Straddles the Northwest Territories–Alberta border. Park headquarters are in Fort Smith, Northwest Territories. Hwy 5 (via the MacKenzie Hwy) provides all-weather access along a hard-packed gravel road to the park and Fort Smith. Charter and commercial air service to Fort Smith is available from Edmonton. There is no all-weather road access to Fort Chipewyan.

HOURS OF OPERATION: Year-round. *Fort Smith visitors center:* Mon–Fri, 9 a.m. to noon, and 1 p.m. to 5 p.m.; summer, Sat–Sun, 1 p.m. to 5 p.m. *Fort Chipewyan visitors center:* Mon–Fri, 8:30 a.m. to noon, and 1 p.m. to 5 p.m.; intermittent weekends June 20–Sept 6 (phone ahead).

CONTACT: Wood Buffalo National Park, Box 750, Fort Smith, NWT X0E 0P0; Tel: 8678727900; Web: www.pc.gc.ca/pn-np/nt/woodbuffalo; email: wbnp.info@pc.gc.ca.

COST: *Entrance:* Free.

ON-SITE AMENITIES: *Fort Smith and Fort Chipewyan visitors centers:* Wheelchair accessible; offer exhibits, park information, backcountry registration, videos, and souvenirs. Campsites and picnic areas are found throughout the park; boating and fishing facilities are available. Fort Smith has a hotel, campground, and B&B rooms; charter and commercial air service. Fort Chipewyan has a hotel and B&B rooms.

BEST TIMES: June through September for optimal wildlife viewing. Mid July starts the bison mating season. All-weather road access is available to Fort Smith and Peace Point.

FIELD NOTES: Bears inhabit all areas of the park; take proper precautions to reduce unwanted encounters. Bison are free roaming and can be very dangerous. Biting insects are a reality on the park grounds. Wearing impenetrable clothing is recommended.

INN AT LORETO BAY

MEXICO

Loreto, the oldest settlement on the Baja Peninsula, was established in 1697 by Juan María Salvatierra, a Jesuit priest. The area served as the capital of all of Las Californias for over 100 years. The Misíon de Nuestra Señora de Loreto, founded by Father Juan Maria, still stands today and includes the original mission bells. This active church is located next to the Museum of the Missions of California, where you can learn about the area's 300 years of religious and cultural history.

Loreto is situated in a naturally protected region between the Sea of Cortez and the Sierra de la Giganta mountains. Here visitors will find a paradise of varied habitats that offers many opportunities for wildlife viewing and other activities such as hiking, cycling, fishing, scuba diving, and snorkeling. The Bay of Loreto National Marine Park, the largest marine park in Mexico, is home to more than 880 species of reef-dwelling and migratory fish not to mention the beautiful corals. Blue, gray, and humpback whales spend the winter in the waters of the marine park. Visitors can also observe seals, dolphins, starfish, and a variety of migratory birds and small reptiles.

A stay at Inn at Loreto Bay is integral to the experience; luxury accommodations and all arrangements can be made through the hotel.

LOCATION: On the Baja Peninsula; 5 hours from Los Cabos and 3.5 hours from La Paz by car.

HOURS OF OPERATION: Year-round, 24/7.

CONTACT: Inn at Loreto Bay, Blvd Misión de Loreto s/n Fracc. Nopolo; C.P. 23880, Loreto, B.C.S.; Tel: 6131330010; Web: www .innatloretobay.com; email: reservations@discoverloretobay.com.

COST: *Standard room* (per day): US$125–$225, depending on season. *Whale watching tours* (per person): 2-person minimum, US$200; 4-person minimum, US$150; children (up to 5 years), free. *Loreto town tour* (per person): 4-person minimum, US$58. *Scuba diving:* US$89–$150; gear rental, US$25; scuba and full certification courses available, US$150–$400 (includes two tanks, beverages, and snacks). *Sport fishing adventures* (7 hours): US$290–$1,200 (includes equipment, filleting, packing, and cleaning); bait licenses, food, and beverage are extra. *Private yachts:* Available for charter; offer a number of cruises, including snorkeling and sunset from US$600. *Coronado Island sand and snorkel tours:* US$60–$100. G*iant Humboldt squid diving:* Check with concierge for booking and current pricing.

ON-SITE AMENITIES: Hotel, restaurant, concierge, tennis courts, tours, mountain excursions, arrangements for water activities and whale watching.

BEST TIMES: February through March.

FIELD NOTES: Commercial air service is available to Loreto. Take a windbreaker for splashing water and waterproof protection for your camera or video equipment if you plan to whale watch. Scuba gear is available for rent. There are nearby towns for sightseeing and shopping, and an artist's colony is in the area.

KUYIMÁ ECO LODGE

BAJA, MEXICO

Dedicated to the habitat protection and eco-tourism in the San Ignacio area, Kuyimá Eco Lodge promotes sustainable development in the Southern Baja region. The lodge organizes tours to observe gray whales in the San Ignacio Lagoon and ancient cave paintings in the San Francisco y Santa Marta Mountains.

The lodge, with its cabins and camping grounds, is designed to exist harmoniously with the surroundings.

Visitors will find the opportunity for easy travel to diverse ecosystems—from desert to mountains to sea—and thus enjoy a range of experiences. The main attraction at Kuyimá Eco Lodge is, however, whale watching. Hundreds of gray whales travel to San Ignacio Lagoon to spend the winter mating and giving birth. Starting in mid December, the whales arrive in the lagoon. Over the next 3 months, the whales become more active as their young begin to

mature; this is prime time to expect close encounters with these huge mammals. The staff is dedicated to both protecting these whales and educating visitors.

A trip to the nearby mountains will give visitors a chance to see some of the 200 caves that are known to contain Native American paintings. It is thought that these cave paintings were created more than 7,500 years ago. Rock art excursions can be arranged through the lodge.

LOCATION: 35 miles south of San Ignacio, on the Baja Peninsula.

HOURS OF OPERATION: Dec–Apr.

CONTACT: Tel: 526151540070; Web: www.kuyima.com.

COST: *Packages* (4 days/3 nights): from US$495. *Camping* (per day): from US$10, space for a 4-person tent; other charges related to camping may apply.

ON-SITE AMENITIES: Whale excursions and cave painting excursions; guided tours by car, foot, bike, and kayak. Food services, rustic rental cabins, environmental-friendly toilets, and sun-heated showers. Campgrounds with equipment rental on-site. Kuyimá also provides summer camps for children on environmental education and conservation.

BEST TIMES: *For whale watching:* January through April.

FIELD NOTES: The lodge can accommodate a maximum of 20 guests so book well in advance; even as much as a year ahead. You can contract camping equipment and food if you are not staying in cabins. Food supplies are not readily available on-site, so plan accordingly. Be sure to have waterproof protection for cameras and other equipment.

SOUTH AMERICA

Argentina, Belize, Bolivia,
Bonaire, Brazil, Costa Rica, Ecuador,
Guatemala, Honduras, Panama, Peru,
Trinidad, Venezuela

EL RAY NATIONAL PARK

ARGENTINA

El Ray National Park is located in a horseshoe-shaped valley bordered by the Sierra del Piquete mountain range and Cresta del Gallo. The natural protection these mountains afford allow for a pristine and environmentally sound ecosystem. This natural barrier is augmented by the efforts of the conservationists working for the park system.

At more than 109,000 acres, the park mainly encompasses high-altitude hill land. Endangered animals such as the caí monkey, white-lipped peccary, and tapir mingle in El Ray with other rare animals like the brocket deer and a tremendous array of brightly plumed birds, including the speedy, red-legged chuña, which populate the jungles. There are, in fact, more than 250 species of birds and roughly 50 species of mammals that make their home in the park. Scrubland foxes, pumas, otters, and anteaters also thrive here. If a visitor were to follow one of the many rivers that run down from the mountains into the jungle valley, he or she would pass through a number of the habitats and have a chance to observe an almost unmatched diversity of species.

There are eight walking trails of various degrees of difficulty, all of which provide front-line wildlife viewing and birding opportunities. The trails lead visitors to some of the park's most scenic regions of jungle interior and sierra landscapes. A visit to the park's three waterfalls, the Pozo Verde, the Popayán, and the Cascada Santa Elena, is time well spent.

LOCATION: 124 miles from Salta, Argentina.

HOURS OF OPERATION: Year-round, 24/7.

CONTACT: Web: www.enjoy-argentina .org/salta-destinations-salta-rey-na tional-park.php.

COST: Depends on accommodations and length of tour.

ON-SITE AMENITIES: Expert guides, horse rentals, numerous hiking trails, auto-touring. There are eight walking paths of different degrees of difficulty, distance, and duration. *Campgrounds:* Two areas for camping, one near the Popayán River and the other near park headquarters.

BEST TIMES: May through November.

FIELD NOTES: A first aid kit, water, and food supplies are recommended for those camping. Binoculars, field books, comfortable walking shoes, and comfortable horseback-riding clothes (if desired) are recommended. Although the park can be explored in many ways, horseback exploration with an expert guide allows you to get closer to the wildlife than you would by vehicle, and to cover more ground than you would by foot.

COCKSCOMB BASIN WILDLIFE SANCTUARY AND JAGUAR PRESERVE

BELIZE

The jaguar is the fastest four-legged creature over short distances on the face of the earth, capable of speeds of over 100 miles an hour. It is an endangered species throughout much of Africa, but not in the Cockscomb Basin Wildlife Sanctuary and Jaguar Preserve, a 150-square-mile area in southern Belize. The preserve, which opened in 1986, has 200 jaguars roaming its grounds—the largest concentration in the world. Unfortunately, because of the jaguar's finely honed sense of stealth and cunning, the animal is difficult to observe in the wild. What is much more likely—and thrilling in its own way—is to spot its paw prints on one of the trails that run through

Cockscomb, particularly when the ground has been softened during the rainy season. The sanctuary receives up to 180 inches a year.

The jaguar is hardly alone in Cockscomb. There are local populations of

several other cats; visitors may be lucky enough to see ocelots, pumas, and margays. Other animals that thrive here are pacas, peccaries, brocket deer, tayras, otters, and coatis; these species have been so well protected that there are few places on earth where you can find them in greater numbers. Cockscomb is also a bird-watcher's delight, with nearly 300 species, including the curassow and the keel-billed toucan. Endangered Morelet crocodiles feed in the major rivers of the basin, and tremendous populations of the splendid red-eyed tree frogs occasionally appear in the thousands.

There is a wide variety of options available for travelers in the preserve. With over 20 miles of maintained trails, hikes lasting from 1 hour to 5 days are available. The River Path and Wari Loop trails are usually the best for wildlife, and the Rubber Tree Trail is the walk for bird-watching.

Cockscomb also features its share of unusual plants, such as the accurately named hot lips bush; its pouting red flowers can often be seen along the edges of trails.

For the bold—if not the downright brave—Cockscomb offers the chance to spend the night in the deep isolation of the basin's forest, surrounded by the roar of howler monkeys, screeching insects, and winds moving through the treetops. Some people would rather spend their nights elsewhere, but for the adventurous, the experience can be thrilling, even magical.

LOCATION: Southern Belize, approximately 20 miles from Dangriga. From Maya Center, reach the park via Southern Hwy. Bus service is available from Dangriga or Belize City to Maya Center; from there, visitors must walk (6 miles) or take a taxi (US$15) to the sanctuary.

HOURS OF OPERATION: Year-round, 7:30 a.m. to 4:30 p.m.

CONTACT: Web: http://ambergriscaye.com/pages/town/parkcockscomb.html. **Belize Audubon Society:** Web: www.belizeaudubon.org/parks/cbws.htm. **Belize Explorer:** Web: www.belize-vacation.com/belize/cockscomb.htm.

COST: *Entrance:* US$5 (non-nationals); purchase at the Maya Center craft shop and then register at the visitors center. Overnight stays are extra.

ON-SITE AMENITIES: Visitors center, gift shop. *Lodging:* Visitors are required to bring their own food and water; rental fee for communal kitchen; dormitory (up to 24 people), US$20 per night; secluded cabins, from US$53 per night. *Camping:* Two backcountry campsites.

BEST TIMES: The most active time for wildlife is the rainy season, especially at its beginning (June to July). The best time for migrant birds is around December. Animals usually are livelier on cloudy, cooler days.

FIELD NOTES: Don't forget to bring: bug repellent, hats, plenty of water, swimsuit, towel, hiking shoes, camera, binoculars, rain jacket, and a bird identification book. No fishing or hunting is allowed. Cooking is allowed in designated areas only.

COMMUNITY BABOON SANCTUARY

BELIZE

Community Baboon Sanctuary is the home to the black howler monkey. These animals have one astonishing trait: They are louder than any other land animal in the world because their large hyoid bone (in the throat) enables them to make a distinctive, incomparably loud sound. In fact, according to *Guinness Book of World Records*, the black howler can be heard for 3 miles, which, when you think about it, is an incredible distance. The monkey's call, however, is not exactly a howling. In the novel *Green Mansions*, William Henry Hudson noted that the monkey's call is not actually a howl. He compared the male's voice to a powerful roar and the female's to a pig's grunt.

There are actually nine species of howler monkeys, some of them with surly personalities, which make them totally unsuitable as pets; the black howler monkey, known in Belize as the baboon (though no relation to the African monkey by that name), has a gentle nature, is not aggressive to people, and does make a good pet—which is why these primates are always in danger of being abducted.

To save the howlers, which were being destroyed by agriculture and other encroachments on their habitat, the 20-square-mile Community Baboon Sanctuary was formed by about 200 private landowners from seven villages. These individuals are committed to conserving their land for the protection of the black howler monkey and its habitat. Owing to these efforts, the monkey population is on the increase. In return, the local economy has benefited from eco-tourism, and many people have been able to take advantage of educational programs.

The sanctuary offers a variety of tours for watching—and listening to!—black howler monkeys. Depending on your tastes, you can stay in a lodge or spend the night in the rain forest. Some tours allow visitors to experience the local wildlife when it's most active—at night; other tours involve canoeing along the river, where crocodiles, monkeys, and other wildlife can be observed.

LOCATION: An hour's drive from Belize City.

HOURS OF OPERATION: Year-round, 24/7.

CONTACT: *Visitors center:* Tel: 501-2202181; Web: www.howlermonkeys.org; email: info@howlermonkeys.org.

COST: *Museum entrance and guided walk* (per person): US$5.

ON-SITE AMENITIES: Visitors center, museum, lodging, campsites. Tours are arranged through the visitors center and museum in Bermudian Landing or by calling or emailing the sanctuary directly.

BEST TIMES: Year-round.

FIELD NOTES: Bring suntan lotion, comfortable walking shoes, bug repellent, sunglasses, hat, long- and short-sleeved shirts, and comfortable footwear. Camping is allowed on sanctuary grounds in small tents and provides a thrilling experience. Consider bringing a tape recorder to capture the sounds of the howler monkeys.

DUPLOOY'S JUNGLE LODGE

BELIZE

Located in the heart of the tropics, duPlooy's eco-retreat offers a unique experience for everyone, whether you are seeking high adventure or simple relaxation, traveling solo or with a family. Considered as a haven for birds—more than 300 species have been recorded within 5 miles of the lodge—and animals alike, this retreat was once a cattle ranch; it's one of the world's most fascinating lodges. Visitors are also treated to the lodge's 45-acre botanical garden.

duPlooy's offers an opportunity for visitors to get close with the forest birds

Other activities provided by du-Plooy's include canoeing, horseback riding, and cave exploration as well as excursions to nearby ancient Mayan sites.

LOCATION: 72 miles from Belize City on the Western Highway.

HOURS OF OPERATION: Year-round.

CONTACT: Tel: 0115018243101; Fax: 0115018243301; Web: www.duplooys .com.

COST: *Rooms* (per night): Individual rooms, double occupancy from US$180; each additional person, US$15. Several group packages are available.

ON-SITE AMENITIES: All accommodations have porches with hammocks, hot water, ceiling fans, and screened windows. Costs include continental breakfast, use of canoes and inner tubes, complimentary coffee or tea, birding on the deck, unlimited entrance to the botanic gardens, and a self-guided tour booklet.

BEST TIMES: September through May. It gets very hot during the summer months.

FIELD NOTES: No red meat is served at the lodge due to environmental issues. The horseback riding tours provide great views of the countryside. Canoeing allows for sightseeing around the Macal, Mopan, and Belize rivers. Bring insect repellent!

on the edge of Macal River. The lodge is situated on a wooded hillside and a walk has been constructed to allow guests to walk right into the forest canopy to observe birds that are rarely encountered at ground level. Relax on the deck and observe collar aracaris, wood thrushes, and the blue-crowned motmots bickering over the plates of fruit set out by the staff each morning.

Lodge guests are awoken each morning by the chattering of plain chachalacas; rose-throated becards, masked tityras, and a variety of flycatchers flit about the trees surrounding the decks. Once you're ready to head into the forest, you'll find a number of trails that will lead you to parrots, toucans, puffbirds, and other exotic species. At the end of the day, bird-watchers can catch sight of owls and nightjars. On the forest floor, iguanas, gray foxes, armadillos, and gibnuts scavenge for food.

MADIDI NATIONAL PARK

BOLIVIA

Madidi National Park, located in the upper Amazon River basin in Bolivia, covers over 10,000 square miles, making it larger than the state of New Jersey. Madidi is part of a group of parks and preserves that make up one of the largest protected areas on earth. Of the roughly 9,000 species of birds in the world, more than 11% of them can be found in Madidi. That number is staggering and has helped designate the park as a world-class destination for the serious student and fan of ornithology.

The biologically and ecologically diverse park offers visitors unparalleled opportunities to visit wildly disparate landscapes, ranging from the glacial caps of the Andes Mountains to the tropical rain forests of the Tuichi River.

River trips through the park allow you to explore the Bolivian Amazon with expert guides as you spend time with both aquatic and riverside animals native to the area. You may witness the pink river dolphin, caimans, and numerous species of monkeys, such as, the night, red howler, brown capuchin, and black spider. Macaws,

toucans, and anacondas are also commonly seen.

LOCATION: Bolivia in the upper Amazon River basin.

HOURS OF OPERATION: Year-round, 24/7.

CONTACT: Tel: 5913 3396470; Web: www.enjoybolivia.com/english/what-new/la-paz-madidi-national-park.shtml.

COST: Depends on length of stay, type of tour, and lodging.

ON-SITE AMENITIES: In addition to the prolific wildlife, the park provides easy access to other sites such as monasteries, local villages, and more. **Chalalan EcoLodge:** The only lodge in the park; cabins and hotel rooms with modern amenities are available; restaurant.

BEST TIMES: October through June.

FIELD NOTES: With such a diverse array of geography, specific note should be taken of the particular region you visit. Climate-appropriate clothing is always recommended because conditions can change dramatically depending on the elevation. Waterproof equipment is recommended for river trips.

SAJAMA NATIONAL PARK

BOLIVIA

Sajama National Park features a spectacular Andean landscape, with elevations ranging from 13,000 to nearly 21,300 feet. The park includes the Nevados de Payachata, a series of inactive volcanoes that straddle the border between Bolivia and Chile, and 200,000 acres that make up the world's highest (in elevation) forest.

The park was formed in 1939 with the goal of preserving the indigenous keua tree, which was almost forested out of existence in the early 1900s. An ancillary benefit was ensuring a protected habitat for endangered animals such as the suri (rare species of alpaca), the quirquincho (South American armadillo), and the vicuña (a wild South American camelid). Birders may delight in the sights of three species of flamingo, various ducks and gulls, and water hens. The Andean avocet, a member of the avocet and stilt bird families is also found here.

The historical highlights in the area include pre-Inca burial tombs and several small churches built by the Spanish during the 17th century.

LOCATION: 180 miles from La Paz, in the Oruro Department, near the Chilean and Bolivian border in southwest Bolivia.

HOURS OF OPERATION: Year-round, 24/7.

CONTACT: *Park:* Tel: 59108135260. *Tours:* www.southamericanfiesta.com.

COST: *Entrance:* US$2. *Tours* (per person): From US$486 (including accommodations, transportation, local tours, and meals).

ON-SITE AMENITIES: Expert guides, extensive ruins, numerous hiking trails, mountain climbing, and camping. Rangers from the station in Sajama village are also able to arrange for transportation, mules, and guides.

BEST TIMES: May through September.

FIELD NOTES: There are sparse amenities in the park. A first aid kit and food supplies are recommended for those camping. Heavy snows fall from October through April. With very fine black lava sand, open camping in the valley can at times become difficult. Severe sand storms can arise out of nowhere, within minutes. No permits are required to camp in the park; however, one must register at the ranger's station in Sajama village near the park entrance. If you intend to climb, additional information will be required during registration (area of climb, experience level, personal equipment).

BONAIRE NATIONAL MARINE PARK

BONAIRE

The 111-square-mile island of Bonaire, one of five islands that form the Dutch Caribbean, has a long history of protecting wildlife. Starting in 1961, the hunting of sea turtles in the island's coastal waters was banned. In 1971, spear fishing was prohibited, and in 1975 the collection of coral (dead or alive) was banned. In 1979 Bonaire's coastal reefs became legally protected, and later that year Bonaire National Marine Park was officially established. The park's mission is to protect, maintain, and restore the biological diversity of the island's shoreline, reef, and marine ecosystems. Bonaire circles the island, covering an area of 6.672 acres, and extends from the high tide line into the sea to a depth of 200 feet. Visitors

can engage in a variety of recreational activities and have the chance to see, appreciate, and learn about the island's rich shore, reef, and marine wildlife.

Growing along the park's sandy shoreline are stands of cacti and divi divi trees, which never grow straight but instead are bent and sculpted by the island's persistent trade winds. Groups of flamingos wade in brackish pools along the shore and many other birds, including grebes, petrels, pelicans, boobies, herons, egrets, rails, and many species of ducks and geese are seen along the shoreline. The lora, an endangered green, yellow-shouldered parrot, lives on the island. Iguana sunbathe in the park's warm sands or lounge lazily high in the trees. An excellent climber, the iguana literally falls when it wants to get down. Incredibly, it can fall 50 feet without injury. The reptile weighs up to 20 pounds and grows to a length of 4–6 feet.

The park's coral reef topography is approximately the same all around the island. Immediately offshore is the shallow reef terrace that gently slopes to a depth of about 30 feet. The slope then becomes steeper, continuing to a depth of about 130 feet where it terminates at the sandy ocean bottom. Snorkelers can expect to see parrotfish, damselfish, blue tang, trumpet fish, and the queen or pink conch. Scuba divers might find wrasses, hogfish, and lettuce sea slugs living on dead coral. The waters are home to the green turtle; the hawksbill turtle, with its beak-like face, serrated carapace, and yellow underside, is another welcome sight. With luck, divers might see the reddish brown loggerhead or the small olive ridley turtle. On rare occasions, visitors can even observe the black and white giant leatherback turtle.

LOCATION: On the island of Bonaire in the Netherlands Antilles, near Kralendijk, and a 5-minute drive from Flamingo International Airport.

HOURS OF OPERATION: 24/7.

CONTACT: *Headquarters and visitors center:* Bonaire National Marine Park, Barcadera z/n, Bonaire, Netherlands Antilles, Stinapa Bonaire, PO Box 368, Bonaire, Netherlands Antilles; Tel: 5997178444; Web: www.bmp.org.

COST: *Entrance* (day pass): With snorkeling, US$10; with scuba diving, US$25. Yearly passes are available; fees can be paid at snorkel/dive shops and at the front desk of hotels.

ON-SITE AMENITIES: Park headquarters, snorkeling and dive shops.

BEST TIMES: Bonaire is sunny year-round with an average air temperature of 82°F and water temperature of 80°F. The island is located outside of the Caribbean hurricane belt.

FIELD NOTES: Because the park boundary is at the high tide line all the way around the island, beachgoers are considered within the park and must pay the entrance ("nature") fee.

JAÚ NATIONAL PARK

BRAZIL

This area brings a whole new meaning to *pristine*. There are no visitor centers, four-wheeled tours, or souvenir shops. This is where those who want to truly experience nature travel. Jaú National Park is the largest park in Brazil and the second largest in South America. Although the size of the park is impressive and certainly noteworthy, what makes Jaú truly stand out is its almost complete lack of development. The government takes its conservation efforts so seriously that it is considered a federal crime to damage flora or fauna in the park. The Brazilian national police make regular visits to the park to ensure that poaching and hunting are eliminated.

Providing expert local guides is a cottage industry in the small town of Novo Airão and in the larger city of Manaus. The established tour services can provide visitors with a variety of experts who will bring you in close contact with the park's stunning wildlife. Be prepared to see dolphins, fish, birds, crocodiles, turtles, monkeys, jaguars, tapirs, and armadillos. The vegetation is quite dense and is virtually undisturbed; thus naturalists have the per-

fect opportunity to see local flora in its natural state.

Three rivers run through the park, including the Jaú, which gave the park its name. The only way to experience the park is by boat and through a tour company.

LOCATION: Northwestern Brazil, in the western Amazon.

HOURS OF OPERATION: Year-round, 24/7.

CONTACT: *Self-guided tours*: Tel: 559236133277, x229 (call at least 1 month in advance). *Eco Discovery Tours:* Tel: 559230824732; Fax: 559232344737; Web: www.freewebs.com/eco_tours/jana tionalpark.htm.

COST: *Permits* (per person, per day): US$2. *Tours:* Depend on point of origin, length of stay, and style of tour. *Boats:* US$10 (per vessel); additional fees may apply.

ON-SITE AMENITIES: Visitors center.

BEST TIMES: December through June.

FIELD NOTES: As there are virtually no amenities in the park, if you are camping, you will need to bring all food and water as well as other essentials such as a first aid kit. There is no road access beyond Novo Airão so boat travel is the only way to go. Rented boats are the most common means of access and most tour companies travel by houseboat, which provides both access to the park and accommodations.

PANTANAL WILDLIFE CENTER

BRAZIL

The highly social and magnificent giant otter, which is as long as a human being, may be the most startling and wondrous creature to be seen in the vast area of savanna and tropical forest that makes up the Pantanal Wildlife Center's grounds, but it is by no means the only attraction for wildlife enthusiasts.

Located on the banks of the Pixaim River, Pantanal Wildlife Center is owned and operated by professional wildlife biologists who are dedicated to the welfare and study of the diverse indigenous wildlife. Each year, a select few visitors have the privilege to view and spend time with the area's animals in an almost pristine environment.

Pantanal offers a world-class experience that includes guided tours, which are offered in several languages; visitors can hike scientifically designed nature trails, attend lectures by renowned experts, engage in birdwatching, and more. The stables house

nearly a dozen gentle, tame horses for riding into the surrounding area. The up-close viewing of different types of monkeys and fruit-eating and nectar-drinking birds is facilitated by the use of observation towers, which can be moved to increase the chances of wild-life observation. These towers have been used by photographers and film-makers from organizations such as National Geographic, the Discovery Channel, and the BBC.

Although this stunning wildlife cen-ter is designed for the study and preser-vation of its 340 species of birds, 5,000 giant otters, and many native silvery marmosets and Brazilian tapirs (the largest land animal in South America), no amenities have been overlooked for the human visitors who venture here. The center offers fully air-conditioned rooms of different sizes, meals, and a pool. After your ventures into the wild, partake in a wonderful Brazilian barbe-cue; the perfect ending to a perfect day.

LOCATION: 33 miles west of Transpan-taneira in central-western Brazil. The park is accessible by van, minibus, or car. Rental cars can be obtained in Cui-aba, a 2.5-hour drive from the center.

HOURS OF OPERATION: Year-round. 24-hour service is available. Times for tours vary.

CONTACT: *Main office:* Pantanal Wild-life Center, Transpantaneira km 66, Po-coné, Mato Grosso, MT, CEP 78.175-000, Brazil; Tel: 556536823175; Web: www .pantanalwildlifecenter.com; email: sales@pantanalwildlifecenter.com.

COST: Depends on tour, booking agency, and length of stay. Four-day packages (2 to 4 travelers) from US$690; single supplement US$180.

ON-SITE AMENITIES: The center has 10 double-occupancy rooms with air-conditioning and private bathrooms. Accommodation includes three meals per day. Multilingual guides.

BEST TIMES: June 1 to December 31.

FIELD NOTES: A good pair of binoculars, bird reference, comfortable light-weight clothing, water-resistant hiking boots, and sunscreen are always rec-ommended. Depending on the season, light jackets are advised.

MANUEL ANTONIO NATIONAL PARK

COSTA RICA

Manuel Antonio National Park is located in Costa Rica's Pacific coastal town of Puntarenas. Within its primary and secondary forests, mangrove swamps, lagoons, and beach vegetation are found a vast array of fauna, including the intriguing two- and three-toed sloths.

White-faced capuchin monkeys, howler monkeys, poison dart frogs, toucanets, hawks, parrots, owls, and eagles can be found in the 145 acres of tropical forest that makes up the biological reserve. You'll spot squirrel monkeys, too—they move swiftly through the

trees, so you have to really concentrate to get a good look! A fun fact about these creatures is that they have the largest proportional brain mass of any primate—including man. Their brain to body mass ratio is 1:17, while that of humans is merely 1:35.

Don't forget your binoculars, as you'll need them to spot up to 270 species of birds that populate the park and surrounding areas. You'll find 15 different types of hummingbirds, including purple-crowned fairies and blue-throated goldentails. Parakeets and parrots are plentiful, and you also can see tanagers, toucans, woodpeckers, and turkey vultures.

Several types of tours are available on the park's grounds. You can explore a butterfly botanical garden filled with brightly colored local species if you decide to take a Nature Farm tour. If you're an adventurous type, you can cross a 410-foot-long, 147-foot-high suspension bridge as part of the Xtreme Canyoning Tour, but you'll get to enjoy lunch beside the breathtaking sight of a cascading waterfall. Perhaps you'd prefer to ride a horse through the hills of the rain forest and learn from your guide about the medicinal and curative properties of many plants you see.

Seashore lovers will enjoy the four beaches at the park. Playa Manuel Antonio features a coral reef, while Espadilla Sur, Escondido, and Playita are just right for sun and fun. Go snorkeling and scuba diving or just enjoy a little sunbathing. Do be aware that rip tides are common and there are no lifeguards at the park.

LOCATION: Just south of Quepos on the Pacific coast of Costa Rica, 82 miles and a 3.5- to 4-hour drive from San José. If renting, choose a 4-wheel-drive vehicle, because the road can be rugged. Bus service is available from San José to Quepos and then to the park.

HOURS OF OPERATION: Year-round. Tue–Sun, 7 a.m. to 4 p.m.; closed Mon.

CONTACT: Web: www.manuelantoniopark.com.

COST: *Entrance* (per person): Adults, US$10; children (under 12 years), free.

ON-SITE AMENITIES: Four gift shops, a rangers station, an open-air museum, and information center. There are no accommodations or snack bars. Tours can be arranged and booked directly through the park's website. A wide range of accommodations are available outside of the park grounds, ranging from five-star resorts to adults-only to inns and villas. Information is available on the park's website.

BEST TIMES: The "dry" season (late December to April) sees the most tourist activity. The park limits visitors to 600 per day during the week and 800 on the weekends in an effort to maintain and protect the ecosystem. Booking your tour in advance is recommended.

FIELD NOTES: Do not feed the monkeys; human food may give the animals heart disease and/or heart failure. It also is important to honor that 4 p.m. closing time; the incoming tide blocks off exit routes and allows alligators to enter the grounds. Wear comfortable clothes, take along the sunscreen, and do not leave valuables unguarded.

MARINO BALLENA NATIONAL PARK

COSTA RICA

The Marino Ballena National Park was established in 1990 as part of Costa Rica's aggressive policy of eco-tourism and sustainable development for its natural resources. The park comprises 270 acres of land and beach as well as 13,300 acres of maritime parkland and can be divided into three distinct habitats: beach, coral reef, and mangrove.

Wildlife in Marino Ballena includes the famed humpback whales of both hemispheres. Regularly scheduled boating tours are available for whale watching. Tours will bring you closer to these whales in their natural environment than any other excursion. In addition to the whales, the beaches of Marino Ballena are home to olive ridley and hawksbill turtles, which nest in the area and leave their eggs to hatch.

Tours are organized to collect the turtle eggs, which are then taken to the hatcheries, where they are protected and nurtured. Visitors can expect to see many turtles, which make terrific subjects for wildlife photography, owing to

their slow and deliberate movements. The best time to visit the area for turtle nesting is from May to November.

Lodging can be found in the village of Dominical, which is a popular surfing area. The village has a number of restaurants, and moderately priced accommodations are available.

LOCATION: West coast of Costa Rica, approximately 120 miles southwest of San José. The park is bordered on the south by Punta Piñuela and extends out to sea for about 5 miles.

HOURS OF OPERATION: Year-round.

CONTACT: *Ranger station:* Tel: 5067438236. *Tour options:* Web: www .lohelani.com/touroptions/ballena .htm.

COST: *Entrance:* US$7 (rarely collected). Other costs depend on choice of tours and organized activities.

ON-SITE AMENITIES: Expert guides, boating, numerous hiking trails, bike trail, fishing, swimming, kayaking, birding, wildlife photography, turtle egg collecting, whale watching. Drinking water, bathrooms, and picnic areas at the ranger station. *Camping:* Allowed on the beaches; no amenities. **Whales and**

Dolphins Hotel: Located directly across from the park; for more information, visit www.ticotravel.com/hotels/ whale.htm.

BEST TIMES: December through April for northern whale migration. May through November for turtle nesting.

FIELD NOTES: Field books, cameras, fishing/hunting permits, snacks, and drinking water are all recommended. Snorkeling is great from shore. Dive trips are available to the islands; inquire at the ranger station. Mosquitoes are most annoying and plentiful at dusk.

SANTA ROSA NATIONAL PARK

COSTA RICA

Santa Rosa National Park combines Costa Rican history with natural wonders. This site, in the northwestern part of the country, was created in 1971 to preserve the area's savanna, deciduous forest, marshlands, and mangroves and to protect the site of the Battle of Santa Rosa. Near the battleground is the Hacienda Santa Rosa (also called La Casona), one of the nation's most treasured landmarks; here in 1856, Costa Rican volunteers defended their country against a mercenary army led by American William Walker. La Casona is now a museum commemorating various battles that took place in the vicinity.

Of the 115 types of mammals found at Santa Rosa National Park, approximately half are different species of bats, and they've even been seen flying in and out of the museum! Lucky visitors will also see jaguars, ocelots, pumas, white-tailed deer, coyotes, armadillos, and tapirs within the boundaries of the 308-square-mile park.

Bird-watchers will delight in seeing orange-fronted parakeets, crested caracaras, common black hawks, and long-tailed manakins as well as many other of the park's 253 species of birds. Santa Rosa is also home to more than 10,000 types of insects, of which almost a third are species of butterflies and moths. A trek along the Indio Desnudo nature trail is a visitor's best bet for animal watching, especially around opening and closing hours.

As many as 10,000 olive ridley turtles gather on the Playa Nancite beach for nesting in early fall (September or October). These olive green reptiles are one of the smallest varieties of sea turtles, and their numbers have been on the decline in the Atlantic Ocean. Special permits are needed to visit Playa Nancite during nesting season.

LOCATION: Guanacaste province, Costa Rica. The park is 165 miles from San José and 22 miles north of Liberia. Bus service is available from San José,

although campers will have to walk about 4.5 miles to the main camping area. The park is accessible by car via the Pan-American Highway.

HOURS OF OPERATION: *Museum and park:* 8 a.m. to 4 p.m. *Camping area:* 24/7.

CONTACT: *Natural history museum and park:* Tel: 6665051; Fax: 6665020; Web: www.acguanacaste.ac.cr.

COST: *Entrance:* Advance purchase, US$10; at the park, US$15. *Camping* (per day): US$2.

ON-SITE AMENITIES: Campgrounds have picnic areas with tables and charcoal stoves, potable water, restrooms, and showers. Drinks and lunch are available at the administration center.

BEST TIMES: Animals can best be seen during the dry season from January to March when many species vie for space at watering holes.

FIELD NOTES: Road conditions vary; the road from the upper-level camping area to the beach is sometimes restricted, even during the dry season. You'll need a 4-wheel-drive vehicle with high ground clearance. Snakes tend to come out during the dry season and are to be avoided. Bring water along, for there is nowhere to get any until you arrive at a main camping site.

TORTUGUERO NATIONAL PARK

COSTA RICA

With a name like Tortuguero, which means "turtle catcher," it's not surprising that this Costa Rican national park is a fantastic spot to see these sea creatures up close and personal. Tortuguero National Park is a major nesting site for hawksbill, loggerhead, green, and leatherback turtles. The green turtle, named for the color of its meat rather than its shell, is endangered because it is the species used for turtle soup and its eggs are supposed to have aphrodisiac properties. During times of nesting, only 200 tourists are allowed on the beach for each night (8 p.m. to 10 p.m. and 10 p.m. to midnight) to watch the turtles lay their eggs. If you are there at the right time you may be able to watch hatchlings running to the sea—a magical and memorable sight.

There's more to Tortuguero than turtle watching. The park encompasses 11 different habitats, including rain forest, mangroves, swamps, beaches, and lagoons. Visitors can hope to see some of the more than 300 species of birds, 57 species of amphibians, 111 species of reptiles, and 60 species of mammals that make their homes within the park's boundaries. Often-seen birds are toucans, swallow-tailed hawks, and several types of herons, kingfishers, parrots, and jacanas. Jaguars; spider, howler, and white-faced capuchin monkeys; and poisonous frogs are among the nonwinged creatures you'll find.

It's highly advisable to take a guided tour if you want to spot the most animals possible. Guides have been trained to find wildlife hiding in the foliage that visitors might miss. Hire a guide at a local lodge or through a San José–based tour company. Although the park maintains hiking trails, the area is best enjoyed by boat. Go kayaking or canoeing on one of the many canals or estuaries or enjoy a guided nature cruise.

LOCATION: Air or boat access only. Air service is available from San José or Limon, where you can take a boat from the port of Moin. Bus service is also available, but it can take up to a day to arrive in Limon.

HOURS OF OPERATION: 8 a.m. to 6 p.m.; visitors may stay later if they are with authorized guides or groups.

CONTACT: Web: www.tortuguerovillage.com; email: tortuguerovillage@gmail.com.

COST: *Entrance:* 1-day pass, US$7; 4-day pass, US$10 (includes admittance to Barra del Colorado Wildlife Refuge).

ON-SITE AMENITIES: Restaurants and shops are found in Tortuguero village, which is just north of the park.

BEST TIMES: February to March is the "dry" season—a relative term because this site is situated in one of Costa Rica's rainiest regions. Any time is a good time to spot sea turtles, but the nesting season for green and hawksbill turtles is July to October and for leatherback turtles, February to April.

FIELD NOTES: Be sure to take your trash along when you leave the park; rubbish disposal is a real problem. Bring boots and rain gear because it can rain unexpectedly at any time. Cameras and flashlights are not allowed while turtle watching, and visitors are advised to be quiet and keep a respectful distance from these creatures.

GALAPAGOS ISLANDS

ECUADOR

The mere mention of the Galapagos Islands invokes thoughts of "enchanted islands" and a place that time forgot as the world moved on. The Galapagos Archipelago, made up of 16 main islands, 6 smaller islands, and 107 islets, is located off the coast of Ecuador, directly on the Equator. The island group covers 4,897 square miles of land and 28,000 square miles of ocean.

Whether you choose a cruise or a stay on the islands, this is an "adventure in evolution" because you'll find the islands little changed from 1835,

a whaler; of the many pirates and buccaneers who frequented the islands, while planning attacks on Spanish galleons; and of many other wondrous tales about these mysterious islands.

Humans have had a detrimental effect on the islands since the 1600s. There was a time when thousands of the islands' tortoises were killed for food. Later, goats, rats, pigs, dogs, and non-native plants were introduced, competing with local species with devastating results. In 1959, Ecuador designated 97% of the total land area as the Galapagos National Park. Today the Charles Darwin Station (on Santa Cruz Island) and the Galapagos National Park ensure the integrity of the islands. The rules for visitors are strictly enforced.

when Charles Darwin set foot here. Each island presents a spectacular showcase in and of itself; each with its own distinctive terrain and wildlife.

Island tours will introduce you to the famed giant Galapagos tortoises, each distinct to its own island. Prehistoric-looking marine iguanas gather to sun on black lava outcrops. Many of the tropical birds you'll see are only found here. You can walk the trails among flightless cormorants and blue-footed boobies and perhaps swim with sea lions and fur seals—or at least watch them close at hand on the beaches. In the seas surrounding the islands, you may see breaching whales or penguins darting in and out of the waves. It is rare, if ever, that one can experience such up-close encounters with such a diversity of wildlife.

While on the islands, you'll learn of how Darwin came to write his *The Origin of Species*, inspired in part from his findings and observations here; of a visit by Herman Melville, when he was

LOCATION: Eastern Pacific Ocean at 525 nautical miles (603 miles) off the west coast of South America, directly on the Equator.

HOURS OF OPERATION: Year-round.

CONTACT: Web: www.galapaguide .com/accommodation_galapagos .html, www.discovergalapagos.com/ bring.html, www.geo.cornell.edu/geol ogy/GalapagosWWW/Discovery.html, www.galapagos.com, www.galapagos online.com.

COST: *Entrance:* US$100. *Accommodations:* Depend on time of year and tour package.

ON-SITE AMENITIES: Hotels, restaurants, and guide services (limited to a few of the islands) are available. Most tours depart from the landing point of Santa Cruz where amenities are plentiful.

BEST TIMES: July to August and December to January. The cool season is from June through November and the warm season is from December to May.

FIELD NOTES: Sunblock and sunglasses; light, quick-drying clothing; good walking shoes (that can also get wet); bathing suit; and water bottle. Most of the travel is by boat; those who experience seasickness should be prepared. The area is best toured via small boat (about 20 passengers), to obtain individualized attention and access to more remote places. Visitors should expect to have to wade because some areas lack docking facilities. Anyone who is relatively fit can enjoy the islands. Although the terrain can be rugged, walking is the best way to experience the islands to their fullest.

SACHA LODGE

ECUADOR

Sacha Lodge is a 5,000-acre private ecological reserve located in the Amazon area of Ecuador. Visitors can feel safe as they venture into this rain forest sanctuary to observe animals that live there. Among the wildlife surrounding the lodge are eight species of monkeys, including the nimble, shy pygmy marmoset and the hooting, acrobatic red howler. Night monkeys often live in small groups, but squirrel monkey troops can be as large as 150 individuals. Visitors may be able to spot flying squirrels gliding among the treetops.

There are over 100 other species of mammals within the reserve, almost half of which are bats. Anteaters, three-toed sloths, and ocelots make their home at Sacha. A special treat is to take a night canoe ride on Pilchicocha Lake to see the resident spectacled caimans, a type of alligator. Sometimes the young hide under the lodge's buildings.

Visitors will get a chance to see a variety of other reptiles along the trails. Boas, vine snakes, and giant anacondas have been recorded in the reserve. Some of the snakes are poisonous, but they are not aggressive and they can be safely observed.

Sacha is home to more than 587 species of birds. With little effort and just a few days, most bird-watchers will be able to see almost half of these birds. Count on spying parrots, toucans, hummingbirds, tanagers, hawks, and oropendolas. Just in case your binoculars are not quite strong enough, bird guides carry telescopes so that species can be clearly seen and identified.

LOCATION: Amazon region, Ecuador.

HOURS OF OPERATION: Year-round.

CONTACT: Tel: 8007062215 (toll-free) or 59322566090, 5932250 9504, or 59322509115, x23; Fax: 59322236521; Web: www.sachalodge.com; email: info@sachalodge.com.

COST: Depends on package.

ON-SITE AMENITIES: There are 26 rooms with private bathrooms and hot showers. All cabins are screened against insects and have ceiling fans. There is a raised lookout above the main bar and lounge, which offers a scenic view and excellent opportunities for bird-watching. Three buffets are served daily; vegetarians can be accommodated.

BEST TIMES: Year-round.

FIELD NOTES: Bring lightweight, quick-drying clothing, rain gear, insect repellent, camera, and loads of film or memory cards because these are not available at the lodge. Night walks and canoe trips by flashlight provide sights seldom seen so be sure to take full advantage of all these excursions.

TIKAL NATIONAL PARK

GUATEMALA

A UNESCO World Heritage Site, Tikal is the largest of the ancient Mayan cities and the most significant excavation site in Central America. In addition to the archaeological site, Tikal National Park offers wildlife enthusiasts the chance to view indigenous animals and birds, such as agoutis, coatis, gray foxes, spider and howler monkeys, harpy eagles, falcons, ocellated turkeys, guans, toucans, and green parrots. Jaguars and cougars also frequent the area. And those interested in local flora will be able to see the sacred tree of the Maya people, the ceiba, as well as tropical cedar and mahogany.

The best way to explore the park is to take advantage of one of the various tours offered. The Canopy Tour enables you to enjoy the jungle and its inhabitants from the forest treetops, providing you with a view unobtainable on foot. All equipment is provided on-site, and professional guides are available for hire. Birding tours abound with both full- and half-day options, all led by experienced naturalists and guides.

LOCATION: Roughly 20 miles from Flores, Guatemala.

HOURS OF OPERATION: Year-round, 6 a.m. to 6 p.m.; tour times vary.

CONTACT: Tel: 50223672837; Fax: 50223370009; Web: www.tikalpark.com.

COST: *Entrance:* US$20. *Guide service* (1–4 people): US$50. *Lodging:* Room rates (per night), US$40–$275. *Tours* (per person): Depends on the package; day tours including entrance, guide, and lunch are available for less than US$100; Canopy Tour, US$25.

ON-SITE AMENITIES: Three hotels, including budget options. Tours can be booked through the park's website; helicopter tours are available. Restaurants and other food options. Museums, visitors center, guide service information desk, souvenir shops. For detailed accommodation information, visit www.tikalinformation.com/hoteltikal .html.

BEST TIMES: September through June.

FIELD NOTES: Equipment to pack depends on your planned activities and style of lodging; contact your hotel to determine what amenities are offered. Comfortable footwear and seasonal clothing are always recommended, especially rain gear. It is advised to stay within the park's perimeters and on the clearly marked trails at all times; it is easy to get lost. Wildlife observation with a qualified guide will ensure your best wildlife experience and safety. The tipping of any of the park's guards is strictly prohibited and is considered an offense. Guests staying at hotels within the park can enter the entrance gate at 5 a.m. Lights are turned off at 9:30 p.m., and guests are asked to return to their hotel beforehand. Access to the Tikal ruin area is by foot only.

PICO BONITO NATIONAL PARK

HONDURAS

Honduras's largest preserve, hosting seven ecosystems in 100,000 hectares of virgin rain and cloud forests, Pico Bonito National Park is a pristine jewel that boasts the perfect combination of forest and beach. According to many reports, the best way to experience the park starts with the Lodge at Pico Bonito, which is the central focus of a wide variety of activities. Birders can enjoy a dense population of over 400 bird species from the abundant platforms and towers; after dinner, guests can revisit the platforms to take in the night sky.

There is a solid representation of Central American mammal life, including jaguars, tapirs, ocelots, kinkajous, peccaries, and monkeys along both trails and rivers. Guided trips of different durations are available; choose to go by foot or by raft or by a combination. Hikers come across pristine swimming holes fed by small waterfalls. Night hikes are also available.

The Cuero y Salado Wildlife Refuge, a short boat ride upstream from the park, is named for the two rivers that feed the refuge's mangrove forest. Visitors will get a chance to look for the endangered manatee as well as see a wealth of birds, monkeys, alligators, and iguanas; the tour ends at the nice swimming beach.

Butterflies and reptiles make a strong showing at the Tropical Butterfly Farm and Serpentarium. Visitors to this working farm not only see the workings of the facility but also stop in an enclosed area called the Butterfly House to experience the mind-blowing effect of the most intense colors in nature. At the Serpentarium, naturalists offer visitors a rare opportunity to see Honduras's snakes up close and in safety.

Other excursions include exploring Maya ruins and horseback riding to the beach with a real horse whisperer. One tour goes to an Adelante village, where you can meet local women who are setting up their own small businesses; part of the fees for this tour goes to a nonprofit foundation that helps support these ventures. Through this tour, visitors can give a gift that will resonate for generations and all over the world.

Packages at the Lodge at Pico Bonito can be combined to provide a variety of activities, depending on your interests: from birding getaways to nature walks, from white water rafting, kayaking, or canoeing to snorkeling or lounging on the beach.

LOCATION: Pico Bonito, Honduras.

HOURS OF OPERATION: 24/7.

CONTACT: *Lodge:* Tel: 5044400388 or 5044400389 (international access); reservations 8884280221 (toll-free, USA and Canada); 3123453288 (international access); Web: www.picobonito.com.

COST: *Rates:* Seasonal; packages, US$445–$1,212, depending on number of people and number of nights.

ON-SITE AMENITIES: Visitors center, well-marked trail system, natural pools and waterfalls. Swimming, hiking, wildlife viewing, and bird-watching. The lodge has 22 luxury cabins, air-conditioning, and restaurant.

BEST TIMES: *Peak season:* January through April. *Summer season:* May through November.

FIELD NOTES: You'll need to carry all essentials, such as suntan lotion, plenty of bug repellent, hats, sunglasses, waterproof or water-resistant lightweight hiking boots, and swimwear. All tours can be arranged through the lodge. Many tour operators offer excursions into the park; however, staying at the lodge will give you the overall best experience.

LA AMISTAD INTERNATIONAL PARK

PANAMA AND COSTA RICA

Bocas del Toro, made up of a series of islands off the Panamanian coast, has been designated as both a World Heritage Site and a BioSphere Reserve. It is an interlocking tapestry of ecosystems that spans more than 2 million acres. The heart of this area is La Amistad International Park, which encompasses one of the largest tracts of undisturbed forests in Central America.

In addition to the deep-sea diving, snorkeling, and amazing fishing that draws adventurers to the region, wildlife enthusiasts will relish spending time with the almost 350 species of birds found in the park. Bird-watchers will be able to spot hawks, thrushes,

and the rare red-billed tropicbird. Although guided tours are readily available, finding beautiful and diverse birdlife in here is as simple as taking a stroll. The wildlife is ubiquitous in the area.

More than 32 mammal species have been recorded on the islands, with numerous two- and three-toed sloths and 13 bat species, including the bulldog and jamaicencis. Pacas, white-throated capuchins, and night monkeys are also common in the park's forest areas.

La Amistad International Park hosts the nation's largest population of Baird's tapirs, and visitors may also be lucky enough to see a giant anteater. All six species of neotropical cats—jaguar, puma, margay, ocelot, tiger cat, and jaguarundi—make their home in the park. The waters of the Bocas are home to various sea turtles, West Indian manatees, an array of fish, lobsters, and several species of dolphin.

Lodging and restaurants are easily found, and guided boat and land tours can be arranged through individuals or large firms. Commercial air service is available from Panama City to Changuinola; a taxi will take you to your hotel for a very small fee. You can also arrive at Bocas del Toro via a boat taxi from Costa Rica.

LOCATION: Between Panama and Costa Rica, a 1-hour flight from Panama City.

HOURS OF OPERATION: Year-round, daily, 8 a.m. to 4 p.m.

CONTACT: La Amistad Caribe, Apdo 10104-1000, Costa Rica; Tel: 5067583170 or 5067542133; Web: www.costarica-nationalparks.com. **Hotel Bocas del**

Toro: Tel: 011507757 9771; Web: www .bocasdeltoro.com.

COST: *Entrance:* Free. *Water taxis:* Roughly US$6. *Bus taxis:* Less than US$1. *Hotel* (per night): US$96–$192.

ON-SITE AMENITIES: Two camping areas with restrooms, showers, drinking water, and electricity. Observatory, research facilities, and hiking trails.

BEST TIMES: Mid December to mid April.

FIELD NOTES: Activities include snorkeling, forest trekking, surfing, sightseeing, hiking, camping, fishing, swimming, cycling, and wildlife photography and viewing.

MANÚ WILDLIFE CENTER

PERU

The Manú Wildlife Center in the western Amazon is home to 1,000 bird species, 200 mammal species— including 13 types of monkey, such as the emperor tamarin—plenty of butterflies, and 15,000 flowering plant species. Located just a short plane ride from Cuzco and a 90-minute boat trip down the Madre de Dios River, the center is found where the great Amazon biosphere meets the Andean foothills. Here visitors can experience not only the nature trip of a lifetime but an un-

forgettable cultural excursion to Machu Picchu and the Inca Trail.

The greater Manú Biosphere Reserve is partly composed of the Manú National Park and the cultural zone.

While most of the park is off-limits to visitors, the wildlife center is in the park's reserve zone, where tourism and commercial interests are welcome.

For birders, huge fruit trees allow excellent canopy viewing, and a boat trip downriver to a quiet catamaran blind brings you within 20–30 yards of a clay lick that attracts red and green macaws and a dazzling spectrum of parrots. Scientifically designed blinds and canopy platforms provide close and exquisite views and photographic opportunities year-round, although July through November are the best months for birdwatching.

The canopy platforms allow birders to see tanagers, toucans, and hummingbirds, but mammal fanciers will enjoy watching a variety of monkeys: red howler, black spider, dusky titi, white-faced capuchin, wooly, and monk saki. On the ground there are 30 miles of trails to enjoy, more than half of which are designed to take hikers through the richest wildlife habitats the park has to offer.

One of the greatest treats is an excursion to a clay lick that justifiably boasts the best tapir viewing in the world. The largest land mammal in South America, weighing in at almost a quarter ton, the tapir is harder to spot than a jaguar in most locales; but from an elevated house blind, visitors are able to observe and photograph this nocturnal mammal.

Opt for a trip into the breathtaking Manú cloud forest where you might catch a glimpse of a giant hummingbird or the mountain caracara to go with your Pre-Inca ruins. And don't forget Machu Picchu and the legendary Inca Trail to lend a little culture to an already magical trip.

LOCATION: Manú, Peru.

HOURS OF OPERATION: Year-round.

CONTACT: Web: www.manu-wildlife-center.com.

COST: *Manú Wildlife Center tours:* From US$1290. *Bio trip from the Andes to the Amazon:* From US$1,635 (includes airfare from Cuzco to Boca Manu). Customized programs, film crews, and student tours featuring Amazon biology are available. For more information visit the center's website. Tours can be booked through www.manuexpeditions.com.

ON-SITE AMENITIES: There are 22 double-occupancy, screened bungalows with private baths and flush toilets. Lodge facilities include dining room, bar, and lounge.

BEST TIMES: Late March through December.

FIELD NOTES: Bring waterproof boots, sunglasses, binoculars, bug repellent, sunscreen, hats, and lightweight, quick-drying clothes. Wear clothes that you don't mind getting wet or dirty because the boat trip required to reach the center is more utilitarian than luxurious.

PACAYA-SAMIRIA NATIONAL RESERVE

PERU

The Pacaya-Samiria National Reserve was created as the result of the passionate work of community activists, preservationists, and other people interested in saving this cultural and biological resource. Rumbo al Dorado, a community association, was formed to promote the sustainable use of biodiversity in fragile ecosystems. The association promotes eco-tourism to provide both funds and training for the local population. The result was the Pacaya-Samiria National Reserve, which offers visitors not luxury but a chance to experience both the natural environment and cultural exchange among people of different countries.

Visitors to the reserve are treated to great biodiversity. Within the area's 7,700 square miles, 965 species of wild plants, and 59 species of cultivated plants, 450 species of birds, 102 species of mammals, more than 130 species of reptiles and amphibians, and 250 species of fish have been recorded so far—studies and investigations are ongoing, and new species are found each year. Many of these animals are protected, such as the black caiman, water turtle, spider monkey, giant otter, and pink and gray dolphins.

Visitors should expect a tropical, wet climate with temperatures of about 80°F and high humidity. The reserve receives about 120 inches of rain a year, which allows for a thick vegetation. The land is fairly level and is crossed by a complex network of rivers, channels, and lagoons that flood seasonally. One favorite destination is a wonderful lagoon that inspired the name of the association: The "Dorado" is not the gold of ancient conquerors or the rubber of caucheros but the experience of meeting nature via responsible tourism that encourages human respect and intercultural exchange.

LOCATION: Amazon region, Peru; approximately 93 miles from Iquitos.

HOURS OF OPERATION: Year-round.

CONTACT: Tel: 005112410559; Web: www.pacaya-samiria.com. **Pacaya Samiria Amazon Lodge:** Tel: 5165225769; Web: www.pacayasamiria.com.pe. *Tour options:* www.pacayasamiria.com.pe/pacaya_tours.htm.

COST: *Entrance:* Fee is included in all tour packages. Other costs depend on the size and type of tour.

ON-SITE AMENITIES: Naturalist observations, bird-watching and wildlife observation, boat and canoe excursions, guided tours through virgin forest, night excursions, and fishing. **Pacaya Samiria Amazon Lodge:** Bungalows equipped with bathrooms, electricity, dining room, bar. and library. Tented camps, mosquito nets, solar electric power, radios, and lavatories.

BEST TIMES: June through January (the dry season), when rainfall is minimal and rivers are low, is the best time to observe caimans, giant otters, and sedentary and migratory birds. During the rest of the year, most of the area is flooded; the highest water levels are seen in February and March, which is the period of bloom and fruit production, when it's easy to see primates and other mammalians in nonflooded areas, but other species have moved well into the forest.

FIELD NOTES: Waterproof rain gear, sleeping bag (for an overnight stay in Tambo German camp), hat, long pants and long-sleeved shirts, rubber boots (you can buy them in Iquitos), long socks, cotton T-shirts, a good flashlight, batteries, binoculars, insect repellent, sunglasses, and sunscreen. Equipment and luggage must be kept to a minimum; storage space inside the refuge is limited. Reaching the reserve is an adventure in itself, involving travel by air, bus, and boat.

PARACAS NATIONAL RESERVE

PERU

The Paracas National Reserve is often called the Galapagos of Peru for its stunning biodiversity and remote, unspoiled wildlife. At one time the unique peninsula was severely threatened by the encroachment of humans. Commercial fisheries, unchecked tourism, and land development all posed a serious threat to the safety of the local flora, fauna, and cultural heritage of Paracas. The government of Peru has extended its conservation efforts in a partnership with The Nature Conservancy in what has been an extremely successful effort to restore the area of the Paracas National Reserve to its former pristine glory. Their joint efforts continue to support the sustainability of the area and the habitats of the local wildlife.

The park itself is more than 750,000 acres and is made up of a unique and contrasting collection of deserts, islands, waterways, mountains, and archaeological landmarks. Animals such as whales, orcas, sea lions, South American fur seals, endangered sea otters, large breeding populations of Humboldt penguins, abalones, and octopi,

are found here. And green, leatherback, and hawksbill turtles make their home in the reserve.

In addition, there are roughly 215 species of birds that spend time within the reserve's boundaries. Visitors might spot pied-billed grebes, white-tufted Peruvian pelicans, Peruvian boobies, turkey vultures, black vultures, and coots. Migratory species that spend time here include the osprey, Wilson's phalarope, semipalmated plover, black-bellied plover, spotted sandpiper, ruddy turnstone, sanderling, red knot, western sandpiper, semipalmated sandpiper, willet, whimbrel, gray gull, Franklin gull, common tern, royal tern, elegant tern, and storm petrel.

Bird-watchers will be able to observe several species that nest in the area, such as snowy egrets, black-crowned night herons, white-cheeked pintails, cinnamon teal, American kestrels, snowy plovers, killdeers, Peruvian thick-knee band-tailed gulls, croaking ground doves, white-winged doves, burrowing owls, chestnut-throated seedeaters, and rufous-collared sparrows. Several species found in the reserve are considered vulnerable, including the kelp gull, black skimmer, and American oystercatcher. According to the World Conservation Union (IUCN), several species found in the reserve require protection: the South American flamingo, condor, Humboldt penguin, and Peruvian diving petrel.

LOCATION: 75 miles from Lima on the Pacific coast of Peru.

HOURS OF OPERATION: 24/7.

CONTACT: Enjoy Peru Tours: 8883173383 (toll-free USA); 08000971749 (toll-free UK); Web: www.enjoyperu .com.

COST: Depends on the tour; for example, 2-day tours of Pisco and Paracas, from US$333.

ON-SITE AMENITIES: Reserve amenities are scarce. Archaeological, cultural, ecological, and wildlife viewing tours are available.

BEST TIMES: May through October.

FIELD NOTES: Take advantage of the tours that offer viewing of the famed Nazca Lines as well as the wildlife of the reserve. Binoculars, field books, cameras, comfortable walking shoes, and seasonal clothing are recommended. To enjoy all that the area has to offer plan on staying 2 to 4 days. Accommodations in Pisco allow you to indulge in the best of both worlds, with city life at your fingertips and the great outdoors within arm's reach.

TAMBOPATA NATIONAL RESERVE

PERU

The Tambopata National Reserve boasts more than 2.5 million acres of natural beauty bordering on the famed Heath River. Along with its sister parks, Bahuajua-Sonene and Madidi, the preserves are two-thirds the size of Costa Rica and offer protection and cultivation of one of the richest and widest array of species in the world.

Lodging in the Tambopata Reserve is available in two distinct and lovely

environs. Deep in the reserve, Sandoval Lake Lodge provides exclusive access to the lake during prime bird-watching hours (early morning and late afternoon). This lake is one of the most biodiverse and pristine of all the bodies of water in Tambobata-Madidi.

The Heath River Wildlife Center is centrally located in the rain forest, with easy access to a wide range of wildlife sites. Visitors can see the macaws that are attracted to the clay licks and the capybaras (120-pound guinea pigs), that forage in the area. Aquatic life, including giant otters, is abundant in the oxbow lakes. And for birders, more than 480 species have been noted around the center.

LOCATION: 25-minute flight from Cusco, near the Peru–Bolivian border.

HOURS OF OPERATION: 24/7.

CONTACT: Tel: 8008921035 (toll-free USA); Web: www.inkanatura.com/tambopatanationalreserveinperu.asp.

COST: Depends on tour and length of stay. **Sandoval Lake Lodge:** 3-night tours from US$295. **Heath River Wildlife Center:** 3-night tours from US$560.

ON-SITE AMENITIES: Sandoval offers roundtrip transportation from the airport, private rooms, and private bathrooms, meals, and bilingual guides and staff. **Heath** offers bungalows with private bathrooms and purified water, meals, bilingual guides and staff, excursions to the macaw licks, and tours of the rain forest. Various tours and excursions are available.

BEST TIMES: August through April.

FIELD NOTES: Bring sufficient lightweight, fast-drying clothing, as the natural environment is damp and regular changing of socks and undergarments is recommended. Waterproof carrying cases, especially for camera and other equipment, is recommended because river travel is required.

ASA WRIGHT NATURE CENTRE AND LODGE

TRINIDAD

The Asa Wright Nature Centre and Lodge is a renowned bird lover's paradise that not only boasts recorded sightings of 400 species of birds but also is unparalleled in the quality of sighting by proximity to the birds. Visitors have a rare opportunity to view nesting birds; both an oropendola colony and a pair of ornate hawk eagles can easily be observed. Hikers will come across white-bearded and golden-headed manakins, and the bearded bellbird is never far away—its bell-like *bong* can be heard throughout the day.

In addition to the bird life, visitors may be able to see some of the 97 species of indigenous mammals, 55 species of reptiles, and 25 species of amphibians. The center is home to 617 varieties of butterflies, including the coolie, banded adelpha, four continent, donkey eye, flambeau, skipper, and checkerspot. And plant lovers will not be disappointed, either; almost 2,500 species of flowering plants have been recorded.

The two major components of the center are the Spring Hill Estate and

the William Beebe Tropical Research Station. The research station was established by Dr. Beebe and functioned as a research station for the New York Zoological Society. Both properties were once cacao plantations that contained large areas of unspoiled rain forest. Famed ornithologist David Snow spent significant time here studying the birds and recording their mating habits.

The Asa Wright Nature Centre is a nonprofit, nongovernment organization that is dedicated to the preservation of the surrounding habitats and the education of both local and international visitors.

LOCATION: Arima Valley of the Northern Range, Trinidad and Tobago.

HOURS OF OPERATION: 24/7. *Visitors center:* 9 a.m. to 5 p.m.; tours leave and return at various hours.

CONTACT: Tel: 8004267781 (toll-free); Web: www.asawright.org.

COST: *Entrance:* Adults, US$10; children (under 12 years), US$6. *Lodging* (per person, per night): From US$125, all inclusive.

ON-SITE AMENITIES: Visitors center, restaurant, expert guides, hiking trails. Lodging is available both on-site and in nearby towns and cities. Tours of different lengths are available.

BEST TIMES: November through April.

FIELD NOTES: Reservations for lodging are highly recommended. Field books and comfortable walking shoes are recommended. Children 8 years of age and over are welcome.

CANAIMA NATIONAL PARK

VENEZUELA

A ngel Falls, which is undoubtedly the most important, but not the only, attraction in Canaima National Park is, in a word, stunning. Almost 20 times higher than Niagara Falls, this is a natural phenomenon that you don't just view but rather experience. The impact is visceral and will never be forgotten.

While Angel Falls certainly deserves its reputation as a must-see destination for world travelers, Canaima National Park boasts countless rivers, sprawling jungles, and Guianan savannas. More than 65% of its 7 million acres is made up of tepui formations

(tabletop mountains), providing one of the most unusual geographic areas in the world.

The park is home to five endangered mammal species—the jaguar, giant anteater, giant river otter, ocelot, and giant armadillo—all of which are subject to intense conservation efforts. Nearly 9,000 species of plants thrive in Canaima and cannot be found outside of Venezuela. And this remarkable variety of vegetation, ranging from mountains to rain forests, can be viewed within the park.

The higher elevations of Canaima provide a home for nearly 100 bird species, including almost 30 species endemic to the tepui region, including harpy eagles, jabirus, oilbirds, 7 species of toucans, and parrots such as the fiery-shouldered parakeet and tepui parrotlet.

LOCATION: South of the Orinico River, Venezuela, near the borders of Guyana and Brazil.

HOURS OF OPERATION: Year-round; tours vary in length.

CONTACT: *Tour options:* Web: www.angel-ecotours.com.

COST: *Entrance:* US$15. Other costs vary, depending on lodging, activities, and tours.

ON-SITE AMENITIES: Expert guides, tours, hiking, and swimming. Accommodations in the park are traditional palm-thatched huts (churuatas) with hammocks, beds, and toilets and showers.

BEST TIMES: Fall through late spring. *For birders:* Winter, when many migratory birds find a home here.

FIELD NOTES: Visitors should be moderately fit because tour activities include walking, hiking, swimming, and river travel. Pack light. Even though the bulk of your luggage will be transported by vehicle or boat, you will need to carry your own necessities for each day's outing.

AFRICA

Botswana, Côte d'Ivoire, Gabon, Ghana,
Kenya, Madagascar, Rwanda, Seychelles,
South Africa, Tanzania, Uganda

ABU CAMP

BOTSWANA

Abu Camp is located on the Okavango Delta, which is the world's largest inland delta. Five distinct ethnic groups are found in the delta region, each with their own traditions and cultures. The delta is also home to abundant wildlife, including the African buffalo, hippopotamus, blue wildebeest, and Nile crocodile. But rising above all the other animals in size and majesty are the beautiful and wise African elephants.

The camp is set well into the forest and offers spacious, permanent tent structures with en-suite bathrooms. Each tent has a tree-shaded deck that overlooks a lagoon providing a wonderful vista. The main deck of the camp was built around and through giant trees, and as so it becomes a natural aspect of the landscape. You aren't just observing the environment, you are part of it. Meals in this salubrious setting are served by on-staff five-star chefs and presented with world-class wines.

If you prefer a bit of privacy, Abu Camp also offers accommodations at Abu Private Villa which is located across the lagoon (roughly 5 minutes from the main camp). The guests at the villa enjoy the services of a private chef, butler, and guide and the exclusive use of a vehicle for guided touring. This villa sleeps four and has a private pool.

LOCATION: Okavango Delta, Botswana.
HOURS OF OPERATION: 24/7.
CONTACT: Tel: 2676861260; Web: www
.abucamp.com; email: ebs@info.bw.
COST: Depends on size of group, length of stay, and choice of accommodations.
ON-SITE AMENITIES: Chefs, butlers, swimming pools, guides, lodging, animal handlers, private vehicle.
BEST TIMES: October through April.

FIELD NOTES: Full vaccinations and a checkup from your doctor are highly recommended. Muted clothing colors help you blend in with the surroundings.

Sweaters are useful for the cool evenings. Educating yourself about the elephants before your arrival will help prepare you for the majesty of these animals.

CHOBE NATIONAL PARK

BOTSWANA

If the romantic kid in you grew up watching Mutual of Omaha's *Wild Kingdom*, then Chobe National Park will place you in your own episode. The park is the destination and capstone of many wildlife lovers' dreams. It's as wild as it gets, because the vast wilderness supports so much wildlife that there's always something to look at, see, and smell.

Chobe National Park is the second largest national park in Botswana and covers about 5,280 square miles. Its greatest feature? It has one of the most supreme concentrations of game found on the African continent. The abundance of wildlife and the true African nature of the region (topography, wildlife, and plant life) offer visitors a safari experience of a lifetime.

People travel to this park for the elephants. Remarkably, the Chobe elephant make up what is probably the largest

surviving continuous elephant population in the world; the herd covers most of northern Botswana plus northwestern Zimbabwe. Botswana's elephant population is estimated at around 120,000. This population has built up gradually from a few thousand since the early 1900s and has escaped the massive illegal off-take that has decimated other populations in the 1970s and 1980s.

In the dry season the Chobe elephants are found near the Chobe and

Linyanti rivers, but in the rainy season they move to the pans in the southeast of the park. These elephants have the largest body size of all modern elephants. They dwarf some of the jeeps and vans that travelers use in safaris. They are breathtaking to behold.

Savuti, one of the areas of Chobe, is heaven on earth for travelers to this region. This area has one of the highest concentrations of wildlife left on the African continent. Animals are visible and active during all seasons, and at certain times of the year their numbers can be quite staggering. Visitors staying at least 3–4 days can expect to see giraffe, elephant, zebra, impala, roan, sable, wildebeest, kudu, buffalo, waterbuck, warthog, and eland. Predators are found here too; look out for lions, hyenas, jackals, cheetahs, and wild dogs.

Luxury lodges found within the park can arrange for a wide variety of guided safaris; but public campgrounds are also available at Ihaha, Savuti, and Linyanti. Toilet and shower facilities available. Each of these campgrounds has its own unique character and visitors should try to see all of them. Self-guided travelers must have a 4-wheel-drive vehicle.

LOCATION: Gaborone is about 200 miles from Johannesburg, with a good road link. Botswana's main airport is Sir Seretse Khama International Airport situated about 10 miles from Gaborone. One park office is next to the police station in Maun and another is in the government enclave in Gaborone.

HOURS OF OPERATION: Year-round; closed Dec 25.

CONTACT: *Maun office:* Parks and Reserves Reservation Office, PO Box 20364, Boseja, Maun, Botswana; Tel: 267661265; Fax: 267661264. *Gaborne office:* PO Box 131, Gaborone, Botswana; Tel: 267580774; Fax: 267580775; Web: www.chobe-national-park.com.

COST: *Entrance:* US$11.

ON-SITE AMENITIES: Gift shop, bar, restaurants, ATM machines, banking services, car rentals, etc. **Chobe Marina Lodge:** From US$300; Tel: 2676252221, 2676252222, or 2676252223; Fax: 267-6252224; Web: www.chobemarina lodge.com. **Chobe Game Lodge:** All-inclusive rates from US$450; Web: www .chobegamelodge.com. **Siyabona Africa Travel:** For reservations call 27214241037 or fax: 27214241036.

BEST TIMES: April through October. The summer season begins in November and ends in March. The summer (rainy season) can be quite hot, but intermittent clouds and rain can temporarily cool things down. The winter season begins in May and ends in August. Winter days (dry season) are invariably sunny and cool to warm; there is virtually no rain. However, evening and night temperatures can drop below freezing. The rest of the year—April to early May and September and October—tend to be dry, but the days are cooler than in summer and the nights are warmer than in winter.

FIELD NOTES: Visitors traveling through the park should remember that this is a wilderness area and no services are available. When traveling without a guide, carry basic safety items such as water, food, fuel, torches, extra wheels, tools, jacks, and pumps. Booking ahead is essential for all campsites. Bring a dustcover and waterproof container for your camera equipment, rain gear (especially in summer), sunglasses, lightweight and neutral-colored clothing, and comfortable walking shoes.

TAÏ NATIONAL PARK

CÔTE D'IVOIRE

The Taï National Park hosts one of Africa's last tropical rain forests and is the object of worldwide conservation efforts. Scientists intensively follow the 2,000–3,000 chimpanzees found in the park, studying their social life, mating habits, and tool use. A native population of African elephants is supported and protected, as conservationists attempt to increase numbers. Visitors to the park can enjoy the sights of leopards, buffalo, warthogs, colobus monkeys, antelope, forest duikers, and the pygmy hippos.

Taï National Park is also home to roughly 230 species of birds, including 8 that are threatened. One of the most spectacular of the threatened birds is the beautiful white-breasted guinea fowl. These birds are found in all the ecosystems from the rain forest to the mountainous areas at the southern end of the park. Hikers will be delighted with the 875 types of plants found within the park. Numerous

walking trails are found throughout the park.

In the south of the park Mount Nienokoue rises above the mists and trees of the rain forest. This unique combination of mountain, rocky coast, and rain forest found at Taï National Park provides visitors with an opportunity for a wildlife experience to fit every interest.

LOCATION: Near the border of Liberia, approximately 235 miles west of Abidjan.

HOURS OF OPERATION: Year-round. Tours of different lengths are available.

CONTACT: *Park main office:* BP 693 San Pedro, Côte d'Ivoire; Tel: 22534712353; Fax: 22534711779; Web: www.parc-na tional-de-tai.org; email: info@parc-national-de-tai.org. **West African**

Tours: Tel: 2204495258; Web: www.west africantours.com.

COST: *Entrance:* Free. Costs depend on lodging, activities, and tours.

ON-SITE AMENITIES: To protect the environment, the park has no tourist facilities. Walking and climbing tours can be arranged through **West African Tours** or directly through the park's main office.

BEST TIMES: December through February.

FIELD NOTES: Amenities are not plentiful so plan your visit accordingly. Binoculars, a light jacket, and comfortable footwear are recommended. If traveling on your own, it is suggested you bring a map and compass, as getting lost in the park is a very real possibility.

LOANGO NATIONAL PARK

GABON

Created in 2002, along with 12 other parks in Gabon, Loango National Park has been dubbed "Africa's Last Eden." Located along Gabon's western coast, the 600-square-mile park's ocean beaches, savannas, wetlands, lagoons, and forests offer visitors the rare opportunity to appreciate the natural wonder and breathtaking beauty of Africa's diverse marine, avian, and terrestrial wildlife.

Whether walking along one of the park's many trails, or taking a vehicle tour along park roads, or watching quietly from a blind, visitors have the opportunity to see two types of antelope: the sitatunga, found in swamplands and the small duiker, found in dense thickets and forests. Lucky hikers may see some of the park's many primates, such as crowned and putty-nosed monkeys, mustached guenons, gray-cheeked mangabeys, and gorillas. African golden cats, civets, and leopards live in the park as do the red river hog, honey badger, and brushtail porcupine. Possible reptile sightings are pythons (often hanging from trees) and the elusive monitor lizard.

Loango provides some of the best bird-watching opportunities in Africa. Visitors may see the rufous-tailed palm-thrushes, long-tailed hawks, Nkulengu rails, red-billed swallows, and blue cuckoos. Other birds found here are white-faced whistling ducks, African pygmy geese, ospreys, Pel's fishing owls, buzzards, and crowned eagles.

Visitors who venture to the park's waters will find Nile, slender-nosed, and dwarf crocodiles; manatees; and swamp otters. Among the many salt-water fish swimming in the coastal waters are bull and sand sharks, chubs, threadfins, rock cods, sea catfish, snappers, and stingrays. World record–size tarpon have been caught in the park's waters. If you decide to surf or fish, don't be surprised to find elephants and hippopotamuses sharing the beach; these animals often venture to the seashore for a dip. If you're there during any time from November through April, you may be lucky enough to observe leatherback turtles laying their eggs in the sand. Otherwise, watch the ocean and you may see dolphins displaying their acrobatic skills or humpback, sperm, or killer whales coming up for air.

LOCATION: Approximately 155 miles south of Libreville.

HOURS OF OPERATION: Year-round, during daylight hours. Contact the park for more information.

CONTACT: Africa's Eden: *Booking office:* Sonsbeekweg 26, 6814 BC Arnhem, The Netherlands; Tel: 31263705567; Fax: 31263705569. *In Gabon:* BP 99, Port-Gentil, Gabon; Tel: 241564818; Web: www.africas-eden.com.

COST: Many visitors opt for a tour group package that includes travel, accommodations, guide, and park entry fees; 8-day tours from US$3,700.

ON-SITE AMENITIES: Lodging, bush camp, beach camp, and savanna camp. Whale watching, turtle seeing, walking safaris, game drives, sport fishing, lagoon tours, and conservation/education programs are available. All tours can be arranged directly through the lodge or by a tour company.

BEST TIMES: Large mammals, primates, elephants, and buffalo can be seen any time. Large mammals visit the beaches and turtles nest from November to April. Whales are offshore July through September. The rainy season is October to May, which is the worst time for mosquitoes.

FIELD NOTES: Visitors should not venture into the park without a guide. Park guides are available for hire at the lodge. Before entering Gabon, US citizens must have a passport, a valid visa, and proof of yellow fever vaccination. Commercial flights from major European cities are available as are flights from South Africa and other African countries. Air France offers four direct flights, per week, from Paris to Libreville. Most visitors arrive as part of an all-inclusive tour group.

MAYUMBA NATIONAL PARK

GABON

Mayumba National Park was founded in 2002 in an effort to protect Gabon's white-sand beaches and nesting grounds for leatherback turtles as well as Gabon's terrestrial and forest wildlife habitats. As a result, Gabon's coastal and forest wildlife habitats are protected and are among the most intact in all of Africa.

Mayumba's beaches are world-famous as the nesting grounds for the critically endangered leatherback, the world's largest living turtle. During the months of October to April, as many as 550 leatherback females may come ashore in a single night. In addition to the leatherback, Gabon is visited by three other turtle species: the olive ridley, the green, and the hawksbill.

Mayumba's coastal savannas and forests are home to a variety of wildlife.

Herds of dark chocolate and chestnut red sitatunga antelope live in and around the coastal swamplands. Forest buffalo graze in small groups in the savannas. Hippopotamuses take strolls from their parkland lagoons to dip in the ocean to remove skin parasites. The marsh mongoose, monitor lizard, mandril, lowland gorilla, chimpanzee, moustached and spot-nosed monkeys, bush pig, and elephant can all be seen in the park.

Owing to the variety of environments within the park, it is home to hundreds of species of birds. Visitors might see the hadada ibis, woolly-necked stork, black-headed heron, kingfisher, darter, European turtle-dove, wattled lapwing, and spotted cuckoo. Vultures, hawks, and falcons circle above the park searching for prey. Migrating waterfowl from Europe and the Arctic visit the parklands in October and November.

LOCATION: By road from Libreville, the trip can take between 12 and 20 hours, due to road conditions.

HOURS OF OPERATION: Year-round, during daylight hours.

CONTACT: *Main office:* Parc National de Mayumba, BP 70, Mayumba, Gabon, Afrique Centrale; Web: www.mayum banationalpark.com; email: info@ maynumbanationalpark.com. *Libreville Tourist Office:* c/o Gabontour, BP 2085, 622 av. du Colonel Parant, Libreville, Gabon; Tel: 241728504; Fax: 241728503; Web: www.gabontour.ga (French language only); email: info@gabontour.ga.

COST: Varies; contact the park. *Area hotels* (per person, per night): US$17–$30.

ON-SITE AMENITIES: Whale watching, turtle viewing, and park tours; the park can recommend a tour operator. Lodging, restaurants, and gift shops are available in the nearby town of Mayumba; visit the park's website for information.

BEST TIMES: Turtles nest from October to April. Whales are offshore July through September. The coolest and driest season is May to September. October and November are best for bird-watching.

FIELD NOTES: Visitors should not venture out on park trails without a guide. Park guides are available for hire through the park's office. Visitors must pack light; flight baggage is limited to 44 pounds. If you can pack in a single carry-on bag, you'll save time and hassle. At the very least, carry on a backpack containing all your essentials, including medical first aid kit, a change of clothes, water bottle, photographic equipment, and any medicines needed.

KAKUM NATIONAL PARK

GHANA

Visitors get a tantalizing taste of life in a tropical rain forest while taking advantage of features that heighten their knowledge and enjoyment. This approximately 140-square-mile section of rain forest was once part of a much larger forest that extended from Guinea through Sierra Leone, Liberia, and Côte d'Ivoire to Ghana. The park was established in 1990 to protect and preserve this area and provide a safe home for the endangered animals within it.

Most visitors start their journey of discovery in the multipurpose visitors center, learning about sights and sounds they are about to see. Trails have been designed to give the best views possible and guides are well qualified to explain how the raw materials of the jungle are transformed into medicines and other products that improve the quality of modern life.

Several endangered animal species live at the park, including the Mona meerkats, siana monkeys, bongos, yellow-backed duikers, and forest elephants. It can be a challenge to see them, because the thick vegetation hides many animals from view. Birdwatchers will enjoy spotting some of the 269 types of birds that make their home in the park, such as parrots, beeeaters, blue plantain-eaters, hornbills, and kingfishers.

If you like butterflies, Kakum National Park is the place for you. An estimated 550 species have been recorded here. You just might spot a *Diopetes kakumiú*, a butterfly species first discovered at the park in 1993!

The park is perhaps best known for its 1,000-foot-long canopy walkway. With viewing platforms along the way, this walk offers a spectacular vantage point for looking at the lush vegetation and birds. This walkway is made up of seven rope bridges, which are 98 feet from the ground at the highest point. Those who are afraid of heights or skittish about walking along a shifting surface might want to stay on terra firma, because the bridge does sway with the wind and movement of pedestrian traffic.

LOCATION: 31 miles north of Cape Coast. A share taxi (*tro-tro*) runs between the park and Cape Coast. The nearest small town is Abrato.

HOURS OF OPERATION: Daily, 8 a.m. to 4 p.m.

CONTACT: *Park:* Tel: 23304233278; Web: kakumnationalpark.info. **Ghana Heritage Conservation Trust:** Tel: 233-04230265; Fax: 23304230264; email: GHCT@ghana.com.

COST: *Entrance:* Adults, US$9; students, US$5; children, US$3. *Camping:* A fee applies.

ON-SITE AMENITIES: Visitors center, guided tours, picnic area, gift shop and restaurant (serves Ghanaian and international cuisine). *Camping:* The Afafranto campsite has room for 12 adults or 16 children; located in the rain forest; raised platforms are available; campers must bring self-standing tents, mosquito nets, and sleeping bags.

BEST TIMES: May through September.

FIELD NOTES: Wear light cotton clothing in neutral colors (not white), long slacks, and sturdy footwear. Bring a water bottle and snacks; don't forget your binoculars and camera!

MOLE NATIONAL PARK

GHANA

A beautiful, secluded, and serene wilderness, untouched by time and civilization will be your first thoughts when you arrive in Mole (pronounced *mo-lay*). Though not for everyone—it is isolated, hard to reach, and lacks many of the luxuries for which many African safari destinations are known—Mole National Park has a beauty and magnetism that draws a diverse group of travelers. Situated in the heart of Ghana's savanna woodland, Mole is the largest

currence and a treat rarely found else-where.

The Mole Motel, located right in the park, is the place you will call home for your stay. The motel offers overnight accommodations; and guests feast on authentic local cuisine. The perfect ending to an exciting day on safari is to relax with a cocktail as you lounge on one of the motel's two viewing plat-forms overlooking watering holes where the wildlife come to drink and bathe daily.

of the country's national parks at 2,600 square miles. Within the park there are a total of 325 miles of game protection and viewing roads.

You'll never be alone is this secluded dreamland, which is home to some 93 different types of free-roaming mam-mals, 33 species of reptiles, 9 kinds of amphibians, and an estimated 300 spe-cies of birds. Encounters with elephants, roan antelope, hartebeests, waterbucks, buffalo, and warthogs are practically guaranteed. Lions, leopards, hyenas, and various primates (such as olive ba-boons, green vervets, and patas mon-keys) also are in evidence. Experienced guides are available to lead you on a number of different tours, including a 3-hour foot safari that promises good sightings of the park's abundant wild-life. In fact, close encounters with the area's many elephants is a regular oc-

LOCATION: The park is 2 miles from Larabanga; accessible by bus, *tro-tro*, chartered taxi, or private car. Arrange-ments can be made in Tamale, the re-gion's capital.

HOURS OF OPERATION: Year-round.

CONTACT: Mole Motel: Tel: 2330712563.

COST: *Entrance:* US$4. **Mole Motel** (per day): US$22–25.

ON-SITE AMENITIES: Mole Motel (only in-park accommodation): single, dou-ble, dormitories, and private chalets with air-conditioning. Flushing toilets and baths, cold water only. Electricity supplied by generator. On-site in-ground swimming pool, restaurant. *Camping:* Campsites are also available for the truly adventurous traveler.

BEST TIMES: November through Febru-ary. The rainy season is April through October. Avoid visiting in March when the temperature is unbearable.

LAKE NAKURU NATIONAL PARK

KENYA

Lake Nakuru was formed 12 million years ago in eastern Africa's 3,700-mile-long by 35-mile-wide Great Rift Valley. Dependent solely on rainfall and with no outlet to the sea, the shallow, strongly alkaline Lake Nakuru varies in depth and size with the seasons and annual rainfall. Lake Nakuru National Park encompasses the lake and the surrounding lands. The Great Rift Valley is subject to periodic droughts, and the word *nakuru* means "dusty place" in the native Maasai language. The area is known for its wind-whipped dust that fills the air during severe dry spells.

Much of the lake is shallow enough for wading waterfowl, making it a popular feeding and nesting ground for one of nature's most spectacular birds, the pink flamingo. Standing 3–4 feet tall,

with long graceful necks and stilt-like legs, flamingos gather along the muddy shores and wade in the lake's warm waters, feeding on brine shrimp and algae, using their specially adapted upside-down beaks to filter out food from the mud. The flamingo's distinctive pink color comes from beta-carotene, which is plentiful in their diet of brine shrimp and blue-green algae. Hundreds of thousands and sometimes 1 million or more of these birds flock at the lake. The brilliant fuchsia of their feathers seems to outline the lake, making it easy to understand why Lake Nakuru has been dubbed "the greatest bird spectacle on earth."

Lake Nakuru National Park was founded in 1968 to protect the flamingo and the hundreds of other bird species that share the lake, such as pelicans, grebes, terns, stilts, avocets, and ducks. Recently, the park added 72 square miles of fenced-in land around the lake to protect the black rhino and Rothschild giraffe. Today, there are 25 black rhinos in the park, the largest population in Kenya. Waterbucks are also common in the park, as are zebras, hippopotamuses, leopards, and lions.

The park can be seen in a day and is a popular destination for tour groups visiting Kenyan parks. Two picnic areas and five overnight campsites are available. A road encircles the lake, and the park has many trails, including a short, winding path leading to a precipice called Baboon Cliff, which overlooks the lake. From atop the cliff, visitors have the best view of the lake and its dazzling fringe of flamingos.

LOCATION: 100 miles north of Nairobi. The park's main gate is 2.5 miles south of the town of Nakuru.

HOURS OF OPERATION: Daily, 6 a.m. to 7 p.m.; entrance is not permitted after 6:15 p.m.

CONTACT: *Park office:* Lake Nakuru National Park, PO Box 539, Nakuru, Kenya; Tel: 25405144069; *Kenya Wildlife Service:* Web: www.kws.org/nakuru.html; email: kws@kws.org.

COST: *Entrance* (per day, nonresidents): Adults, US$30; children, US$10.

ON-SITE AMENITIES: Warden's headquarters, field study center, well-marked trails, maintained roads, two picnic areas, and five campsites (with water, toilets, and showers). Toilet facilities are available at other locations in the park.

BEST TIMES: Year-round. Mosquitoes are worst during the rainy season, October to May. Note that 4-wheel-drive vehicles may be necessary on park roads during the rainy season.

FIELD NOTES: Baboon Cliff is the best place to view the lake and flamingos. Do not drive too close to the lake because the shoreline is very soft.

MOUNT KENYA NATIONAL PARK

KENYA

With its rugged, glacier-clad peaks and forested slopes, Mount Kenya has one of the most spectacular landscapes in East Africa. This central feature of the Mount Kenya National Park is the second highest mountain in the region and home to the supreme being, Ngai of the Kikuyu and other local peoples. Ngai is sometimes called the Professor of Brightness; thus this eco-destination has earned the name "Mountain of Brightness."

The park is located between 11,000 and 17,058 feet on the mountain, enabling visitors a rare opportunity to experience the diversity of flora and

wildlife that grow and live along the mountain slopes. From grasslands to bamboo forests, to the edge of glaciers that grace its highest points, Mount Kenya is an eco-traveler's dream. Above and beyond the magnificent backdrop of mountain peaks, pristine lakes, forests, and glaciers is the opportunity for some gratifying wildlife viewing. Lower altitudes are home to the olive baboon, genet cat, waterbuck, black rhino, black-fronted duiker, leopard, giant forest hog, bush pig, and hyena. More obscure is the bongo, a rare type of forest antelope.

In the middle elevations visitors will find black and white colobus and sykes monkeys, buffalo, bushbucks, and elephants. Zebras and elands inhabit the higher regions. A number of rare and endangered species are found within the parklands: Mount Kenya mole shrews, skinks, Sunni bucks, and a few different species of owls. Sightings of albino zebras are also a possibility while in the park. The bird life around the mountain is prolific; bird-watchers may see olive pigeons, giant kingfishers, multicolored sunbirds, red-fronted parrots, and eagles.

Truly adventurous souls may consider scaling one of the three major peaks in the park. Point Lenana (16,355 feet) can be reached by most relatively fit people. Batian (17,058 feet) and Nelion (17,022 feet), however, are accessible only to skilled mountaineers. If you are planning a safari or trip to the Kenya area, a journey to Mount Kenya National Park would nicely round out your African experience.

LOCATION: Approximately 108 miles from Nairobi. The closest commercial airstrip is located in Nanyoki.

HOURS OF OPERATION: Daily, 6 a.m. to 6:30 p.m.

CONTACT: *Park office:* Senior Warden, Mount Kenya National Park, PO Box 69, Naru Moru, Kenya; Tel: 01712383; Web: www.kws.org/mt-kenya.html.

COST: *Entrance* (nonresidents): Adults, US$15; children 3–18 years old, US$5; children under 3, free. Other costs depend on the type of trip chosen.

ON-SITE AMENITIES: Concessions available, gift shop, lodging.

BEST TIMES: High season is July to March, which offers optimal animal viewing due to short grasses and plentiful food sources. Low season is April to June; rains are likely at this time of year. Most roads require the use of 4-wheel-drive vehicles.

FIELD NOTES: Appropriate clothing varies with altitude so think "layering," which allows you to accommodate to warming temperatures during the day. Lace-up or comfortable walking shoes, long pants, shirt/T-shirts of natural or khaki colors are advised. Also bring a flashlight, insect repellent, and, of course, a camera and plenty of film (or extra memory cards).

NAIROBI NATIONAL PARK

KENYA

Nairobi National Park, located just 4 miles from Kenya's capital, could not be more of a contrast to that bustling city. The city is home to 2.8 million people, and the park provides a habitat for some of the world's best-known "zoo" animals: lions, giraffes, zebras, hippopotamuses, leopards, elephants, cheetahs, rhinoceroses, and ostriches. But Nairobi National Park is no

zoo. It is a treasured, natural wildlife sanctuary about which the park's first warden, Captain Archie Ritchie, wrote some 50 years ago, "I want to give an assurance, a guarantee that the park is wholly 'genuine'. Persons...may well imagine that its faunal population, varied and teeming as it is, has been laboriously built up, and that many of the animals...have been brought from elsewhere, or at least induced by artifice to come in and dwell. The exact opposite is the case, and the area is essentially the same as when I first took charge of it [in 1924]."

The 29,000-acre park, established in 1946, is Kenya's oldest and most popular park. Its varied habitats, ranging from areas of lowland grass and thick brush to dry highland forests, are home to more than 80 species of mammals and more than 400 different species of birds. World-renown as a rhinoceros sanctuary, the park has more than 50 white and black rhinos, making it very likely that visitors may see at least one during their stay. The park has an active recovery program for the critically endangered black rhino—dark gray, really; their color varies with soil conditions—which was hunted to near extinction for their highly valued horns, incorrectly thought to be an aphrodisiac or to be capable of curing fever and even reviving the comatose. Hundreds of thousand are thought to have roamed Africa at the beginning of the 20th century. In 2004, scientists estimated there were fewer than 2,500 black rhinos left. A 2006 estimate suggests that their numbers have rebounded slightly, thanks to the park's efforts and the work of many other like-minded organizations.

Visitors frequently start with the Nairobi Safari Walk, a guided tour, led by a trained naturalist, who provides introductory information about Kenya and its many parks and reserves, emphasizing the various conservation efforts the country is making to protect its diverse, natural wildlife. On the walk, visitors will learn to identify many of the trees, plants, and animals they see from their vehicle safari through the parklands. A great way to end the stay is to visit the Wild Animal Orphanage, where visitors may see baby elephants, monkeys, and other animals.

LOCATION: The park is 4 miles from the city center of Nairobi.

HOURS OF OPERATION: Daily, during daylight hours.

CONTACT: *Park Headquarters:* Nairobi National Park, PO Box 42076-00100, Nairobi, Kenya; Tel: 254020602121. **Kenya Wildlife Service:** PO Box 40241-00100, Nairobi, Kenya; Tel: 254020600800; Web: www.kws.org/nairobi.html.

COST: *Entrance* (per day; nonresidents): Adults, US$40; children, US$20. Tour groups generally include the entrance fee in the package.

ON-SITE AMENITIES: Park headquarters, gift and African art shop, Wild Animal Orphanage, picnic areas, toilet facilities, road system with signage, and nature trails. There are no overnight accommodations in the park, but the **Masai Safari Lodge** is near the park and there are many hotels in Nairobi.

BEST TIMES: Year-round. Mosquitoes are worst during the rainy season, October to May.

FIELD NOTES: The park can be experienced by vehicle tour or by taking part in the safari walk. Allow a minimum of 4 hours. Park staff, located at the entrance gate, can tell you where to find each species, so ask. The park is located a short distance from the city, making it an ideal stopover destination. US visitors to Kenya require vaccination against cholera and yellow fever.

SAMBURU NATIONAL RESERVE

KENYA

Located in the Great Rift Valley, along the banks of the Ewaso Ngiro River in Kenya's arid northern region, Samburu National Reserve is a great place to see Africa's dry plains and savanna wildlife. Nairobi, Kenya's capital city, is 200 miles away, making Samburu more difficult for foreign visitors to reach; but the trip is well worth any extra effort. The reserve is less crowded than other Kenyan parks. Some of you may recognize the area from the movie *Born Free*, which was filmed in the reserve.

Large herds of elephants roam the park's scrublands and dry hills. The world's largest land animal, standing 12 feet tall and weighing 12,000 pounds, the elephant was mercilessly hunted during the 20th century for sport and for its prized ivory tusks, measuring 5–8 feet in length. In 1990, a worldwide ban on the trade and import/export of ivory was imposed, greatly reducing the number of elephants killed, although an underground illegal market for tusks still exists.

Samburu safari adventurers can see giraffe, gazelle, impala, waterbuck, ze-bra, leopard, lion, and the incredibly fast cheetah. The fastest animal on earth, the cheetah can run 70 miles an hour for short distances and can go from a dead start to 60 miles an hour in less than 3 seconds!

Samburu is also home to 350 species of birds. Visitors may see king-fishers, sunbirds, bee-eaters, storks, and tawny eagles. Vultures can be seen circling overhead. Wrongly portrayed as nature's bad guys, vultures are really an important part of the Samburu ecosystem. Visitors can see the flightless ostrich living in flocks of 5–50 birds. If frightened, the ostrich tries to hide itself by lying flat against the ground—contrary to popular belief, it doesn't actually stick its head in the ground; sometimes the birds run away, reaching speeds of 40 miles per hour.

LOCATION: 200 miles north of Nairobi.

HOURS OF OPERATION: Daily, during daylight hours.

CONTACT: *Reserve office:* Tel: 2540-20600800; Web: www.go2africa.com/kenya/sambura-national-reserve.

COST: Most visitors arrive with tour groups. Entrance fees and vehicle permits are included in most tour packages. *Lodging* (per night): from US$400, all inclusive.

ON-SITE AMENITIES: Park headquarters, gift shop, restroom facilities, various tours, and lodging. *Lodging:* www.safarinow.com/go/SamburuIntrepids. *Tours:* Visit www.go2africa.com/kenya/samburu-national-reserve/tours or www.thos.co.za/Kenya_Lodging_Options-travel/safari-lodge-samburu-intrepids-lodge.html.

BEST TIMES: January through October.

FIELD NOTES: Camel-back tours, walking tours, and driving safaris accompanied by skilled guides can be booked through your accommodations provider. The reserve also offers an educational safari for children. Rafting trips are available when the river levels are high.

MASOALA NATIONAL PARK

MADAGASCAR

Picture yourself walking under a dense rain forest canopy enjoying primeval sounds of birds, monkeys, and flying squirrels. The occasional chattering and hooting is suddenly broken by the sound of crashing water. Walk a little farther and you'll see what you've been hearing, the Indian Ocean and its resident fauna. Not only is Masoala National Park the largest national park in Madagascar but it is one of the only places in the country where the rain forest meets the sea. The parklands protect the forest all the way from the coast to the mountaintops, and its three marine reserves protect the coral reefs. A pristine shore and a forest rich in biodiversity await travelers on the Masoala Peninsula and the forested island of Nosy Mangabe.

In addition to being an excellent destination for eco-tourism it draws research scientists who come to study the animals and plants that are found nowhere else on the planet, such as the red-ruffed lemur. Madagascar is among the top five countries in terms of biodiversity richness. And Masoala park lives up to this reputation. Visitors will find many rare species of flora and fauna, including spectacular palms, serpent eagles, and 10 species of lemurs. The park is covered by rain and coastal forests that together make a home for carnivorous plants, red owls, and a variety of reptiles and birds.

Visitors can engage in hiking, trekking, whale watching, and boating. Choose a day hike to the beach or to see old tombs; if you venture out at night you may spot a leaf-tailed gecko

or the elusive aye-aye. At Tampolo, hikers can travel into the forest to see red-ruffed lemurs or stroll to the beach beneath canopies of *Pandanus*. In Cap Est, plant lovers might find the exotic *Nepenthes*, or pitcher plant.

Within the park's boundaries, 10 species of lemurs have been recorded; 4 of these are considered to be threatened. Lemurs, which are cousins to monkeys, are incredibly agile, social, and intelligent animals.

LOCATION: Masoala Peninsula.

HOURS OF OPERATION: Year-round.

CONTACT: *Park office:* Masoala National Park, BP 86–Maroantsetra 512, Madagascar; Tel: Maroantsetra 111; Web: www.masoala.org. **Cortez Expeditions:** Web: www.air-mad.com. **Kayak Africa:** Web: www.kayakafrica.net. **Libertalia:** Web: www.libertalia-mada .com/voyage.php.

COST: Depends on the tour package.

ON-SITE AMENITIES: Hotels, motels, bar, travel services, gift shops. *In-park accommodations:* **Ocean Momo:** Tel: 261320234069; Web: www.ocean-momo .com. **Arollodge:** Tel: 261331290277; Web: http://arollodge.free.fr/home.htm.

BEST TIMES: This tropical park is humid and hot year-round, so visit during the drier season, May through November, after the rains, when everything is lush and green.

FIELD NOTES: While a visit to the peninsula can be self-guided, most veterans recommend that you hook up with a tour. Get ready for warm, sticky weather. Bring rain gear, boots, comfortable walking shoes, sunglasses, sunscreen, first aid kit, etc. Watch where you swim because the Gulf of Antongil is notorious for its shark population. Getting to and from the park can be difficult; Masoala can be reached only by boat.

VOLCANOES NATIONAL PARK

RWANDA

In 1925, the first national park in Africa was created in the Virunga Mountains of the Belgian Congo, in what is today the countries of Uganda, Democratic Republic of Congo, and Rwanda. The purpose of the 3,000-square-mile park was to protect the largest primate in the world, the mountain gorilla, from the relentless hunting of poachers. In 1962, after the three countries gained their independence, the park was split, and the Rwanda portion became Volcanoes National Park, named after the five Vurunga volcanoes that lay within the park's borders. The park and the plight of the mountain gorilla were brought to the world's attention by the work, writings, and tragic death of American zoologist Dian Fossey.

There are two subspecies of gorilla, the lowland and the mountain gorilla, with the latter being larger and stronger than its lowland cousin. The mountain gorilla's natural habitat is restricted to only one place in the world: the Virunga Mountains. It is estimated there are only 630 mountain gorillas living in the

wild, approximately half of which live in Volcanoes National Park.

The park's other featured species is the endangered golden monkey. In 2002, a group of golden monkeys was introduced to the park from Rwanda's southern Nyungwe forest, where the species was struggling to survive. Currently, the park is home to about 40 golden monkeys, which are thriving. These monkeys, which are much smaller than gorillas, are often found in dense thickets of bamboo; thus they can be difficult to spot in the wild.

LOCATION: Northwest corner of Rwanda, bordering Magahinga Gorilla National Park in Uganda and Virunga National Park in the Republic of Congo. The park entrance is near Musanze, a 90-minute drive from Kigali. Taxis are available from Musanze to the park entrance.

HOURS OF OPERATION: Year-round. *Tours:* 7 a.m., from the visitors center in Musanze.

CONTACT: *Park office:* Office of Rwanda Tourism and National Parks (ORTNP), Boulevard de la Revolution No. 1, PO Box 905, Kigali, Rwanda; Tel: 250576514; Web: www.rwandatourism.com/guide .htm.

COST: *Tour fee permits* (per person, non-nationals): gorilla, US$500; golden monkey, US$75; available from the park office in Kigali; visitors must arrange their own transportation to the park.

ON-SITE AMENITIES: The ORTNP visitors center in Musanze is a short driving distance from the park entrance. Park activities include daily gorilla and golden monkey visits, tours of lakes and caves, a visit to Dian Fossey's grave site, and hiking tours up Karisimbi and Bisoke volcanoes.

BEST TIMES: Gorilla and golden monkey tours are best during the drier season, June through January.

FIELD NOTES: Gorilla tour entails a 4-hour walk at an elevation of 6,000–8,000 feet above sea level. Tour groups are limited to eight people. Wear long pants and long sleeves; avoid touching the plants because nettles are common.

THE SEYCHELLES ISLANDS

SEYCHELLES

Vallée de Mai, on the main island of Praslin, once believed to be the original site of the Garden of Eden, may be the main—but far from the only—attraction of Seychelles, a remarkable collection of 115 islands off the east coast of Africa. It is also home to Aldabra, the world's largest raised coral atoll, home to abundant marine life and a sanctuary for some of the rarest species of plants and animals on earth.

The government of Seychelles is serious about conservation. The nation has set aside almost half of its limited land as national parks and reserves. Visitors to this paradise come to appreciate the forward-thinking conservation policies that have preserved the islands and the variety of ecosystems found here.

The islands boast unique and rare endemic specimens. Here, visitors can see and learn about the coco-de-mer, a palm tree that produces the largest seed in the world. The Seychelles are also home to the only known living specimens of the jellyfish tree. Wildlife observers can look for the paradise flycatcher, the Seychelles warbler, the world's smallest frog, the heaviest land tortoise, and the only flightless bird of the Indian Ocean. The beautiful and peaceful islands are home to an amazing variety of plants, animals, and marine life.

The islands are covered with lush, green vegetation, which is stunning in itself. The real treat, however, is the remarkable variety of life that lives under the foliage. Many animal species are found nowhere else in the world. A number of endangered animals are protected here. Bird-watchers should look for the Seychelles white-eye (a rare warbler-like perching bird, endemic to the area, once thought to be extinct), the black paradise flycatcher (on La Digue), the Seychelles black (on Praslin and Curieuse), and the scops owl (on Mahé). The hawksbill, green, loggerhead, and leatherback sea turtles can all be found here.

Visitors will want to see as many of the Seychelles islands as they can because each offers a unique eco-experience. A well-organized system of air and water transport makes island-hopping easy, and it is reasonable to see more than one island a day. Most services operate out of Mahé. Buses and rental cars are available for land travel.

LOCATION: West Indian Ocean, 260 miles off the east coast of Africa.

HOURS OF OPERATION: 24/7.

CONTACT: *Tourism information:* Seychelles Tourism Board (STB), PO Box 1262, Victoria, Mahé, Seychelles; Tel: 248671300; Fax: 248620620; Web: www.seychelles.travel.

COST: Depends on hotel or guesthouse; see the STB's website for more information.

ON-SITE AMENITIES: Hotels, guesthouses, restaurants, shopping, sailing, fishing, diving, and island exploration expeditions.

BEST TIMES: The islands' tropical climate provides for an optimal experience year-round.

FIELD NOTES: Bring sunglasses, sunscreen (SPF 30 or higher is recommended), hats, camera, batteries, film, and comfortable walking shoes. Each island offers a unique set of opportunities. It is a good idea to try to plan ahead by researching the possibilities for each island and to learn about any special events; start with the STB's website.

EDENI PRIVATE GAME RESERVE

SOUTH AFRICA

Edeni Private Game Reserve is a world-class safari and wildlife destination that provides both five-star accommodations and the very best in guided tours, hiking, and safaris. The reserve encompasses 21,000 acres of unspoiled land with flourishing wildlife located a mere 45 minutes from the entrance to the internationally renowned Kruger National Park.

Visitors to Edeni are able to join walking tours of the area where they are led by Shangaan, who are expert, native guides eager to share their pride in and enthusiasm for the land they call home. As you are guided through the bush you will be exposed to virgin vegetation and come close to many of the animals indigenous to the area. For those who prefer to roam farther afield,

the reserve offers both day and night tours in open 4-wheel-drive vehicles. The guides ensure that you will get as close as possible to animals that you may never otherwise see. Led by the same expert guides as the walking tours, the driving tours allow you to cover more ground in the same amount of time.

Visitors can expect to see many species in Edeni. Among the carnivores that live here are caracals, cheetahs, civets, large and small spotted genets, honey badgers, and brown and spotted hyenas. You'll delight in observing black-backed and side-striped jackals, servals, leopards, and lions. Three types of mongooses, several primates (including the chacma baboon, lesser and thick-tailed bushbabies, and vervet monkey) roam about the grounds. Visitors will come across grazing herds of buffalo, bushbucks, duikers, elands, gemsboks, giraffes, hippos, impalas,

kudos, nyalas, white rhinos, waterbucks, blue wildebeests, and Burchell zebras. And, of course, African elephants are also here.

The Edeni Private Game Reserve provides three different types of lodging. River Lodge, on the banks of the Makhutswi River, offers five-star accommodations. Right from the comfort of their own suite, guests can watch animals visit a nearby watering hole. The other two areas consist of private tented accommodations in the midst of the wilderness. But this isn't rough camping; all "tents" have at least some modern conveniences, such as electricity, coffeemaker, toilets, and a shower.

LOCATION: 37.3 miles south of Tzaneen. Daily commercial air service available from Hoedspruit or KMIA. The reserve staff is able to book your transportation from the airport.

HOURS OF OPERATION: 24/7, with day and night guided tours.

CONTACT: *Reserve office:* Tel: 271-53839909 or 27153839910; Cell: 278-36264491; After hours: 27153830044; Fax: 27153839911; Web: www.edeni .com; email: lodge@edeni.com or reservations@edeni.com.

COST: *Entrance:* US$6. *Rooms* (per person, per night): River Lodge: US$280–$379; Hoyo Hoyo: US$224–$261; Bush Lodge: US$224–$261; meals and snacks, morning and afternoon game drives, and game walks included.

ON-SITE AMENITIES: Three styles of lodging, guided walking and driving tours, and all meals.

BEST TIMES: May through August.

FIELD NOTES: Reservations are strongly suggested. Binoculars, camera, comfortable walking shoes, raincoat in summer (September through April), and seasonal clothing are recommended. Children are welcome, and every effort is made to include all family members in activities. See the reserve's website for current information and restrictions.

INYATI PRIVATE GAME RESERVE

SOUTH AFRICA

Inyati Private Game Reserve abuts Kruger National Park and is located within the Sabi Sand Game Reserve. Visitors to this prime wildlife destination will be able to observe Africa's big five mammals and a host of other species. Dawn and dusk game drives in specially equipped open vehicles, early morning walks into the bush, and drifting down the Sand River on a barge are ideal methods for close encounters with lions, leopards, buffalo, elephants, and rhinoceroses. Experienced trackers and skilled rangers ensure that animal sightings and bush adventures are truly inspiring experiences.

After a day in the bush, relax in your chalet or spend time on the deck watching the animals that have come down to the river. Before dinner, visit the lounge, sample one of the lodge's many

wines, and swap stories with the other guests. You can have dinner outdoors at either a traditional braai (barbecue), while enjoying the night sounds of the bush, or at a boma, while hearing native tales and listening to African drums. If you'd rather, take your dinner on the patio, which overlooks the Sabi River.

LOCATION: A 5-hour drive from Johannesburg. The reserve has a private airstrip suitable for light aircraft. There are three daily flights from Johannesburg International Airport.

HOURS OF OPERATION: Year-round.

CONTACT: *Reserve office:* Inyati Private Game Reserve, PO Box 38838, Johannesburg, South Africa, 2016; Tel: 270118805907/9; Fax: 270117882406; Web: www.inyati.co.za; email: inyatigl @iafrica.com.

COST: Depends on season and level of accommodations.

ON-SITE AMENITIES: Main lodge, luxurious chalets, bar, swimming pool, gymnasium, curio shop, and view deck. Game drives; foot and river safaris.

BEST TIMES: Select encounters occur at different times of year: choose the wet season for plentiful wildlife, the birthing season to see the new arrivals, or dry season when animals are more competitive. Reserve staff will help coordinate your ideal itinerary.

FIELD NOTES: Comfortable walking shoes, sunglasses, and sunscreen are recommended. Summer is generally from September through April; winter is from May through August. For summer, bring lightweight clothing, swimsuit, and warm clothes for the night game drives. In winter, bring light clothing for daytime and a warm insulated jacket for evenings and early mornings. Binoculars and cameras with a good supply of batteries, film, and/or memory cards are a must. Children under the age of 8 are not permitted at the reserve. Children must be at least 10 years old to go on the drives and 15 years to participate in the walks.

IVORY TREE GAME LODGE

SOUTH AFRICA

Approximately 1,300 million years ago, the site of Ivory Tree Game Lodge was an extremely active volcano. Today the volcano is long gone, and the area is now the setting of the popular Pilanesberg National Park. Guests can explore the park and take in the sights and sounds of the bushveld, a transition zone between the dry Kalahari Desert and wetter lowveld vegetation. The mammals, birds, and vegetation from the two ecozones overlap here, so guests can expect exciting animal-watching opportunities.

Ivory Tree Game Lodge offers a chance to spot both rare and common species. Although some species, such as the lion, were introduced to the area in the last century, many animals are native to parklands of Pilanesberg. The lodge's open-vehicle safaris allow guests to observe and photograph—lions, African elephants, cape buffalo, black and white rhinoceroses, and leopards—as well as brown hyenas, sables, giraffes, zebras, bushpigs, warthogs, and Jamesons red rock hares.

At Ivory Tree, guests can choose to learn about wildlife management or even participate in animal conservation activities. For example, scientists who are interested in collecting data about the movements of individual animals must have a way of tracking them. Once a conservationist has tranquilized an animal, visitors can help him or her place a radio collar or remove a microchip, for instance. This is a once-in-a-lifetime experience and a chance to see some of the animals on a one-to-one basis.

Another wildlife activity takes bird-watchers into Pilanesberg to spot some of the 280 species that live in the park. The lodge guides can also teach guests how to identify the 18 species of frogs and toads in the area by both sight and sound. The guide for the botany safari will not only identify species but will teach participants about the medicinal uses of many indigenous plants found in the park. Guides are also available for stargazing tours in which guests can learn about the constellations and the traditional stories told about them.

LOCATION: A 2-hour drive from Johannesburg.

HOURS OF OPERATION: Year-round.

CONTACT: *Lodge offices:* Tel:270117811661 (reservations) or 270145568100 (information); Web: www.ivorytreegamelodge .com; email: francois@anthology.co.za.

COST: *Rooms* (per person, per night): depends on season and type of accommodation; US$218–$594; meals, tea, snacks, dawn and dusk safaris, and VAT inclusive.

ON-SITE AMENITIES: The lodge has 57 air-conditioned suites, with patios, en-suite bathroom, outdoor shower, and boma (open-air enclosure). There are also 3 luxury executive suites. Other amenities are spa, conference room, and curio shop. Hot air ballooning, elephant-back safaris, and open-vehicle game drives.

BEST TIMES: Winter (May to September).

FIELD NOTES: Children under 6 years are not permitted on safaris. Participation by children aged 6–12 years is at the discretion of the guide.

KAPAMA PRIVATE GAME RESERVE

SOUTH AFRICA

Among the largest of South Africa's private game reserves, Kapama Private Game Reserve, situated in the Limpopo Province, is known for its density of big game animals, which makes it one of the best reserves for an African safari. The options that Kapama offers for safari is where your adventure begins.

From the safety of an open vehicle, you can go on a dawn search for big cats who are getting ready to relax after a night's hunt. As daybreak progresses to morning, you'll really start to marvel at the abundance of wildlife that lives here. After returning to the lodges at around 9 a.m. for a hearty breakfast, remember to keep a keen eye on the surroundings; you'll likely be able to spot antelope and other game right from the comfort of the lodge. After having high tea in the afternoon, you'll be ready to head back into the bush for an evening drive, in which you'll see the big predators getting ready for the night's hunting.

Guests can also go on walking safaris to learn how to identify tracks, birds, and plants. Other ways to view wildlife involve elephant-back riding and soaring high in a hot air balloon, searching for the wild game in the bush below as you enjoy a glass of bubbly high above.

At the Hoedspruit Centre for Endangered Species you will gain insight into the issues involved in protecting Africa's animals. The center also works to rehabilitate cheetahs and other animals so they can be returned to the wild.

LOCATION: Limpopo Province.

HOURS OF OPERATION: Year-round.

CONTACT: *Reserve office:* Tel: 270-123680600; Fax: 270841977952; Web: www.kapama.co.za; email: res@kapama.co.za.

COST: Depends on options and accommodations; from US$214 per person, per night.

ON-SITE AMENITIES: The reserve provides guides, game drives, safari walks, and elephant rides. There are full-service accommodations, including fine dining, bars, pools, gym, and wellness center. Spa treatments are also available. Additional fees may apply. Accommodations range from the large River Lodge to the lakeside Kapama Lodge to the luxury tents of Buffalo Camp.

BEST TIMES: Year-round, depending on personal choice, however, spring (August through October) is usually the best for game viewing.

FIELD NOTES: Clothing should be lightweight and in neutral colors (not white).

Also have a windproof jacket or fleece for early morning drives, a good pair of walking shoes (sandals are not a good choice), high SPF sunblock, and supe- rior binoculars. Make sure you have enough film, memory cards, tape, and batteries because they may not be available on-site.

KGALAGADI TRANSFRONTIER PARK

SOUTH AFRICA AND BOTSWANA

Named after a term that means "the land that dried up" or "the thirsty land," Kgalagadi Transfrontier Park is located in the southern African Kala- hari Desert. Encompassing more than 9 million acres, the Kgalagadi Trans- frontier Park is one of the largest con- servation areas in the world. Red sand dunes, sparse vegetation, and the dry riverbeds of the Nossob and Auob show antelope and predator species off to spectacular advantage and provide ex- cellent photo opportunities. Kgalagadi is also a known haven for birders, espe- cially for those interested in birds of prey.

Among the many unusual species is the gemsbok, a large striking desert an- telope, which also serves as the emblem of the park. The park is also home to suricates, also widely known as meer- kats, which display an intricate family structure.

Visitors should also be on the lookout for sociable weavers, small birds known for constructing huge communal nests, and pygmy falcons, the smallest falcons of Africa. Blue wildebeests, springboks, elands, and red hartebeests are also found in the park. Bird lovers travel here to catch sight of a variety of raptors, the most common being the tawny and black-breasted snake eagles, bateleurs, and white-backed and lappet-faced vultures. The smaller pale chanting goshawk, gabar goshawk, and greater kestrel are also seen here.

The predator mammals are the park's main attraction. The black-maned Kalahari lions are physically impressive and truly the kings of the desert. Visitors may also see cheetahs, leopards, and brown and spotted hyenas.

Although weather and climate depend on the season, the best time to travel to the Kalahari is in winter, when the temperatures are cooler. The dry season lasts from May through October, and November through April are marked by hot and wet weather. On the other hand, there are plenty of wildlife opportunities in the dry days of summer.

The park maintains several trails and two are for 4×4s. Visitors can join guided morning and afternoon walks along different trails.

There are several rest camps within the park. These areas offer different amenities, including swimming pool, lodges, tent camping, food store, and fuel. Note that some rest areas are much more primitive and the only restaurant is at Twee Rivieren. Visitors wishing to drive in the park should allow a minimum of 1 full day; a 4-wheel-drive vehicle is recommended.

LOCATION: The entrance at Twee Rivieren gate is approximately 130 miles north of Upington.

HOURS OF OPERATION: Year-round; summer, 6 a.m. to 7:30 p.m.; winter, 7:30 a.m. to 6 p.m.

CONTACT: *Park office:* Tel: 270545612000; Fax: 270545612005; Web: www.sanparks .org/parks/kgalagadi.

COST: *Entrance:* US$17.

ON-SITE AMENITIES: Shops, restaurant, swimming pools, and filling stations. The park has six rest camps of varying size that have excellent facilities; three are traditional rest camps and three are wilderness camps. All are well equipped with the basic necessities. The shops sell a variety of goods, including fresh meat, dairy products, beer, and spirits.

BEST TIMES: Dry season (May through October), when the animals tend to gather around the remaining watering holes.

FIELD NOTES: Boots are essential for protection against possible scorpion stings. A 4-wheel-drive vehicle makes for easier travel because the roads can be rough. Rental cars are available at

Twee Rivieren (book in advance). Before driving into the park be sure to read and understand the regulations. Drivers should be on the road by noon to ensure arrival at a rest camp. Visitors may not travel in the park after dark. Have your binoculars and cameras readily accessible at all times.

LALIBELA GAME RESERVE

SOUTH AFRICA

Located only 1 hour from Port Elizabeth, Lalibela Game Reserve is an amazing repository of flora and fauna and is an excellent representative of African wildlife in an unpaved, natural environment. The five distinct ecosystems and variety of animals allows visitors a glimpse into the totality of Africa while never leaving the grounds of the game reserve. Safaris through the park are conducted in open vehicles that allow close encounters with a range of animals from elephant, lion, rhino, and buffalo to the tiny blue duiker, rock hyrax, and more. Nighttime tours offer visitors the chance to observe the bat-eared fox, aardvark, black-backed jackal, aardwolf, and spring hare.

A stay at any of Lalibela's three lodges includes an evening and morning open-vehicle game drive and all meals and drinks. Each lodge has its own ambiance, but all include swimming pool, viewing deck, and lounge.

LOCATION: An hour's drive from Port Elizabeth. Transfers to the reserve are available.

HOURS OF OPERATION: Year-round, 24/7.

CONTACT: *Reserve office:* Tel: 274-15818170; Web: www.lalibela.co.za; email: res@lalibela.co.za.

COST: *Lodge* (per person, per night): US$369–$412, includes game drives, meals, and drinks; discounts available for children; family suites available.

ON-SITE AMENITIES: Dining (all meals), lodging, daily game drive safaris, swimming pools, expert guides. An on-site landing strip can accommodate light aircraft.

BEST TIMES: April through August.

FIELD NOTES: This reserve is an ideal family vacation destination because it is so close to a major airport and offers a specific program for children as well as child care services. Children must be 8 years old to join the adult game drives.

MALAMALA GAME RESERVE

SOUTH AFRICA

Within the unfenced borders between the famed Kruger National Park and the Sabi Sand Reserve, lies MalaMala Game Reserve, the largest private big-five game reserve in South Africa. Add a 13-mile stretch of the Sand River to this and you are at the center of one of the largest concentrations of free-roaming lions, leopards, rhinos, elephants, buffalo, and hundreds of other mammals. Except for two safaris that slowly and quietly wander through the wilds each day, with no more than six guests in each vehicle, MalaMala's 33,000 acres remain undisturbed. These are a few of the reasons why MalaMala is the choice of a multitude of photojournalists and filmmakers.

Besides the big five, visitors can expect to spot many other mammals, including blue wildebeests, tsessebes, impalas, kudos, and black-backed and side-striped jackals. MalaMala is also home to chacma baboons, vervet monkeys, Burchell zebras, cheetahs, giraffes, and African wild cats.

The reserve has three camps and thus offers an array of accommodations to meet individual needs. All camps offer luxury suites, air-conditioning, viewing decks, swimming pool, historic bar, lounge, library, and fitness center. The main camp has 8 suites and 10 rooms tucked away in the greenery along the banks of the Sand River. From the camp's observation deck, guests can watch antelope or elephants looking for lunch in the lush surrounding growth. There is also a fully equipped suite for the disabled. The 5 suites at Sable offer a more intimate and private safari adventure. Guests at Rattray's on MalaMala feel as though they have entered an Africa of a century ago. The 8 *khayas* (Zulu for "home") are furnished in colonial-style crystal and leather and each has a private view deck.

LOCATION: Between Kruger National Park and the Sabi Sand Reserve.

HOURS OF OPERATION: Year-round.

CONTACT: *Reserve office:* Tel: 270-114422267; Fax: 270114422318; Web:

www.malamala.com; email: reserva tions@malamala.com.

COST: *Lodge:* US$575–$925, includes meals, snacks, game drives and walks, bush laundry services, and transfers to and from the airstrip.

ON-SITE AMENITIES: The reserve conducts wildlife tours led by qualified rangers and experienced trackers; there are daytime and nighttime game drives and game walks.

BEST TIMES: Depends on what game you'd like to observe; visit the reserve's website to determine what time of year will best serve your viewing desires.

FIELD NOTES: *Suggested clothing:* Summer—lightweight clothing for daytime, warm clothing for game drives, and swimwear; winter—lightweight clothing for daytime, warm insulated jackets for game drives; general—the dress code is casual but neutral colors are recommended on game drives. It is requested that men wear long pants to dinner in the evenings. Be sure to bring comfortable walking shoes, sunscreen, sun hat, sunglasses, binoculars, cameras with plenty of film and/or memory cards (plus chargers and batteries). Antimalarial prophylactics are essential year-round. Children of all ages are permitted at the Main Camp. Children must be over 12 years of age to stay at Sable Camp and over 16 years to stay at Rattray's.

MONKEYLAND

SOUTH AFRICA

In the heart of the scenic Garden Route, between Capetown and Port Elizabeth, is Monkeyland, the world's only multispecies primate sanctuary. Here, deep within the Tsitsikamma forest, more than 400 primates, including many endangered species, live wild and roam free.

When you enter Monkeyland, you instantly become a forest dweller, sharing the lives of fascinating animals in a natural environment. Because the animals are not caged, the monkeys may not be instantly visible, but this is part of the fun and adventure of your visit. Experienced guides are available to help you locate the animals and to share their extensive knowledge.

You'll thrill to discover many endangered or vulnerable species. Visitors have the chance to spot black lemurs, black and white ruffed lemurs, ringtail lemurs, cottontop tamarins, golden-handed tamarins, and black-handed spider monkeys. White-handed gibbons, Angolan black and white colobuses, tufted and brown capuchins, common marmosets, douroucouli or northern gray-necked owl monkeys,

and spectacled langurs can also be found here.

Monkeyland is also home to the longest rope bridge in Africa. At 387 feet long, it rises above the forest canopy, providing a bird's-eye view seldom seen by humans. If you're daring enough, you'll have an adventure right out of *Indiana Jones*. After an exciting day close to the wildlife, you may choose to dine at the Banana Gialla, an open-air restaurant on the edge of the reserve. There, while enjoying cocktails and a delicious meal, you can gaze out at the exquisite landscape and watch the primates at play in the trees.

LOCATION: About 9 miles east of Plettenberg Bay, Eastern Cape.

HOURS OF OPERATION: Daily, 8 a.m. to 5 p.m.

CONTACT: *Sanctuary office:* Tel: 270-445348906; Fax: 270445348907; Web: www.monkeyland.co.za; email: info@ monkeyland.co.za.

COST: *Entrance:* free. *Ranger-guided tour:* Adult $US100, children, $US50; may go on as many 1-hour tours as you like on the day of your visit.

ON-SITE AMENITIES: Main lodge, with restaurant, bar, and gift shop.

BEST TIMES: Cooler months (May to September) early or late in the day for maximum wildlife activity.

FIELD NOTES: Comfortable walking shoes for the guided safari tours. For birders, visit the Monkeyland's sister site, **Birds of Eden**, the largest free-flight aviary in the world; explore at your own pace or book a guide.

MOTSWARI PRIVATE GAME RESERVE

SOUTH AFRICA

Located in the hub of big five game land, the 15,000-hectare Motswari (a word meaning "to conserve and protect") Private Game Reserve offers a one-of-a-kind bush experience. Famous for its dedicated staff and friendly service, the lodge at Motswari provides a hands-on ranger-training program—a behind-the-scenes bush education, seldom found elsewhere. Lion tracking and accompanying the lion camera crew on any one of their many expeditions are just two aspects of this informative program.

Qualified rangers and skilled Shangaan trackers guide safaris, ensuring the best possible viewings the reserve has to offer. Sightings of elephants, white rhinos, lions, leopards, and Cape buffalo are almost guaranteed. The black-backed jackal, blue wildebeest, chacma baboon, spotted hyena, genet, small spotted giraffe, and the gray duiker live in the reserve and are often seen.

Visitors can also look for painted wolves, antelope, vervet monkeys, cheetahs, and many other species. Motswari is also a bird-watcher's destination because it is home to more than 350 species of birds.

Safaris run in the early morning hours and late afternoon when the animals are most active; guests can travel in open vehicles or on foot. Known for its pristine habitat, wide horizons, untamed wilderness, and wild game, the lodge itself also provides accommodations for up to 30 guests in 15 luxury bungalows, all with air-conditioning and overhead fans. There is an open-air boma, spacious lounge and bar, wildlife art gallery, and swimming pool.

LOCATION: 43 miles from Hoedspruit, 5–6 hours by car from Johannesburg. South African Express provides daily service from Johannesburg. The reserve has an air strip for chartered flights.

HOURS OF OPERATION: Year-round.

CONTACT: *Reserve office:* Motswari Private Game Reserve, PO Box 67865, Bryanston 2021, SA; Tel: 0114631990; Fax: 0114631992; Web: www.motswari.co.za; email: reservations@motswari.co.za.

COST: *Lodge* (per person, per night): From US$304; includes meals, game drives, and guided walk; visit the website for current pricing.

ON-SITE AMENITIES: Curio shop, swimming pool, boma and bush dinners, two bars, library, art gallery, brunch, and high tea. Morning and evening safaris and walking trails. Optional activities (booking required) include microflights, elephant-back safaris, and cultural township tours.

BEST TIMES: May through October.

FIELD NOTES: Children under 6 years of age are not permitted.

MOUNTAIN ZEBRA NATIONAL PARK

SOUTH AFRICA

By 1937 the Cape mountain zebra, which is distinguished from the more common plains zebra by its narrower stripes, lack of shadow stripes, and orange coloration on its face, was in danger of going extinct. That same year, Mountain Zebra National Park was established to protect this endangered animal. And today there are approximately 300 Cape mountain zebras living in and around the park.

Although this 124-square-mile park was named for one particular species, visitors will find plenty of other mammals to see here. Look for red hartebeests, elands, springboks, and kudus. The African buffalo and black rhino have recently been reintroduced to the park. The main predator here is the caracal, a type of lynx. Birders will put their binoculars to good use in the park, where they can spot Verreaux's (black) and martial eagles, pale-winged starlings, ostriches, becretary birds, and many more.

Most visitors explore the park in their own vehicles. The park does main-

tain short nature trails and 3-day trails; guided day and night drives and a visit to see the San cave paintings must be booked in advance.

Visitors who wish to sleep under the stars can camp at several spots around the park. Campsites have 220V electrical outlets and restrooms. The less adventurous can find lodging in family cottages that offer more creature comforts, including a partially equipped kitchen. Doornhoek Guest House is a restored Victorian home with three bedrooms, en-suite bathrooms, and a fully-equipped kitchen.

LOCATION: Less than 10 miles from Cradock on the Middelburg-Graaff Reinett Road.

HOURS OF OPERATION: Daily; Oct 1–Mar 31, 7 a.m. to 7 p.m.; Apr 1–Sept 30, 7 a.m. to 6 p.m.

CONTACT: *Park office:* Tel: 270488812427 or 488813434; Fax: 270488813943; Web: www.sanparks.org/parks/mountain_zebra or www.nature-reserve.co.za/mountain-zebra-national-park.html.

COST: *Entrance:* Adult, US$8; children, US$4.50. Tours, hiking trails, and cave paintings entail additional fees. *Lodging* (per night): Campsites (up to 6 people), US$16; family cottage (up to 4 people), US$67; guesthouse (up to 4 people), US$108.

ON-SITE AMENITIES: Reception center, picnic area, restaurant, gift shop, restrooms, campsites, accommodations, conference facilities, fuel station, and swimming pool.

BEST TIMES: October through March.

FIELD NOTES: Visitors who arrive by car should note that most of the roads leading to and through the park are gravel with only a few paved sections. Visitors are allowed to exit vehicles only at designated areas, which are clearly marked. The park can be seen as a day trip for those staying in Cradock.

MVURADONA PRIVATE GAME LODGE

SOUTH AFRICA

M vuradona Private Game Lodge overlooks a magnificent setting in South Africa's Lowveld region on the edge of the famous Kruger National Park. Wildlife lovers will delight at the sight of some of the 146 mammal species, 520 bird species, and 114 reptile species found within the park's 12,500 square miles. Lions, hyenas, leopards, cheetahs, and wild dogs are the top mammalian predators that roam the park and primarily can be found in its southeastern corner. Visitors may also be lucky enough to see some of the rarer animals, like aardvarks, black rhinos, pangolins, and suni and roan antelope.

Mvuradona Private Game Lodge offers several safari packages, ranging

from three nights in the national park to a full week spent moving around to several locations, including Byde River Canyon. There are many day and half-day options available for those who want to experience unique adventures. For example, guests can spend time in the city of Maputo, Mozambique, visit a tribal village, or pan for gold. The lodge itself offers horseback riding, golfing, and stargazing. Colonial African cuisine is a special treat; visitors can enjoy piri piri chicken on the fire or ostrich steaks as they relax after a day filled with memorable sights.

LOCATION: In the Marloth Conservancy on the Crocodile River, a 4.5-hour drive from Johannesburg. Commercial air service is available to the Malelane airport (15 minutes from the lodge) and to Kruger Mpumalanga airport (45 miles from the lodge).

HOURS OF OPERATION: Year-round.

CONTACT: *Main office:* Tel: 27083326-2835; Web: www.mvuradona.co.za; email: jay@africaunleashed.co.za.

COST: *Lodging* (per night): Depends on type of accommodation; from US$81 for a shared room, to US$125 for a self-catering rondavel; to US$691 for a private room that sleeps up to 12; check the lodge's website for included amenities; additional fees for safaris, excursions, and other activities may apply.

ON-SITE AMENITIES: Lodging, restaurant serving colonial African cuisine, safari tours, and specialty packages.

BEST TIMES: Winter, which tends to be mild and dry. Summer is from October to April, when the temperatures and the threat of malaria are highest.

FIELD NOTES: Malaria inoculations are a must before a visit, as is wearing mosquito repellent. Cool cotton shirts, shorts, and long pants are suggested for summer; layering long pants, T-shirt, sweatshirt, and jacket is the wisest strategy for winter.

NGALA PRIVATE GAME RESERVE

SOUTH AFRICA

Ngala means "lion" in the Shangaan language, and like its namesake, Nagala Private Game Reserve is magnificent and unforgettable. It's difficult to decide between the reserve's luxurious lodge, with all the amenities, and a tented camp, which puts you right in the middle of nature. Fortunately, whichever you choose, you'll have the trip of a lifetime.

Ngala is part of the world-famous Kruger National Park in South Africa. The more than 36,000 acres are owned and operated by the Conservation Corporation Africa, and their dedication to the wildlife in their care is evident in everything they do. In addition to preserving and maintaining the reserve, the corporation funnels part of its annual profits back into the National Parks Trust, helping ensure that future generations will be able to enjoy the majesty of Africa's unspoiled wildlife.

Guests at Ngala can participate in guided walking safaris, led by expert rangers. Some of these safaris take several days, as visitors track elephants, rhinos, and buffalo during the mornings and watch nocturnal predators search for prey in the evenings. Because visitors are on foot, they have the opportunity to immerse themselves in an Africa that can't be appreciated from a moving vehicle.

Staff at Ngala not only make visitor safety a priority but also protect the wildlife and environment. But more than that the reserve cares about their community and has made generous donations to and has become involved in programs designed to help change the lives of local inhabitants, with a special emphasis on children. They have spearheaded HIV-awareness programs, offered scholarships for local kids, and set up a media center with computers and other supplies for local schools.

Guests can relax in colonial style at the lodge. A premium suite and 20 thatched cottages come with all the amenities, including air-conditioning and private verandas. There is also a swimming pool and common room. The tented safari camp is located near the Timbavati River. The six tented suites come complete with bathrooms, fans, and viewing decks. There is also a riverside lap pool.

LOCATION: Mpumalanga, a 5-hour drive from Johannesburg. Air service is available from Cape Town/Johannesburg to Eastgate or Skukuza; charted flights can fly directly to the reserve's private airstrip.

HOURS OF OPERATION: Year-round.

CONTACT: *Reserve office:* Tel: 271-18094300; Web: www.ngala.co.za.

COST: *Lodging* (per person, per night): Tented, from US$350; lodge, from US$240; rates are all inclusive.

ON-SITE AMENITIES: The lodge has a restaurant, swimming pool, game viewing decks, and African gift gallery. The luxury suite offers a private swimming pool, exclusive safari vehicle, butler service, and private meals upon request. The tented camp offers en-suite bathrooms with outdoor showers, intimate game viewing decks, and contoured lap pool.

BEST TIMES: Winter (March through October).

FIELD NOTES: Bring lightweight clothing in neutral colors (not white), a jacket or fleece for early mornings and evenings, and comfortable footwear. Cameras, binoculars, and/or field glasses are essential. Visiting local communities is recommended. Guests must be at least 16 years old to participate on walking safaris.

PAKAMISA PARADISE

SOUTH AFRICA

Reality often pales when compared to the cinema. When it comes to Pakamisa Paradise, it is the cinema that pales in comparison. If you can imagine a setting that is more lush, more vibrant, and more beautiful than *Out of Africa*, you are getting a glimpse of what awaits you at this luxurious game reserve, nestled in the heart of this glorious land.

Pakamisa Paradise, situated in the Pakamisa Private Game Reserve, offers the best of European epicurean delights and amenities amid the breathtaking mountainous surroundings. The mix of fine European and African stylings provide a unique and unforgettable ambiance. From the world-class dining to awe-inspiring views from every private suite, guests come away with memories for a lifetime.

The word *pakamisa* means "to lift up" in Zulu, and the reserve's almost 9 square miles of tranquil, serene beauty is sure to lift your spirit. Entry to the area is restricted, which helps protect the ecosystem and gives privacy for the guests. The staff's dedication to hospitality is unmatched, giving visitors an enriching and memorable experience.

Visitors can look forward to observing giraffes, zebras, waterbucks, red hartebeests, warthogs, and bushpigs as well as many other mammals. In addition, the reserve is home to more than 200 species of birds, including eagles and sunbirds. Horse lovers will be delighted with the on-premises Pakamisa Arabian studs. These amazing horses were brought to Pakamisa from Andalusia, Spain, by Isabella von Stepski, internationally renowned as an Arabian expert. And guests can experience the bush from horseback on guided tours.

Amenities at Pakamisa Paradise include the local restaurant, El Prado, which offers both regional and European selections. The lodge includes conference rooms, a rock pool, a library, and more. Private guided vehicle tours, available upon request, traverse the entirety of the reserve. Both guided and unguided nature walks are also available.

LOCATION: Northern Zululand in the KwaZulu-Natal Province.

HOURS OF OPERATION: Year-round.

CONTACT: *Main office:* Tel: 27344133559; Web: www.pakamisa.co.za; email: pakamisa@pakamisa.co.za.

COST: *Lodging* (per person, per night): US$154–$232, includes meals, two daily game viewing activities (on horseback, vehicle, and foot), taxes, fees, and tourism levy.

ON-SITE AMENITIES: Lodge, stable, pools, restaurant, library, archery, and clay shooting.

BEST TIMES: Year-round.

FIELD NOTES: Bring comfortable riding clothes if you're interested in equestrian activities. Lightweight clothing and sturdy footwear are recommended. You'll want to have good binoculars, a camera, and plenty of film or memory cards. Dinner attire is casual.

SABI SABI PRIVATE GAME RESERVE

SOUTH AFRICA

The Sabi Sabi Private Game Reserve, always numbered among the best reserves in the world, offers the whole package. Guests can expect exciting wildlife encounters as well as luxury accommodations, excellent service, and delicious dining. Situated in the southwestern region of Kruger National Park, the reserve is home to Africa's big five (elephant, rhino, lion, leopard, and buffalo) as well as hundreds of other species of native animals, birds, and plants.

The Sabi Sabi philosophy of "yesterday, today, and tomorrow" is based on decades of safari experience; and its safari lodges bring guests in touch with the rich South African history and warm hospitality. Day and night safaris in open vehicles are led by highly trained game rangers and qualified trackers so that guests can follow animals on and

CONTACT: *Head office:* Sabi Sabi Private Game Reserve, 4 Jameson Ave, Melrose Estate, Johannesburg, South Africa or PO Box 52665, Saxonwold, 2132, South Africa; Tel: 27114477172; Fax: 27114420728; Web: www.sabisabi.com; email: res@sabisabi.com.

COST: *Lodging* (per person, per night): US$480–$1740, including game drives, walking safaris, and meals.

ON-SITE AMENITIES: Luxury accommodations, including full room and board, exercise rooms, private libraries, steam rooms, a private study, private pools, butler service, gift shop, guided driving and walking tours.

off the road, deep into the heart of the wild African bush. For a more personal encounter with nature, visitors can participate in guided walking safaris.

Sabi Sabi is also home to a remarkable 350 species of birds. On a single summer's day, visitors from the Northern Hemisphere will probably see more bird species than they are likely to see in a lifetime in their home country. In fact, almost 5% of the world's bird species have been recorded in this region of South Africa.

BEST TIMES: Anytime during the year there are fascinating things to do. Low season is May to August; high season is September to April.

FIELD NOTES: Dress is informal. Neutral colors are recommended. (A full range of safari clothing is available in the Curio Shop.) Must-haves are windbreaker or warm jacket for winter and night safaris, comfortable walking shoes, sun hats, sunglasses, sunscreen, bug repellent, swimwear, binoculars, camera, and video camera.

LOCATION: 250 miles from Johannesburg, an easy 5-hour drive on national roads.

HOURS OF OPERATION: Year-round.

SAMARA PRIVATE GAME RESERVE

SOUTH AFRICA

South Africa is ranked as one of the world's top mega-diversity countries; among them these countries hold more than two-thirds of all known biological resources (animals and plants). Samara Private Game Reserve alone provides a habitat for more than 60 mammal species, some of which are rare, unusual, endangered, or threatened. The reserve is also home to common species such as kudus, duikers, aardvarks, and once-endangered white rhinos.

Situated in the malaria-free eastern cape, Samara is 70,000 unspoiled acres of savanna, plains, and rolling hills that are home to elephants, rhinos, giraffes, birds, reptiles, amphibians, and insects.

Of particular interest at Samara is the cheetah. Here, visitors can watch cheetah families that have been the subject of carefully managed conservation efforts. The reserve has been successful in reintroducing the cheetah here, which is thriving without threat from larger predators. Important efforts are made to return the endangered species to Samara and to preserve global biodiversity in this unique, pristine environment. Free from the restrictions of larger preserves, the professional, trained guides help visitors participate in an exclusive interaction with the animals here.

The botanical wealth here is also stunning. Some 20,000 plant species are found spread across seven types of environments such as impenetrable thickets, savannas, and grasslands. Paleontology buffs will find fossils that predate the dinosaurs, and budding anthropologists can see well-preserved Bushman paintings; all guests will gain a fascinating insight into the region's past.

LOCATION: 157 miles north of Port Elizabeth.

HOURS OF OPERATION: Year-round.

CONTACT: *Reserve office:* Tel: 270-498910880; Fax: 270498923751; Web: www.samara.co.za; email: reservations @samara.co.za.

COST: *Lodging* (per person, per night): US$168–$601, depending on season; Manor at Samara, US$3,000, includes personal ranger, chef, and butler; all accommodations include game drives, airstrip transfers, meals, beverages, and tourism fees.

ON-SITE AMENITIES: Luxury accommodations, restaurant, bar, guided safari walks, and vehicle tours.

BEST TIMES: Mid December to mid February is the ideal time for optimal weather conditions and animal activity.

FIELD NOTES: Always wear comfortable shoes and layered clothing to prepare for early morning game drives and cool evenings. Don't forget plenty of bug spray, protective eyewear (sunglasses), binoculars, and hats with brims.

SHAMWARI GAME RESERVE

SOUTH AFRICA

On the Bushmans River, between Port Elizabeth and Grahamstown, and home to Africa's big five mammals, Shamwari Game Reserve offers the finest in luxury safaris including lavish accommodations and unparalleled African adventure. The 25,000-hectare reserve has been named the World's Leading Conservation Company and Game Reserve for several consecutive years and supports five ecosystems and numerous plant, animal, and bird species.

At Shamwari, guests can expect days and evenings of wildlife sightings. Skilled guides lead 3- to 4-hour safaris so that visitors can see and photograph lions, rhinos, elephants, buffalo, cheetahs, hippos, leopards, brown hyenas, caracals, and servals, and sometimes even aardvarks. For a more intimate wildlife experience, consider participating in the reserve's ranger school. During this hands-on program, guests have a chance to camp in the African bush and learn safety procedures,

telephone. A splendid stone-walled and thatch-roofed lodge, Bayethe offers a large deck area overlooking a wildlife watering hole. Here guests stay in private luxury tents that have air-conditioning, plunge pool, and viewing deck. Some of the lodges include spas or private spa services.

LOCATION: 50-minute drive from Port Elizabeth airport, Eastern Cape.

HOURS OF OPERATION: Year-round.

CONTACT: *Reserve office:* Tel: 270-414071000; Fax: 270414071001; Web: www.shamwari.com.

COST: *Lodging* (per person, per night): Depends on lodge; US$407–$899; includes meals, game drives, taxes, and some beverages; other fees may apply.

ON-SITE AMENITIES: Vary according to chosen accommodations. All offer guided game drives, bush walks, and the ranger school experience.

BEST TIMES: The reserve boasts optimal game viewing year-round.

FIELD NOTES: The reserve is located in a malaria-free zone. You'll need walking shoes, sun hats, sunglasses, sunblock, cameras, and binoculars. Warm clothing for vehicle tours at all times of year. Light clothing and swimwear for summer. Children aged 6 years and younger are not permitted on safari; a child-friendly program is available for youngsters while their parents are on tour. Two longer programs are the 6-week field guide training course and the

tracking, and identification. If camping isn't for you, bush walks can be arranged through your personally assigned game ranger.

The five-star accommodations within the reserve will exceed your expectations, no matter which of the six lodges you stay in. Located in the valley, Eagles Crag includes nine private rooms with secluded deck with pool showers. Deep in the bushveld, Lobengula Lodge offers a more traditional African experience; three of the six suites have private plunge pools. Built in 1910, Long Lee Manor has a colonial ambiance with 15 rooms and two luxury suites. Bushmans River Lodge is a Victorian homestead that offers privacy for a small group or family. Guests staying in this 4-bedroom house will bask in South African hospitality. The colonial-style Riverdene Lodge has nine luxury rooms. It's geared toward families and includes a supervised playroom, spacious grounds, jungle gym, television, and

yearlong volunteer program; visit the reserve's website for details. **Born Free Big Cat Sanctuary**: Founded to draw the public's attention to the plight of wild animals that are living in captive environments and to promote educa- tion and public awareness. The sanctu- ary has successfully rescued many big cats from dangerous situations and provides them with safe lifetime care. Guests of Shamwari are able to visit with the rescued cats.

TSWALU KALAHARI RESERVE

SOUTH AFRICA

Ever since the television program *Meerkat Manor* debuted in 2005, viewers have been captivated by these sociable small mammals that are part of the mongoose family. Meerkats, which live in colonies of 20–30 mem- bers, are called "sun angels" in African folklore because they are thought to protect villages from moon devils or werewolves that attack solo tribesmen and cattle. Meerkats are a common sight in the Kalahari Desert, and Tswalu Kalahari Reserve is the place to view these captivating critters up close.

Tswalu also provides guests with an excellent chance of seeing the rare des- ert black rhino. About 30% of the South African population of this species can be found at the reserve. Visitors learn how to track these animals by looking for clues like broken branches, and when tracking is successful, they can watch the rhinos' movements from a respectful distance. Other rare and threatened species that have been spot- ted at the reserve include the mountain zebra, pangolin, roan antelope, tsess- ebe, and wild dog. Birds are a common sight, and visitors will be able to see many of the 240 species found here, in- cluding raptors and pygmy falcons.

Located beside the Korannaberg mountain range, Tswalu offers open- air safaris as well as guided trips that spotlight archaeological treasures and rock engravings in and around the re- serve. Visitors can gain a bird's-eye view of the gorgeous surroundings from the peacefulness of a hot-air balloon. Visitors should take advantage of the reserve's classes in archaeology, ethnobotany, and photography; sports-minded guests can take a break from wildlife viewing to play a round of golf, go horseback riding, or give archery a try.

Tswalu has accommodations for only 30 guests at any given time; thus staff is able to provide each person with plenty of attention and pampering. The Motse is an African village with eight stone-walled and thatched-roof bungalows, each with indoor/outdoor showers and private decks. Tarkuni is a private dwelling that can house a family or small group. Tswalu prides itself on being a child-friendly facility. Game drives and bush walks provide learning experiences that can't be taught in a traditional classroom, and children are welcome to participate in all activities. Children will also find board games, miniature golf, and finger painting. Babysitting is also available.

LOCATION: Marshalltown, about 1.5 hours by air from Johannesburg.

HOURS OF OPERATION: Year-round.

CONTACT: *Reserve office:* Tel: 270-112472299; Fax: 270114842757; Web: www.tswalu.com; email: res@tswalu.com.

COST: *Lodging* (per night): Depends on occupancy; US$617–$1,104: *Exclusive use:* depends on facility; US$3,152–$14,299. *Private guide and pilot:* US$327–$371.

ON-SITE AMENITIES: Spa, library, wine cellar, gift shop, children's day care, laundry and valet services, restaurant, room service, private clinic, with 24-hour emergency care. Guided safaris are offered by foot, horseback, and vehicle. Hot-air ballooning; reservations required and additional fees apply; write to bookings@lifeballooning.co.za for more information.

BEST TIMES: June through September.

FIELD NOTES: The reserve is located in a malaria-free zone. For horseback riding you will need to bring comfortable riding attire. The reserve supplies helmets, chaps, gloves, and boots.

ULUSABA PRIVATE GAME RESERVE

SOUTH AFRICA

Nestled in the heart of the Sabi Sand Game Reserve and bordering Kruger National Park, Ulusaba Private Game Reserve gives guests a slice of sheer heaven. Virgin mogul Sir Richard Branson founded the reserve to be an ultimate wildlife destination in the genuine spirit of Africa. With its earthy aromas, sun-drenched skies, and light dry winds, this unspoiled African bush is virtually teeming with wildlife and is a must-stop on every wildlife traveler's to-do list.

Whether you want a guided drive safari, or an on-foot game walk, visitors are able to enjoy 10,000 acres of unspoiled bush on a near-exclusive basis. Twice-daily safaris allow guests to see and observe the big five—elephants, rhinos, lions, leopards, and buffalo, but that's just the beginning of the grand adventure. Hyenas, wildebeests, baboons, monkeys, and impalas are not far off; and visitors can expect to be entertained by zebras, giraffes, waterbucks, kudus, hippopotamuses, and duikers. If the time is right, guests may spot wild dogs (the wolves of the savanna), bushbabies, and even servals (African wild cats).

Luxury accommodations come in two grand lodges. Rock Lodge, perched high on a rocky summit, offers stunning views of the lowland bush country and the wildlife within. Safari Lodge offers a more traditional ambiance, located along a dry riverbed and built "tree house style." From here, guests are treated to nonstop wildlife observation as animals gather around the watering hole to drink. Whichever location you choose, expect first-class service, exceptional African cuisine, and boutique spas. Safari Lodge has its own well-stocked wine cellar for those wishing to have a taste or two of some South African splendor.

LOCATION: Western sector of the Sabi Sand Game Reserve, northeast South Africa.

HOURS OF OPERATION: Year-round.

CONTACT: *Reserve office:* Tel: 0800056343 (toll-free) or 270113254416; Fax: 270113254416; Web: www.ulusaba .com.

COST: *Lodging* (per person, per night): From US$560, all-inclusive.

ON-SITE AMENITIES: Safaris, bush walks, spa/wellness center, gym, tennis, and shopping. *Special Tours:* Cascades and Canyons Spectacular, Community, Breeding Project, and Canyon's Cultures and Contrast; prebooking required.

BEST TIMES: Year-round; each season offers its own unique experience. Summer (October to April) provides lush vegetation and warm nights. Winter (May to September) offers warm days and cool evenings. Wildlife is more active in the winter as food and water become scarce.

FIELD NOTES: Lightweight, neutral-colored (not white) clothing is preferred for safari; a sweater or jacket for cool evenings and early mornings in winter. Hat, sunglasses, and insect repellent are needed year-round. This is a malaria-endemic area; take proper precautions well in advance of your trip. Camera film, for those who still use it, is available in the gift shop. The Cascades and Canyons Spectacular tour offers fantastic views of waterfalls, the bushveld below, and various other photographic opportunities.

WELGEVONDEN PRIVATE GAME RESERVE

SOUTH AFRICA

If the thought of cheetahs lounging in trees, rhinos wallowing in the mud, or a mother leopard teaching her cubs the laws of survival excites you, a trip to Welgevonden Private Game Reserve is an experience not to be missed. Deep ravines, imposing gorges, and rolling hills create a spectacular setting where more than 50 mammals, including one of Africa's largest populations of white rhinos, live wild and roam free. Located in the Waterberg Plateau, just north of Johannesburg, the reserve offers an exclusive, intimate experience of the African bush.

Visitors to the reserve's 34,000 hectares will thrill to observe the unusual brown hyena and the rare aardwolf and should be on the lookout for black-backed jackals; bat-eared foxes; small and large spotted genets; slender, banded, and dwarf mongooses; and blue wildebeests. Other mammals that wander the grounds are lesser bushbabies, chacma baboons, vervet monkeys, lions, African wildcats, and servals. And visitors will also see Burchell zebras, giraffes, elephants, klipspringers, impalas, gems-

boks, nyalas, tsessebes, common and mountain reedbucks, and elands.

Committed to conservation research and development, Welgevonden Private Game Reserve caters to a limited number of guests at any one time. No private vehicles are permitted, ensuring minimal human impact and the ultimate wildlife experience.

LOCATION: About 2.5 hours by car from Johannesburg.

HOURS OF OPERATION: Year-round.

CONTACT: *Reserve office:* Tel: 27014-7554392; Fax: 270865018400; Web: www .welgevonden.org; email: info@welge vonden.org.

COST: Depends on accommodations and tour packages chosen.

ON-SITE AMENITIES: *Lodging:* A variety of in-park accommodations offering all-inclusive packages. **Kudu and Tshetshepi Lodge:** Tel: 27218895514; Fax: 27218897880; Web: www.clearwater lodges.co.za. **Wooded Peaks Game Lodge:** Tel: 270824461325; Fax: 270114675334: Web: www.wooded peaks.com. **Makweti Safari Lodge:** Tel: 27118376776; Fax: 27118374771; Web: www.makweti.com. **Martial Heights Game Lodge:** Tel: 270827872776: Web: www.martialheights.co.za. **Mhondoro Game Lodge:** Tel: 0861106648 (South Africa) or 27738194233 (international); Fax 0163642470; Web: www.mhondoro .com. **Pitse Lodge:** Tel: 270827744639; Web: www.pitselodge.co.za. **Shibula Game Lodge:** Tel: 0218828206; Web: www.shibulalodge.co.za. **Shidzidzi and Nungubane Private Game Lodges:** Tel: 0313106900 or 0313103333; Web: www.shinunlodges.co.za.

BEST TIMES: Cooler months (May to September) early or late in the day for maximum wildlife viewing.

FIELD NOTES: When choosing your accommodations make note of the rules and regulations regarding children. Not all sites or game drives are suitable for all ages; many have minimum age requirements.

WHITE SHARK PROJECTS

SOUTH AFRICA

White Shark Projects (WSP), a world-leading organization focusing on great white shark diving, is an adventurer-lover's dream. Their mission statement is clear: "We are humble and grateful for the privilege and opportunity to work with one of the earth's greatest predators face to face, causing no harm, but further enhancing the chances of survival of this rare species." White Shark Projects has been instrumental in getting the white shark protected under South African law, and today visitors can enjoy the presence and experience of this magnificent animal in South African waters.

WSP is located in a unique marine reserve in the heart of the world's great white shark waters, including Dyer Island, which is home to 20,000 African

jackass penguins, and Geyser Rock, which hosts 60,000 Cape fur seals. In season there is also an abundance of southern right whales.

The project offers Great white shark cage diving and viewing, a student education program, shark expeditions, and specialized shark discovery trips. Visitors reach the sharks on *Shark Team*, a 36-foot, custom-built dive catamaran. There is a limit of 18 passengers plus crew on each trip to ensure comfort and best shark viewing. The project carries comprehensive public insurance and passenger liability and proper safety precautions are taken.

A typical day starts with a buffet breakfast at White Shark Lodge, followed by a day at sea. While on board, all diving and viewing equipment is supplied and visitors are treated to information talks about the white sharks they are about to see. After cage div-

ing and viewing the sharks, the boat returns to land. The day ends ashore with afternoon tea and scones at the lodge where you will be awarded with a "White Shark Experience" certificate.

LOCATION: Gansbaai, a 2-hour drive from Cape Town. Pickup is available from Cape Town city center, Hermanus, or Gansbaai.

HOURS OF OPERATION: 7 a.m. to 6 p.m.

CONTACT: *Main office:* White Shark Project, 16 Geelbek Street, Kleinbaai, SA 7200; Tel: 270214054537 (waterfront office), 270283841774 (lodge), 270-762455880 (24/7); Web: www.white sharkprojects.co.za; email: bookings@ whitesharkprojects.co.za.

COST: *Fee* (per person): US$500.

ON-SITE AMENITIES: Meals, including breakfast and a packed lunch, and afternoon tea; all scuba equipment including wet suits; shark talk.

BEST TIMES: Year-round.

FIELD NOTES: Suntan lotion, a warm jacket, swimwear, and towel. Seasickness pills should be taken 2 hours before launch. The diving cage can hold two to three people at a time. Each person will spend approximately 20 minutes in the cage and 4–6 hours at sea.

ARUSHA NATIONAL PARK

TANZANIA

Arusha National Park, in northern Tanzania, is a multifaceted gem, often overlooked by safari goers, despite offering visitors the opportunity to explore a wide range of habitats within just a few hours. As visitors enter the 53-square-mile park they are in a shadowy montane forest inhabited by inquisitive blue monkeys and colorful turacos and trogons. Here one gets a sense of being watched—and that's because there are many eyes in the trees. It's the only place on the northern safari circuit where the acrobatic black-and-white colobus monkey can be readily seen. Visitors are also treated to the Ngurdoto Crater, a spectacular area that is home to buffalo and warthogs.

Those who venture north find grassy hills surrounding the Momela Lakes; each peaceful body of water a different hue of green or blue. Here visitors get a chance to watch thousands of pink flamingos and many species of resident and migrant waterfowl. Shaggy waterbucks come down to the shores to drink and giraffes and zebra roam the land. Although elephants are rarely seen here, be on the lookout for leopards and spotted hyenas in the early morning and late afternoon, when they venture out to feed. Dusk and dawn are also the best times to see the famous snows of Kilimanjaro, only 30 miles away.

But Arusha has its own mountain. Mount Meru is the fifth highest on the continent, rising to 14,990 feet and dominating the park's horizon. Visitors who choose to drive up the mountain will pass by buffalo and giraffes grazing in the wooded savanna. Plant lovers will get a chance to see red-hot pokers and Spanish moss.

LOCATION: Northern Tanzania. An easy 40-minute drive northeast from the town of Arusha, approximately 35 miles from Kilimanjaro International Airport.

HOURS OF OPERATION: Year-round.

CONTACT: *Park office:* Director General, Tanzania National Parks, PO Box 3134 Arusha, Tanzania; Tel: 255272503471 or 255272504082; Fax: 255272508216; Web: www.tanzaniaparks.com/arusha .html. *Tours:* Visit www.tanzaniaodys sey.com/northern-tanzania-safaris/ tanzania-safari.htm.

COST: *Entrance:* Adults, US$35; children under 16 years old, US$15.

ON-SITE AMENITIES: *In the park:* A lodge, two rest houses, campsites, two mountain huts inside the park. *Near the park:*

Two lodges at Usa River and many hotels and hostels in Arusha; for more information, visit the park's website or www.tanzaniaholidays.com.

BEST TIMES: For visitors wishing to climb Mount Meru, June through February are best, although it may rain in November. For the best views of Kilimanjaro, visit December through February.

FIELD NOTES: The lakes, forest, and Ngurdoto Crater can all be visited in the course of a half-day outing at the beginning or end of a northern safari. Bring good walking shoes or climbing boots (if you're so inclined), rain gear, binoculars, camera, sunglasses, insect repellent, suntan lotion, and clothing to layer.

GOMBE STREAM NATIONAL PARK

TANZANIA

During a visit to Gombe Stream National Park, visitors are assaulted with the sound of *pant-hoo*, described on the park's website as a "frenzied, shrieking crescendo." It is the sound of chimpanzees calling to one another to find out which individuals are in the area. Dr. Jane Goodall introduced the Gombe Stream chimpanzees to the world through her stunning research. In 1960, she founded a behavioral research program that has become the longest-

than 200 bird species here. Some, like the Peter twinspot, hop tamely around the visitors center.

LOCATION: 10 miles north of Kigoma on the shore of Lake Tanganyika in western Tanzania.

HOURS OF OPERATION: Year-round, 24/7.

CONTACT: *Park office:* Tel: 255272503471 or 255272504082; Web: www.tanzania parks.com/gombe.html.

COST: *Entrance* (per day): Adults, US$100; children (5–12 years), US$20, children (under 5 years), free.

ON-SITE AMENITIES: Visitors center, restricted camping, and guided chimp walks.

BEST TIMES: Because the chimps don't roam far in the wet seasons (February to June and November to mid December), they may be easier to find. Photography opportunities are better in dry weather (July to October and late December).

FIELD NOTES: Allow at least two days for viewing the chimps. Remember that the park is not a zoo and the chimpanzees roam free. When visiting the chimps it is highly suggested that you wear old clothing; we'll leave it to your imagination as to why!

running study of its kind in the world. When Goodall began to study this community, she named one 3-year-old chimp Fifi. Today, Fifi is the last living member of the original study group of chimpanzees; and lucky visitors can get a chance to see her.

The Gombe Stream chimpanzees live on the steep slopes near the northern shore of Lake Tanganyika. The chimpanzees here are well acclimated to human visitors and the scientists who observe them so closely. Primatologists have also spent decades studying a group of beachcomber olive baboons, and these monkeys are used to humans. The red-tailed and red colobus monkeys stick to the treetops. In fact, chimpanzees frequently hunt the red colobuses. Bird-watchers will find more

MAHALE MOUNTAINS NATIONAL PARK

TANZANIA

Mahale Mountains National Park is difficult to get to. Its 1,002 square miles are situated directly on Lake Tanganyika, with the Mahale Mountains rising up behind the beach. Here is one of the most concentrated and habituated groups of chimpanzees left on the planet. This is a remote area, and there are limited options for accommodations in the area. The best choice may be the Greystoke Mahale Camp, located about 150 miles south of Kigoma Town, which can be reached only by boat, or dhow. The camp is made up of a half dozen thatched cabanas on the beach with immediate access to the trails that lead up to Nkungwe Peak, at more than 6,500 feet high.

To see the area's more than 700 chimpanzees, visitors must hike through heavy jungle and cross many mountain streams. But along the way, walkers will see red colobus monkeys, roan antelope, red- and blue-tailed monkeys, warthogs, and an occasional elephant or anteater. Bird-watchers should pick up their binoculars once they reach the higher elevations. Here speckled mouse birds, bee-eaters, rollers, crown eagles, red-collared widowbirds, Ross turacos, and ground guinea fowls make their home.

After the long hike, visitors are treated to a true thrill when suddenly they hear a terrifying scream, followed by roars, grunts, barks, and shrill yelling. They have entered chimp territory and suddenly they are everywhere.

When an adult male chimp stands on his back legs, he is about 4 feet tall. This 150-pound animal is often found on the forest trails. The females and their young tend to stay in the trees feeding while the males engage in ritual games and battles in an effort to gain or retain power over the others. The fighting can become intense, and the huge males often use tree limbs and rocks as weaponry. What is most amazing is that all of this occurs directly in front of you; the chimps completely ignore their human visitors while they interact in a natural manner.

After spending about an hour with the chimps, visitors walk back to camp for a swim in the crystal clear waters of Lake Tanganyika and snorkel among the 250 varieties of tropical fish that are found only in this lake. You may find some Tanganyika mussels for dinner while always keeping an eye open for the local crocodiles and hippos.

LOCATION: 150 miles south of Kigoma, with air service to Mahale, then a 2-hour boat ride to Greystoke Camp.

HOURS OF OPERATION: Year-round, closed March 17–May 29 for maintenance.

CONTACT: Greystoke Mahale: Does not accept direct booking; contact your travel agent; visit www.greystoke-mahale.com for a list of tour operators.

COST: Depends on tour, booking agency, and length of stay.

ON-SITE AMENITIES: A self-contained camp for up to eight visitors with all meals, guides, snorkeling trips, and hikes to see the chimps included. Six double bandas that overlook the beach, with en-suite bathrooms, hot running water, toilets, showers, relaxation decks, dining room, and bar.

BEST TIMES: June through November.

FIELD NOTES: Allow 4–5 days because there is no guarantee that chimps will be spotted on a particular day. Comfortable hiking boots or walking shoes are a must! The hikes to visit the chimps can be very demanding and a certain level of good physical fitness is required to enjoy this grand adventure. Children must be 8 years or older to stay at Greystoke but must be at least 12 years to participate in the chimp hike.

PRIMATE LODGE KIBALE

UGANDA

The Primate Lodge Kibale offers unparalleled access to 13 species of primates, most of which are protected and preserved by local officials. Visitors can expect to see the common chimpanzee, and several species of central African monkeys, such as gray-cheeked mangabeya, central African red colobuses, and the L'Hoest monkeys. These animals can be seen and heard from the lodge.

The lands around Kibale include evergreen and deciduous forests as well as grasslands and swamps. This variety of environments means that guests can expect to see everything from elephants, leopards, and bushpigs, to three species of duikers and two species of otters. Kibale is also home to an amazing variety of birdlife, such as hornbills, two species of pittas, and the African gray parrot.

The Kibale Primate Lodge offers you several different accommodations. The Sky Tree House has only one bedroom and few amenities, but it overlooks an elephant wallow and places guests among their primate cousins. For those who want to experience African tenting,

the Luxury Tented Camp offers raised tents with en-suite bathrooms, and private verandas. Small cottages with private decks are also available. And the truly adventurous can pitch a tent in the campgrounds and still take advantage of the lodge's facilities and activities.

LOCATION: Kaborale, roughly 20 miles from Fort Portal.

HOURS OF OPERATION: Year-round, 24/7.

CONTACT: *Main office:* Tel: 256-0414267153; Web: www.primatelodge .com; email: reservations@primate lodge.com.

COST: *Lodging* (per person, per night): depends on accommodations; US$7–$290.

ON-SITE AMENITIES: Restaurant, bar, lounge, campsite, expert staff. Chimp tracking, chimp habituation experience, educational walks, nocturnal walks, and birding. Nearby activities and attractions include Bigodi Wetland Sanctuary, Bigodi village walk, Crater Lakes exploration, Sebitoli Forest Camp, Cultural Heritage and Nature Trail, hiking in the Rwenzori Mountians, and visiting the green tea plantations.

BEST TIMES: Year-round.

FIELD NOTES: Recommendations vary, depending on your choice of lodging. Campers should bring their own tents and equipment. All visitors are encouraged to bring comfortable lightweight, neutral-colored clothing, including light jackets for the evenings.

EUROPE

Austria, Belarus, Croatia, Denmark,
Finland, Ireland, Italy, The Netherlands,
Norway, Poland, Portugal, Russia,
Spain, Sweden, Switzerland

NOCKBERGE NATIONAL PARK

AUSTRIA

The mountains of Nockberge are among the oldest and most weathered in Austria. When the glaciers of the last ice age retreated from Europe more than 20,000 years ago, they left the mountain's crystalline rock beautifully sculpted with rounded mountaintops, honed mountain slopes, and carved bowl-like depressions, called cirques. In 1987, the Austrian government created Nockberge National Park, with the name of the mountains and park coming from the Austrian word *nicken*, which means "dumpling," because the mountain's peaks are shaped like rounded domes (dumplings).

Nockberge's 70 square miles encompass a mixture of pristine mountains and alpine meadows with carefully cultivated and managed family-owned pasturelands and forests. The contrast between wild and rural gives the park its stunning beauty.

Nockberge provides the visitor with excellent walking, hiking, and climbing opportunities as well as a variety of summer and winter sports activities. There are many well-marked trails; the Nocklam Road, a 21-mile-long roadway that winds up to an elevation of 6,500 feet along the mountain ridges, provides access by vehicle. The mountain ridge offers great views of the park's forests, mountain slopes, and corrie lakes, which are formed in round-shaped hollows on hillsides. During the summer, visitors can see herds of red deer grazing in the alpine pastures next to domestic cows. Red deer usually graze in small single-sex groups; however, in the fall, the mating ritual begins. Visitors during this time may be able to observe rival males standing on their back legs, bellowing and trying to ward off competing males and attract females.

Bird-watchers will find many of the 66 species of birds that breed in the park. Look for rock partridges, a game bird in the pheasant family, and dotterels. The dotterel is unmistakable, with its yellow legs, chestnut-colored breast with white above, and black belly and beak. Unlike most bird species, the female is more colorful than the male. It nests on the ground in a bare, scraped area, and lays 2–4 eggs.

LOCATION: North of Klagenfurt, in the northern region of Carinthia.

HOURS OF OPERATION: Year-round.

CONTACT: *Office:* National Park Nockberge, A-9565 Ebene Reichenau 117, Klagenfurt, Austria; Tel: 4304275665; Web: www.nationalparknockberge .stream.at. *Austrian Tourist Office* (in the USA): 2129446880.

COST: *Entrance:* Free.

ON-SITE AMENITIES: Visitors centers, museum, cable car (gondola) lift, hiking trails, biking trails (ranging from easy to difficult), horse stables and riding, guided nature tours, and skiing.

BEST TIMES: May through October.

FIELD NOTES: Regular scheduled events are held throughout the summer season, visit the park's website for details. Dress appropriately for the season.

BEREZINSKY BIOSPHERE RESERVE

BELARUS

The Berezinsky Biosphere Reserve was created in 1925 after the discovery of a type of beaver that had been thought to be extinct. Today, the reserve offers so much more to ecotourists and scientists. Its 210 acres are a fine example of the southern European taiga zone, which includes boreal coniferous and broad-leafed forests, lakes, marshlands, and floor plains. The reserve also is the site of a 27-acre undrained peat bog, one of the largest in eastern Europe.

Beavers are doing rather well at the reserve, as are European bison, a species that was reintroduced to the area in

1974. Visitors can also see wild boars, wolves, otters, bears, and lynx, which are just some of the 55 species of mammals that live there. Smaller mammals include shrews, voles, and dormice. The reserve is home to 230 species of birds, from golden eagles and several species of grouse. Bird-watchers will not want to forget their binoculars. The park is also home to 34 species of fish, 10 species of amphibians, and 5 species of reptiles. Some of the animals are housed in open-air cages, while others roam freely on the grounds. The avid wildlife photographer will be captivated by the 718 species of plants and 416 varieties of fungi found within the reserve's boundaries.

Berezinsky Biosphere Reserve offers eco-tours that are customized to meet the specific interests of its visitors. Treks along trails and guided tours are a large part of the experience. Group tours are also available from commercial tour operators. Do note that the reserve is not a spur-of-the-moment destination; visitors must contact the reserve in advance so that an individualized tour can be arranged.

LOCATION: About 80 miles north of Minsk; the reserve will provide transportation from the airport or train station.

HOURS OF OPERATION: Year-round, daily, 7 a.m. to 6 p.m.

CONTACT: *Tourist information:* Republic of Belarus, 211188, Lepel District, Vitebsk Region, Tsentralnaya str., 3; Tel: 3750213226403; Fax: 375021322-6342; Web: www.berezinsky.com; email: tourism@berezinsky.com.

COST: *Lodging* (per night): **Hotel Plavno,** from US$69; **Hotel Serguch,** from US$39.

ON-SITE AMENITIES: Visitors center and nature museum. Besides the **Hotel Plavno** and **Hotel Serguch,** several guest cottages and lodges are available at a reasonable cost.

BEST TIMES: It's easiest to spot small mammals in September and early October.

FIELD NOTES: Obtaining a visa for travel to Belarus is a must; the reserve will send the paperwork upon request. Hikers must always be accompanied by a guide.

PRIPIATSKY NATIONAL PARK

BELARUS

The popular notion of Belarus might be cold, dark, and damp, but Pripiatsky National Park will dispel any such notions for visitors. Established in 1969, Pripiatsky National Park encompasses both ancient floodplains and mixed-species forests. Visitors to this 325-square-mile park will find interesting landscapes that change dramatically as they travel through Pripiatsky. Depressions formed by many years of regular flooding have caused the vegetation to grow in peculiar settings. These are of special interest to many of the park's visitors.

A number of rivers and streams wander through the park, which, along with 30 small lakes, provide a serene habitat for the wildlife and fish species that thrive in this area. The temperate climate provides an ideal setting for a variety of plant species. The environment supports food and shelter for the abundant wildlife found in the park. Visitors will be treated to 45 species of mammals, 256 species of birds, 7 types of reptiles, 11 varieties of amphibians, and 37 species of fish. Highlights of the park are the European bison, wolf, fox, badger, lynx, black stork, gray crane, short-toed eagle, greater spotted eagle, horned owl, bog turtle, running toad, smooth snake, and sterlet.

LOCATION: 160 miles south of Minsk and 220 miles east of Brest. Park headquarters is located at Turov, 17 miles from the Brest-Briansk highway.

HOURS OF OPERATION: Year-round, daily, 8 a.m. to 6 p.m.

CONTACT: *Park office:* Tel: 0037-5172269840 or 00375172269056; Fax:

00375172231143; Web: www.belarus
.org.uk/pripiatsky.html.

COST: *Lodging:* US$50–$80 at local hotels.

ON-SITE AMENITIES: Campground, hotel, hotel motor boat, lodge, restaurant, guarded parking.

BEST TIMES: March through December.

FIELD NOTES: It is recommended that visitors fly to Minsk or Warsaw, Poland (if intending to arrive via Brest or Vilnius, Lithuania). The best way to travel locally is to hire a driver, most of whom are available for a reasonable fee. A number of different types of tours can be arranged; walking, boating, or driving. A water journey from Turov along the Pripiat River is highly recommended and provides plenty of opportunity for fishing. *Be advised:* Hunting is permitted on the grounds.

PLITVICE LAKES NATIONAL PARK

CROATIA

With nearly 1 million visitors a year, Plitvice (pronounced *pleet-veet-seh*) Lakes National Park is Croatia's most popular park and one of the world's most spectacular natural wonders. The 72,850-acre park includes a thick forest of fir, spruce, and beech trees, 16 lakes totaling approximately 500 acres, numerous ponds, and more than 90 waterfalls. Located in a basin of dolomite and limestone, among the Lička Plješevica, Mala Kapela, and Medvedak mountains, the park lakes are distinctive because of their colors, varying from cobalt blue to azure, turquoise, green, and gray, depending on the organisms and quantity of dissolved minerals present in the water as well as by the angle of sunlight. The lakes are separated by natural travertine stone dams, built up over tens of thousands of years.

Plitvice's lush forests support a wide range of plant and animal life. It is home

to more than 120 different species of birds, 70 of which are known to breed in the park. Plitvice is home to the largest population of brown bears in Europe. Look for the rare European brown bear in the early mornings and at dusk, when these animals forage through the park's forest. The park is also home to the solitary, shy lynx, which were once extinct from this area. Three pairs of lynx were reintroduced to the parklands in the early 1970s, and today there are at least 60 of the beautiful cats. The dense woods make a great habitat for deer, boar, fox, and the gray wolf.

Bird-watchers may find black storks searching the lakes and pools for small fish, insects, and shellfish. Overhead, Ural owls patrol the forests for small rodents, squirrels, and hares. The Olm, a rare salamander with no pigmentation or eyes makes its home in the park's watery limestone caves. The Olm, which reaches a length of 14

inches and lives upward of 80 years, can go for years without eating. It hunts small fish, protozoa, and other cave-dwelling organisms using its ability to detect faint electrical currents to locate its prey.

Visitors to the park can take a 20-minute boat ride on Lake Kozjak, the largest in the park. There are hiking trails through the woods and trails and boardwalks around the waterfalls, giving visitors an exhilarating and spectacular closeup look; some walkways pass right through the waterfalls.

LOCATION: A 2-hour drive south of Zagreb, the capital city, on road E71; 3 hours by bus.

HOURS OF OPERATION: Year-round, 24/7. *Ticket booths, boat rides, and shuttle bus:* Vary by season; summer, 7 a.m. to dusk; rest of year, 9 a.m. to dusk.

CONTACT: *Croatian tourist office:* Tel: 8008294416. *Park Preservation Department:* Tel: 385053751132. *Park sales office:* Tel: 385053751015; Web: www .np-plitvicka-jezera.hr (accommodations, travel and tourist information).

COST: *Entrance:* Varies by season; April to October, US$24; November to March, US$15; includes park boat and shuttle bus. Additional fees apply for guided tours.

ON-SITE AMENITIES: Well-marked trails and boardwalks, guided tours, boat rides, shuttle buses, several restaurants and hotels, and toilet facilities.

BEST TIMES: May through September. To avoid large tour groups in the high season and to get the best experience of the wildlife, visit in the early morning and late afternoon.

FIELD NOTES: Wear good walking shoes that you don't mind getting wet. No fishing is allowed. Guided tours are available in English, German, Italian, and Spanish. Booking in advance is necessary; contact the park's sales office.

THE FAROE ISLANDS

DENMARK

The Faroe Islands, an archipelago of 18 small islands covering about 500 square miles, sit between the Norwegian Sea and the North Atlantic. An autonomous province of Denmark since 1948, its rocky terrain, with dramatic cliffs at the coastline, makes this a photographer's dream and is of special interest to birders.

There are approximately 300 bird species that make their home in the Faroes. The oystercatcher is the national bird and can be distinguished by its long pointy orange/yellow beak. Visitors will find it easy to spot the common starling, thanks to its shiny plumage. The Faroes are home to abundant seaside birds like puffins and gulls. Bird-watchers will find colonies of puffins on the ledges and grasslands

above the cliffs. Their breeding areas can be spotted because the they take on a distinctive blue-green color because of years of natural fertilization. Puffins are the small birds flying just

above the water; they tend to flap their wings in a frantic manner, as if they were large insects. The gannet nests only on Mykines and Mykinesholm and are often spotted in flocks as they dive for food. Visitors to the island of Nólsoy will find the largest colony of storm petrels in the world. You'll need to venture out at night, because these nocturnal birds shouldn't be missed.

Take a bus from Torshavn to visit the Vestmanna bird cliffs, located in north Streymoy. This is a must-see location for bird-watchers who will have a chance to spot guillemots, razorbills, and kittiwakes. Gray seals and several species of whales, including short-finned pilot whales and killer whales, inhabit the surrounding waters. Take a boat tour in the waters off Sandoy and Skúvoy; this will allow you the possibility of witnessing these amazing creatures.

Don't miss seeing the Faroese horse, which is a domesticated breed that is said to be something between an Icelandic horse and a Shetland pony. In the 1960s there were only a handful of purebreds left, but today there are more than 50 individuals.

LOCATION: Between Iceland and Norway, northwest of Scotland. Atlantic Airways offers commercial air service between the islands and Europe. Visit www.flyfaroe.com for more informa-

tion. Smyril Line provides ferry service between the island and several nearby countries.

HOURS OF OPERATION: Year-round.

CONTACT: *Tourist information:* Tel: 355800; Fax: 355801; Web: www.visit-faroeislands.com.

COST: The Faroe Islands can be a bit pricey because many goods have to be imported from Denmark and other countries. The currency is the krona, which has the same exchange rate as the Danish krone.

ON-SITE AMENITIES: The islands are linked by underocean tunnels, bridges, and causeways and bus service around and between islands is readily available; no car is necessary. *Camping:* Permitted at designated campsites, most allow only tents. Accommodations, restaurants, stores and so on are available in almost every town; visit the tourism website for specific information. Visitors will find the opportunity to engage in diving, canoeing, and kayaking; playing golf and tennis; and fishing. Bicycles and motorcycles are available for rental. Wildlife viewing and various island tours can be arranged.

BEST TIMES: The long summer days of June, July, and August.

FIELD NOTES: Warm clothing and waterproof rain gear is a must for this trip due to frequent wind and precipitation. Dress in layers. Waterproof hiking boots or rubber boots are suggested for hiking. Have sunglasses and sunscreen on hand. Before arrival to the Faroes, all fishing equipment should be thoroughly cleaned and treated to kill any fish pathogens. Cats, dogs, and other animals are not permitted on the islands for stays of less than 3 months.

ARCHIPELAGO NATIONAL PARK

FINLAND

Covering more than 600 square miles, Finland's Archipelago National Park, as the name implies, is made up of a group of more than 2,000 islands, which are a paradise for trekking, walking, and canoeing. While some of the islands near the mainland are accessible by car, the real treasures are accessible only by boat. Many of the islands are surreal in their beauty with their dense forests, rugged boulders, and jagged inlets. But it's the inner, protected archipelago that attracts most visitors.

In the shallow waters, fish and birds are always visible and active. Birdwatchers should look for black guillemots, which are common in the islands and nest between the rocks. White-tailed eagles can often be seen wheeling over the forested islands. Visitors are treated to more than 132 species of birds that make use of the parklands as breeding grounds, including gulls, arctic terns, eiders, and razorbills. Other nesting birds are the mute swan, graylag goose, and shelduck also nest here. Large mammals such as moose, and sea mammals, including the gray

and Baltic ringer seals, make their home here. Close to 25 species of mammals can be observed in the park.

LOCATION: Kasnäs, southwest Finland.
HOURS OF OPERATION: Mon–Fri, 9 a.m. to 4 p.m.
CONTACT: *Metsähallitus customer service:* Tel: 35820564125. *Blåmusslan visitors center:* Tel: 358205644620. Web: www.visitpanparks.org/ourparks/ Archipelago.
COST: *Entrance:* Free; groups should make reservations in advance. *Guided tours:* Depends on nature of tour.

ON-SITE AMENITIES: Visitors centers and outdoor centers; Blåmusslan visitors center is best place to obtain up-to-date information on the wide range of available services and facilities. Marked hiking and skiing trails, nature trails, campsites, lean-to shelters. The underwater nature trail in Stora Hästö is not to be missed. Rental cabins. The park has handicap-accessible services and trails.

BEST TIMES: May through October.
FIELD NOTES: It is not possible to drive to the park; however, Blåmusslan visitors center is accessible by car. There are ferries to all inhabited lands; visit www.fma.fi/e for more information. Hiking is very popular here. Bring hiking boots or comfortable walking shoes, rain gear, insect repellent, sunscreen, sunglasses, and a hat.

HIIDENPORTTI NATIONAL PARK

FINLAND

The Hiidenportti Gorge and its surrounding woodlands have attracted visitors and settlers as far back as the national memory of Finland can recall. Legends tell of a demon that sought the solace and peace of what is now Hiidenportti National Park and made his home there. Like the demon of myth, many people journey to these forests to find refuge.

The area protected by the park has expanded since the 1940s, and over time, wolves have found a home at Hiidenportti. Bears, wolverines, and lynx

There are roughly 18 miles of marked trails running through the park. The trail system is well designed, with three departure areas and intersection points so hikers easily created a path that meets their needs. One starting point is at Palolampi, which also has an information center, campfire site, a cooking fire area, and a well. Besides the gorge, trails lead along the river and to Kovasinvaara Hill.

are also found here. Visitors will see many signs of the park's beavers, which work industriously to create dams, changing the surrounding environment.

Birding enthusiasts will most commonly see the chaffinch, the willow warbler, siskin, spotted flycatcher, and tree pipit. Although usually found much to the south, the wren is another resident of the park. Visitors hiking through the forest can often hear this bird's song.

The parklands were once a major logging area, an industry that threatened the habitat for the native flora and fauna. Because logs were floated downstream to mills, the natural course and conditions of the rivers were altered. Conservation efforts have helped restore woodlands and the rivers to their original condition.

Hiidenportti Gorge is roughly 100 feet deep and more than a half mile long and can be accessed via hiking trails. Here, visitors will find numerous dark ponds with moss-covered banks.

LOCATION: Kainuu Region, southeast Sotkamo, approximately 4 miles from Helsinki.

HOURS OF OPERATION: 24/7.

CONTACT: *Petola visitors center:* Tel: 358205646380.

COST: *Entrance:* Free.

ON-SITE AMENITIES: Visitors center, marked trails, campgrounds with toilets. Nearby towns offer a range of lodging choices. *Camping:* Permitted in the park at the lean-to shelters and campfire sites as well as near Palolampi information point.

BEST TIMES: March through August.

FIELD NOTES: There is no official lodging within the confines of the park. Come prepared for camping if you are staying overnight. Limited handicap access. Local establishments and farms sell food and equipment for campers. Activities include camping, fishing, boating, hiking, bird-watching, skiing, and berry and mushroom picking.

PETKELJÄRVI NATIONAL PARK

FINLAND

If your desire is to find an enchanting oasis in the middle of the forest look no further than Petkeljärvi National Park. Nestled among the park's steep-sided ridges are areas of virgin forest, including 150-year-old shield bark–covered pines. Summer hikers will be able to hear the cries of black-throated divers and will sometimes have to climb over trees that have been downed by beavers.

The park's ridges were formed when a glacier melted nearly 11,000 years ago. Southern Finland was covered by an ice lake, and as the waters lowered, Petkeljärvi was the first region of dry land. The park's ridges have pits in them, know as "suppa holes," which were formed by clumps of ice left behind as the glacier receded.

In the wake of the melting ice, the first animals to migrate to the area were the Arctic fox and wild forest reindeer. Today, visitors who hike the park's trails will find moose and wolves wandering along the pine-covered ridges or following the waterways. The park offers guided tours for individuals and groups, which can be booked through the outdoor center. Fishing, hiking, swimming, and canoeing are favorite park activities. Berry and edible mushroom picking is permitted and encouraged.

LOCATION: On the east side of main road 74, which runs between Joensuu and Ilomantsi. The outdoor center and nature information hut are located at the tip of Cape Petraniemi at the end of Petkeljärventie Road.

HOURS OF OPERATION: Year-round; daily, Mon–Fri, 9 a.m. to 4 p.m.

CONTACT: *Outdoor center:* For information and group reservations, Tel: 358414361790; Web: www.luontoon.fi.

COST: *Entrance:* Free. Fees required for guided tours, camping, and overnight lodging.

ON-SITE AMENITIES: Outdoor center and nature information hut, cafe/restaurant, restrooms, sauna, boat and canoe rentals, guided tours. Campgrounds have showers, toilet, camp kitchen, and dining area. Groups should make advance reservations for camping, tours, or lodging. *Lodging:* Contact **Karelia Expert** at www.kareliaexpert.fi.

Fishing permits can be purchased on-site. The closest shop is in Mohko, and most services can be found in Ilomantsi, about 15 miles from the park.

BEST TIMES: April through October.

FIELD NOTES: Hiking is very popular so bring comfortable walking shoes or boots, rain gear, insect repellent, sunscreen, sunglasses, and hats. Lake, river, and stream water should be boiled or filtrated before drinking. Drinking water can be obtained at the cafe. Canoes and boats can be rented from the outdoor center.

BALLYCROY NATIONAL PARK

IRELAND

At more than 73 square miles, Ballycroy National Park is one of the largest expanses of peat land in Europe. Irish law has adapted the European Union Habitats Directive, which requires certain species and habitats be protected to ensure their continuing existence or to restore them to their original condition. Because it is the largest blanket bog in western Europe,

Ballycroy was automatically included in the list of mandated government parks. Formed in 1998, the park encompasses a variety of ecosystems and is of particular importance within the European Union.

Primarily known for its intact and preserved Owenduff bog, the centerpiece of the park, the area also includes mountains, heath, upland grassland,

pipers, woodcocks, dunlins, skylarks, meadow pipits, ravens, and hooded crows are all found here.

Nonnative species have also been introduced to the park, such as the red deer. Indigenous mammals, such as the fox, badger, mountain hare, otter, feral American mink, and pygmy shrew, coexist with the imported species to create a new and more diverse ecosystem.

lakes, and river catchments. Located on Ireland's northern coast, the park is named for the small town of Ballycroy, which is also a popular destination in its own right as well as for fishing enthusiasts. Park visitors will find accommodations in the town of Ballycroy. Lodging is also available from the Aughness and Park Vies.

The Owenduff River, which runs through Ballycroy, is the home of local salmon, eels, brown trout, and sea trout. Otters are popular in the area and prey on the brown trout and eels. Birdwatchers will be able to work on their life lists because the greater Owenduff area is vital for the feeding, roosting, and breeding of many migratory birds, including the Greenland white-fronted goose. The park is also home to rare species such as the whooper swan, peregrine falcon, and corncrake. Visitors may also spot some of the indigenous birds: kestrels, dippers, common sand-

LOCATION: Owenduff/Nephin Mountains, northwest County Mayo. The visitors center is located in the village of Ballycroy on N59 between Mulranny and Bangor.

HOURS OF OPERATION: 24/7.

CONTACT: *Park office:* Tel: 09849996; Web: www.ballycroynationalpark.ie.

COST: *Entrance:* Free. *Fishing:* Permit required; call John Campbell, Ballyveeny, Ballycroy, County Mayo at 09849116.

ON-SITE AMENITIES: Visitors center, public fishing, private fishing lodges, hiking, and nature photography. Self-catering cottage rentals are available; visit www.parkviewmayo.com.

BEST TIMES: May through September.

FIELD NOTES: It is advised that you do not venture out onto the hills alone given the ruggedness of the terrain. Suitable clothing for hiking is recommended. Wildflowers cannot be picked; dogs must be kept on a leash at all times.

BURREN NATIONAL PARK

IRELAND

At first glance, you may think Burren National Park were made of nothing but rock; however the park's 3,706 acres encompass a variety of complex, overlapping ecosystems, creating a unique habitat structure for the area's flora and fauna. Over 75% of the plants found in Ireland are represented in the park, and some of the rarer species are protected under European legislation. Orchid enthusiasts will find several rare specimens, including the bee, fly, and frog orchids.

Although the majority of the park's mammals are active only at night, daytime visitors will be able to see hares, foxes, pygmy shrews, and stoats. The shy and elusive pine marten makes its home here, but it is very difficult to spot. The park is home to 7 species of bats, and visitors can hope to see the endangered lesser horseshoe bat.

The feral goat is a familiar sight in the Burren landscape. Visitors can often see a herd roaming free over the grounds. On sunny days, look for them in higher elevations, but in bad weather they tend to gather in the woodlands and hazel scrub.

Other mammals that can be found throughout the park are the red squirrel, badger, and otter. The mink is not a native to the area, but individuals that escaped from fur farms thrive in the park. More than 89 species of birds have been recorded here, 50 of which use the park as breeding grounds. Of particular interest are the peregrine falcons, ravens, kestrels, and merlins; winter visitors may be able to spot hen harriers.

LOCATION: Southeastern side of the Burren, north County Clare.

HOURS OF OPERATION: Year-round.

CONTACT: *Park office:* National Parks and Wildlife Service, 7 Ely Place, Dublin 2; Tel: 35318882000; Fax: 35318883272; Web: www.burrennationalpark.ie.

COST: *Entrance:* Free.

ON-SITE AMENITIES: There are no on-site facilities in the park, and camping is not permitted. Lodging is available in nearby towns. Hiking, wildlife viewing, and picnicking can all be enjoyed here.

BEST TIMES: Summer months are considered to be best for wildlife viewing, though keep in mind this season also brings extra tourism to the area.

FIELD NOTES: There are no marked trails, but many people visit the park for walking. The terrain is very rocky with deep fissures and cracks; there are also loose rocks and steep cliff areas. Visitors are advised to keep well away from any cliffs and steep rocky areas, as they may be dangerous. The limestone can get very slippery when wet so extreme caution must be taken. Sturdy walking boots and a map and compass are essential. The weather is also very changeable so waterproof clothing is in order.

CONNEMARA NATIONAL PARK

IRELAND

Most travelers are attracted to Ireland for its friendly people, the picturesque Twelve Bens mountain range, and shimmering golden beaches. But wildlife enthusiasts come for the almost 5,000 acres that make up Connemara National Park. The park is famous for the Connemara pony. Though domesticated, the ponies roam the park freely and are a familiar sight throughout the area's rolling hills.

Bird-watchers will have much to see at Connemara. Look for meadow pipits, skylarks, stonechats, chaffinches, robins, and wrens. Birds of prey include kestrels and sparrowhawks; and merlin and peregrine falcons also make occasional visits. Winter visitors may spot woodcocks, snipes, starlings, song thrushes, and mistle thrushes. The park is home to a number of mammals as well. The fox, rabbit, stoat, shrew, bat, and the pine marten are all found here. The non-native mink has thrived here and is considered a threat to indigenous wildlife.

With its endless beauty and true green ambiance Connemara National Park is a trip not to be missed. Spend a day walking the magnificent countryside or cycling, fishing, or horseback riding while enjoying Ireland's nature lands.

LOCATION: Letterfrack Village, west Ireland.

HOURS OF OPERATION: Year-round. *Visitors center:* Mar–May and Sept–Oct, 10 a.m. to 5:30 p.m.; June–Aug, 9.30 a.m. to 6:30 p.m.

CONTACT: *Park office:* Connemara National Park, Letterfrack, Co. Galway, Ireland; Tel: 3539541054 or 3539541006; Fax: 3539541005; Web: www.heritageireland .ie/en/West/ConnemaraNationalPark.

COST: *Entrance:* Free.

ON-SITE AMENITIES: Guided tours and nature walks during July and August. Self-guided trails, exhibitions, toilets (some handicap accessible), parking lots, all-weather picnic areas, restaurant, tearooms, and coffee shop.

BEST TIMES: March through October.

FIELD NOTES: Allow 2–3 hours. The last daily admission is 45 minutes before closing time. Bring your camera because the park offers wonderful photographic opportunities. The sunsets can be breathtaking.

GLENVEAGH NATIONAL PARK

IRELAND

There are three distinct topological areas in Glenveagh National Park's more than 27,000 acres, and each area has its own mix of thriving wildlife populations. In the hilltops, scarce in vegetation, visitors will find the hardy arctic mountain hare and be treated to the sweet call of the now-rare golden plover. Other birds found in this area are ravens and peregrines.

The bogs provide food for visiting kestrels and migratory pipits, which can be seen here during migration seasons. The red deer feed on the grasses and sedges found in and bordering the bog areas. Though contained by a deer fence the Glenveagh herd is completely wild and can be difficult to approach. The best time for viewing the deer is during the fall mating season, or rut. Visitors to the bog areas will find numerous mice, shrews, and lizards. This area supports a number of grasses, such as molinia, sundew, butterwort, and the saffron-colored bog asphodel.

The park also contains almost 250 acres of mixed woodlands. Besides the common oak and birch, visitors will see rowan, holly, hazel, yew, and aspen. It is in this area that badgers and foxes roam looking for rodents, which they prey on. The birds of Glenveah's forests include the rare wood warbler and more common crossbill, siskin, goldcrest, and coaltit.

The parkland was consolidated in the 19th century by a wealthy land speculator, who used it as a private deer farm; the park has been under government control since 1975. A visit to the park would not be complete without seeing the world-famous Glenveagh castle and its beautiful gardens. The gardens, located between the sloping fields of Lough Veagh and the castle itself contains both native species and exotics that have been transplanted from the far corners of the world. Daily tours are available.

LOCATION: Derryveagh Mountains, County Donegal. The visitors center is located on the northern end of Lough Veagh, near the edge of the park.

HOURS OF OPERATION: Mar–Oct, 10 a.m. to 6 p.m.; Oct–Mar, 9 a.m. to 5 p.m.

CONTACT: *Park office:* Tel: 0749137090; Fax: 0749137072; Web: www.glen veaghnationalpark.ie. **Glenveagh gardens:** Tel: 0749137391.

COST: *Entrance:* Free. **Glenveagh castle** tours: Adults, US$5; seniors, US$3; children, US$2. *Bus to and from park:* US$8. *Garden tours:* Free.

ON-SITE AMENITIES: **Glenveagh gardens,** hiking, guided tours, **Glenveagh castle,** visitors center, ranger-led walks. The extensive displays contained within the visitors center provide an introduction to the park's natural and built history as well as providing information on walking trails and events. Guides are happy to provide visitors with information about the park and surrounding area; they also sell tickets for the park buses. Guided tours of the gardens are available by appointment with the head gardener; call the gardens for details.

BEST TIMES: May through September.

FIELD NOTES: Wear comfortable hiking and/or walking boots/shoes. If you are not driving, learn the bus schedule. There are tours available for almost every facet of the park; visitors should plan to stay more than 1 day. The weather can be extremely changeable and wet; carry suitable attire. **Glenveagh castle** tours fill up quickly in the summer; arrive early.

ABRUZZO NATIONAL PARK

ITALY

The choice can be maddening. All roads lead to Rome, but is that where you want to spend your vacation? The Eternal City offers everything that a visitor could ask for: incredible nightlife, opulent palaces, museums, and the wonders of the ancient world. Yet only a 50-mile drive away in the majestic Italian mountains is Abruzzo National Park, where you can experience encounters with nature that you may never have imagined this close to one of the world's great cities. So, spend your time in Abruzzo and then do some shopping in Rome—the best of both worlds, and only a short drive apart.

Abruzzo National Park is a 150,000-acre protected area with only one paved road. More adventurous visitors can travel by bicycle or foot along the countless unpaved roads and 150 marked and mapped walks, which lead to an amazing variety of habitats, landscapes, and wildlife. The walks vary in length and difficulty, allowing you to find just the right hike for your abilities.

Visitors will notice that much of the park is forested; and it is here that several formerly endangered species have begun to thrive. Look for Apennine wolves, marsican bears, foxes, mountain goats, and Apennine lynx.

The Titolo trail, which begins at the Santa Venere Bridge in Pescasseroli, allows visitors to tread the same path that generations of shepherds followed as they have moved their flocks back and forth from winter to summer pastures.

Whether you spend the day watching the deer, roebuck, and marsican bear or visiting the old world villages where the customs, regalia, and architecture recall an earlier, more simple time, Abruzzo National Park offers everything a naturalist could look for. And it's easily accessed from Rome.

LOCATION: 2-hour drive from Rome.

HOURS OF OPERATION: 24/7.

CONTACT: *Park office:* Tel: 0635403331; Web: www.parcoabruzzo.it. *Further information:* Web: www.initaly.com/regions/abruzzo/parco.htm; www.paradoxplace.com; or www.parks.it/parco.nazionale.abruzzo/Ecen.html. *Tours:*

Web: www.seeabruzzo.com/Abruzzo-National-Park.html.

COST: *Entrance:* Depends on visitors center. *Lodging* (per night, midweek, hotel): US$110.

ON-SITE AMENITIES: Visitors centers, museums, and nature centers, bicycle and walking paths, zoos with semi-tame animals, local villages, churches, and other architectural sites.

BEST TIMES: Early spring to mid fall.

FIELD NOTES: Hotel reservations in the immediate area are recommended, especially in high season. Guide books, comfortable footwear, and cameras are also recommended. Rental cars are useful if you are considering traveling to and from Rome but not essential; regular train and bus service is available.

GRAN PARADISO NATIONAL PARK

TORINO, ITALY

Too many people think of the sun-dappled coast of Sicily or the ancient city of Rome when thinking of Italy. After a life-changing sojourn to Gran Paradiso National Park in the mountains of northern Italy you will never make that mistake again. Every mountainous or winter activity is possible here, and visitors will want to experience it all. Located near Mount

find many males venture down into the valleys, where they can be easily photographed. People who frequent the park often quip that visitors will see more ibex and chamois than humans.

The park offers many specialized nature walks, including one that is specifically designed for the blind and for those of limited mobility. The hiking facilities are second to none and offer views rarely seen outside this region. Lodging for almost every taste is available, ranging from luxury hotels to tent camping.

Blanc, Gran Paradiso is the largest mountain in Italy and is the second highest peak in the Graian Alps. The park was established in 1856 and is the oldest national park in the country.

From larch and fir woods to alpine grasslands and scenic rocks and glaciers, visitors to the park encounter the amazing natural beauty of the Italian mountains. A trip to this park is almost like stepping into another world, and photographs and movies have never done justice to the area's magnificence.

Strict environmental protection laws mean that wildlife is less skittish here than in other areas. The indigenous alpine ibex, red fox, and chamois (locally called *camoscio*) can be frequently spotted in the park. During the spring, ibex (locally called *stambecco*) are often seen using their horns to scratch themselves or other herd members as they shed their winter coats. You can

LOCATION: Torino, in the Piemonte and Valle d'Aosta.

HOURS OF OPERATION: 24/7; with guided climbs and hikes departing at specific times.

CONTACT: *Park office:* Tel: 0118606211; Web: www.pngp.it.

COST: Depending on activities and lodging options.

ON-SITE AMENITIES: Numerous visitor centers. *Camping:* At commercial sites only. *Lodging:* A variety of hotels, rooms, and mountain huts. Guided and marked walking tours and picnic areas. Nature paths for the disabled and sight impaired.

BEST TIMES: April through October.

FIELD NOTES: Hiking and climbing equipment recommended. Cameras, field books, and binoculars are standard for those visiting for the wildlife. No dogs or fire making allowed.

DE HOGE VELUWE
NATIONAL PARK

THE NETHERLANDS

The shifting dunes of De Hoge Ve-Luwe National Park, The Netherlands' largest national park, were plowed by glaciers during the Ice Age. In the south and east portions of the park, these same glaciers left behind tailings of 200- to 300-foot-high piles of fragmented rock, called moraines. Primeval forests grew in and around the moraines, but many of the forests were cleared during the Middle Ages for cultivation and the grazing of sheep.

Anton Kröller, a business tycoon, and his wife, Helene Müller Kröller, were lovers of nature and art. In the early 1900s they purchased a 13,750-acre moorland and woodland, which became De Hoge VeLuwe National Park.

Plant lovers will find a wide variety of plants in the park's wetland heaths and dry sandy forests; look for bog-rosemary, marsh gentian, bog aspho-del, heath sedge, viper's grass, clover dodder, fan and stag horn clubmoss, and water crowfoot. Animal observers and photographers will find many spe-cies of mammals in the park's pro-tected habitat. Visitors may spot red deer, wild boars, and moeflons, which are threatened red-brown sheep that have large curving horns. Red deer are most active during the September rut-ting season. During October the moef-lons begin their rut, and visitors may be witness to rams engaging in brutal fights in an effort to attract mates. The park is also home to the wheatear thrush and the red-backed shrike, a carnivorous bird that feeds on insects, voles, and lizards. Many species of but-terflies and moths live in the park, in-cluding the tree grayling, dark green fritillary, niobe fritillary, and grizzled skipper.

In 1938, the Kröller-Müller Art Mu-seum opened in the northern, wooded area of the park, featuring among other masterpieces, the second largest col-lection of Van Gogh paintings in the world; the largest is not far away in Am-sterdam. The museum grounds include a 75-acre modern and contemporary sculpture garden that is also the start of 26 miles of walking and biking trails.

LOCATION: Approximately 70 miles southeast of Amsterdam, 10 miles from the Apeldoorn train station.

HOURS OF OPERATION: Year-round; daily; Nov–Mar, 9 a.m. to 5:30 p.m.; Apr, 8 a.m. to 8 p.m.; May–Aug, 8 a.m. to 9 p.m.; June–July, 8 a.m. to 10 p.m.; Sept, 9 a.m. to 8 p.m.; Oct, 9 a.m. to 7 p.m.

CONTACT: *Park office:* Nationaal Park De Hoge Veluwe Visitor Center, Apeldoornseweg 250, Hoenderloo, Gelderland 7351 TA, Netherlands; Tel: 031055378 8100; Web: www.hogeveluwe .nl; email: information@hogeveluwe.nl.

COST: *Entrance:* Adults US$10, children (6–12 years), US$5; children (under 6), free. *Camping* (per person, per night): US$6 (children half price); Hoenderloo entrance, tents and RVs; first-come, first-served basis.

ON-SITE AMENITIES: Visitors center provides maps to the walking and biking paths (bicycles are available for rent); **Kröller-Müller Art Museum;** sculpture gardens.

BEST TIMES: April through November.

FIELD NOTES: Wear layered clothes as the weather can be changeable, and comfortable shoes for the long walking paths.

DRENTS-FRIESE WOLD NATIONAL PARK

THE NETHERLANDS

People have occupied the northern portion of modern-day Netherlands since the Iron Age, some 3,000 years ago. For centuries, the area's heath lands were stripped for peat fertilizer and heavily farmed. As the beech, oak, and conifer forests were clearcut, the area began to lose its topsoil and became barren and covered by shifting sands. In an effort to save the remaining heath and forests as well as farmland and villages, reforestation projects began as early as the mid-19th century. In 2000, the 15,000-acre Drents-Friese

Wold National Park was established to continue the recovery efforts. The park not only protects and manages the heath and forest but also provides recreational and educational opportunities for the public. Biologists come to the park for the natural wildlife laboratory found within its borders.

The park's forests are nearly 80% conifers. The 75-foot-tall Scots pine, the only pine tree native to northern Europe, dominates the restored forests, but visitors will find beech groves as well. Among the great variety of plants that thrive here, visitors will find bell-heather; cotton grass; bog gentian, a 4-inch-tall deep blue wildflower found primarily in wet heathlands; bog asphodel, a 10- to 15-inch-high wetland lily with bright yellow flowers; marsh club moss; and the mouse-eared hawkweed, with its lemon yellow flowers.

Bird-watchers can look for stonechats, curlews, woodlarks, and tawny pipits. A trek to the wetlands will put you in sight of wading birds like the long-billed, long-legged godwit and gray-brown redshank, recognizable by its thin bright orange legs. High above, the honey buzzard, hawk, sparrow hawk, and barn owl search for prey.

Areas of the park are still used as grazing land, so visitors are likely to see sheep and cattle on the heath. The park is home to a number of wild mammals, including the common roe deer, hares, hedgehogs, and squirrels and the rarer pine martens, badgers, stoat or ermines, and polecats or skunks. The park is home to reptiles and amphibians, too: look for adder and ringed snakes, lizards, brown and pool frogs, newts, and several species of salamander.

LOCATION: Approximately 150 miles northeast of Amsterdam.

HOURS OF OPERATION: Year-round; hours vary seasonally. *Appelscha visitors center:* Daily; Tue–Sun, 10 a.m. to 5 p.m.; weekends only, Nov–Mar. *Diever information center:* Generally 10 a.m. to 4 p.m., closed Thur and Sun.

CONTACT: *Appelscha visitors center:* Tel: 31516464020. *Diever information center:* Tel: 31521591748; Web: www.nationaalpark-drents-friese-wold.nl.

COST: *Entrance:* Free.

ON-SITE AMENITIES: Visitors center at the Appelscha entrance, with wildlife exhibits, book/gift shop, and park maps. Information center, near the Diever entrance. *Hiking:* More than 80 miles of well-marked footpaths with more than 30 different routes of various lengths. *Horses:* 40 miles of bridle paths and sandy roads for horses and horse-drawn carriages. Paths and trails have wildlife information signs along the way. Organized, family-friendly excursions are available. Two watchtowers provide wide views of different areas.

BEST TIMES: Open year-round, but the park can be very wet during late autumn and winter. Spring and summer are best for wildlife viewing.

FIELD NOTES: Wear good walking shoes. The park's footpaths can be very soggy in late autumn and throughout the winter. Visitors must stay on marked paths.

SERRA DA MALCATA NATURE RESERVE

PORTUGAL

The critically endangered status of the Iberian lynx is underscored by the fact that the International Union for the Conservation of Nature has named this species to be the world's most threatened carnivore. Their numbers shrank by 75% in 5 years. While there were 400 known Iberian lynx in the wild in 2000, by 2005 there were only 100.

This species of lynx is found only on the Iberian Peninsula, and their habitats have been encroached on by humans. For example, the Iberian lynx preys primarily on the hare, which has been slowly eliminated from the peninsula. This alone has had a disastrous impact on the area's ecosystems. Attempts have been made to reintroduce the hare, to create protected zones, and to educate hunters, all which has helped.

Serra da Malcata Nature Reserve was created with a focus on protecting the Iberian lynx. As a result other wildlife have reaped the benefits. Visitors will find foxes, wildcats, badgers, genets, weasels, rabbits, hares, wild boars, Egyptian mongoose, otters, toads, salamanders, vipers, snakes, kites, eagles, eagle owls, and partridges all living within the boundaries of the reserve.

The reserve encompasses 40,000 acres of heather-clad hills and oak forests. The variety of woodlands and elevations means that visitors hiking along one of the many trails are treated to diverse habitats and ecosystems. Trail maps, in many languages, are available at the park office and the associated Environmental Education Center. Personal guides are available from commercial tour companies.

LOCATION: Central Portugal along the border with Spain. The entrance to the Serra da Malcata Nature Reserve is about 9 km northeast of Penamacor.

HOURS OF OPERATION: Year-round.

CONTACT: *Main office:* Serra Da Malcata Nature Reserve, Rua Dr. Ribeiro Sanches, 60, Apartado 38, 6090–587 Penamacor; Tel: 351277394467; Fax: 351277394580. **Environmental Education Centre:** Centro de Educacao Ambiental da Sra da Graca, 6320–052 Aldeia de Sto Antonio; Tel: 351271752825; Fax: 351271754425; *Tours:* Web: www.aportugalattraction .com/portugal-attractions/serra-da-malcata-nature-reserve.htm or www .visitportugal.com.

COST: *Entrance:* Free. Tours vary in cost.

ON-SITE AMENITIES: Environmental Education Centre with trained guides. Other amenities are scarce, but there are towns and cities near the park that offer a variety of accommodation options.

BEST TIMES: February through September.

FIELD NOTES: Proper hiking apparel is recommended. Although there are driving and marked walking tours, a guided tour is recommended for those who prefer an in-depth exploration of the reserve. **Sabugal castle:** About 11 miles away, the castle, restructured by King Dinis (1275–1325), has an unusual five-sided, 90-foot-high keep known as the Torre das Cinco Quinas.

BIESZCZADY NATIONAL PARK

POLAND

Bieszczady National Park is Poland's largest mountain national park, located in the mountain range of the same name. Approximately 80% of the park's 112 square miles is heavily forested, much of it still virgin timber. In an effort to preserve Poland's diverse, natural ecosystems and wildlife, the park was established in 1973 and almost 70% of the park remains closed to visitors.

First-time visitors should stop at the information and education center for maps of the park's extensive hiking, biking, and cross-country skiing trails. The elevation of the park changes dramatically; and the trails vary in length and difficulty. One trail winds to the peak of Mount Tarnica. Along the way, visitors will find themselves encounter Bieszczady's beech forest, which is part of Europe's largest remaining untouched beech forest.

Rising to 4,420 feet, Mount Tarnica offers spectacular views of the park and surrounding rugged, forested area. As visitors change elevation they will be passing through distinct ecosystems and habitats for a wide variety of plant life. The park is home to 778 plant species, of which 29 are endemic. Here, cow-wheat grows in thickets, meadows, and pastures; as the name suggests, cows are particularly fond of it. It is said that medieval farmers believed the plant, with its thin grass-like leaves, would somehow turn into wheat, which is how the grass got its name. Wildflower lovers will spot plants like catchfly and monkshood—so-named because its flower looks like the hood worn by medieval monks—growing in the meadows and along the forest's edge. More than 250 different species of moss and an estimated 1,000 species of fungi grow in the park.

The varied habitats and abundant plant life mean that visitors can expect to find good wildlife viewing. In fact, the park is home to 144 species of birds and 58 species of mammals. This is a well-known bird-watching destination, where Ural and eagle owls, water pipits, black storks, corncrakes, river warblers, lesser spotted eagles, and the white-backed woodpeckers can be seen. Visitors should also look for 7 other species of woodpeckers, honey buzzards, ring ouzels, crested tits, and spotted nutcrackers. Large mammals are always exciting, and European brown bears, wolves, wild boars, beavers, lynx, deer, and Polish bison, can all be found here.

LOCATION: Podkarpackie Region, near the borders of Slovakia and Ukraine.

HOURS OF OPERATION: Year round, 24/7.

CONTACT: *Park office:* Bieszczady National Park, 38-714, Ustrzyki Górne, Poland; Tel: 48134610650; Web: www .panparks.org/network/ourparks/ bieszczady.

COST: *Entrance* (per day): Adults, US$2; children, US$1.

ON-SITE AMENITIES: Information and education center, snack bar, museum, toilet/break facilities along park trails, educational facilities for school groups, guided tours by horseback.

BEST TIMES: May through October.

FIELD NOTES: Dress in layered clothing. Wear comfortable walking shoes. Horseback riding is a great way to explore the park. Licensed guides are available for booking through the website. Tours are available in Polish, English, and German.

KENOZERSKY NATIONAL PARK

RUSSIA

Established in 1991, Kenozersky National Park is a refuge for more than 300 species of animals. Covering an area of 530 square miles in Russia's far northwest corner, the park encompasses rolling hills, meadows, dense forests, wooded shorelines, and two lakes—Lake Lekshmozero and Kenozero. Within the park are a number of pastoral villages that contain historic wooden buildings and churches dating from the 16th–19th centuries. The park offers visitors hiking, bird-watching, boating, sight-seeing, and a variety of cultural and historical activities.

Among the park's 50 species of mammals are beavers, red and flying squirrels, mountain hares, Siberian chipmunks, shrews, deer, moose, wild boars, five species of bats, and a variety of rodents. Visitors will find 14 species of mammal predators at Kenozersky. The pine marten hunts hare, birds, squirrels, and other rodents at dusk in wooded areas. The red fox is found in scrub brush and meadows, searching for small mammals and birds. The threatened European lynx, the largest cat of the lynx genus, stalks birds and small mammals. Packs of gray wolves, also called timber wolves, follow herds of moose through the park during their spring and fall migrations. In turn, wolverines, the largest members of the weasel family, follow the wolves, looking for an opportunity to steal prey or feed on carrion. The solitary raccoon dog, which has markings similar to a raccoon, hunts birds and small mammals at night.

Perhaps the best-recognized park resident is the brown bear, an omnivore that feeds mostly on vegetable matter. They catch fish and will occasionally hunt small mammals and even deer. These huge bears have no natural competitors; not even wolves and wolverines are a match for the bears' size, strength, and ferociousness.

LOCATION: Northern European Russia, in the Plesetsk and Kargopol districts in southwestern Arkhangelsk Province.

HOURS OF OPERATION: 24/7.

CONTACT: *Park office:* Center for Russian Nature Conservation Director, 163061

Arkhangelsk, ul., Vyucheiskogo, 18 Shatkovskaya, Russia; Tel: 78182271867; Web: www.wild-russia.org/bioregion2/2-KenozerskyNP/2_kenoz.htm; email: kenozero@arkhangelsk.ru.

COST: Most visitors come in tour groups with park fees included. Contact the park for current entry fees.

ON-SITE AMENITIES: Park headquarters and visitors center are located in Vershinino on Lake Kenozero. The visitors center offers rooms for overnight stays. The park encompasses small villages with additional accommodations. Children's ecological camp, hiking trails, guided hikes, and boat excursions. Russian banya (steam bath), meals, and areas for swimming. Transportation to and from the train stations at Nyandoma and Plesetsk. The park staff can arrange for family, individual, and group tours.

BEST TIMES: Late spring and summer. Autumn is rainy and winters are long and cold with snow blanketing the ground from October through April.

FIELD NOTES: Visitors to Russia require passport and Russian visa. Wear comfortable, layered clothing and good walking shoes.

DONANA NATIONAL PARK

SPAIN

Due to its unique landscape and proximity to Africa, Donana National Park offers avid bird-watchers the opportunity to view and photograph an array of species that would be difficult to find anywhere else in the world. More than half the bird species in Europe have been recorded in Donana. As the last piece of land between Europe and Africa, Donana National Park is of critical importance to the promulgation and protection of the birds that migrate to and from Africa annually.

During the winter, visitors to the park would be hard-pressed to not see an array of magnificent birds. Although this is a bonus for those who are interested in the stunning beaches and varied landscapes, for both amateur and professional ornithologists it is the primary reason to be at the park.

The park's 125,000 acres are spread over several provinces in southern

Spain and make up the country's largest national park and one of Europe's most important protected areas. The current parklands started out in the mid 1900s as a private hunting ground for Spanish royalty. By 1969, it was turned into a national park and was later named a national Heritage site.

Donana is split into two parts: the natural park and the national park. It seems counterintuitive, but the natural park is the less protected of the two and is open to public use. The national park offers visitors marked paths and an extensive visitors center. True enthusiasts will make the national park the centerpiece of their visit, because here they can see the most birds. Look for Spanish imperial eagles, geese, colonies of flamingos, ducks, gray herons, waders, terns, lanner falcons, spoonbills, wood sandpipers, doves, partridges, griffon vultures, booted eagles, and red and black kites. When you need a break from birding, you may even spot the extremely rare Iberian lynx, which lurks in the park's pine forests.

There are many nearby towns and villages that offer lodging and restaurants. Some are located on the water and offer magnificent views of the river, ocean, and park grounds. There are daily river tours, which provide an excellent visual overview of the park; they stop twice along the way for walking tours.

LOCATION: Roughly 45 miles from the city of Huelvo in southern Spain.

HOURS OF OPERATION: Year-round, 8:30 a.m. to 5 p.m.

CONTACT: *Tourist promotion board* (Patronato Provincial de Turismo): Web: www.diphuelva.es; email: buzon@diphuelva.es. *Reservations:* Tel: 349-59430432 or 34959430451. *Tour options:* Web: www.discoveringdonana.com. *Lodging:* **Cooperativa Marismas del Rocio/Hotel Toruño:** Plaza Acebuchal 22, 21750 El Rocio (Huelva), Spain; Tel: 34959442323; Fax: 34959442338.

COST: Depends on lodging and tours. Tours are provided by park officials (more controlled and reasonably priced) and commercial licensed agencies (more extensive and expensive).

ON-SITE AMENITIES: Visitors centers, extensive trails, guided bird-watching, walking tours, and 4-wheel-drive vehicle tours.

BEST TIMES: November through March.

FIELD NOTES: Due to the size, the controlled protected areas, and the diversity found in the park, guided tours are highly recommended. No more than 256 visitors are allowed on any given day. Contact the reservations number to book your tour with a park official. **Marismas de Doñana Cooperative:** Runs the Toruño, a small hotel that overlooks the park in the village of El Rocio and not far from the pilgrimage shrine.

LOBO PARK

SPAIN

The European, timber, Iberian, and tundra Alaska wolves make their home in the huge tracts of enclosed land that make up Lobo Park. The wolves are acquired from other parks as pups and raised with and by humans, which helps desensitize their innate fear of people. The wolves run through the woodlands in an environment that is as close to the wild as possible.

Wolves are extremely social animals and the pups maintain their relationship with the humans with whom they have interacted throughout their lives. Only park officials are allowed in the encampments, and wolves will often congregate when one of the park owners ventures into their area. Noted wolf biologist John Theberge remarked, "Their social bonding and care-giving behavior are second only to those of humans and other social primates."

Although the wolves are the main attraction of the park, the owners work hard to maintain the pristine condition of the environment, which allows other wildlife, such as the foxes that roam the park, to thrive. The family-friendly atmosphere of Lobo Park is supported by the domestic farm animals that are kept on-site and the petting zoo available for children. Andalusian horses are available for petting as well as riding in the park.

The park's roughly 100 acres are less than an hour's drive from Malaga. Lobo was, unlike most parks that serve a similar purpose, designed and created by two individuals, Daniel Weigend and Alexandra Stieber, whose passion for wildlife is manifest in this park, which they started in 2002. They recognized that there was a dearth of information and resources about wolves as well as a lack of organized and structured care for these animals.

Weigend and Stieber accept wolf pups from around the world and care for them personally. Although they work with the pups to acclimate them to humans, they are extremely careful to avoid any semblance of domestication. The wolves in the park accept humans and allow themselves to be seen at a closer distance than their brethren in the wild. The park provides huge expanses for the wolves in which to roam and mate while human access is limited to specific areas. In direct opposition to the way most areas for observing wildlife are structured, in Lobo Park it is the wolf that is free.

LOCATION: About 40 miles from Malaga in Andalusia.

HOURS OF OPERATION: Year-round, 10 a.m. to 6 p.m.

CONTACT: *Park office:* Tel: 34952031107; Web: www.lobopark.com; email: info@lobopark.com.

COST: *Tours* (in English and Spanish): Adults, US$13; children, US$9. *Petting zoo:* US$2.

ON-SITE AMENITIES: Restaurant, visitors center, petting zoo, walking tours, horseback riding, and wolf museum (under construction at the time of publication).

BEST TIMES: Year-round.

FIELD NOTES: Visitors can enter the park only as part of a guided tour. Bring comfortable walking shoes and, if you are so inclined, appropriate riding clothes. Family oriented.

SIERRA NEVADA NATIONAL PARK

SPAIN

Sierra Nevada National Park is home to the greatest number of endemic plant species in Europe. More than 2,100 species of vascular plants can be found in the park, of which roughly 70 species can be found only here, making this a naturalist's paradise. In addition to the commonly found Nevada violet and the Sierra chamomile, the area is also home to threatened species of daffodil, Sierra Nevada sandwort, and

wormwood. At the highest elevations, visitors will find holm oak, sweet chestnut, and Pyrenean oak.

For wildlife enthusiasts, the attraction of the park is the more than 60 species of birds, including birds of prey, such as golden eagles, Bonelli eagles, peregrine falcons, and kestrels. Alpine accentors, black redstarts, and northern wheatears are found in the highlands and hoopoes, green woodpeckers,

coal tits, and golden orioles are found in the wooded areas.

Visitors most often see Spanish ibex, a mountain goat famed for its curling horns. Those who travel to the mountainsides will find pine voles and weasels if they are quick enough to spot them. At lower elevations, look for host boars, wild cats, badgers, foxes, and beech martens.

The park is also known for its 120 species of butterflies, such as the Apollo butterfly. Amateur entomologists will be busy finding the 37 native species of beetles that live here, including the rare endemic rhinoceros beetle.

The park has a number of excellent hiking and walking trails. The GR7 trail links numerous villages of the Alpujar-ras and crosses the Sierra Nevada foothills. The 5-mile Vía Verde of the Sierra Nevada trail is a converted rail route. The various visitors centers for the park offer maps and guidebooks so you can select the right trail for your needs.

LOCATION: Granada and Almería provinces, southeast Spain.

HOURS OF OPERATION: Year-round. *Visitors centers:* Daily, 10 a.m. to 2 p.m.; Oct–Mar, 4 p.m. to 6 p.m.; Apr–Sept, 6 p.m. to 8 p.m.

CONTACT: *Park office:* Tel: 011 34 958 340 625; Web: www.andalucia.com/environment/protect/sierra-nevada.htm.

COST: *Entrance:* Free.

ON-SITE AMENITIES: Two visitors centers; one area of free camping in the eastern edge of the park, in Monterrey.

BEST TIMES: March through June.

FIELD NOTES: The heat in the summer gets oppressive, so be prepared. It is essential to have sunscreen and a hat. The park contains many villages and some towns, so finding guides, food, and lodging should be fairly easy. There are numerous resorts in the area if camping is not for you; many offer package deals, with guides and tours. Activities here include skiing, snowboarding, hiking, climbing, bird-watching, fishing, and wildlife photography. The ancient architectural sites are another attraction of this area.

FÄRNEBOFJÄRDEN NATIONAL PARK

SWEDEN

Färnebofjärden National Park, situated along the banks of the southern Dalälven River, contains more than 200 islands, making it a unique park that encompasses a great variety of fauna and flora.

Färnebofjärden offers the most spectacular bird-watching in all of Sweden. More than 100 species nest in the park regularly and another 270 species have been recorded visiting or migrating through. Due to the contrasting ecosystems in the park, the diversity of birds found here is unmatched. All of the Swedish woodpeckers can be seen here as can numerous species of owls.

Other wildlife includes 20 species of fish and more than 70 red-listed insect species. The fish, insects, and birds share the park with elk, moose, roe deer, mountain hare, red fox, pine marten, beaver, wood lemming, and lynx. Within the park, Sweden's wetlands and evergreen forests meet broadleaved forests of oak and linden. Färnebofjärden also encompasses riverside fens and meadows, floodplains and ancient forest.

The park entrances at Sevedskvarn, south of Gysinge, and Östa Camping offer permanent displays that provide information about the park's flora and fauna. Sevedskvarn has a wheelchair-accessible trail. Guided water tours, which allow visitors access to some of the park's most exciting areas, are available, but experienced boaters should feel comfortable on their own.

LOCATION: The main entrance to the national park is at Sevedskvarn, just south of Gysinge along the Dalälven River.

HOURS OF OPERATION: Year-round. *Visitors center:* Apr 1– Sept 30, daily, 10 a.m.

to 5 p.m.; Oct 30 to Mar 31, Wed, Sat, and Sun, noon to 5 p.m.

CONTACT: *Park office:* Tel: 4686981000; Web: www.farnebofjarden.se.

COST: *Entrance:* Free. *Guided tours:* depends on the individual purveyor.

ON-SITE AMENITIES: Exhibits, activity station, guided tours, boating, and fishing.

BEST TIMES: April through September.

FIELD NOTES: Guides are highly recommended to get the most out of this experience especially for novice birders. Tyttbo Rapids, located in the western section of the park, is definitely worth a visit. Between January 1 and June 15 select areas of the park are off limits to visitors to avoid disturbing nesting sites. Boundaries to these areas are clearly marked.

TYRESTA NATIONAL PARK AND NATURE RESERVE

SWEDEN

Tyresta National Park is located just 12 miles from Stockholm and encompasses 12,000 acres that abut a larger nature reserve of the same name. The lakes, cliffs, swamps, and forests provide nesting places and homes for about eighty species of birds in the park. Because of the variety of habitats found within the park, visitors can expect to see a diverse array of species. Capercaillies, woodpeckers, and owls are commonly seen in the park and are the subjects of many photos and sketches by visitors.

The entrance to the park is located at Tyresta village, a community that dates back to the Iron Age. Some of the

standing buildings were built in the 1700s.

Hikers will find almost 40 miles of marked trails, all coded for experience and difficulty. The 2-mile Primeval Forest Trail is the perfect introduction to the park. Specially designed signboards are strategically placed along the path to provide hikers with information; a number of these are specifically designed for children. The park trails hook up the reserve's trails and the adventurous hiker can go all the way to the Baltic Sea.

LOCATION: 12 miles southeast of Stockholm in Haninge Municipality. From Tyresö, the park and reserve can be reached via several routes. There are parking areas at several places, including Prästängen, Storängen, Brakmaren, and Ängsudden.

HOURS OF OPERATION: 24/7.

CONTACT: *Park office:* Tyresta National Park, Stiftelsen Tyrestaskogen, 136 59 Vendelsö. Web: www.tyresta.se. *National park house:* Tel: 0874 53 94. *Tyresta Forest Foundation:* Tel: 0874 10876 (Mon–Fri, 8 a.m. to 10 a.m).

COST: *Entrance:* Free. *Tours:* Depends on options. *Transportation from Stockholm:* Depends on method, but all options are reasonable.

ON-SITE AMENITIES: National Parks Center, located in the park, offers information on all of the country's park systems, including Tyresta. Tyresta village offers food at a variety of prices and quality. There is a cafe (closed Mondays), rest cabin, farm shop (open weekends only), and **National Park House** (free entry, closed Mondays). National Park House is handicap accessible. A 3-mile-long trail from the village circles Lake Bylsjön and can accommodate strollers, and wheelchairs with large wheels or drive motors; individuals in chairs with smaller wheels may need assistance. Some sections of the trail are steep.

BEST TIMES: April through September.

FIELD NOTES: Comfortable hiking shoes/boots and socks are recommended. Follow the suggestions of the drivers if busing in from Stockholm. Dogs must be kept on a leash at all times. Bicycles must stay on gravel road surfaces.

SWISS NATIONAL PARK

SWITZERLAND

Swiss National Park is Switzerland's only national park. Founded in 1914 and located in the Swiss Alps, the 68-square-mile park is central Europe's oldest Alpine national park and one of the oldest national parks in all of Europe. The elevation in the park ranges from 4,500 to over 10,000 feet above sea level. The park is made up of three habitats of fairly equal size: alpine forest, alpine meadow, and rugged mountain terrain above the tree line. The park includes an extensive hiking trail system so that visitors can enjoy the spectacular alpine scenery and vistas while having the least impact on alpine wildlife.

The park is home to about 30 species of mammals, including the red deer, hare, weasel, and marten. The ibex, a large, wild mountain goat weighing 200–270 pounds is also found here. Male ibex have large, backward curving horns that grow throughout their lives. At the tree line, visitors will find a smaller mountain goat, the sure-footed chamois. About half the weight of the ibex, these goats have smaller horns, a white face and rump, and thick brown fur in summer and a light gray coat in winter.

Visitors may be lucky enough to see the nocturnal stoat, a weasel-like carnivore. The stoat's body is long and thin with short legs, perfectly adapted for chasing smaller prey into its burrow or den. The fur from this mammal is commonly known as ermine, which was a favorite with European royalty. The park's alpine meadows provide the perfect habitat for marmots. These colony-living mammals look much like a very large ground squirrel. When members of the group are busy feeding on meadow grasses and wildflowers, others keep a watchful eye out for danger. Visitors are often treated to the marmot's loud whistle.

Bird lovers will find more than 100 species, including the woodpecker, wheatear, water pipit, and skylark. Golden eagles, kestrels, ravens, alpine choughs, grouse, ptarmigans, and rock partridges have been recorded within the park's boundaries. The bearded vulture, once locally extinct, has been reintroduced to the area.

LOCATION: Eastern Switzerland in the Canton Graubünden, 2.5 hours from Zürich by train.

HOURS OF OPERATION: Year-round, daily; some roads close during the winter. *Visitors center:* Daily June–Oct, 8:30 a.m. to 6 p.m.

CONTACT: *Visitors center:* Tel: 410818514141; Web: www.about.ch/various/nationalpark.

COST: *Entrance:* Free. *Film:* Adults, US$7; children (6–16 years old), US$3; children (under 6 years), free.

ON-SITE AMENITIES: Visitors center with exhibits and film; 50 miles of well-marked trails, varying in length and difficulty (trail maps are available at the visitors center).

BEST TIMES: Open year-round, but access may be limited during the winter. The visitors center is not open during the winter.

FIELD NOTES: Wear good hiking shoes and dress in layers, because temperatures can change quickly and unexpectedly. Visitors are not permitted to leave marked trails; pick flowers; or gather plants, fungi, or dead wood. Hunting, fishing, and fires are not allowed. No overnight camping and no dogs allowed. The park's motto, while not original, is worth remembering: Take nothing but pictures, leave nothing but footprints!

ASIA

China, India, Indonesia, Japan,
Malaysia, Nepal, Taiwan, Thailand

DAFENG MILU NATIONAL NATURE RESERVE

CHINA

For nearly 1,000 years, Pere David's deer did not exist in the wild. This species, which the Chinese call *milu*, was saved from extinction because it was bred and raised on farms, in zoos, and in private parks in China and elsewhere. The last milu in China disappeared in the early 1900s around the time of the Boxer Rebellion, when the deer's marshland habitat was flooded.

Woburn Abbey Park in Bedford, UK, gave 39 Pere David's deer to China and thus sparked the formation of the Dafeng Milu National Nature Reserve. This million-plus-acre site, which also includes the Yancheng Nature Reserve, strives to increase the deer's numbers and to reintroduce it to the wild. There are now 302 deer living wild in the reserve. Pere David's deer, which have bright red summer coats, branched antlers, wide hooves, and a long tail, are named for a French Catholic priest who first wrote about them in 1865.

Visitors will see much more than this rare deer at the reserve. Look for river deer, yellow weasels, otters, marmots, and badgers. Bird-watchers will find egrets, seagulls, peacocks, and golden pheasants.

Yancheng Nature Reserve was founded to protect rare birds and their habitats, particularly the red-crowned crane. Also known as the Japanese and Manchurian crane, it is the heaviest and second rarest of these birds. Only about 1,500 are thought to exist in the wild, and visitors will see some of the 1,000 that make their home in this reserve. Yancheng is also a major stopover for migratory birds along the east Asian–Australasian flyway.

LOCATION: The reserves are southeast of Dafeng City in Jiangsu Province on

China's eastern central coast. Two buses daily from Yancheng, one in the morning and one about 3 p.m. Bus service is also available from Dafeng.

HOURS OF OPERATION: Year-round, 24/7.

CONTACT: *Reserve office:* National Nature Reserve, Dafeng City, Yancheng, Jiangsu 224136, China; Tel: 865153391912; Web: www.chinamlw.org (Chinese language only).

COST: *Entrance:* US$3.

ON-SITE AMENITIES: Dafeng Milu National Reserve has a museum, artificial lake with boating, bird garden, restaurant, and souvenir shops as well as a hall devoted to its namesake deer. Yancheng Nature Reserve has two museums specializing in fossils and seashells, a conference room, offices, a waterfowl lake, fish ponds, and parking. There is a hotel and restaurant in the village of Xinyanggang.

BEST TIMES: October to February is considered best for bird-watching.

FIELD NOTES: The reserve can be explored on one's own or with a hired guide; www.chinaleisuretours.com.

MOUNT FANJING NATIONAL NATURE RESERVE

GUIZHOU, CHINA

China's Mount Fanjing is a holy site to the followers of Buddha, and the name of the mountain means "the pure land." It is an apt name for Mount Fanjing National Nature Reserve, which encompasses 27,711 acres of what is considered the best example of a virgin subtropical forest. The 352-square-mile reserve is 80% forest, particularly in the valleys and at the foot of the mountain.

Created in 1976, the reserve protects the rare and endangered species found within its borders. The most crucial is the Guizhou golden monkey, of which only about 100 are known to survive. Because of its threatened status this

primate has not been exhibited abroad. The reserve is home to about 850 Guizhou snub-nosed monkeys, and it is believed that this monkey is found nowhere else. Just 20 years ago there were only 350 individuals, so the reserve is doing its job well.

Visitors may be lucky enough to spot a clouded leopard, south China tiger, or giant salamander, although their numbers are low. Pangolins and antelope are two more protected animals that can be seen in the reserve. Wildlife enthusiasts can look for some of the 57 mammals, 173 birds, 34 amphibians, and 40 reptiles that make their home here. Plant lovers may find one of the 15 rare plant species among the almost 2,000 types of plants that grow here. The dove tree, whose flowers resemble doves from a distance, is found in the reserve.

Geology buffs should keep an eye out for sericite-quartz-schist rock formations. The iron, manganese, and mica within these rocks create multicolored patterns that are a photographer's dream. These rocks are estimated to be more than 1.4 billion years old, and are prized by collectors. However, no samples can be taken from the reserve.

LOCATION: The reserve straddles Jiangkou, Yinjang, and Songtao counties in northeast Guizhou Province.

HOURS OF OPERATION: Year-round, 24/7.

CONTACT: *Hotel reservation and tour booking* (customer service): Tel: 861059059011 (China), 8584275213 (USA) or 8666522041 (toll-free), 4169079850 (Canada), 442079932117 (UK), 8207070488202 (Korea), 813-45300606 (Japan); Fax : 861051659622 or 861061763374 (China); 8582250716 (USA); Hotline: 4008106868 (China; mobile and direct phone); email: sales@sinohotel.com.

COST: *Entrance:* November 1 to April 30, US$5; May 1 to October 31, US$7.

ON-SITE AMENITIES: Tourist center, tea stalls, communal toilets. **Hotel at Golden Summit:** Referred to as Jinding; simple accommodations but ideally situated.

BEST TIMES: October through February.

FIELD NOTES: Bring rain gear and umbrellas. Temperatures range from 33.8°F to 50°F in January and from 62.6°F to 82.4°F in July. *Mount Fanjing:* The climb is strenuous, check with your doctor before attempting the hike; the climb includes 7,000 vertical steps. Foreigners must register with the police before climbing. Minivans are available for US$2 per person; a porter costs US$29 one way. Numerous tea stalls are located along the path.

Tent camping is allowed at the top, though be prepared for wet and windy conditions and bring your own equipment.

MOUNT WUYI NATURE RESERVE

CHINA

The area around China's Mount Wuyi has an important historical role; it is considered the cradle of New Confucianism and today is protected within the boundaries of Mount Wuyi Nature Reserve. Established in 1979 and named a World Heritage Site, this 220-square-mile area is the site of the largest continental subtropical forest ecosystem in southeast China—90% of the reserve is forest. Mount Hianggang, the tallest peak in southeast China at 7,080 feet above sea level, is also found in the reserve.

The reserve is known for its rich diversity of wildlife, including many rare and unique species. The fauna is amazingly diverse and abundant here, with 5,000 species of animals and almost that many types of insects. And researchers believe there are still unrecorded organ-

isms in the area. Visitors may spot David's parrotbills, Chinese tigers, clouded leopards, black muntjacs, Cabot's trogopans, Chinese black-headed pheasants, Chinese giant salamanders, golden kaiserihind butterflies, white and silver pheasants, macaques, zibets, Mandarin ducks, and pangolins.

People interested in cultural history will be treated to the site of a Min Yue village, which was discovered in 1958. Pottery kilns, rock paintings, and cave dwellings are among the sights. And those looking for a thrilling and different perspective on the reserve can take an invigorating raft ride down Nine-Bend Stream.

LOCATION: About 3 miles from Wuyishan City in Fujian Province in eastern China.

HOURS OF OPERATION: Year-round, 24/7.

CONTACT: *Reserve office:* Wuyishan Nature Reserve Administration, Sangang, 354315 Wuyishan City, Fujian Province, China; Tel: 865995305198; Fax: 865-995305118.

COST: *Entrance:* US$12.

ON-SITE AMENITIES: A tourist service area beside the reserve offers shopping, museums, a memorial hall, a painting academy, hotels, viewing points for the reserve, and medical and rescue services.

BEST TIMES: October through February.

FIELD NOTES: The Biodiversity Protection Area within the reserve strictly controls the number of visitors that are allowed onto the grounds. The area around Mount Wuyi is humid and foggy, with plenty of rain, so be sure to bring rain gear and shoes that handle mud well. The reserve can be explored on one's own or by guided tour. For more information on tours and booking visit www.chinadiscover.net/china-tour/fujian guide/fujian-wuyi-mountain.htm.

BANDIPUR NATIONAL PARK WILDLIFE SANCTUARY

INDIA

There is a certain magic in sitting on the back of the elephant as you move through the wilds to see a variety of exotic plants and animals. Bandipur National Park Wildlife Sanctuary is one of India's oldest and most prestigious preserves. An important part of Project Tiger, the sanctuary encompasses more than 300 square miles, and the Moyar, Kabini, and Nagur rivers all wind their

way through the park, offering visitors a wide array of options for their naturalist activities.

Visitors to the sanctuary have the chance to see the magnificent animals of the Indian subcontinent in their natural environment. Look for tigers, elephants, sloth bears, and four-horned antelope. In addition, bird-watchers will be able to observe the woodpecker, warbler, weaverbird, kingfisher, and the drongo.

For those who appreciate the natural splendor of preserved and protected sanctuaries, the Bandipur will not disappoint. The park offers guided safaris, which will help you make the most of your experience here.

A variety of accommodations, designed to suit every lifestyle and pocketbook, is available. There are resorts, hotels, guesthouses, and forest guesthouses. The resorts and premium hotels offer every possible amenity. Visitors can also choose four safaris a day (two in the morning and two in the evening) conducted by expert guides.

Bandipur is part of India's Project Tiger, a government program designed to ensure the safety and welfare of the indigenous tigers. Bandipur is one of the leaders of conservation efforts in the area. The guides and site officials will be happy to help visitors learn how to coexist harmoniously with their surroundings.

LOCATION: Southern India, about 50 miles from Mysore and 130 miles from Bangalore, between the Western Ghat and the Nilgiri mountains.

HOURS OF OPERATION: Guided safaris by van, jeep, or elephant begin at 6:30 a.m.; the last one ends at 6:30 p.m.

CONTACT: *Park office:* Web: www.bandipur.net. *Tour options*: Web: www.india-wildlife.com/bandipur-national-park.html.

COST: *Safaris:* From US$32 (non-nationals); depends on mode of transport.

ON-SITE AMENITIES: Different size vehicles for parties of varying sizes. Expert, knowledgeable guides conduct safaris.

BEST TIMES: Year-round.

FIELD NOTES: Book accommodations and safaris in advance. Recording devices and other music players are not allowed on the safaris. Lightweight, neutral-colored clothing is advised for warmer weather. Binoculars or field glasses are helpful.

CHINNAR WILDLIFE SANCTUARY

INDIA

Nestled in the rain shadow region of the Western Ghats, Chinnar Wildlife Sanctuary offers a wide range of wilderness opportunities; visitors can try river trips, hiking expeditions, or nature walks and can even visit observation tree houses or camp in the thorny scrub forest. The sanctuary, at more than 60 square miles, is the second largest habitat for the giant grizzled squirrel, an endangered species of India. On a trip to Chinnar, visitors may encounter the elephant, gaur, panther, spotted deer, sambar, and Hanuman monkey as well as the largest number of reptilian species in Kerala, including the mugger crocodile, and the illustrious and extremely rare white bison. Tigers, leopards, nilgiri tars, the common langurs, and bonnet macaques make their home in the sanctuary. And bird-watchers will find more than 225 recorded species of birds. The flora is as captivating as the fauna, with more than 1,000 flowering plants, providing a unique habitat for Chinnar's many animals.

Visitors shouldn't miss the Marayoor sandal forest and the beautiful Thoovanam waterfalls. With its habitats ranging from high-altitude shoal-grassland to dry thorny scrub and its ecological, floral, geomorphological, and cultural significance, Chinnar is regarded as one of the most distinctive protected areas in the Western Ghats region.

LOCATION: About 71 miles from Coimbatore, southwest India.

HOURS OF OPERATION: Year-round, 24/7.

CONTACT: *Forest information center:* Wildlife Warden's Office, Munnar PO-685612; Tel: 04865231587; Web: www .chinnar.org; email: roywlw@chinnar .org.

COST: *Entrance* (non-nationals): Adults, US$13; students and children (under 12 years), US$1. *Video and movie camera fees:* US$19. *Camera fee* (still picture): US$3. *Vehicles:* heavy, US$19; light, US$6.

ON-SITE AMENITIES: Wildlife viewing, trekking, camping, wildlife watchtower, interpretational activities, and medicinal garden. Various accommodations can be found in the near town of Munnar; for more information visit www.munnar.com.

BEST TIMES: January through September.

FIELD NOTES: Chinnar offers visitors the unique opportunity to watch wildlife at close quarters from the road without the need to go deep into the jungle. *Tours:* Tours for Chinnar and Kerala can be booked through www.luxurykerala.com.

GIR NATIONAL PARK AND WILDLIFE SANCTUARY

KARNATAKA, INDIA

Located 242 miles from Delhi, the Gir National Park and Wildlife Sanctuary is one of India's most impressive wildlife preserves. It is best known for its bird-watching, facilities, and experts, but the park offers world-class fauna and flora. More than 877 square miles of varying ecosystems provide the visitor with the opportunity to journey into five distinct habitats and view animals living as nature intended.

This is one of the most important large feline sanctuaries in India; 300 lions and as many leopards make their home here. Visitors are also likely to see spotted deer, blue bulls, chousinghas (the world's only four-horned antelope), jackals, striped hyenas, jungle cats, rusty-spotted cats, langurs, porcupines, and black-naped Indian hares.

If you get tired of furry mammals, take the opportunity to find some of the more than 40 species of amphibians and reptiles at the park, including the marsh crocodile. The invertebrates and butterflies demand their due, with more than 2,000 varieties found at the park.

But it would be a crime not to spend some time acquainting yourself with

the ornithological benefits of the area—even if you're not a birder. More than 250 species of birds can be found at Gir at any one time. From the majestic and endangered lesser florican and saras crane to the predators such as the long-billed vulture, Indian white-backed vulture, red-headed (king) vulture, and various eagles, the park offers a stunning array. Other birds can be seen right from the park's lodge, such as the painted sandgrouse, gray francolin, quail, and Asian paradise flycatcher.

The park's safaris can be individually customized; but the standard package is a comprehensive 9-day and 10-night trip. Gir also sports a beautiful lodge, with one main building and four cottages, all located in a mango grove.

LOCATION: Roughly 30 miles from Veraval and 240 miles from Delhi.

HOURS OF OPERATION: Year-round.

CONTACT: *Park office:* Tel: 911202551963; Web: www.girnationalpark.com (commercial site that provides good information about the park).

COST: Depends on tour selection.

ON-SITE AMENITIES: Tour facilities and guides, lodge with shared rooms and separate cabins, a variety of cuisines available for full-meal services.

BEST TIMES: October to April.

FIELD NOTES: Book accommodations, tours, and safaris in advance. Temperate clothing is advised. Binoculars and field glasses are helpful. The nearest town (Veraval) is renowned for its fishing and seafood.

JIM CORBETT NATIONAL PARK

INDIA

India's oldest national park has had several names since its inception in 1936, but in 1956, it was renamed Jim Corbett National Park in honor of a hunter and naturalist well known for his writings and photos of the area's wildlife and Bengal tiger. He was known to have successfully hunted several man-eaters, but later he was better known for his research than for his hunting skills.

Today, there are only 3,000–4,000 Bengal tigers remaining, spread across several countries. The tiger is subject to intensive preservation efforts at the park. In fact, Project Tiger, working in conjunction with the World Wildlife Fund, has its headquarters here. Because these magnificent cats blend so well into their surroundings, they can be difficult for visitors to spot during a visit to the 201-square-mile park. Tigers may be the big draw but wildlife lovers will find a variety of other rare animals throughout the park's mountainous area. Look for the hog deer and the Indian pangolin, for example. Wild boars are plentiful, as are elephants and leopards. Common otters, Himalayan black bears, and ghorals (goat/antelope hybrids) also roam the parklands. Birders will enjoy looking for many of the 585 types of birds that live at or stop by the park during migration.

Visitors can join an elephant safari or a more modern open-vehicle safari. Be warned that this park is very popular, and the 70,000 yearly visitors may harm the ecosystem. Park officials are trying to find a balance between protecting the environment and welcoming guests to this appealing site.

LOCATION: Ramnagar, approximately 108 miles from Delhi.

HOURS OF OPERATION: Nov 15–June 15, 6 a.m. to 11 a.m. and 2:30 p.m. to 5:30 p.m.; closed June 16–Nov 14, during the monsoons.

CONTACT: *Park office:* Tel: 919719251997, 915947284200, or 919811403431; Web: www.jimcorbettnationalpark.com; email: info@corbettnationalpark.com. *Safari:* visit the park's website.

COST: *Entrance:* US$8.

ON-SITE AMENITIES: Park admission center, rest houses. For more information on accommodations and tours visit www.indianwildlifeportal.com.

BEST TIMES: Mid November through January.

FIELD NOTES: Visitors need to obtain permits from the park admission center at Ramnagar; allow 30 minutes for the paperwork. Park officials advise wearing brown and green clothing to best fit in with the environment, avoid wearing perfumes, and speak softly. Vehicle safaris are the most convenient way to travel within the park; vehicles can be rented from the park admission center at Ramnagar.

KANHA NATIONAL PARK

INDIA

Established as a national park in 1955 and a key part of the Kanha Tiger Reserve, Kanha National Park is dedicated to the preservation and protection of the tiger while offering an astounding array of other wildlife. The staff here has been instrumental in saving several species from local extinction, so visitors to the park are able to see threatened species such as swamp deer (barasingha), bison, barking and black deer, blackbucks, chousinghas, nilgais, and mouse deer. The park is also home to sloth bears, jackals, Indian foxes, porcupines, hyenas, jungle cats, pythons, monkeys, mongoose, and leopards. Visitors are never far from an exhilarating wildlife encounter.

Known as the land of the tiger, Kanha offers a variety of safari options. Experienced guides are available to lead visitors on a number of tours from elephant-back safaris to vehicles. Self-drives are allowed if you have a guide with you. Kanha clearly offers something for every traveler's needs.

There are several resorts a short walk from the park proper, and all provide modern conveniences in a beautiful locale. Expert tours of the park and the region can be arranged through your accommodation provider. The park is close to Khajuraho and Pana in Madhya Pradesh, making for convenient and accessible sightseeing and touring in the heart of India.

LOCATION: 165 miles from Nagpur Airport, Madhya Pradesh, India.

HOURS OF OPERATION: Daily, Dec–July; closed July–mid Nov, during the monsoons.

CONTACT: *Park office:* Tel:911127948870. Website: www.kanhanationalpark.com.

COST: Depends on tour and accommodations.

ON-SITE AMENITIES: Museum. *Lodging:* The park's website has a link to **Garhwal Himalayan Expedition,** but many travel and expedition companies are available. The following resorts are located close to the park's main entrance. **Kanha Jungle Lodge:** 19 twin-bed rooms, with en-suite baths, running hot/cold water; dining room, serving Indian and Continental cuisine; call 912224042211. **Tuli Tiger Resort:** 18 well-appointed rooms with 24-hour room service, laundry/dry-cleaning, telephones; fax and conference facility; restaurant serving continental and Indian cuisine; call: 91712253478488 or 91712661216064; fax 917122534473,

or visit www.tuligroup.com. **Wild Chalet Resort:** Self-contained cottages with modern amenities; restaurant serving Indian, Chinese, and continental cuisine; call 912224042211.

BEST TIMES: Late November to March.

FIELD NOTES: Advance booking of tours and safaris is highly recommended. Field glasses and/or binoculars and a camera are must-haves. It can get pretty warm even in the cool season so pack a hat, light and neutral-colored clothing, and a jacket for cooler evenings. Comfortable footwear is always important, although visiting the park is generally by vehicle.

KAZIRANGA NATIONAL PARK

INDIA

Founded in 1905, Kaziranga National Park has played a crucial role in protecting the endangered Indian one-horned rhinoceros, the second-largest type of rhino, which has been poached for its horn's supposed healing powers. At one time, its numbers dwindled to approximately 100, but owing to conservation efforts there are now

about 2,500 individuals. Visitors to Kaziranga have the chance to see this rare mammal.

Within the park's 106,245 acres, visitors may also spot hog deer, capped langurs, and leopards. The park was named a Tiger Reserve in 2006 and is a major breeding site for the Indian elephant, wild Asiatic water buffalo, and eastern

swamp deer. The only Indian ape, the hoolock gibbon, lives here, too.

Birdlife International has recognized Kaziaranga for its conservation efforts. Bird-watchers will have ample opportunity to add to their life lists. Species such as Oriental honey buzzards; Pallas fishing, white-tailed, and gray-headed eagles; black-shouldered, black, and Brahminy kites; and Himalayan griffons can be spotted. During migration season, visitors will find graylag and bar-headed geese, ruddy shelducks, and falcated ducks taking a break from their journey.

Kaziranga offers guided tours in open 4-wheel-drive vehicles and on elephant back; these are a great way to experience up-close viewing of wildlife, especially rhinos. The tours leave from the park's administration center in Kohora and must be booked in advance. Other wildlife viewing includes a boat trip down Brahmaputra River and observation from the five towers located throughout the park.

LOCATION: Northeast India's Assam Province, 14 miles from Bokakhat and 135 miles from Guwahati, the major gateway city in the area.

HOURS OF OPERATION: Nov 1–Apr, 8 a.m. to 11 a.m. and 2 p.m. to 4:30 p.m.

CONTACT: **Kaziranga-National-Park .com:** 611, D.D.A. Complex, Plot No. 4, District Center, Laxmi Nagar, New Delhi, 110092, India; Tel: 911142153655, 911142153755, or 911142153955; Fax: 911122456488; Web: www.kaziranga-national-park.com. (commercial site that provides good information about the park).

COST: *Entrance:* US$5. *Camera:* US$1.50. *Elephant ride:* US$5. *Vehicle tour:* US$20, includes entrance fee.

ON-SITE AMENITIES: Park administration center at Kohora, observation towers. *Lodging:* Five nearby resorts offer a variety of accommodations and amenities. **Bonhabi Resort:** The closest to the park, with 12 cottages in sight of tropical rain forest and rice paddies, modern facilities, en-suite bathroom, hot/cold water; on-site safaris directly into the park; visit www.Kaziranga-National-Park.com.

BEST TIMES: March and April.

FIELD NOTES: Hiking is not allowed because of the possibility of unpredictable encounters with wild animals. Motorists must be accompanied by a park guide. During the summer, the area is subject to heavy rains; flooding can occur.

LITTLE RANN OF KUTCH WILDLIFE SANCTUARY

INDIA

Established in 1972, Little Rann of Kutch Wildlife Sanctuary encompasses a terrain ranging from rocky and thorn scrub to lakes and marshes that includes desert, plains, and grasslands ecosystems. And, despite its name, it is one of the largest sanctuaries in India, covering almost 2,000 square miles.

The animal that put the sanctuary on the map for wildlife enthusiasts is the Asiatic wild ass, the last survivor of the wild horse family on the Indian subcontinent. A tall mammal with chestnut brown fur, it moves at an extremely swift pace. Approximately 2,800 individuals are thought to exist at the present time. Other especially notable animals found at the sanctuary are the blue bull (India's largest antelope), chinkara (Indian gazelle), and desert wolf. Visitors can also look out for Indian foxes, hares, and jungle cats.

The sanctuary is a breeding ground for flamingos; houbara bustards; spotted and Indian sandgrouses; bustard quail; and steppe, imperial, and short-toed eagles. It also serves as a staging ground for pelicans, cranes, and storks. Bird-watchers should consider a winter visit because migratory birds stop here during that time.

LOCATION: 93 miles from Ahmedabad in north India near the Pakistan border.

HOURS OF OPERATION: Year-round.

CONTACT: *Tour options:* Web: www.indianwildlife.com; email: info@indianwildliferesort.com.

COST: *Entrance* (per person, per day): US$7.

ON-SITE AMENITIES: There are several lodging options, including a government guesthouse in Dharangedra, a government department rest house at Dasada, and the **Desert Courser Camp** in Zainabad. Forest lodges are available at Madarihat, just outside the sanctuary. Hot lunches are available with advance notice at **Fatima Manzil**, a nearby hotel.

BEST TIMES: November through March.

FIELD NOTES: Be sure to bring plenty of water while on safari; temperatures have been known to climb to 110°F. During monsoon season, from July through September, the entire region can become flooded.

MANAS NATIONAL PARK AND TIGER RESERVE

INDIA

Designated a UNESCO Natural World Heritage site, a Project Tiger Reserve, an Elephant Reserve, and a Biosphere Reserve, Manas National Park and Tiger Reserve is not to be missed. This park is located in the Himalayan foothills and is home to a wealth of wildlife and a haven for many highly endangered species.

On any given day, visitors may come across assamese macques, rhesus macques, common langurs, or large or small Indian civets, common palms or Himalayan civets, and binturongs (Asian bear cats). The sharp-eyed observer may spot the common mongoose, small Indian mongoose, dhole, jackal, and, with luck, Indian fox. Other mammals living here are the Himalayan black bear, yellow-throated materna, Chinese badger, and yellow-bellied weasel, sambar, hog deer, wild boar, three- and five-striped palm squirrel, and Mayan giant squirrel.

Once abused by poaching, political unrest, and general neglect, the park is now a sanctuary for some 20 of the world's endangered species, including

the royal Bengal tiger and the famed black panther. The one-horned rhino, all but lost to poachers, is being reintroduced to the park. Visitors still have a chance of seeing capped and golden langurs, slow lorises, Asiatic elephants, and Asiatic water buffalo, clouded leopards, Indian pangolins, sloth bears, golden cats and fishing cats, swamp deer, hispid hares, particolored flying squirrels, and Gangetic dolphins, also known as river dolphins.

LOCATION: 109 miles from Guwahati, the gateway city to northeast India.

HOURS OF OPERATION: Year-round.

CONTACT: *Park office:* Field Director, Manas Tiger Reserves, PO Barpeta Road, Kamrup, Assam, India 781315; Tel: 00913666261413; Fax: 00913666260253. *Tourist information office:* Barpeta Road, Assam, India 781315; Tel: 0366632749. *Tours:* Station Road, Guwahati, Assam, India 781001; Tel: 0361547102.

COST: *Entrance:* Vehicle, US$7.50, plus US$6 per person. *Camera:* Additional fees apply, depending on the type of equipment. *Tours:* Elephant-back tour, 3 hours, US$20 per person; boat, 8 hours, US$190 per eight-passenger boat.

ON-SITE AMENITIES: There are no special permit requirements to visit Manas; however, to stay inside the park you must obtain permission from the field director's office. Rest houses operated by the tourism department are located at Banshari and Barpeta Road. The state department offers two bungalows to rent at reasonable rates inside the forest at Mathanguri, but you have to bring your own provisions; you can hire a cook, if desired. Campsites are also available.

BEST TIMES: November through April.

FIELD NOTES: Safaris providing the ultimate wildlife experience are offered from Mothanguri on elephant back or by boat. Open-vehicle safaris through the park are also available by private hire. Because each tour is unique, try to do all three. Be sure to check if the tour includes food, or else you will need to buy provisions and general supplies locally and carry them into the park. A few of the tour companies offer meal-inclusive packages, but pay attention to what is offered. Plan on a 3-night visit to see the park.

NAGARHOLE NATIONAL PARK

INDIA

It seems that India has many wildlife preservation parks, but some offer more opportunities than others. Nagarhole National Park, also known as Rajiv Gandhi National Park, should be at the top of your list, even when compared to Bandipur (see page 269), its better-known neighbor. Formerly the private hunting grounds of the royal family of Mysore, Nagarhole was established as a park in 1955. Its almost 425 square miles are bordered by the Kabini Reservoir, which separates it from Bandipur. Nagarhole park has a healthy tiger-to-predator ratio and is part of the nation's renowned Tiger Reserve system. Tiger, bison, and elephant populations are denser and better cared for here than in almost any other park in the world. In addition, the jackal, panther, gaur, muntjac, sambar, spotted deer, mongoose, civet cat, and hyena all find a home in the park.

The park is also known for its reptile population. Visitors will see king cobras, kraits, pythons, vipers, tortoises, monitor lizards, and various toads all within the park's boundaries. The can-

opy of the rosewood, teak, sandalwood, and silver oak trees is home for rare birds, including the endangered Malabar trogon, the Malabar pied hornbill, and the crested hawk-eagle.

LOCATION: About 31 miles from Mysore. The forest reserve office is located within the confines of the park and is the starting point for all safari options.

HOURS OF OPERATION: Year-round, daily, 6 a.m. to 6 p.m. Game drives are conducted in the early morning, 6 a.m. to 9 a.m., and early evening hours, 3 p.m. to 5 p.m.

CONTACT: *Park office:* Conservator of Forests, Wildlife South Circle, Aranya

Bhavan, Ashokapuram, Mysore 570008; Tel: 0821480901.

COST: *Entrance* (per person): US$5.

ON-SITE AMENITIES: Forest reserve office. Safaris by open-top vehicle, boat, and elephant back, book by contacting the conservator of forests or through your accommodations. *Lodging:* **Kabini River Lodge:** Within the confines of the park, offers luxury accommodations with all modern amenities; 14 rooms with river views; restaurant serving Indian, Chinese, and continental cuisine; from US$65 per night; will book tours; call Jungle Lodges and Resorts, 918228264402 91822826440203 or visit www.jungle lodges.com. **Jungle Inn:** Located near the main Veeranahosahalli entrance; provides basic accommodations; write jungleinn@nivalink.com. **King's Sanctuary:** offers luxury accommodations; visit www.kingssanctuary.com.

BEST TIMES: October through May. Optimal wildlife viewing March through April.

FIELD NOTES: Kabini River Lodge was rated by the British *Tatler's Travel Guide* as one of the top five wildlife resorts in the world. Boat rides on the Kabini River provide optimal elephant viewing, because the animals tend to congregate on the banks; visitors are often treated to as many as 150–200 elephants on any given summer evening. A minimum 3-night stay is recommended.

PANNA NATIONAL PARK

INDIA

Panna National Park, roughly 543 square miles in size, is located almost adjacent to Khajuraho, one of India's most popular tourist destinations. Established in 1981 as an official Tiger Reserve, the primary goal of the park is the preservation and support of the big cat population, specifically the tiger. In addition to the tigers, which are given priority here, Panna is home to the panther, blue bull, sambar, chinkara, spotted deer, sloth bear, wild dog, wolf, jackal, monkey, and crocodile.

Bird-watchers can have fun trying to see as many of the 200 species of birds that are found in the park. Many are common to India and can be photographed and viewed with little effort.

More exotic birds, such as the white-necked stork, bareheaded goose, honey buzzard, king vulture, blossom-headed parakeet, paradise flycatcher, and slaty-headed scimitar babbler can be spotted, especially when on a guided tour.

The park's deciduous forests are interspersed with verdant grasslands, providing the perfect big cat environment. The teaks and other trees plus the thorny woodlands support the nesting, hunting, and survival of much of the park's wildlife.

Most daily safaris must be arranged before arrival and are led by expert local guides. The park officials offer an hour-long boat ride that showcases the waterside wildlife and natural beauty of the park.

LOCATION: Chattarpur, Madhya Pradesh.

HOURS OF OPERATION: Year-round, 6:30 a.m. to 10:30 a.m. and 2:30 p.m. to 5:30 p.m.

CONTACT: *Field director:* Tel: 077-32252135; Web: www.forest.mp.gov.in/pannal.html. *Tours:* Web: www.wildlife-tour-india.com/wildlife-in-india/panna-national-park.html.

COST: *Entrance* (3-day pass, non-nationals): Single drive, US$65; two drives, US$95; three drives, US$130. Additional fees apply for elephant safaris, use of watchtowers, and personal guides.

ON-SITE AMENITIES: Vehicle safari, elephant rides, Sher darshan and Ken River boat safaris. For more information contact the field director. *Lodging:* Accommodations are available at **Ken River Lodge, Lawania Jungle Resort,** and **Jass Trident Hotel** (visit www.khajuraho.org.uk/hotels/hotel-jass-trident-khajuraho.html) located in nearby Khajuraho; for more information, contact the field director.

BEST TIMES: October through June.

FIELD NOTES: Guides are highly recommended. Refrain from using perfumes and colognes while on safari because the scents attract honeybees. Early morning and late afternoon safaris provide optimal wildlife viewing. Private vehicles can be hired at Khajuraho/Panna; 4-wheel-drive vehicles are needed for wildlife watching and traveling through the park owing to rough terrain, unpaved roads, and steep inclines. Carry drinking water. Nearby sites worth visiting are the ancient temples at Khajuraho and the Panna diamond mines.

PENCH TIGER RESERVE

INDIA

The Pench Tiger Reserve has been called God's own country. Others know it as the area in which Mowgli, the wolf child, was discovered by British officer John Moor; Rudyard Kipling's *The Jungle Book* was based on this boy.

Declared a national park in 1983 (and part of the Tiger Project in 1992), Pench is home to an abundant diversity of land animals and birds. Visitors will try to see the park's primary carnivores—the tiger and leopard, which stay hidden among the foliage. The big cats are waiting for spotted deer, sambars, nilgais, barking deer, langurs, chinkaras, wild boars, and four-horned antelope. Both the gaur, a coarse grazer, and the sloth bear, an omnivore, are found here. Be on the lookout for the wild dog, wolf, jackal, fox, hyena, or jungle cat.

Bird-watchers will find many species to grab their attention. The park is home to orioles, hornbills, flycatchers, warblers, and raptors, among others. Teak, bamboo, and tendu provide habitat for these birds. Reptiles also inhabit the area. Visitors can see monitor lizards, rat snakes, the leaf nosed vine snake, Indian pythons, cobras, and both the krait and Russell viper.

Attractions include a boat ride on the river Pench to view the fantastic landscapes and the riverine forests, teeming with water birds and other wildlife, and to visit Mowgli's Den, just 5 miles from Khawasa.

LOCATION: Entrance to the park is Turia Gate, 7 miles from Khawasa on Nagpur Jabalpur NH-7 on the border of Madhya Pradesh and Maharashtra.

HOURS OF OPERATION: Oct 1–June 30. *Jungle drive:* 6 a.m. to 11 a.m. and 3 p.m. to 6 p.m.

CONTACT: *Main office:* Pench Tiger Reserve, Turia, District Seoni, Madhya Preadesh, India; Tel: 917695232832. *Jabalpur office:* 917612620072; Web: www

.mowglisden.com. **Pench Jungle Camp:** Avarghani, District Seoni, Madhya Pradesh, India; Tel: 9107695232817; Web: www.wildlife-camp-india.com. *Tours:* http://pench.naturesafariindia.com.

COST: *Entrance* (per person): US$4. Accommodation costs depend on options and tour; contact **Pench Jungle Camp** directly for current rates.

ON-SITE AMENITIES: Rest houses. **Pench Jungle Camp:** 12 deluxe safari tents with all modern conveniences; dining hall serving vegetarian and non-vegetarian, Indian, continental, and Chinese cuisine; bar and library.

BEST TIMES: March through June.

FIELD NOTES: Tours of the park can be conducted in your own vehicle or by hired vehicle. Tourists visiting the park are required to have a guide with them at all times.

RANTHAMBHORE NATIONAL PARK

INDIA

The Ranthambhore National Park is an official Project Tiger Reserve, dedicated to protecting and promoting the native tiger. Project Tiger's efforts in wildlife management, eco-development, and protective measures have helped preserve not only the tigers but their natural habitat as well.

A trip to the Ranthambhore offers numerous options for nature-loving visitors. The safaris are the jewel in Ranthambhore's crown, but enthusiasts will find world-class bird-watching, nature walks, and hiking. Furthermore, local rural villagers welcome visitors and look forward to sharing their culture and heritage with others. Several ancient temples and forts are found throughout the park, which is the only

dry, deciduous tiger habitat in the world.

The park's Ranthambhore Bagh is a resort that sits comfortably between luxury and nature; guests enjoy two safaris a day (from October to June). Casual birdwatchers and ornithologists alike come to the park to see and photograph the 330 species of bird here. Dastkari Kendra is a local market where visitors can purchase locally made crafts, art, and clothes.

LOCATION: Approximately 195 miles southeast of Delhi.

HOURS OF OPERATION: Safaris depart mornings 6:30 a.m. to 7:30 a.m. and afternoons, 3 p.m. to 4 p.m., depending on the time of year.

CONTACT: *Park office:* Tel: 917462221728; Web: www.ranthamborenationalpark

.com; email: info@ranthamborena tionalpark.com.

COST: *Entrance:* Included in most safari packages. **Ranthambore Bagh** (per day, per person): Depends on accommodations; rooms, US$57–$114; permanent tents, US$72–$129; safaris, US$22–$29; for more information visit www.rant hambhore.com.

ON-SITE AMENITIES: Various accommodation and tour options are offered. Most of the lodgings have all the amenities required; the park has none.

BEST TIMES: October through June.

FIELD NOTES: Visitors cannot travel through the park independently. Due to the nature of the Project Tiger Reserves, booking vehicles early is strongly recommended. Vehicle use is strictly limited, and on-site bookings are rarely available.

TIGERLAND RESORT

INDIA

In spite of the sound of its name, Tigerland Resort is no amusement park, nor is it exclusively about tigers, although they are the chief focus. The resort's property is situated in the Kanha Forest, the location of Kanha National Park. The quality of the fauna and flora found here demonstrate the best of India's nature preservation efforts. Along with the tigers, the Kanha area is the home to animals that are rarely seen elsewhere, such as the sloth bear, leopard, and Indian wild dog. The most common prey for these carnivores is the

chital (a type of deer), which is plentiful in Kanha.

Within the Kanha Forest, visitors find an impressive variety of environments: lowland mixed forests, meadows, highland forests, dry areas, bamboo stands, sloping terrain, open grasslands, lakes, and wetlands. This variety of natural habitats offers shelter and food for abundant wildlife, including indigenous deer and their predators and the numerous species of birds.

Tigerland Resort has been hosting visitors to India's famed Kanha Forest since 1996. Their 23 rooms and cottages offer a respite for the weary traveler. The on-site restaurant offers multiethnic cuisine suitable for every palette, and

their resident experts are happy to assist guests in obtaining vehicles, guides, and everything necessary to make their stay the vacation of a lifetime.

LOCATION: Kanha National Park in the Maikal Hills at Satpura Range.

HOURS OF OPERATION: Year-round.

CONTACT: *Main office:* Tel: 917612678198, 917614045528, or 917614045907; Web: www.tigerlandresort.com; email: tiger land_in@yahoo.com.

COST: *Lodging* (per person): 2 nights/3 days, US$275; 3 nights/4 days, US$395; contact lodge for longer or shorter visits.

ON-SITE AMENITIES: Private reserve, private restaurant, cabins and lodge rooms, laundry services, private tours, guided safaris.

BEST TIMES: October through September.

FIELD NOTES: Due to the nature of tiger reserves, booking vehicles early is strongly recommended. Vehicle use is strictly limited, and on-site bookings are rarely available. Binoculars, field books, comfortable walking shoes, and lightweight clothing are recommended.

VELAVADAR NATIONAL PARK

· INDIA ·

Velavadar National Park's 21 square miles were once used as a grazing area for the maharajahi of Bhavnagar's cattle. Today the park, which was founded in 1976, is dedicated to the preservation and support of the indigenous blackbuck and the threatened population of the lesser florican, a large bird in the bustard family. The population of the florican is plummeting throughout India, but the largest current group is found within the confines of the Velavadar.

The blackbuck, an endangered member of the antelope family, possesses phenomenal speed and grace. Visitors can also see the blackbuck's prime predator, the endangered Indian wolf, plus the blue bull antelope, Indian fox, jackal, jungle cat, hyena, wild pig, and hare.

The birdlife in Velavadar is impressive and extensive. Birding enthusiasts have the opportunity to see sandgrouse and larks as well as one of the world's largest harrier roosts. Special tours are available to help birders make the most of their time in the park, whether they want to observe or photograph.

The park is mostly made up of tropical savanna grasslands, which are under constant threat from encroaching human settlements, the need for arable land, and the use of the existing grasslands for cattle grazing.

LOCATION: 40 miles from Bhavnagar, Gujarat Province in northwest India.

HOURS OF OPERATION: Daily, Oct–June; 7:30 a.m. to 6 p.m.

CONTACT: *Park office:* Tel: 0278428644. *Reservations:* Assistant Forest Conservator, Velavadar Black Buck National Park, Velavadar, PO Vallabhipur, Bhavnagar. *Tours:* Web: www.indiawildlifesafari.net/Velavadar_NationalPark.htm.

COST: *Entrance*: US$5. *Guide:* US$8. *Vehicle:* US$10.

ON-SITE AMENITIES: Interpretation center. On-site amenities are negligible so carry what you think you will need or contact your guide to ensure that he or she will provide the necessities. *Lodging:* The forest department runs **Kaliyar Bhavan Forest Lodge**, situated near the park; pay your entrance fee here. Contact the range forest officer at the park's address.

BEST TIMES: October through March; evening hours are best for wildlife viewing.

FIELD NOTES: Guides are mandatory and can be hired at the main gate entrance. Cameras, field books, and appropriate clothing are all suggested. Fees apply for still and video cameras. The harrier roost here is one of the world's best, with numbers reaching into the thousands at a single sighting.

BALI BARAT NATIONAL PARK AND MARINE RESERVE

BALI, INDONESIA

One of the species listed by the World Conservation Union as being critically endangered is the strikingly beautiful Bali starling, which lives and fights against the odds in Bali Barat National Park and Marine Reserve. Researchers have estimated that there are only 1,000 of these birds left in captivity; furthermore it is the only endemic bird species in Bali. At one time it was believed that there were less than six of these birds left in the wild; in a concerted effort by park managers and international conservation the Bali starling has so far survived.

Although the park was specifically created for the preservation of the Bali starling, an important secondary concern at Bali Barat is the support and preservation of the wild banteng, the stock from which most of the Bali cattle are derived. Once the parklands were

set aside, wildlife within the boundaries has again begun to flourish.

There are numerous habitats within the park's 470 square miles, including savanna, mangroves, montane forests, mixed-monsoon forests, and coral islands. The middle of the park is highlighted by four volcanic mountains.

Visitors to the area are able to be in close contact with an amazing array of animals. Tourists and avid nature photographers alike take advantage of the opportunity to capture wonderful images of animals such as the Hawksbill turtle, Indian muntjac, Javan lutung, large flying fox, leopard cat, rusa deer, water monitor, and wild boar. Bird-watchers are on the lookout for barn swallows, black-naped orioles, black racket-tailed treepies, crested serpent eagles, crested treeswifts, dollarbirds, Java sparrows, lesser adjutants, and the sacred kingfishers.

A wildlife trip to Bali Barat would not be complete without a trip to the Marine Reserve. The reserve's cape shores and sanctuary islands make the perfect haunt for seabirds. The island of Menjangan and its surrounding coral reefs in the bay of Gilimanuk is a popular diving destination for locals and tourists alike.

LOCATION: Northwest Bali.

HOURS OF OPERATION: Year-round.

CONTACT: *Office:* Bali Barat National Park and Marine Reserve, Kantor Pos Gilimanuk, Cekik 82253, Bali; Tel: 61060 or 6236561173.

COST: *Entrance:* US$57. *Permits and obligatory guides:* Available at the PHPA héadquarters in Cekik, PHPA visitors center in Labuhan Lalang, and PHPA office in Denpasar.

ON-SITE AMENITIES: Headquarters/visitors center; guided tours.

BEST TIMES: August through December (end of the dry season and start of the wet season).

FIELD NOTES: Guides are available for hire from the park headquarters. Be sure to determine the costs in advance; some visitors have reported being charged as much as US$5,800 for a 2-day hike. A variety of hikes are offered; the 7-hour option is very popular because it provides exposure to a variety of environments. Aside from the naturist activities, water-based sports are a huge attraction, including snorkeling, swimming, fishing, diving, and boating.

BUKIT BAKA-BUKIT RAYA NATIONAL PARK

CENTRAL KALIMANTAN, INDONESIA

Formerly two different nature reserves, Bukit Baka-Bukit Raya is now one national park of more than 445,000 acres. Situated at the border of the east and central Kalimantan provinces, the mountainous rain forests in the park support an array of mammals that are uncommon in other parts of Indonesia and are either rare or nonexistent in other parts of the world. Animals such as the clouded leopard, orangutan, sun bear, maroon leaf monkey, slow loris, gibbon, barking deer, spotted giant flying squirrel, and spotted civet all make their home in this moist, high-altitude habitat.

Birds that are both migratory and indigenous to the area thrive on the prolific flora found in the park. Patient observers will note the helmeted, rhinoceros, and black hornbills; emerald and little cuckoo doves; and the great argus. A prime example of the successful preservation efforts of the park authorities is the elusive Bornean peacock pheasant, which has been threatened by human and predatory encroachment almost everywhere with the exception of Bukit Baka-Bukit Raya National Park.

Of the 1,817 different species of plants that have been documented in the park, many have been used by the indigenous peoples for medicine, food, and tools. There is a large variety of beautiful and innocuous species of forest orchids in the park, which are the counterpart to the more exotic, ominous plants such as parasitic flowers.

LOCATION: Central Kalimantan, Indonesia. Bus service is available from West Kalimantan to Nanga Pinoh; from there public riverboat service provides access to the park.

HOURS OF OPERATION: Year-round.

CONTACT: *Park office:* Tel: 056134613; *Tours:* Web: www.indahnesia.com or www.indecon.or.id/ecosites/baka.html.

COST: *Entrance:* US$1. *Hiking permits and information:* Available at the KSDA office in Pontianak or Palangkaraya or from the park office in Sintang at Jl. Dr. Wahidin S. No. 75. *Lodging and tours:* Depends on desired options.

ON-SITE AMENITIES: Visitors center, lodge, marked trails, and guard post. Basic accommodations can be arranged at the timber company in Popai. Other accommodations and guides can be found among the local Limai Dayaks, located near Belaban village.

BEST TIMES: June through September.

FIELD NOTES: Visit the park office in the town of West Kalimantan for permits and information. The area with the most orangutans is along the Ella River beyond Belaban village. Hiking through the park is the primary means of exploration, but can become quite rough at times. Climbing Bukit Raya is another option; if you decide to do so, it is best to travel by boat to Jelundong via Serawai.

GUNUNG LEUSER NATIONAL PARK

NORTH SUMATRA, INDONESIA

Orangutans are the big attraction for most visitors to Gunung Leuser National Park, which is the site of the Orang-Utan Rehabilitation Station at Bohorok-Bukit Lawang, one of two remaining homes for Sumatran orangutans. This species is considered critically endangered, with an estimated 3,500 individuals recorded in 2002. Baby orangutans are sought-after pets, and poachers often kill the mothers when they steal the young. The station strives to rehabilitate orphans so they safely can reenter the wild. The other research station in Ketambe is not open to the public.

But orangutans are far from the only animal that can be seen at Gunung Leuser. Visitors will be exposed to about 176 types of mammals, 320 birds, and 194 reptiles and amphibians. Some of the more exciting mammals that live in the park are Sumatran elephants, red giant

flying squirrels, Malayan sunbears, and barking deer. The endangered two-horned rhinoceros, which is smaller than other rhinos, is also here. The park is the last known home of the swamp crocodile in North Sumatra. Birders can look for the rhinoceros hornbill, argus pheasant, Asian pied hornbill, white-bellied sea eagle, and blue-crowned hanging parrot.

Covering more than 3,000 square miles, Gunung Leuser National Park is vast and mountainous, encompassing more than 60 miles of the Bukit Barisan Mountains. Other ecosystems of the area are beach forest, swamp, lowland rain forest, alpine, and mountain forest.

LOCATION: About 50 miles from Medan, the capital of Northern Sumatra.

HOURS OF OPERATION: Year-round, daily, 7:30 a.m. to 6 p.m. *Rehabilitation center:* open to visitors at feeding times only, 8 a.m. and 3 p.m.

CONTACT: *Park office:* Lembaga Pariwisata Tangkahan–LPT (Tangkahan Tourism Institution) Visitor Center, Kawasan Ekowisata Tangkahan (Tangkahan Ecotourism Area), Desa Namo Sialang, Tnagkahan, Indonesia; Tel: 08126567432, 081361662387, or 081-361674113; email: tangkahan_eco tourism@yahoo.com.

COST: *Entrance* (per person): US$3. *Permit:* Visitors must have a park service (PHPA) permit, available from the park offices in Medan, Tanah Merah, Bukit Lawang, Pondok Wisata, and Wisma Gurah in Ketambe.

ON-SITE AMENITIES: Orang-Utan Rehabilitation Center. Ketambe, a village at the western edge of the park, has lodging and restaurants.

BEST TIMES: June through September.

FIELD NOTES: Weather at the park tends to be very humid at all times; during the rainy season, visitors need to take boats to get around many flooded areas. Wear shoes that are good in muddy terrain. Treks can get somewhat adventurous so you will want to be relatively fit to take part. Guides are on-hand to take you deep into the jungle for various wildlife-viewing experiences and can be hired at a rate of about US$65 per day, but don't hesitate to bargain for the price. For an unusual thrill, you can go tubing down one of the rivers at the park; at a cost of less than US$1 per person, it is a bargain for 2–3 hours of water fun. If you visit the rehabilitation center, don't carry a shoulder bag; orangutans looking for food might snatch it!

UJUNG KULON NATIONAL PARK

JAVA, INDONESIA

For wildlife enthusiasts who would like to know more about endangered animals and how to support them, the Javan rhinoceros is considered ecotourism's holy grail. It is estimated that there are approximately only 70 individuals left, divided between two locations. Ujung Kulon National Park is home to 60 of these rhinos. In a cruel twist of fate, these magnificent pachyderms were hunted not just for the mythical properties of their horns but also at the behest of the government, which wanted to curb the rhino's negative effect on local agriculture.

In addition to these crown jewels, there are three species of deer in the park, the largest of which, the Javan rusa deer, often come near visitors' lodging, making them easy to observe and photograph. The smaller barking deer is also readily spotted. Visitors will have less luck finding the remarkably tiny mouse deer; the adults barely reach 18 inches long and weigh about 4.5 pounds.

Formerly domesticated banteng now roam the grassy clearings of Ujung Kulon. This species of cattle have made these lands their home since antiquity and were used by humans for farm labor until the 1800s. Visitors to the park will be exposed to 5 species of primates. The macaque is commonly seen. Silver-leafed monkeys are found in only Java and thrive in the park. The endangered Javan gibbon now lives under the protection and support of the park. Wild pigs, civets, big cats, and wild dogs also find a home here.

Because many of the more than 250 species of birds live in the canopies of the high forests, bird-watchers will want to bring along their binoculars.

Ujung Kulon offers visitors a unique assortment of wildlife. The parklands, which include the Ujung Kulon Penin-

sula, the Panaitan, and various other small islands, was declared a UNESCO World Heritage Site in 1992. It contains the largest remaining lowland rain forest in Java.

LOCATION: Ujung Kulon Peninsula, Indonesia.

HOURS OF OPERATION: Year-round, 24/7.

CONTACT: *Park office:* Ujung Kulon National Park, Jl. Perintis Kemerdekaan 51, Caringin, Labuan 42264, Pandeglang, West Java, Indonesia. *Tours:* Web: www.ujungkulontour.com.

COST: Depends on lodging and tours chosen. *Permits:* Required for park use; available from the park service, Perlindungan Hutan dan Pelestarian Alam (PHPA), in Labuan.

ON-SITE AMENITIES: Information center located at the main gate in Tamanjaya and Cibiuk. *Lodging* (Peucang Island and Handeuleum islands): **Flora and Fauna:**

Two comfortable guesthouses equipped with double- or twin-bedded units with bathroom, air-conditioning, refrigerator, private terraces, and spacious communal lounge. **Tamanjaya Guesthouse:** Four cottages, each with two or three bedrooms, shared living area, and bathroom. **Sundajaya Homestay:** Locally operated, offers a Sundanese home with two bedrooms. For more information, visit the tour website.

BEST TIMES: May through September.

FIELD NOTES: Hiking is the best way to explore the park and its various habitats. For safety reasons, guides are highly recommended and can be hired at the park's information center or through independent tour companies. Peucang Island is a recommended spot for snorkeling the shallows. Panaitan Island's northern and eastern shores, including the reef of Batu Pitak, are great scuba diving spots, though not recommended for beginners.

OZE NATIONAL PARK

JAPAN

Renowned for its vistas of wildflowers and majestic mountain scenery, Oze National Park is a popular destination for visitors. In some seasons, the

park, which includes the largest area of highland marsh in the country, is filled with vibrant flowers. In mid May, brilliant white flowers of the Japanese skunk cabbage proliferate; the end of the summer brings the yellow Alpine lilies. The marshland can be walked easily through, thanks to boardwalks that have been constructed throughout the grounds. Japanese deer can often be spotted foraging in the marsh areas, an attraction that is seldom seen elsewhere. Other mammals that reside here are the Japanese serow and the Asiatic bear, which co-inhabit the lands with more than 110 species of birds and 40 insect species.

The park contains a number of mountains, and visitors often note that they could never tire of the vast beauty of this area. Mount Huchigatake, technically an active volcano, rises 7,696 feet, and likely created the marshlands, which owe their existence to a volcanic eruption that dammed the Tadaganigawa River with lava. Mount Shibutsu (at 7,309 feet) is within the park but is off-limits to visitors because it has been designated a Special Protection Zone. The peak's serpentine rocks, which are rich in magnesium and iron, allow flora and fauna to grow well. Its lower slopes are granite, making for a dramatic sight.

Getting to the park itself involves a trek into nature. Visitors enter through a lodge, but then must hike up and over a mountain before entering the park.

The path has been laid out well, complete with wooden paths. Because part of the walk is uphill, the park staff suggest that visitors spend a couple of weeks getting into shape before their trip. The walk to the park is beautiful and you'll want your camera close by, but it's long with very few rest areas.

LOCATION: Northwestern Japan, approximately 2 hours by car from Tokyo.

HOURS OF OPERATION: Early May–Nov 3, weekdays: 8 a.m. to 7 p.m.; weekends and holidays, 7 a.m. to 7 p.m.

CONTACT: *Park office:* Oze Ranger Office (May through October) 1 Aza Hiuchigatade, Hinoemata-mura, Minamiaizu-gun, Fukushima, 967 0531. Tel: 81241752247. *Information:* Web: www.japanvisitor.com.

COST: *Entrance:* US$15–$35, depending on season.

ON-SITE AMENITIES: Lodge, restaurant, bar, gift shop, boardwalks through the marshes. Access to the park is through the lodge, where entrance fees are paid.

BEST TIMES: May through October.

FIELD NOTES: Because a large part of the park is marshland, biting insects are a problem; long pants and long-sleeved shirts (bug-repellent fabric is a good idea) and insect spray are highly recommended.

SHIRETOKO NATIONAL PARK

JAPAN

The popular image of Japan is of a place of extremely dense population, but Shiretoko National Park belies that. At around 150 square miles, it forms about half of the 44-mile-long peninsula that juts into the Sea of Okhotsk. *Shiretoko* means "land's end" or "end of the earth," and the park is one of true wilderness, with very limited access by road; and some areas accessible only by foot or boat.

The park is as unusual as it is beautiful. The peninsula was formed from volcanic rock, and there are huge black boulders strewn along its length as a potent reminder of the birth of the land. The park also contains majestic volcanic mountain ranges, rough cliffs pounded by wild seas, magnificent waterfalls, ponds, lakes, woods, thermal vents, and hot springs. In the winter, the Sea of Okhotsk has the southernmost ice floes in the Northern Hemisphere. This seasonal drift of sea ice is a popular tourist attraction; ice breakers tours are available from nearby Abashiri.

Hikers can follow a trail to shiretoko-go-ko, five famous lakes, and the Ka-muiwakka falls. One of the few roads in the park leaves Utoro and allows drivers to visit both the lakes and the falls. Another popular trek, which takes about 8 hours, leads hikers on an uphill climb to Io-Zen volcano. This is a rugged and difficult hike, but well worth it. Active visitors may choose to walk the backbone of Shiretoko from Iwaobetsu to Rausu to the 5,450-foot-high peak of Rausu-dake volcano. This 4.5-hour walk offers wonderful views of the park and out to Russian-held islands.

In addition to offering lots of eye candy for birders, Shiretoko has a huge deer population and the greatest number of

Hokkaido brown bears in Japan; so do not travel solo and arm yourself with a bear bell. Foxes are plentiful and can be easily seen.

LOCATION: A short drive from urban area of Rausu-cho, in the east of Hokkaido, the northernmost of Japan's four main islands. *Rausu visitors center:* 32-1 Rebuncho, Rausu-cho, Menashi-gun, Hokkaido, 086-1834.

HOURS OF OPERATION: Apr–Oct, 9 a.m. to 5 p.m.; Nov–Mar, 9 a.m. to 4 p.m.

CONTACT: *Rausu-Kunashiri observation tower:* Tel: 81153874560. Web: www.jnto .go.jp/eng/location/regional/hokkaido/ siretoko.html. *Information:* Ministry of the Environment, Rausu Ranger Office, 388 Yunosawa, Rausu-cho, Menashi-

gun, Hokkaido, 086-1822; Tel: 8115387-2402; Fax: 81153872468; Web: www.ja pan-guide.com.

COST: *Entrance:* Free.

ON-SITE AMENITIES: Rasau visitors center. A variety of accommodations can be found in the town of Utoro on the west coast of the peninsula.

BEST TIMES: Year-round, particularly in the fall, summer, and spring.

FIELD NOTES: In Utoro, you can board a sightseeing boat that sails along the west coast of the peninsula and continues below the cliff line, providing views that cannot be seen from land. This can be rugged territory so dress accordingly with sturdy hiking or walking shoes. Rain gear is also recommended because the weather can be changeable.

BAKO NATIONAL PARK

BORNEO, MALAYSIA

Bako National Park is Sarawak's oldest national park and the premier park in the system. Small enough to be seen in a day, Bako is a self-contained environment that offers an array of landscapes and habitats. Access to the park is strictly by boat from Kampung Bako (a 20-minute

ride), which is about 23 miles from Kuching.

Formed by millions of years of erosion, the coastline consists of steep cliffs and beautiful white, sandy bays, but diverse landscapes are found within the 27 square miles of the park. Visitors can explore beaches, rain forests, jungle

LOCATION: Tip of the Muara Tebas peninsula at the mouth of the Bako and Kuching Rivers.

HOURS OF OPERATION: Year-round.

CONTACT: *Park office:* Tel: 6011225049; Web: www.forestry.sarawak.gov.my/forweb/np/np/bako.htm. *Permits and reservations:* Acquired at the National Parks Booking Office in Kuching.

COST: *Lodging* (per night): Campsites, from less than US$5; two-room house, from US$23.

ON-SITE AMENITIES: Education and information center, lodging, campsites (with bath and toilets), day shelters, lockers, and canteen, expert guides, boating facilities, and numerous well-marked hiking trails. Telok Delima and Telok Paku are the best trails for viewing proboscis monkeys. Lodging information can be found on the park's website.

BEST TIMES: November through June. Wildlife viewing is best early in the morning or in the hours before dusk. You will need to be in position by 6 a.m. or 5 p.m.

FIELD NOTES: For day tripping, bring along snacks and drinking water. You will need to provide your own camping equipment.

streams, and waterfalls within a relatively small area. These diverse regions make up seven ecosystems, in which 25 distinct types of vegetation thrive, including a variety of carnivorous plants. Almost every type of vegetation found in Borneo can be found here.

Bako National Park is the host to about 150 endangered proboscis monkeys and works for the preservation of long-tailed macaques, silvered langurs, monitor lizards, plantain squirrels, and Bornean bearded pigs. Hikers will find 16 fully developed trails designed to offer a variety of lengths and difficulties, from short easy jaunts to full-day treks to trips involving overnight camping. The trail system offers visitors a fairly complete experience of all the diversity of the park.

GUNUNG MULU NATIONAL PARK

BORNEO, MALAYSIA

The Gunung Mulu National Park is set in a lush and verdant rain forest and has the famed Sarawak Chamber as its centerpiece. The park is most easily accessible by air and is a 30-minute flight from Miri Airport. For the more adventurous, a 12-hour boat ride is available for charter in Miri and will bring you to the area. The Sarawak Chamber, one of the many enormous caves in the area, is large enough to accommodate a jumbo jet!

The park, a UNESCO World Heritage Site, includes the famed caves and caverns as well as equatorial rain forests and karst formations, which result from the erosion of limestone. The area was the focus of a 15-month Royal Geographic Expedition, in which more than 100 scientists gathered together to learn about this geologically unique location.

The Bat exodus experience is one not to be missed. Visitors wait for nightfall at the Bat Observatory, while bat hawks roost on the cliff face, waiting with you. Each evening the millions of bats that live in Deer Cave gather at the cave's entrance in large ring-shaped formations and begin to circle up the cliff face before moving out across the rain forest, forming black spirals in the night sky. Researchers have recorded 12 species of bats within Deer Cave, including the wrinkle-lipped bat, which lives in a colony of between 2.5 and 3.5 million individuals.

The Royal Mulu Resort is the base for most explorations of the park. This world-class resort was built in the traditional longhouse style. The buildings are on 90-foot wooden stilts, so that visitors are eye level with the forest canopy.

LOCATION: Miri, Sarawak, Borneo, Malaysia.

HOURS OF OPERATION: Year-round.

CONTACT: *Park office:* Tel: 082441377; Web: www.mulupark.com; email: enquieries@mulupark.com.

COST: *Entrance* (per day): US$3. *Lodgings:* **Royal Mulu** (per night): US$85–$665; tours are priced separately. Visit the park's website for more options.

ON-SITE AMENITIES: Park headquarters, information center, gift shop, a canteen that sells drinks and light meals, and a variety of accommodation options. Overnight stays in the rain forest are permitted and can be arranged through park headquarters. Guides are mandatory. There are several guided treks available, lasting from a few hours to a few days. All can be arranged through local tour operators or directly through the park itself. For more information visit the park's website.

BEST TIMES: November through June.

FIELD NOTES: Guides are mandatory for your own safety. A minimum 3- to 4-day stay is recommended. If you are planning a trek to Camp 5 or along the Summit Trail, you will have to carry your own food and water. **Café Mulu** stocks a range of groceries and drinks and several small canteens near the park also sell food and groceries. Camp 5 facilities include open-air sleeping rooms with raised platforms, fully equipped kitchens, dining areas, and toilets and showers. Experienced trekkers may reach the top of the Pinnacles trail in 2–3 hours, the not so fit should allow 4–5 hours or more.

SEPILOK REHABILITATION CENTER

BORNEO, MALAYSIA

The orangutan, which today is found only in Malaysia and Indonesia, is thought to be the smartest mammal next to man, and more intelligent than the previous title-holder, the chimpanzee. A study of orangutans by Carel van Schaik, a Dutch primatologist at Duke University, found them capable of tasks well beyond chimpanzees' abilities, such as using leaves to make rain hats and leak-proof roofs over their sleeping nests. Van Schaik also found that, in some food-rich areas, the apes had developed a complex culture in which

adults teach youngsters how to make tools and find food.

The orangutan, from the Malaysian/Indonesian meaning "man of the forest," is the only ape that spends all its time in trees, and sleeps in them each night by creating nests out of branches, leaves, and other foliage. And those nests must be strong because an adult male can weigh up to 260 pounds and stand 5 feet 9 inches. Females are a bit smaller at 4 feet 2 inches.

The problem with orangutans is that the babies make incredibly cute pets, and human predators have made a business of supplying them to pet owners worldwide, killing the mothers in the process. In response to this growing problem, the Sepilok Rehabilitation Center was founded in 1964, to rehabilitate orphan orangutans. The site is 22 square miles of protected land at the edge of the Kabili Sepilok Forest Reserve. Today 60–80 orangutans are living free in the reserve and about 25 young orphaned orangutans live in the nurseries.

On a visit to the rehabilitation center, visitors can also see some of the area's other animals, such as proboscis monkeys, monitor lizards, river otters, civet cats, bats, and a huge variety of birds.

Sepilok Orangutan Appeal UK offers a Borneo orangutan adventure that leads visitors in a variety of activities, including forest trekking, wildlife spotting, gong playing (musical instrument), rice pounding, tree planting, river cruises, and night drives to spot wildlife. There is also cycling and bamboo rafting for the more adventurous.

LOCATION: Sabah, Borneo, Malaysia.

HOURS OF OPERATION: Year-round, daily, 9 a.m. to 11 a.m. and 2 p.m. to 3:30 p.m. *Feeding times:* Daily, 10 a.m. and 3 p.m., Fri, 10 a.m. only.

CONTACT: *Center office:* Sepilok Orang Utan Rehabilitation Centre, Sabah Wildlife Department W.D.T. 200, 90000 Sandakan, Sabah, East Malaysia; Tel: 6089531180; Fax: 6089531189. **Orangutan Appeal UK**, 11 Forest Hall, Brockenhurst, New Forest SO42 7QQ, Tel: 4401590622966; Web: www.orangutan-appeal.org.uk/sepilok-rehabilitation-centre; email: info@orangutan-appeal.org.uk.

COST: *Entrance* (per person): US$3. **15-day Borneo Orangutan Adventure:**

US\$4,080, all-inclusive (including flight from UK and most of your meals).

ON-SITE AMENITIES: Reception center, guides, walking trails, forest canopy walkways.

FIELD NOTES: The adventure trip is for people of all ages and the variety of options allows you to custom-design your own tour. The Mangrove Forest Trail takes 2–3 hours each way. Expect to spend a full day at the center to explore all that this site has to offer. Wear comfortable shoes and bring rain gear, hats, sunglasses, insect repellent, and suntan lotion.

TABIN WILDLIFE RESERVE

BORNEO, MALAYSIA

Proclaimed as the finest wildlife viewing spot in Borneo, great care has been taken to make Tabin Wilderlife Reserve an eco-tourism destination that boasts a finely tuned balance of harmony between humans and nature. Tabin provides a feeling of total disconnection to the outside world. As you wander beneath the jungle canopy, glimpse pygmy flying squirrels gliding across your path and listen to the calls of gibbons and other primates from high above. There are more than 300 species of birds that will serenade your walk along the trekking trails amid the wild orchids, pitcher plants, and other jungle flora. Pay close attention to the trees as you wander the reserve for the "men of the jungle," the impressive and majestic orangutan.

An ideal area to view wildlife or search for tracks left by nighttime visitors is the mud volcano. The salt and minerals of the mud make this a veritable hot spot for wildlife. Visitors can look for the Borneo pygmy elephant, tembadau, and the elusive and seldom seen Sumatran rhinoceros. Bearded pigs simply delight to wallow in the mud.

Other must-see areas are the extensive caves in the northern section of the reserve, believed to have been carved by an underground river system. There are a total of 36 caves with 23 openings for visitors to explore. Another stop, the Lipat Waterfall, will provide for a cool and relaxing swim after a long day of trekking through the jungle.

Whether it is in a chalet nestled into the lush hillside or one overhanging the riverbank, guests awaken each morning to the sheer excitement of the rain forest, the call of unseen birds, and movements of the primates high above in the canopy—the very hum of the jungle itself.

LOCATION: Eastern Sabah, eastern Malaysia, on Borneo.

HOURS OF OPERATION: Year-round.

CONTACT: *Reserve office:* Tel: 608-8267266; Fax 6088258266; Web: www.tabinwildlife.com.my.

COSTS: Depends on package chosen.

ON-SITE AMENITIES: Chalets and **Sunbird Café**.

BEST TIMES: Sabah has an equatorial climate. The wetter season is between October and February, the drier season between March and September, but there is often no sharp division between the two.

FIELD NOTES: Recommended items to bring: insect repellent, leech socks, tropical-weight long-sleeved shirts and long pants, shorts, raincoat, sun hat, swimwear, two pairs of comfortable trekking shoes, slippers, flashlight, water bottle, and personal toiletries.

TAMAN NEGARA NATIONAL PARK

MALAYSIA

Spread over three states in Malaysia and encompassing almost 2,700 square miles, Taman Negara National Park is the most famous eco-tourism destination in the country. One of the oldest parks in the area, it was established in 1938 as the King George National Park and then was renamed and rededicated after the nation's independence.

The park is home to Gunung Tahan, the highest peak in the Malay Peninsula and a major attraction for climbers and hikers. However, the park offers a range of attractions for everyone.

Many rare mammals are indigenous to the area and are protected and supported by the efforts of the national park, including the Indochinese tiger,

Sumatran rhinoceros, Malayan gaur, Asian elephant, and Malaysian mahseer fish. The rich ecosystems found in the park provide homes for a diverse array of other wildlife such as tapir, sambar deer, serow, wild pig, barking deer, mouse deer, and Malaysian wild dog.

Bird-watching is a prime activity in the park because roughly 300 species of birds have been recorded here. The birds found in the area run the gamut of being hard to spot, with dull colors designed to blend into the background, to birds with spectacular plumage that seems to put the rest of nature to shame. Highlights include the argus and firebacked pheasants.

LOCATION: Jerantut, a town in Pahang, is the main entry point to the park, 3–4 hours by car drive from Kuala Lumpur.

HOURS OF OPERATION: Year-round.

CONTACT: *Reservation office:* Tel: 032634434. *Mutiara Taman Negara:* Web: www.malaysiaforestresorts.com. **Taman Negara Resort:** Tel: 888359 8655 (toll-free USA); 6185298033 (international); Web: www.tamannegararesort.com.

COST: *Entry permit* (per person): US$1. *Cameras tariff:* US$1.50. *Fishing rod tariff:* US$3. *Lodging:* from US$150.

ON-SITE AMENITIES: Park headquarters with information and guides; the world's longest canopy walkway, picnic and swimming areas, guided fishing and boat tours, guided jungle trekking, cave exploration, and observation hides. **Mutiara Taman Negara Resort:** 108-rooms, located at park headquarters, world-class dining, spa, and other first-class amenities.

BEST TIMES: November through June.

FIELD NOTES: Taman Negara is a restricted area and all arrangements to visit must be made in advance at the reservations office in Kuala Tahan. The Department of Wildlife office located at the Kuala Tembeling jetty can also help with reservations. And many companies offer inclusive tours. For climbers and hikers, access to Gunung Tahan is from Kuala Tahan or Merapoh, two local villages that offer accommodations, guides, and other amenities.

ROYAL BARDIA NATIONAL PARK

NEPAL

South of the Shivalik Mountain Range of the Himalayas, bordering the Karnali River in western Nepal, is the largest and most undisturbed wildlife reserve in the lowland Terai region. Royal Bardia National Park is a subtropical jungle with thick forests and several open grasslands, where viewing the park's flora and fauna is prime.

Visitors to the park will have the chance to look for more than 30 species of mammals, 200 species of birds, and many lizards, snakes, and fish, which have been recorded in the park's forest, grassland, and river habitats. The park provides a perfect home for the endangered animals that live here. The one-horned rhinoceros was once extinct in this area but 13 rhinos were reintroduced into the park's lands, where they now thrive. Other endangered species that live here are the Bengal tiger, swamp deer, and blackbuck. Furthermore, the park offers refuge to one of the last known herds of wild elephant in South Asia. Visitors should also be on the lookout for the other large mammals in the

park: the gaur, the largest wild oxen in the world; wild boar; sloth bear; and blue bell antelope, the largest on the Indian subcontinent. The langur monkey, jackal, mongoose, Indian otter, and leopard are some of the smaller mammals to watch for.

The Geruwa River runs through the reserve, providing a home to the endangered gharial and marsh mugger crocodiles, not to mention the Gangetic dolphin. Those who visit the river area and hike on the forest trails may spot some of the six species of deer: chital, hog, sambar, swamp, barasingha, and barking.

An early-morning or late-afternoon elephant ride provides a different view of the park and its surroundings. Also available in the park are guided nature walks, bicycling, canoeing, rafting, and game drives through the jungle. Although the wildlife and vegetation are similar to those found in Royal Chitwan National Park, Royal Bardia National Park offers visitors a greater chance to view the tigers than anywhere else in Nepal.

LOCATION: 250 miles west of Kathmandu. Daily commercial air and public bus service from Kathmandu to Napalgunj; from there it is a 5-hour drive to the park office at Thakurdwara.

HOURS OF OPERATION: Year-round.

CONTACTS: *Main contact for park:* **Bardia Jungle Cottage**, Royal Bardia National Park, Thakuradwara, Bardia, Nepal; Tel: 97784429714; Web: www.visitnepal.com/bjc.

COST: *Entrance* (per person): US$68; children (under 10 years), free. *Accommodations:* Depends on lodging and tour selection.

ON-SITE AMENITIES: Camping (bring your own tent and food); in-park lodges—Bardia Jungle Cottage, Karnali Safari Lodge, Tiger Tops Karnali Lodge, and **Rhino Lodge Bardia**.

BEST TIMES: October through April (dry weather, warm days, cool nights).

FIELD NOTES: A minimum 3-night stay is recommended. Comfortable lightweight clothes, a hat, and good walking shoes for game viewing and treks. Also recommended: swimwear, flashlight, bug repellent, and sunblock.

ROYAL CHITWAN NATIONAL PARK

NEPAL

Known as one of the country's treasures of natural wonders and the oldest national park in Nepal, the Royal Chitwan National Park lies between two mountain ranges: the Shivalik and the Mahabharat. The parklands encompass the Churia Hills, oxbow lakes, and the floodplains of Rapti, Reu, and Narayani rivers.

The park is home to more than 43 species of mammals. Renowned for its protection of endangered species, which include the Bengal tiger, gharial crocodile, and one-horned rhinoceros (population of about 400). Other endangered species that make a home here are the wild elephant, four-horned antelope, striped hyena, pangolin, Gangetic dolphin, monitor lizard, and python.

Visitors may spot the sambar, chital, common leopard, ratel, palm civet, wild dog, langur, rhesus monkeys, and four species of deer. The birds of the park include the Bengal florican, lesser florican, giant hornbill, and black and white storks. Peafowls, red jungle fowls, herons, kingfishers, and woodpeckers are commonly seen. The marsh mugger crocodile, greenpit viper, cobra, and various species of frogs and tortoises are among the amphibians and reptiles that inhabit the lands.

Royal Chitwan National Park provides a tremendous opportunity to view these wonderful animals at close range by elephant back, on foot, by canoe, or by 4×4 vehicle. Visitors who decide to stay inside the park can choose from seven resorts that provide lodging and access to wildlife activities.

LOCATION: At the foot of the Himalayas in the subtropical inner Terai low-

lands of south-central Nepal, southwest of Kathmandu.

HOURS OF OPERATION: Year-round.

CONTACT: *Park office:* Web: www.south-asia.com/dnpwc/roy-chi-nat-park.htm. *Lodging:* Web www.hotelnepal.com/wildlife_resort/chitwan.php.

COST: *Entrance:* US$10; children (under 10 years), free.

ON-SITE AMENITIES: Display center, library, visitors center, museum, two breeding centers, and view tower. Seven in-park resorts providing lodging and access to wildlife activities, such as elephant-back safaris.

BEST TIMES: October through February are the coolest months in the region.

Monsoon season begins at the end of June and continues until September, during which time road closings may occur.

FIELD NOTES: A minimum of 3–4 nights is recommended to experience all this site has to offer. For safety reasons, no one is allowed to walk on park grounds between sunset and sunrise. The **Gharial Breeding Center**, just a short walk from the park's headquarters, is home to the marsh mugger and a variety of turtles. The **Elephant Breeding Center**, located at the Khorsor, Sauraha, entrance provides information on elephants and the babies born there.

ROYAL SUKLA PHANTA WILDLIFE RESERVE

NEPAL

The Royal Sukla Phanta Wildlife Reserve, named for the famed Sukla Phanta grasslands, is one of the last protected habitats of the threatened hispid hare and pygmy hog and the world's largest population of endangered swamp deer. But the reserve is able to claim reporting the highest number of tigers per square mile as well as being home to 35 royal Bengals out of Nepal's population of about 140. It is also home to about 50 endangered wild elephants. Additional wildlife in this area includes the spotted deer, hog deer, nilgai, wild dog, and jackal.

Visitors, especially bird-watchers,

colonel, who is very knowledgeable about the area and offers guided walks and game safaris. Meals are included. Lodging is also available at nearby Mahandranager, and transportation to the reserve can be easily arranged.

should make sure not to miss Rani Tal Lake. Herons, ducks, storks, kingfishers. and egrets all make their way here to find food and respite.

The reserve offers viewing and tours by 4-wheel-drive vehicle as well as guided nature walks near the river, lakes, and grasslands with trained trackers. There is an elevated viewing tower near the shore of Rani Tal Lake that allows visitors to extend their view of the grasslands and surrounding area. The staff at the park ranger's office can help you arrange for vehicle tours, elephant rides, and other activities in the park.

The reserve may be visited independently or by tour but not on foot. Information is available at the reserve office, but many visitors choose to stay at the only accommodations in the reserve, Silent Safari, a tented camp that provides simple and comfortable lodging. The camp is run by Himkat Bsiht, an ex-army

LOCATION: 3 miles southwest of Mahandranagar, Nepal.

HOURS OF OPERATION: Daily, 8 a.m. to sunset.

CONTACT: Silent Safari Tented Camp, PO Box 4631, Kathmandu or PO Box 1, Mahendranagar, Kanchanpur; Tel: 09921230; Fax 09922220; email hikmat@camp.wlink.com.np.

COST: *Entrance* (per day): US$10–$12. **Silent Safari** (per day): from US$150.

ON-SITE AMENITIES: Reserve office (at main gate), viewing towers, safaris, elephant rides, nature walks, guided vehicle tours.

BEST TIMES: October through April.

FIELD NOTES: Reservations for tours, activities, and accommodations are highly recommended. Essentials include insect repellent, good walking shoes, binoculars, and layered clothing, especially for cool nights in the winter months. Another popular destination for visitors is a nearby Tharu village.

KENTING NATIONAL PARK

TAIWAN

Located on the southern tip of Taiwan and covering 112 square miles of land and 94 square miles of sea, Kenting National Park was established in 1983 in part to protect endangered animals that would otherwise be hunted for mythical healing properties. Animals such as the Formosan Reeve muntjac, Formosan gem-faced civet, and Formosan rock monkey live harmoniously with the nearly 30 species of lizards, frogs, and turtles. There are approximately 26 species of snakes, including five of the poisonous variety, such as the hundred-pacer snake, green bamboo viper, turtle-designed snake, Taiwan banded krait, and Chinese cobra.

The park is visited by roughly 230 species of birds, of which about 80 make their home within the confines of the park. And visitors will delight in some of the almost 220 species of butterflies found here, including the rare and magnificent heng-chun bird-wing.

The unique physical character of the park includes mountains to the north, coral reefs to the south, and lake- and stream-studded plains in the central section. Mount Nanren is located in the park and rises from a virgin forest that is as lush today as it was thousands of years ago.

LOCATION: Southern tip of Taiwan, near Hengchun.

HOURS OF OPERATION: Year-round, 24/7.

CONTACT: *Park office:* Kenting National Park Administration Office, 946 No. 596, Kenting Rd, Hengchun Township, Pingtung County 946, Taiwan (ROC); Tel: 088861321; Fax: 088862047; Web: http://np.cpami.gov.tw.

COST: *Entrance:* US$17. *Resort and tour fees:* Vary according to choice.

ON-SITE AMENITIES: Visitors centers, botanical gardens, exhibition and recreational areas. *Lodging:* There are

numerous resorts near and in the park, including **Kenting Nan Wan Resort** on the park grounds, visit http://nanwan .sinotour.com; and the nearby **Kenting-ton Resort**, visit http://kentington.sino tour.com or http://tourguide.sinotour .com/kenting. *Camping:* Campgrounds are available in the park; contact the park directly for more information and booking.

BEST TIMES: November through March.

FIELD NOTES: The park's website suggests several 1- to 3-day driving tours, with recommendations for sightseeing and accommodation within the park. The **National Museum of Marine Biology and Aquarium** is located close by and well worth a visit. Other activities to enjoy here include swimming, fishing, hiking, and boating.

KHAO SAM ROI YOT NATIONAL PARK

THAILAND

Sam Roi Yot National Park, Thailand's oldest coastal national park, was established in 1986 in an effort to stem the encroachment of human activity in the area and to stop the tide of erosion to the natural habitats found here. The park is made up of almost 45 square miles of land and roughly 15 square miles of marine area.

Visitors are able to view the abundant wildlife, including endangered animals that are starting to thrive once more; such as the serow. The park is home to more than 300 species of birds and is a bird enthusiast's paradise. On any given day visitors will see amateur and professional bird-watchers taking notes and photos that will further the science of ornithology for everyone.

When you wish to take a break from the bird-watching, there is abundant mammalian wildlife in the park. Animals such as the wild dusky langurs, crab-eating macaques, and ponderous lorises are all part of the park's larger ecosystem. Commonly found in the area are gray-bellied squirrels, spectacled langurs, barking deer, fishing cats, and Siamese hares. Frolicking in the waters of the park are the beautiful and mysterious Irrawaddy dolphins.

The name of the park translates to "Mountains with Three Hundred Peaks," which is an apt description of the locale. The hills in the area are predominantly limestone and rise at the shore of the Gulf of Thailand. Khao Krachom is the highest peak in the park, rising over 1,000 feet above sea level. Located between the hills are freshwater marshes, many of which have been converted to shrimp farms.

One added bonus is that visitors will be able to find accommodations at a reasonable rate. World-class resorts sit on amazing beaches that lead to pristine water. In other parts of the world, the resorts themselves would be the destination, not just a place to rest after a day of sightseeing.

LOCATION: Thailand, south of Hua Hin and east of Pranburi.

HOURS OF OPERATION: Year-round, 24/7.

CONTACT: *Park office:* Khao Sam Roi Yot National Park, Mu 2, Ban Khao Daeng, Tambon Khao Daeng, Amphur Kui Buri Prachuap Khiri Khan Thailand 77150; Tel: 6638364700. *Bookings:* Web: www.thaiforestbooking.com.

COST: *Entrance:* US$12. *Resorts* (per night): from US$32.

ON-SITE AMENITIES: Park headquarters, visitors center, food services, campsites, restrooms. Accommodations, tours, and bicycle rentals can be arranged for at the headquarters.

BEST TIMES: November through June.

FIELD NOTES: The mosquito population is great so always carry lots of repellent. And seek out accommodations on the coast where the ocean breeze can provide some temporary relief from the bugs. Because the park isn't visited as much as it once was, several areas have returned to their virgin state and wildlife viewing is at its best. Activities to enjoy here include swimming, biking, fishing, cave exploration, camping, and hiking.

KHAO SOK NATIONAL PARK

THAILAND

Thailand's Malay Peninsula was at one time the most biodiverse area on earth. Due to logging, industrial farming for rubber tree plants and oil palms, and poaching, the botanical and animal life in the area has been decimated. Where once you could reliably expect to see wild elephants, tigers, and hornbills throughout the peninsula, these animals are now becoming just a memory or a tourist attraction even to locals. The last-known gibbon on Phuket Island was recently taken to the Gibbon Rehabilitation Center because she appeared to be starving.

The Khao Sok National Park is the area's best hope to stem the tide of human encroachment and to preserve Thailand's botanical heritage for future generations. The park includes the world's oldest evergreen forest and hosts an amazing array of wildlife. Endemic species that are rare outside of the park are plentiful here. Endangered species, such as the palm langkow and the *Rafflesia kerri meijer*, are the focus of the park's conservation efforts here, and these plants can now live in safety.

Barking deer, clouded leopards, tapirs, tigers, Malaysian sunbears, elephants, and gibbons still thrive within the park's borders.

While other parks in southern Thailand are known for their wildlife and draw more people in a day, Khao Sok should be considered the hidden treasure of Thailand's park system. Visitors have most often been avid naturalists and backpacking eco-tourists. As the word has spread about the beauty and splendor to be found here, interest in the park has grown commensurately.

There are eight independently owned lodging facilities available to visitors to the park. The operators of these facilities have joined together with the park officials to form the Khao Sok Environmental Protection and Tourism Agency. The agency is dedicated to preserving the local habitats and ecosystems while ensuring responsible and regulated eco-tourism in the area. In a move that the Western hospitality industry would consider counterintuitive, the agency is investigating the feasibility of limiting the amount of visitors to the area. Conservation and commerce work harmoniously in the area for the betterment of the park and the visitors.

The park itself is almost 2,500 square miles, making it one of the nation's largest, and it is easily accessible from most parts of southern Thailand. There are numerous tours available for visitors, including 1-, 2-, and 3-day visits. Tours are both terrestrial and aquatic and are led by expert guides.

LOCATION: Surat Thani Province, southern Thailand, a 2.5-hour drive northeast of Phuket.

HOURS OF OPERATION: Year-round, 24/7.

CONTACT: *Park office:* Web: www.khao sok.com or infor@khaosok.com.

COST: *Tours* (1- to 3-day trips): Adults, US$95–$334; children, US$66–$206. *Booking:* **Siam Safari Nature Tours;** Web: www.siamsafari.com.

ON-SITE AMENITIES: Visitors center; natural swimming pools. Elephant trekking, guided canoe trips, and jungle hiking.

BEST TIMES: November through May.

FIELD NOTES: Although the amenities offered in the park are scarce, you are within easy driving distance of anything you need, especially if you are not traveling to the park as part of a tour. In-park lodging offers full dining and will attempt to accommodate special requests. Activities to enjoy here include birding, camping, fishing, climbing, hiking, and boating. The mosquito population is dense, so bring a strong insect repellent. An 11-tier waterfall within the park is well worth a visit.

KHAO YAI NATIONAL PARK

THAILAND

Made famous for its waterfalls—including the 262-foot-high Heo Narok and the Haew Suwat shown in the movie *The Beach*—Khao Yai National Park is not only Thailand's second largest park but the country's first national park.

The park's 1,300 square miles are rich with evergreen forests, grasslands, and virgin jungle. Khao Yai, which was declared a nature reserve in 1959, is host to 67 species of mammals, 300 species of birds, and more than 2,500 plant varieties. Khao Yai is a pristine environment for many endangered animals, such as elephant, gibbons, macaques, tigers, clouded leopards, and Malaysian sun bears. Birders will enjoy the sight of parrots, parakeets, and a wide variety of hornbills, among many others.

In addition to the 31 miles of wildlife trails, the park also offers a unique site with bat caves. At dusk hundreds of thousands of bats can be seen flying out of their homes in unison.

LOCATION: A 3-hour drive north of Bangkok.

HOURS OF OPERATION: Year-round, 24/7.

CONTACT: *Park office:* Khao Yai National Park, PO Box 9 Amphur Pak Chong Nakhorn Ratchasima Thailand 30130; Tel: 0818773127, 0860926531, or 0810639241; Web: www.khaoyai.com; email: khaoyainp@hotmail.com. **Palm Garden Lodge:** Ban Kon Khuang, Moo 10, Dong Keleek, Amphoe Muang, Prachin Buri 25000, Thailand; Tel: 00660899894470 (cell) or 00660871661282; Fax: 0066-037403390 (English and Thai languages only); Web: www.palmgalo.com.

COST: *Entrance:* US$12. *In-park bungalow rentals* (per night): from US$24. *Campgrounds:* Laem Ta Kong and Pa Gluai Mai; tents available for rent; erect your own for a small fee. *Lodging:* **Palm Garden Lodge** (per night): near the entrance to the park; prices de-

pend on options; double room with air-conditioning, US$20; double room with overhead fan, US$12; family bungalows, US$37; additional beds are available for US$3.

ON-SITE AMENITIES: Exhibition center, restroom, small library, restaurants, campgrounds, bungalows and wildlife watchtower, guided walks, and night safaris. Contact the park directly for tour options. Both campgrounds offer restaurants and Pa Gluai Mai has a souvenir shop with snacks and drinks.

BEST TIMES: To avoid the crowds, visit away from local holiday times. Wildlife viewing is eventful year-round.

FIELD NOTES: Trekking with a guide is recommended for the most informative experience.

AUSTRALIA

Australia, New Zealand

TIDBINBILLA NATURE RESERVE

AUSTRALIAN CAPITAL TERRITORY, AUSTRALIA

Tidbinbilla Nature Reserve has recently become a member of the Australian Alps National Parks, a 12-park system sharing a vast tract of land in southeast Australia, whose midline straddles New South Wales and Victoria.

The region hosts around 700 species of plants, from tall mountain ash to delicate wildflowers, and is home to some of Australia's rarest animals—many found only in the Alps—such as the mountain pygmy possum and the corroboree frog. It is also home to some of wildlife enthusiasts most-loved animals: lyrebirds, wombats, koalas, platypuses, and several species of wallabies, and kangaroos.

The reserve, which spans more than 13,000 acres, encompasses a large valley floor, the Tidbinbilla mountain range, and the Gibraltar range. The lower slopes and the valley floor are partially cleared of trees, whereas ecosystems on the heavily forested and steep sides of the Tidbinbilla Valley are relatively undisturbed.

Visitors to this beautiful setting can often see eastern gray kangaroos, red-necked wallabies, swamp wallabies, cockatoos, and the occasional emu, which were introduced to the area. In addition, regular spotlight surveys have shown that the brushtail possum, ringtail possum, and greater glider are also present; they are always a treat for visitors.

The reserve provides habitat for a wide range of native vertebrate fauna, including 164 bird species; a variety of reptiles, fish, and amphibians; and a diversity of mammals, including several bat species. Tidbinbilla also includes a site that serves as a shelter or staging site for the bogong moth in October to November.

The reserve plays an important role in captive wildlife management; in particular, staff is involved in the breeding program for the endangered northern Corroboree frog and the brushtail rock-wallaby. Sadly, brushtail rock-wallabies have not been seen in the wild since 1959. They are believed to be extinct in the wild in Australian Capital Territory (ACT) and are critically endangered in Victoria. The staff at Tidbinbilla is part of a recovery team that is contributing to the survival of the Victorian brushtail rock-wallaby populations. Tidbinbilla maintains a captive colony of New South Wales brushtail rock-wallaby.

Northern Corroboree frogs, currently under the threat of extinction, live exclusively in the subalpine areas of the ACT and adjacent parts of New South Wales. To help ensure their long-term survival eggs have been collected from the wild in Namadgi National Park and successfully reared in captivity at Tidbinbilla.

In addition to wildlife conservation, Tidbinbilla provides many other activities with a universal appeal. Here visitors can attend a family barbecue in a highly managed setting or participate in an adventure experience that requires a high level of competence in outdoor and navigational skills. Activities in the park may be undertaken independently, or with ranger guides. Specific environmental educational programs are also offered.

The park's visitor center provides a great introduction to the reserve. Friendly staff is available to help visitors plan their day. Guided walks and special events are also scheduled and available. There are hands-on displays to explore, an interactive computer program about the park's birds, and live animal displays. The gift shop also sells an interesting range of clothes, toys, books, cards, and souvenirs. Coffee and light refreshments are available.

LOCATION: 40-minute drive from Canberra.

HOURS OF OPERATION: *Visitors center:* Weekdays, 9 a.m. to 4:30 p.m.; weekend and public holidays, 9 a.m. to 5 p.m.; reserve grounds: 9 a.m. to 6 p.m. (Standard Time); 9 a.m. to 8 p.m. (Daylight Saving Time).

CONTACT: *Reserve office:* Tidbinbilla Visitor Centre, Tidbinbilla Nature Reserve, Paddys River Rd, Tidbinbilla ACT 2620, Australia; Tel: 61262051233; Web: www.australianalps.deh.gov.au/parks/index.html.

COST: *Entrance:* Free.

ON-SITE AMENITIES: A newly opened sanctuary. Scenic drives through the reserve, where you can absorb the panoramic views of the Tidbinbilla Valley. Picnic areas with electric and wood-fired barbecues, available free of charge. Various bush walks, on formed walking trails, ranging from easy strolls to challenging day trips. Bicycle riding is allowed along the sealed roads and fire trails. Special events may be accommodated within Tidbinbilla as long as the environmental impact is not significant—for example, cross-country running or orienteering.

BEST TIMES: Year-round.

FIELD NOTES: Prohibited activities include camping, fishing, horseback riding, car rallies, off-road and 4-wheel-drive activities, and trail bike riding. Dogs, cats, and other pets are not permitted except for guide dogs. Firearms are not permitted.

CARAWIRRY WILDLIFE REFUGE

NEW SOUTH WALES, AUSTRALIA

Some people choose their vacation spots for the fantastic accommodations. Some people opt for the scenic locale. Carawirry Wildlife Refuge offers the best of both. Two spacious cabins are ideal for families and groups. Each cabin accommodates 8–10 guests. The cabins are private and provide the bounty of nature at your doorstep. Guests are free from the distractions of other visitors as they relax and enjoy their surroundings.

The recipient of the prestigious Golden Axe award for Environmentally Sustainable Business Practice, the mission of the Carawirry Cabins and Wildlife Refuge is to "continue to manage the property as an Uneven Aged native forest structure to provide maximum native vegetation and habitat values for wildlife."

The refuge offers more than 5 miles of nature walks. During a typical visit, guests can view up to a dozen endangered species, including the Parma wallaby, the koala and the tiger quoll. The reserve is bordered by state forests that offer idyllic swimming pools, additional hiking locations, and picnic areas.

Guests can also enjoy the Carawirry Creek and the secret swimming hole at Telegherry River. The area offers numerous mountain bike routes, self-drive 4-wheel driving options, and horseback riding. Most important, Carawirry Cabins offers you the opportunity to unwind, relax, and recharge amid some of the most beautiful scenery in the world.

LOCATION: 100 miles from Sydney at the foot of the Black Bulga Range.

HOURS OF OPERATION: Year-round, 24/7.

COST: *Midweek* (2 days): US$194–$670. *14 nights:* US$1,038–$1,630.

CONTACT: *Main office:* Carawirry Wildlife Refuge, 73 Cabbage Tree Road, Main Creek, NSW, Australia, 2420; Tel: 610249921859; Web: www.carawirry .com.au.

ON-SITE AMENITIES: Each of the two fully stocked cabins features toilets and showers, full operating kitchens, wood heater, and stacked firewood, and op-

tional linen packages as well as amenities that encourage conservation, such as mulching bins, eco-friendly cleaning supplies, and garbage-sorting bins.

BEST TIMES: Year-round. The refuge offers unique experiences for each season.

FIELD NOTES: The town of Dungog is 8 miles away and is the best place to stock up on food and other necessities you'll need since very little is provided at the cabins

LORD HOWE ISLAND

NEW SOUTH WALES, AUSTRALIA

Since the advent of human exploration and habitation on Lord Howe Island, a number of endemic species have become extinct. The efforts of the current conservators have helped reverse the slow but continual degradation of the area, and now more than 130 species of birds live and thrive on the island. Sooty terns can easily be seen at Ned's Beach common and the Northern Hills from September through January. A trek on the Little Island Track between March and November will give visitors the firsthand experience of the magnificent aerial courtship

displays by the winter-breeding Providence petrel. One of the world's rarest birds, the Providence petrel returns to the island to nest and can be sum-

moned out of the air by voice, landing at your feet, and maybe even climbing into your lap.

Although the inland forests and landscapes of Lord Howe Island are the prototypical island paradise, the true attraction for visitors to the island is the water. There are more than 400 species of fish mingling among the 80 species of corral in the island's coastal waters. The water is so clear and clean it's almost as if you were swimming in the world's most beautiful pool.

Roughly 50% of the plant life at Lord Howe Island is endemic to the area. The *Howea* is a genus of palms and are commonly known as kentia palms. These are popular houseplants and their cultivation and exportation make up the only major industry aside from tourism. The glowing mushrooms found on the island are harvested after heavy rains, and their glow lasts for days. Particularly vibrant samples provide enough radiance to read by.

Lord Howe Island is a crescent-shaped remnant of a 7-million-year-old volcano. Roughly 6 miles long and 1 mile wide, the island was discovered in the late 1700s and has been used since that time as a layover for sailors and as a private paradise for nature enthusiasts. The area was designated a World Heritage Site in 1982.

There is a tremendous range in the options for lodging on the island. This is not a typical resort island. No international corporations run industrial resorts here. Visitors can choose from simple rooms to all-inclusive boutique lodging; all owned and run by local inhabitants. One of the remarkable benefits to visiting the area is that there is a limit of only 400 guests allowed at any one time. You can enjoy the hospitality of the native population while avoiding intrusive shoulder rubbing with other tourists.

LOCATION: 375 miles northeast off the east coast of Australia, about 2 hours flying time from Sydney or Brisbane.

HOURS OF OPERATION: Year-round, 24/7.

CONTACT: *Tourist information:* Tel: 6126563 2114; Web: www.lordhoweisland.info; email: lhi.visitorcentre@bigpond.com.

COST: There is no fee for most activities in and of themselves, but you will need to rent equipment (such as for scuba or boating), acquire lodging, arrange for transportation, and pay for meals.

ON-SITE AMENITIES: Accommodations range from self-catering cottages to boutique luxury lodges. For more information visit the island's website.

BEST TIMES: August through March.

FIELD NOTES: At Ned's Beach kingfish, wrasse, and various other species of fish frequent the shallow waters. Take some spare bread with you for a hand-feeding adventure. Activities are plentiful and include kayaking, scuba diving, water sports, nature walks, climbing, hiking, bird-watching, and more. At low tide, reefs can be explored by foot from the beach. Bring water shoes or an old pair of sneakers.

KAKADU NATIONAL PARK

NORTHERN TERRITORY, AUSTRALIA

Kakadu National Park is an ultimate destination for wildlife enthusiasts. Travelers to this park can enjoy the net result of conservation of both plants and animals. In fact, it's like stepping back in time. After all, Kakadu is one of the few places in Australia where there have been a very few, if any, extinctions of plants or animals over the last 200 years. Traveling by foot, boat, or car, visitors can enjoy watching magpie geese, which were once found throughout eastern and southern Australia. The park actively protects the habitats of animals that live only in the Kakadu/ Arnhem Land region, such as the white-throated grass wren, black wallaroo, and chestnut-quilled rock pigeon—all long-time native residents to the area.

Located in the wet-dry tropics of northern Australia, covering about 40,000 square miles within the Alligator Rivers Region, the park consists of

many different environments that support an astonishing array of animals. Charles Darwin would have loved this place. It is evolution and the origin of species in action. Responding to the extreme heat and humid weather conditions experienced in the park, many animals have changed their physical and behavioral patterns to adapt and are seen at different times of the day and night compared to their counterparts in milder climates.

Guests can enjoy watching crocodiles, wallabies, 26 species of bats, black wallaroo, black-footed tree-rats, brown bandicoots, dingos, dugongs, flying foxes, pythons, and geckos as well as many other reptiles and snakes. Feral horses, pigs, and water buffalo have also been known to frequent the park.

Activities include ranger-guided tours, seven different walks, and, for the more adventurous, flightseeing and night safaris are available. Unique to this park are the numerous rock art sites. In fact, Kakadu boasts one of the largest concentrations of rock art sites known to the world, with 5,000 recorded sites and another 10,000 thought to exist. The rock art sites can be found along the escarpment, in gorges, and on rock outliers. Ranging in age from 24,000 years old to more modern times, the art represents one of the longest historical records of any group of people in the world.

LOCATION: Kakadu National Park is located about 490 miles east of Darwin. It extends from the coast in the north to the southern hills and basins about 290 miles to the south, and from the Arnhem Land sandstone plateau in the east, about 230 miles through wooded savannas to its western boundary.

HOURS OF OPERATION: Year-round, 24/7. *Bowali visitors center:* Daily, 8 a.m. to 5 p.m. *Warradjan Aboriginal Cultural Centre:* Daily, 9 a.m. to 5 p.m. *Ubirr*

Rock: Daily, Apr 1–Nov 30, 8:30 a.m. to sunset; Dec 1–Mar 31, 2 p.m. to sunset.

CONTACT: *Park manager:* Kakadu National Park, PO Box 71, Jabiru NT 0886 Australia; Tel: 61889381120; Fax: 61889381115; Web: www.environment.gov.au/parks/kakadu; email: kakadunationalpark@environment.gov.au.

COST: *Entrance:* Free. *Camping* (per night): US$5; children (under 16 years), free. Fees can be paid at the Bowali visitors center and on-site at the major park camping areas.

ON-SITE AMENITIES: Picnic areas, 18 campgrounds, restrooms, and showers throughout the park, flightseeing, boat and 4-wheel-drive tours, and fishing and boating. *Boat ramps:* Located at South Alligator River, East Alligator River, Yellow Water, Mardugal, Jim Jim Billabong, Waldak Irrmbal, Muirella Park, and Home Billabong; crocodiles frequent boat launches, be on guard. *Swimming:* In natural plunge pools and gorges is on an "at your own risk" basis. The park is surveyed each dry season for crocodiles as some may have traveled in. *Camping:* Several free camping areas in the park, which have limited or no facilities; drinking water is usually not available at these sites, so you'll need to bring your own. *Lodging:* Various hotels, motels, and backpacker accommodations, ranging from high end to low end are available. **Aurora Kakadu:** Call 61889790166 or visit www.auroraresorts.com.au; **Kakadu Lodge:** Call 61889792422 or visit www.auroraresorts.com.au. **Gagudju Lodge Cooinda:** Call 61889790145 or visit www.gagudjulodgecooinda.com.au. **Lakeview Park Kakadu:** Call 61889793144 or visit www.lakeviewkakadu.com.au. **Wirnwirnmila Mary River Road House:** Call 61889754564.

BEST TIMES: April through September, when the humidity is low, and wildlife most active.

FIELD NOTES: *Crocodile warning:* Two types of crocodiles inhabit Kakadu: estuarine (saltwater) crocodiles and freshwater crocodiles: Estuarine crocodiles can be found in fresh, estuarine, and saltwater environments (floodplains, billabongs, rivers, and coastal waters). They are aggressive and dangerous and have attacked and killed people in Kakadu. Freshwater crocodiles generally inhabit the upper reaches of freshwater creeks and rivers. They are usually shy animals but can become aggressive if disturbed, particularly during the breeding season (September and October). For your own safety it is advised that you look out for crocodile signs, obey all swimming warnings, remove rubbish from your campsite, clean fish away from the water's edge. When camping in areas near water, set your site far from the water's edge. And, most important, never approach freshwater or estuarine crocodiles. Crocodiles are not the only threat in Kakadu, feral buffalo and pig can also become dangerous if approached. It is in your best interest to maintain a safe distance between yourself and the animals at all times. *Flash flooding:* Another concern, especially during October through April, can occur without notice and cut off return paths. Extra caution should be used when crossing waterways, or swimming, during these times. Bring insect repellent, long-sleeved tops, rain gear, sunscreen, sunglasses, comfortable footwear, cameras, and binoculars. Due to the elevated temperatures in Kakadu, water should be kept with you at all times; no less than one half gallon per person should be taken even on the shortest of walks. *Permits:* Required for camping outside the designated areas, bush walking off marked trails, and for various commercial endeavors. Permits are available at the park's website. If you are unsure if your desired activity requires a permit contact the park headquarters before visiting.

MARY RIVER PARK

NORTHERN TERRITORY, AUSTRALIA

Mary River Park is a family-owned and -operated eco-tourism complex that provides visitors with a unique and relaxing experience in a true wilderness that's specifically tailored to "fisherfolk," bird-watchers, animal lovers, and anyone who really enjoys the spectacular raw beauty of the natural world. Mary River offers country charm and hospitality amid a tropical paradise loaded with incredible wildlife: birds of prey, flocks of waterfowl, wallabies, water buffalo, dingos, lizards, snakes, saltwater and Johnson River crocodiles—not to mention enough species of fish to fill a scientific volume.

Along the Mary River, which meanders 160 miles or more into the Kakadu,

an area of more than 4,000 square miles, the permanent human population is less than 30. In fact, there are more numbers and varieties of animals than there are people! What's also so spectacular is that it's only an hour's drive from the capital city of Darwin. Halfway between Darwin and Kakadu, Mary River Park boasts nearly 2 miles of river frontage and is a remarkable sanctuary for both woodland and wetland flora and fauna.

There's something for everyone at Mary River Park from the creature comforts of air-conditioned cabins to secluded riverside campsites, plus eco-river cruises, sunset and stargazing dinner cruises, Barnamundi fishing trips, and 4×4 wetland and wildlife safari tours. There are also woodland, grassland, and wetland bush walks, perfect for bird-watching or simply being close to nature

Country hospitality at its best: Home-style meals are served in dining rooms that overlook woodlands and landscaped gardens. Even mealtimes are flexible, and are adjusted to suit guests leaving or returning on tours away from Mary River Park.

LOCATION: Mary River Crossing on the Arnhem Hwy, about 50 miles from Darwin and 16 miles from the Kakadu National Park entrance.

HOURS OF OPERATION: Year-round.

CONTACT: *Main office:* Mary River Park, PO Box 37420, Winnellie, Northern Territory, Australia, 0821; Tel: 0889788877, 1800788 844 (toll-free), 61889788877 (international); Fax: 0889788899; Web: http://maryriverpark.com.au.

COST: *Cabins:* Single air-conditioned, US$144, family, US$184. *Packages* (1 or 2 nights): US$240–$398, includes accommodations, wildlife tour, and Mary River Park experience.

ON-SITE AMENITIES: BBQ deck, bar, restaurant.

BEST TIMES: December through June.

FIELD NOTES: Binoculars, bug spray, light clothing, sunglasses, hats, boots—and an adventurous spirit.

ULURU-KATA TJUTA NATIONAL PARK

NORTHERN TERRITORY, AUSTRALIA

About 500,000 million years ago, central Australia was covered by an inland sea. Sand and mud sediment slowly built up over time, forming sandstone rock. Eventually, the sea receded and the seabed eroded away, leaving behind enormous harder, mineral-rich rocks of sandstone. For thousands of years, the Anangu people of central Australia lived in respectful harmony with their desert environment and believed the enormous, dome-shaped rocks to be sacred places. They called the largest rock Uluru, which means "Earth Mother," and a group of 36 various sized rocks, located approximately 20 miles away, are called Kata Tjuta, or "Many Heads." In 1872 the English explorer Ernest Giles called the single largest rock "the remarkable pebble." The following year, the South Australian surveyor William Goose named the remarkable pebble Ayers Rock in honor of the chief secretary of South Australia, Sir Henry Ayers. He named the group of other rocks the Olgas, after the queen of Wurttemberg. In 1985 the 510-square-mile Uluru Na-

Another park animal that never drinks water is the mulgara, a small marsupial with kidneys evolved to excrete extremely concentrated urine to conserve water. A total of 72 species of reptiles and amphibians live in the park, including the woma python, the great desert skink, and four species of frogs. The park has 178 different species of birds, including the gray honeyeater, striated grass wren, hawk, kestrel, falcon, and the rare scarlet-chested parrot, with plumage the color of the rainbow: blue head, orange throat, red chest, yellow belly, and green back.

tional Park was established under joint-management by the Anangu people and the Australian National Parks, and in 1993 the name was changed to Uluru-Kata Tjuta National Park. Today, the 106-foot-high, monolithic rock is called both Uluru and Ayers Rock.

The park is home to a variety of unusual plant species, such as the endangered adder's tongue fern. Unlike other ferns, only one frond grows out of the ground, resembling a single standing tongue. Visitors can also count 27 mammal species, 6 of which are not native: rabbit, dog, cat, fox, house mouse, and camel. The park is reintroducing locally extinct mammals, such as the nocturnal marsupial, the brushtail possum, the endangered rufous hare-wallaby (mala), and the bilby. The bilby is a small omnivore with large ears and a keen sense of hearing. It derives all the water it needs for survival from its diet of insects, seeds, fruits, and bulbs, which it finds by scratching and probing the soil with its long tongue.

LOCATION: Ayers Rock, Australia, southwest region of Australia's Northern Territory, approximately 300 miles southwest of Alice Springs.

HOURS OF OPERATION: Park hours vary slightly with the seasons, but generally daily, 6 a.m. to 8 p.m. *Cultural center:* Daily, 7 a.m. to 6 p.m. *Headquarters:* open 8:30 a.m. to 4:30 p.m., closed between noon and 1 p.m.

CONTACT: *Park headquarters:* Uluru-Kata Tjuta National Park, PO Box 119, Yulara, NT, 0872, Australia; Tel: 61889561100. Web: www.environment.gov.au/parks/uluru; email: uluru.info@environment.gov.au. *Cultural center information:* Tel: 61889561128.

COST: *Entrance* (3-day pass): US$25; children (under 16 years), free.

ON-SITE AMENITIES: Cultural center with parking lot, picnic areas with gas BBQs and accessible toilet facilities. Lodging and food establishments are available at **Ayers Rock Resort** located just outside the park. Various walking, vehicle, and helicopter tours are available. There is even a camel tour!

BEST TIMES: Open year-round, but during the months of November through January it is frequently over 110°F.

FIELD NOTES: There are commercial flights into Alice Springs and bus and tour groups are available from Alice Springs. Commercial flights are also available to Connellan Airport in Ayers Rock. The Anungu people consider Uluru rock sacred and discourage visitors from climbing it. Nevertheless, there is a trail leading to the top and approximately 1 out of 10 visitors make the 3-hour round-trip climb. For the protection of wildlife, visitors must stay on defined trails and roads.

BLACK MOUNTAIN (KALKAJAKA) NATIONAL PARK

QUEENSLAND, AUSTRALIA

This is a place of surreal, gothic imaginings—so distinctive and otherworldly it is the source of as many legends as it is home to a unique array of wildlife. With its imposing mountain range of massive black granite boulders, Black Mountain (Kalkajaka) National Park is situated at the northern end of the wet tropics World Heritage Area and is renowned not only for its topography but for its appeal to birders and its unique animal specimens. The park is home to the Black Mountain boulder frog, as well as the Godman's rock-wallaby, the ghost bat (vulnerable to extinction), the Black Mountain gecko, and the rare Black Mountain skink.

Also seen throughout the park are three species of flying fox, the endangered northern quoll, and, for the lucky or mendacious few, the Queensland tiger, allegedly a resident in the mountain. It is interesting that the tiger has been described as a large striped cat closely resembling the marsupial lion, which inhabited Queensland more than 20,000 years ago, at which time it was believed to have gone extinct. Sightings have been rare in the last few decades, with few documented encounters.

Snakes and reptiles are fairly common on the mountain, such as the giant amethystine python, which can grow to more than 15 feet, and the ringtailed gecko, which is found at only a few other locales.

Watching nature in action is clearly a favorite pastime for visitors, who, from constructed lookouts throughout the park, can search out the surprisingly large fig trees growing among the boulders on the distant mountain and can discover the natural light color of the rock in the distance on freshly broken boulders, before algae blackens it.

LOCATION: About 12 miles south of Cooktown, on the Cooktown Developmental Rd.

HOURS OF OPERATION: Year-round, 24/7.

CONTACT: *Park office:* Tel: 1300130372 or 1300130372 (toll-free); Web: www .epa.qld.gov.au/projects/park/index .cgi?parkid=136.

COST: *Entrance:* Free.

ON-SITE AMENITIES: None. From the car park there are accessible lookout points with interpretive signage. There are no trails; camping is not permitted. Accommodations can be found nearby in Cooktown; for more information visit www.queenslandholidays.com.au.

BEST TIMES: May through October. Many roads and tracks become impassable during the hotter-wetter season, from late November to April.

FIELD NOTES: Four extraordinary sites of interest exist in the park, including the Kambi, a rock structure and cave where flying foxes can be found; Julbanu, a kangaroo-shaped rock; Birmba, a rock facing in the direction of Helenvale, where sulfur-crested cockatoos are seen; and a taboo place named Yirrmbal, located near the foot of the range.

Though the park can be explored by vehicle or by foot, visitors are advised not to try to venture out onto the boulder fields. Be aware of snakes at all times, and always keep a safe distance. Stinging plants are common in the area so take care when walking in close proximity of the vegetation. Bring sunglasses, long-sleeved shirts, hats, sunscreen, and drinking water. Pets are not permitted on the park grounds.

CAPE TRIBULATION

QUEENSLAND, AUSTRALIA

Cape Tribulation, a section of the Daintree National Park, is said to be one of the richest biological places on the planet. The area is where the Great Barrier Reef and the Daintree rain forest meet, the only place on earth where two World Heritage areas exist side by side.

The 135-million-year-old rain forest of Cape Tribulation is of the most ancient and primitive in the world. Many species of animals and plants originated here over 120 million years ago.

The wet tropics region is a recognized major world center of the highest level of biodiversity; species are found only within particular areas of Australia. Add this to the presence of the Great Barrier Reef, and you have the ultimate destination for biologists, ecologists, ornithologists, and any other serious kind of -ologist. Animal and nature lovers alike will find much to see and do.

Although the wet tropics region represents just 0.1% of the land surface of the Australian continent it contains more than 3,500 plant species, including Australia's largest range of ferns

and the world's largest concentration of ancient flowering plants. It also boasts the highest number of endemic mammals of any region in Australia, almost half of Australia's bird species, about two-thirds of Australia's butterflies, and a quarter of Australia's frog species, more than 20 of which are endemic. Although Australia contains less than one thousandth of the world's tropical rain forests, the forests found here are some of the most significant ecosystems on the planet. World Heritage status was granted in recognition of the area's wide range of scientific significance and conservation of biodiversity.

Cape Tribulation offers guided tours (which are always recommended to get the most out of your trip), backpacking, a wide variety of accommodations from campsites to B&Bs to farm stays to motels and resorts. A unique adventure in the park is the Jungle Surfing Canopy Tour, which offers a zip-line flying fox that allows the rider to "surf" through majestic, old-growth rain forest with spectacular views over the parklands and out to the Great Barrier Reef. Tours can be booked online by visiting www .junglesurfing.com.au. The Daintree coast area offers a range of services to meet most travelers' needs from rain forest information to a spa, pharmacy, supermarkets, fuel, Internet access, daily newspapers, and bus transport.

LOCATION: Daintree National Park is bounded by the Mossman Gorge and Bloomfield River.

HOURS OF OPERATION: Year-round, 24/7.

CONTACT: *Tourist information:* Web: www.daintreecoast.com.

COST: Depends on accommodation, tours, etc.

ON-SITE AMENITIES: Rain forest tours, ocean and reef tours, river cruises, horseback riding, guided night walks, Discovery Centre, and 4-wheel-drive safaris. *Lodging:* Vary from high-end resorts to campsites. Tours can be booked directly through most hotels and resorts. visit www.daintreecoast.com for

more information. *Campsites:* **Cape Tribulation Camping, Jungle Lodge,** and **Lync Haven Rainforest Retreat.** *Other:* **Deep Forest Lodge:** Cape Tribulation Rd, Daintree Coast, PO Box 916, via Mossman. 4873 Qld, call 617-40989162, fax 617 40989242, or visit www.daintreedeepforestlodge.com.au. **Cape Tribulation Rainforest Hideaway:** 19 Camelot Close, Cape Tribulation, 4873 Qld, call 61740980108 or visit www.rainforesthideaway.com. **Coconut Beach Resort:** Lot 10, Cape Tribulation Rd, Cape Tribulation, 4873 Qld, call 61740980033 or visit www.capetribulationresort.com.au.

BEST TIMES: May through November. The wet cyclone season is from December to April.

FIELD NOTES: Bring it all: suntan lotion, layered clothing, sunglasses, hats, bug repellent, umbrella, and cameras. Water-resistant protective gear is recommended for your equipment.

FRASER ISLAND

QUEENSLAND, AUSTRALIA

Located at the southern end of the Great Barrier Reef just off Australia's northeast corner lies the largest sand island in the world. With spectacular beaches, lush rain forests, and magnificent lakes, the island's Aboriginal inhabitants called it K'gari, or "paradise." In 1836, a 70-gun, two-decked, heavy warship the HMS *Sterling Castle* ran aground on a reef off the island. The ship broke apart, but 18 of its crew, including Captain James Fraser and his wife, Eliza, made it to the island. Planning to walk south to Brisbane, the group encountered the island's Aboriginal people. Captain Fraser and many of his crew lost their lives struggling with the Aborigines, but Eliza Fraser and seven others managed to make it

off the island. Eliza toured Europe telling many versions of her harrowing island tale, gaining sympathy and wide notoriety in the process. In response, the island was named Fraser Island.

Starting in the 1860s the island's rain forest was logged, which continued until 1991, when the 700-square-mile island was listed by the World Heritage Foundation as a site of outstanding universal natural and cultural significance. Since then, the island's unique geography and wildlife have been protected.

The island has more than 40 lakes, which can be classified into three distinctive types: window, barrage, and perched. The island's window lakes lie below the water table, and as water seeps in, the fine white sand filters the water. Window lakes, like Ocean Lake and Yankee Jack are so pure they support little wildlife. Barrage lakes, like Wabby Lake, formed when natural spring water was dammed by wind-blown sand. Perched lakes formed above the water table and are fed by rainwater collected in dish-shaped depressions with impervious bottoms of sand covered by organic, peat-like matter, giving the lakes a tea-stained color. Lakes

McKenzie and Boomanjin are perched lakes, with the latter having nearly 80 acres of surface area, making it the largest perched dune-lake in the world.

Fraser Island supports over 750 species of flowers, plants, and trees. While many of the trees have deep root systems, most of the wildflowers and plants draw their nutrients directly from the sand, which is quickly depleted and replenished. More than 350 different species of birds live on the island, such as the kingfisher, cockatoo, pelican, tern, seagull, peregrine falcon, osprey, sea eagle, and the rare and endangered ground parrot. A wide variety of reptiles and amphibians, including a variety of frogs, snakes, lizards, and skinks can be found on the island. The island is home to some of the last remaining pure dingoes in eastern Australia, wallaby, opossum, flying fox, sugar glider, and flying opossum. Visitors can see brumbies, or wild horses, descendants of those used in the lumber industry of the 19th century. From August through October, more than 1,500 humpback whales can be seen traveling through Hervey Bay during their migration south to the Antarctic, with mothers and babies arriving from mid September on.

LOCATION: Eastern coast of Queensland, offshore from the city of Hervey Bay. A 45-minute flight or 3.5-hour drive from Brisbane and a 30-minute ferry ride to Fraser Island from Hervey Bay.

HOURS OF OPERATION: Year-round.

CONTACT: *Tourist information:* Fraser Island Tours, PMB 1, Urangan, Hervey Bay, Qld 4655; Tel: 61741949222; Web: www.fraserisland.net.

COST: *Ferries* (round trip): Per person, US$30; 4-wheel-drive vehicle with passengers, US$140. **Kingfisher Bay Resort** (per night): Peak US$285–$325, with 3-night minimum; off season, US$235–$275, no minimum; visit www.kingfisherbay.com.

ON-SITE AMENITIES: Kingfisher Bay is a world-class resort with lodging, restaurants, gift shops, swimming pool, spa, tennis courts, conference center, general store, and gas station. Four-wheel-drive tours and eco-tours are available.

BEST TIMES: August through October.

FIELD NOTES: No paved roads outside of **Kingfisher Bay Resort**; 4-wheel-drive vehicles only are allowed; vehicles can be rented, ask at the lodge. Private hire and ranger-guided tours. To explore all that this island has to offer it is recommended to take advantage of the tours offered and then try it on your own. Beaches are legal roads on Fraser Island and normal road rules apply. No dogs or other domesticated animals are allowed on the island.

GREAT BARRIER REEF MARINE PARK

QUEENSLAND, AUSTRALIA

Australia's Great Barrier Reef is perhaps the most famous marine wildlife habitat in the world. It is the largest reef structure in the world and stretches over 1,000 miles along the Queensland coastline. The Australian government protects this precious natural resource, including a buffer zone as part of the park. Named the Great Barrier Reef Marine Park, it is larger than Great Britain, and the variety of marine life is staggering.

The reef itself is made up of 400 kinds of hard, soft, and multicolored coral and is home to brightly colored fish, turtles, and an amazing array of sea life. Visitors to this paradise can see from the air or from a boat that many exotic islands surround the reef. There are also shark-feeding stations and intact shipwrecks to explore.

Visitors have many options from which to choose. Adventure seekers can do day tours of snorkeling or diving. Another option is to stay dry and view the coral and fish through underwater observatories. Visitors can choose from a sailing catamaran, a fast wave-piercer, or a more personal dive vessel to immerse yourself and your fellow travelers into this incredible, mysterious world. There are many ways to get in the pristine water. Some of the best diving spots and dive platforms can be easily accessed from the mainland by boat, and many companies operate day trips. Walking from the beach to the water and snorkeling your way around islands or in the nearby shallow corals off the mainland is yet another option.

Tours are offered by naturalists and marine biologists, who share their insights on this incredible natural place. Helicopter and seaplane tours are available from a variety of tour companies.

Visitors are welcome to join an extended dive trip or stay on an island of the Great Barrier Reef.

There are different things to do on different islands; each has its own thrilling activities. Some islands have resorts, ranging from family friendly to exclusive hideaways. Other islands are uninhabited paradises in which visitors can pitch their tents under the stars on the beach and hike through rain forest–covered hills.

LOCATION: Coastal Queensland, Australia with main access from Cairns, although many coastal towns offer good points of departure.

HOURS OF OPERATION: Year-round.

CONTACT: *Park website:* www.gbrmpa.gov.au. *Tours:* www.queenslandholidays.com.au.

COST: Depends on tour package, length of stay, and travel preference.

ON-SITE AMENITIES: From luxury resort accommodations to camping, restaurants, bars, shopping, spas, gift shops, etc.

BEST TIMES: Queensland is blessed with an enviable climate of warm sunny days. Warm summers and mild winters are what you can expect, plus loads of sunshine (with just the occasional shower). Queensland is divided into a subtropical region in the south, where summers are warm, winters are mild, and autumn and spring offer the very best of climates, as well as a tropical region in the north, where the wet season (throughout summer) can be quite humid and hot, while the dry season (throughout winter) is quite dry and mild.

FIELD NOTES: From Mission Beach, the closest mainland access, you can be on the reef within an hour's time by boat. Queensland has an average of 265 days a year of sunshine. Load up on sunscreen, sunglasses, hats, snorkel gear, fins, towels, layered clothes, etc. Don't go unprepared.

O'REILLY'S RAINFOREST RETREAT

QUEENSLAND, AUSTRALIA

An enchanting escape into the lush beauty of the largest subtropical rain forest in the world, O'Reilly's Rainforest Retreat is located in one of Queensland's best-loved parks. Lamington National Park is the core of the Central Eastern Rainforest Reserves Australia World Heritage Area along the adjoining Border Ranges National Park in New South Wales. Visitors enjoy rugged mountain scenery, tumbling waterfalls, caves, stands of unusual plants, and some of the largest variety of exotic birds in the world.

The park and its surrounding lowlands support an abundance of mammals of about 70 species in 18 families. Some are shy and hard to see, like the much sought-after lyrebird or the echidna. Others, like the koala, are friendly and go about minding their own business while you watch and enjoy the magic of the natural world all around you.

Visitors can also see flying foxes, flying squirrels, red-necked and red-legged pademelons, ring-tailed possums, mountain brushtails, bandicoots, quolls, bats, wallabies, kangaroos, gaters, and platypus.

The Tree Top Walk at O'Reilly's is an innovative structure that gives visitors what can only be described as an exhilarating experience, a chance to observe life in the rain forest canopy at close range. Two observation decks have been constructed in a strangler fig above the walkway; the highest one being about 110 feet above the ground. Access to the decks is by a ladder that is protected by wire screens. The decks allow a close look at the orchids and ferns growing on the tree as well as the splendid view out over the rain forest canopy.

In January, during Wildlife Week—an annual survey of the mammal fauna of this region—visitors are provided with an opportunity to be shown these fascinating creatures up close and by experts in the field. O'Reilly's also sponsors other specialty programs on birds, the forest, and photography throughout the year and provides individualized and private guiding service. And for those seeking a respite from the onslaught of nature, O'Reilly's recently opened spa gives weary adventurers a full menu of pampering treatments for a unique relaxing experience.

The O'Reilly family pioneered ecotourism in Australia when they began showing visitors around the park in 1915. Their story is a classic example of how a local landholder was able to find a sustainable alternative to farming in an area of great environmental significance.

LOCATION: In the heart of Lamington National Park, 2 hours by road south of Brisbane and 90 minutes by road west of the Gold Coast.

HOURS OF OPERATION: 8 a.m. to 6 p.m.

CONTACT: *Main office:* O'Reilly's Rainforest Retreat, Lamington National Park Rd Canungra Valley, Queensland, 4275, Australia. *Mailing:* PO Box 392, Nerang, Qld, 4211, Australia. Tel: 1800688722 (reservations, within Australia) or 61755024911 (reservations), 61755434011 (reception), Fax: 6175543 4162; ABN: 99080634948. Web: www.oreillys.com.au; email: reservations@oreillys.com.au.

COST: Depends on accommodations; US$109–$590 per night for one or two; US$360–$610 per night for a villa; minimum stays may apply; linen charge, US$40 per stay.

ON-SITE AMENITIES: Discover program, treetop walk. Accommodations feature hi-def TV, outside bath spa, full kitchens, BBQ, private decks. Information and bookings for tours and transfer services.

FIELD NOTES: Bring comfortable walking shoes and rugged boots and layered clothing. The rain forest cools down considerably during the evening. Bug spray and hats and binoculars are a must for nature lovers.

WARRIGAL HIGHLAND RAINFOREST PRESERVE

QUEENSLAND, AUSTRALIA

The Warrigal Highland Rainforest Preserve, a private reserve owned by Wild Watch, in the Misty Mountains region of Queensland, is Australia's largest single track of tropical rain forest and home to an amazing array of rare and exotic fauna and flora. The unique ecosystem has promoted biodiversity in a hospitable climate. Wild Watch, which has dedicated itself to the area's preservation, believes that the best way to promote long-term protection of this natural treasure is through education. And their expertly guided tours, ranging from half to multiple days, are replete with options for the avid naturalist. If you are interested in native plant life, you will have the opportunity to view the giant rain forest trees, which are remnants from the ancient forests that once covered most of Australia. If your desire is bird-watching, you will be among more than 50% of Australia's renowned species, including 6 species of owls. If mammals are your main interest, there are guided nocturnal tours to see tree kangaroos, lemuroids, and Gliding possums as well as red-legged pade-

melons, swamp wallabies, musky-rat kangaroos, and tiger quolls. Also to be observed are insectivorous bats, bandicoots, forest dragons, leaf-tailed geckos, platypuses, and perhaps flying foxes.

LOCATION: Southwest of Cairns in the Misty Mountains, Queensland.

HOURS OF OPERATION: Year-round.

CONTACT: *Preserve office:* Tel: 617-40977408 (international) or 07-

40977408 (local); Web: www.wildwatch.com.au; email: jmunro@wildwatch.com.au.

ON-SITE AMENITIES: Wild Watch provides transport to and from your accommodation, air-conditioned tour vehicles, personal guides, loaner binoculars or scopes if needed, species lists and other printed details, night/day tours, and tours of varying length.

BEST TIMES: March through November.

FIELD NOTES: Accommodations are not provided on-site. See the preserve's website for recommended hotels and other nearby accommodations. To maximize the opportunity of seeing wildlife, timing, temperature, and lighting situation are critical. Platy-

puses are crepuscular and nocturnal and the very best time to observe them is very early morning, 6 a.m. to 7 a.m. before the sun reaches the water and before there are too many people moving around! They are relatively common and easy to find and see, providing certain procedures are observed. Possums and tree-kangaroos are mostly nocturnal. Tree kangaroos can also be found in some locations sleeping in favorite trees during the morning, warming themselves after a cool night. They disappear into vine thickets as the day warms up and are impossible to find. Kangaroos are best observed in either early morning or late afternoon or early in the evening.

KANGAROO ISLAND

SOUTH AUSTRALIA, AUSTRALIA

The third largest island off the southern coast of mainland Australia, Kangaroo Island is just a short flight or a 45-minute scenic ferry ride from Cape Jervis, often accompanied by an escort of dolphins, to what one can only call paradise. Kangaroo Island separated from the mainland of Australia some 10,000 years ago, leaving its creatures to

evolve differently from those on the mainland, meaning that some of the island's species and subspecies, such as the Kangaroo Island kangaroo, cannot be found anyplace else in the world. In addition, visitors can expect to see the more familiar Aussie animals, including the Tammar wallaby, short-beaked echidna, southern brown bandicoot,

koalas, heath goannas, brushtail possum, several species of snakes and bats, and even the elusive duck-billed platypus. Because many of the native animals are nocturnal, night tours are recommended and offered by local guides.

Along the many beautiful sandy beaches, visitors will see a variety of sea animals, such as Australian sea lions and New Zealand fur seals, fairy penguins and, on occasion, southern right whales.

For scuba divers, there are about 60 shipwreck sites around the island to explore. If you'd rather a day of superb fishing there are day charters that will supply tackle. Or you can spend your time relaxing on the magnificent beaches.

Accommodations range from hotels and B&Bs to cabins and houses on the beach to campsites. This is a place where luxury travelers and backpackers and everyone in between can find perfect accommodations.

LOCATION: 70 miles southwest of Adelaide, off the southern coast.

HOURS OF OPERATION: Year-round.

CONTACT: *Tourist information:* Web: www.tourkangarooisland.com.au or www.kangaroo-island-au.com.

COST: Depends on type of accommodations or tour.

ON-SITE AMENITIES: Nature and wildlife tours, and whale-watching tours.

BEST TIMES: With moderate temperatures, the island is an ideal year-round vacation and wildlife-viewing destination.

FIELD NOTES: A minimum 3- to 4-day stay is recommended to take advantage of all the island has to offer. You will need a good set of binoculars and a flashlight for night viewing, which is a particular highlight not to be missed. Activities to be enjoyed here aside from the abundant mammalian wildlife include scuba diving, charter fishing, bird-watching, and swimming. It should be noted that kangaroos and wallabies can move quickly so maintain a safe distance at all times.

FREYCINET NATIONAL PARK

TASMANIA, AUSTRALIA

Founded in 1916 and named after the French navigator Louis de Freycinet who explored Tasmania's coastline in the early 19th century, Freycinet National Park is Tasmania's oldest park. The 65-square-mile park includes forested hills, rugged coastline, and rocky granite peaks called the Hazards. The secluded, picturesque Wineglass Bay, with azure blue water, is one of the best white sand beaches in the world. With more than 300 days of sunshine, the park offers visitors scenic car touring, hiking, strolls along the beach, swimming, kayaking, sailing, snorkeling, rock, climbing on the Hazards with breathtaking views, and wildlife-spotting.

Park visitors are likely to see many kinds and sizes of wallabies. Wallaby is a general term for a variety of marsupials of the Macropodidae family that have the distinctive kangaroo-look but are smaller. The park is home to a variety of possums, like the common brushtail and ringtail possums. Sleeping in the hollow of a tree during the day, the possum ventures out at dusk to forage for food, much like its Northern Hemisphere cousin, the opossum. Visitors may see quoll, a carnivorous marsupial that is sometimes called the native cat because of its cat-like fur, eating habits, and size. The quoll is a close relative of the larger and much better known Tasmanian devil, which can also be found in the park.

The Tasmanian devil is the largest carnivorous marsupial in the world. With a body the size of a stocky, muscular small dog, the devil, as it is sometimes called, has the strongest bite relative to body size of any mammal in the world. The devil earned its name because of its ferocious and noisy eating habits. Although wallabies and wombats are its favorite food, it is willing to eat just about anything dead or alive. Able to consume as much as 40% of its body weight in 30 minutes, mealtime is a bizarre social event for the Tasmanian devil. As many as a dozen eat together, frantically tearing carrion or their kill apart, loudly crushing bones with their strong jaws and teeth, pausing to yawn viciously and strike terrifying poses to scare one another, and vocalizing so loudly the ruckus can be heard a mile away. When mealtime is over, nothing remains; the devils devour every scrap, including bone and fur. If startled, the devil can excrete a pungent odor rivaling that of the skunk. Until 1941, the devil was hunted by farmers and ranchers concerned about their livestock. As a result, the devil is extinct in mainland Australia and exists in only Tasmania, where their numbers are estimated at 20,000–50,000.

LOCATION: Freycinet Peninsula on the east coast of Tasmania, approximately 80 miles north of Hobart. The closest town is Coles Bay, about 7 miles away.

HOURS OF OPERATION: Year-round. *Visitors center:* Generally daily, 9 a.m. to 5 p.m.

CONTACT: *Park office:* Freycinet National Park Private Bag, Bicheno, Tasmania 7215 Australia. *Visitors center:* Tel: 0362567000; Web: www.parks.tas .gov.au/natparks/freycinet/index.html.

COST: *Entrance* (per day): US$20. Campgrounds require an additional fee, depending on location and campground amenities.

ON-SITE AMENITIES: Visitors center with nearby outdoor amphitheater, campgrounds with restroom facilities, park trails of varying lengths and difficulty, and ranger-led guided tours. *Lodging:* **Freycinet Lodge:** Located in the park and managed by a concessioner; visit www.freycinetlodge.com.au.

BEST TIMES: August through May.

FIELD NOTES: Wear good walking shoes and carry a good set of binoculars. Bring sun protection and carry water because some areas of the park, like Wineglass Beach, do not have water. Wineglass Beach is accessible only by boat or 3-hour hike. The lodge offers a variety of walks to experience this unique site. Pets and firearms are not permitted, and visitors should not feed the animals.

HUON BUSH RETREATS

TASMANIA, AUSTRALIA

Variety is the spice of life in this breathtaking section of Tasmania. There are gorgeous dolomite caves, warm thermal springs, deep blue waters, brilliant white beaches, cool fresh rain forests, and spectacular purple, orange, and golden sunsets. As remote as it is, it is also spiritually refreshing. Huon Bush Retreats are self-contained cabins, teepees, and campgrounds in an extensive private nature reserve just a 50-minute drive south from Hobart. To get to the retreat you drive a long gravel public road, which is narrow and winding in places and which takes careful driving not only because of the curves but because the wildlife, which roams free, is used to living in secure

privacy, and is not used to vehicular traffic.

Most Tasmanian animals are nocturnal. During the day, visitors will not see much activity, but come nightfall, the bush becomes, as it were, a beehive of activity, with animals foraging, feeding, and building. A unique part of the preserve is that the creatures at Mount Misery Habitat Reserve are free to come and go as they please and are protected. While this is not the easiest place to spot them, it is the best place to learn about their habitat. Sightings do occur, of course, and are thrilling when they do. Nearly guaranteed sightings are brushtail possums and rufous hare-wallaby (mala). Highly likely sightings are bats, moths, and perhaps a quoll, bandicoot, or Bennett wallaby. You will probably also hear an owl or two and maybe a ringtail possum, which is likely to be too high in the trees to spot, but you might be lucky. Bettongs are very shy, but you might see evidence of their diggings on the forest floor.

Also a treat for bird lovers, the retreat is habitat to several dozen species, including the threatened wedge-tailed eagles, black cockatoos, sulfur-crested cockatoos, and currawongs. Many of the smaller species can be found and heard in the shrubs throughout the village and high in the forest canopy. Several species of owls and nightjars are heard and can be seen after nightfall. In sum, night or day, you won't be disappointed.

LOCATION: Southwest of Hobart.

HOURS OF OPERATION: Year-round.

CONTACT: *Main office:* Huon Bush Retreats, 300 Browns Rd, Ranelagh, Huon Valley, Tasmania; PO Box 168, Huonville 7109, Tasmania, Australia; Tel: 0362642233; Fax: 0362642288; Web: www.huonbushretreats.com.

COST: *Cabin rentals* (per night): from US$240.

ON-SITE AMENITIES: Insulated cabins with kitchens; solar-powered, 12-volt electric systems; rainwater recycling systems; mobile phone capabilities; campground, and BBQ facilities. The on-site commercial kitchen serves local organic foods (24-hour notice required); for more information, visit the retreat's website. Four bush-walking tracks and facilitates interpretive walks.

BEST TIMES: October through June.

FIELD NOTES: The catered menu is limited so special diets and food restrictions should be considered; most of the cabins have cooking facilities, although the nearest supermarket is 10 miles away. Layered clothing, boots, and comfortable walking shoes are a must. Waterproof jackets and footwear are highly recommended due to changeable wet weather patterns.

MACQUARIE ISLAND NATURE RESERVE

TASMANIA, AUSTRALIA

If you want to visit a place that's totally off the beaten path consider Tasmania's Macquarie Island Nature Reserve. But then some might say that the whole of Tasmania is off the beaten path. With a surface area of 79 square miles, the reserve is made up of Macquarie Island, surrounding islands, and ocean up to three nautical miles from the coast. Named a World Heritage site due to its geological significance, Macquarie is the only spot on earth created entirely from oceanic crust and rocks formed on or below the seabed, deep beneath our earth's surface.

Macquarie Island is a breeding ground for some 3.5 million birds and 80,000 elephant seals. Other native animals include four types of seals: elephant, Antarctic, southern elephant, and New Zealand. And there are 25 bird species, of which 90% are penguins. Macquarie is the only place where royal penguins breed. There's an estimated 850,000 of them in the area. Until 1919, these birds, which have a distinctive white face and chin, were routinely killed for their oil. King, southern rockhopper and gintoo penguins also live on Macquarie, along with other seabirds, such as albatrosses, gulls, cormorants, ducks, and petrels.

Macquarie Island has had problems caused by the introduction of invasive species by travelers. The feral cats that killed seabirds and disrupted the island's balance of nature are now gone, but their absence has led to an explosion in the numbers of rodents and rabbits. The former eat young chicks, while the latter ruin seabirds' nests. Plans are under way to rid the island of these pests.

It is not possible to visit Macquarie Island on a whim. Due to environmental concerns, the Tasmanian State Reserve, managed by the Tasmanian Park and Wildlife Service, limits the number of tourists to 750 people a year. All visitors must have advance access authority, or be accompanied by an authorized person. All visitors must be part of an authorized group with a leader, and no more than 15 people per group for a maximum visit of two consecutive days, and overnight stays are prohibited, unless in the case of an emergency. No food can be brought to the area, and tourists are not to enter any of the offices and homes of the 20–40 scientists and support staff that live on the island.

Yes, there are plenty of restrictions. But the chance to visit this reserve so close to the bottom of the world is well worth the trouble. Tourists can walk along designated trails on the tree-free island and contemplate the ocean in peace. The big payoff is seeing thousands upon thousands of seabirds and seals in their native habitat and knowing that few others have witnessed such a sight.

LOCATION: 932 miles south-southeast of Tasmania, Australia.

HOURS OF OPERATION: Year-round, daily, 7 a.m. to 7 p.m.

CONTACT: *Permits:* Available from Tasmania Parks and Wildlife Service; Tel: 1300135513; Web: www.parks.tas.gov .au/macquarie.

COST: Depends on tour package and transportation.

ON-SITE AMENITIES: Guided tours.

BEST TIMES: September through mid March to observe thousands of royal penguins during their mating season.

The spring and summer months, on the northern part of the island, are ideal for spotting the breeding elephant seal colonies.

FIELD NOTES: Combination tours of varying length and destinations can be booked through Heritage Expeditions, visit www.heritageexpeditions.com. For a listing of additional tour operators contact the Tasmania Park and Wildlife Service directly. The weather is harsh, so plan on wearing plenty of layers and wet-weather gear because it rains an average of 310 days out of the year. Access to the southwest corner of the island is restricted due to its use as a mating ground for the wandering albatross, an endangered species. While animal viewing is relatively close, you'll want to bring a good set of binoculars.

MARIA ISLAND NATIONAL PARK AND MARINE RESERVE

TASMANIA, AUSTRALIA

In 1825 a penal colony of log and bark huts was constructed on Maria Island, 10 miles off Tasmania's east coast. Subsequently, more permanent penitentiary buildings were constructed of sand and limestone bricks, quarried and manufactured on the island. By the 1880s the penitentiary had closed, and in 1888 the Grand Hotel, with a banquet hall and billiard room, opened, and the island was promoted as a sanatorium and pleasure resort. Bricks from the penitentiary cells were reused to build guest cottages, a coffee house called the Coffee Palace, and roads. From the 1930s to 1972 the island was mainly used for farming. In 1972, the island was turned into a national park, administered by the Tasmania government. Various mammal and bird species were released on the island, and today, Maria Island National Park and Marine Reserve contains a wealth of history and natural wildlife for visitors to explore

A variety of marsupials live on the island, like the endangered Tasmania bet-

tong, a small kangaroo-like animal that eats fungi, roots, and tubers. Bettongs became extinct in the wild in Australia in the 1920s. Since then, breeding programs have been successful in reestablishing their numbers, and visitors may see them on Maria Island. The island is home to the wombat, a short-legged marsupial that lives in colonies and digs complex burrow systems, with its powerful claws and rodent-like teeth. During the 1970s, emu were reintroduced to the island. Extinct in Tasmania by the early 1800s, the emu is the second largest bird in the world after the ostrich. Standing 6 feet 6 inches tall, it can trot for long distances or gallop for short distances at a speed of 30 miles per hour. The endangered forty-spotted pardalote, one of the smallest birds in Australia, can be found on the island by patient bird-watchers. Maria Island is one of the few refuges in the world where this very rare, small greenish brown bird survives.

Off the west coast of Maria Island lies a spectacular underwater world of fish and invertebrates. The Marine Reserve is home to abalone, rock lobster, and sea dragons. The threatened tiny fairy penguin, just 16 inches tall and weighing only 2.2 pounds, swims and fishes along the island's shores. Seastars and five species of handfish, found nowhere else in the world, walk along the reserve's sea bottom. A type of anglerfish, the handfish is so-named because its peculiar pectoral fins spread out at the ends like hands and the fish uses them to pull itself along on the ocean floor. White sharks troll the Marine Reserve in search of prey, while porpoises and migrating whales frolic about in the reserve's protected waters.

LOCATION: Approximately 10 miles (half-hour by boat) off the east coast of Tasmania near the town of Triabunna, accessible only by ferry, boat, or plane.

HOURS OF OPERATION: Year-round, daily, closed 2 weeks in mid-July for site maintenance.

CONTACT: *Park office:* Maria Island National Park, c/o Post Office Triabunna, Tasmania 7190. Tel: 03625 1420; Web: www.parks.tas.gov.au/marine/maria/index.html.

COST: *Entrance* (per day): Adults, US$11; family, US$22. *Ferry* (round trip): Adults, US$50; children (3–16 years): US$25.

ON-SITE AMENITIES: Darlington visitors center, ranger station, public toilets, picnic areas with gas barbecues, overnight campgrounds with pay showers. There are no tourist shops on the island. Historic guided tours are available, numerous walking trails, tide-pool exploring, snorkeling, diving, and kayaking. *Lodging:* Accommodations are basic, including the bunkhouse-style accommodations in the refurbished Darlington Convict Penitentiary Cells or in campsites, visit http://tassie.org.au/mariaisland for more information.

BEST TIMES: Year-round.

FIELD NOTES: Wear good walking shoes. Water temperature varies between 68°F in December (Tasmania's summer) and 52°F in July. Dive tanks can be refilled on the island. Hunting, fishing, and collecting wildlife are not allowed. There are no shops on the island, so visitors are required to bring their own food, warm gear, etc. (There are plenty of shops in Triabunna.) There is no ferry service for about 4 weeks around July; contact the park and ferry service for exact days.

MOUNT FIELD NATIONAL PARK

TASMANIA, AUSTRALIA

At more than 39,000 acres, Mount Field National Park is just right for tourists who wish to experience multiple ecosystems—and the flora and fauna they support—in one visit. Around the base of the mountain tall swamp gum forests and huge tree ferns predominate. Along Lake Dobson Road, the park takes on the appearance of a rain forest. Subalpine woodland starts and continues on from there as the amount and variety of vegetation increases as the altitude rises.

The first of two major sections of the park are centered on Russell Falls, a three-tiered waterfall that flows into a fern forest. The second is the Lake Dobson area, which offers plenty of opportunities for scenic hikes and skiing in the winter.

Mount Field is a walker's dream, for there are many trails of varying difficulty that provide good opportunities to see the abundant natural wonders. The Tall Trees Trail, which takes approximately a half hour to complete, focuses on the swamp gums that are the world's tallest flowering plants. Another relatively simple journey, the Lyrebird Nature Walk, winds past the rain forest. Tarn Shelf, a moderately challenging route, takes visitors past small glacial lakes. Park rangers lead walks during the summer months and offer nature discussions as well.

Every trail offers good chances to see a variety of animal species that are now extinct on the Australian mainland, such as the eastern barred bandicoot and eastern quoll. Other species are also found on the continent, such as common wombat, long-nosed potoroo, Bennett wallaby and the laughing kookaburra. The Tasmanian devil, a carnivorous marsupial that has been placed on the endangered species list, also uses the park as one of its prime habitats. (Devil tumor facial disease, a form of cancer, has been killing off this animal since the mid 1990s.) There are many bird species to delight in at Mount Field, including the Tasmanian native hen, black currawong, cormorant, pacific black duck, and Latham snipe.

LOCATION: 37 miles northwest of Hobart.

HOURS OF OPERATION: Year-round.

CONTACT: *Park office:* Mount Field National Park, 66 Lake Dobson Rd, National Park TAS 7140; Tel: 0362881149; Fax: 0362881170; Web: www.parks.tas.gov.au/natparks/mtfield. *Hobart visitor information center:* 20 Davey St, Hobart; Tel: 0362308233.

COST: *Entrance:* Individual, US$11; vehicle (up to 8 passengers), US$22. *Cabin* (per night): US$40.

ON-SITE AMENITIES: Picnic areas, visitors center, cafe, rest rooms, gift shop, campground. *Camping:* Mount Field campground offers both powered and unpowered sites for tents or caravans operated by a private on-site contractor; call 0362881526. *Lodging:* **Lake Dobson cabins:** In the higher elevations; accessible by car, each sleeps up to six people; bunks with mattresses, cold water and sink, a wood heater, firewood, and a table with benches. Visitors should bring items that will make this sparse structure more comfortable, like sheets, pillows, and a lantern; there is no electricity. A communal restroom is nearby. Book through the Parks and Wildlife Service.

BEST TIMES: Enjoy spectacular fall foliage during late April to early May. Wildlife viewing is optimal year-round.

FIELD NOTES: Wear sturdy walking boots, warm clothing, and a waterproof jacket. The weather at Mount Field can change dramatically during the day, so check the weather forecast before your trip. Park officials advise carrying a good map as well.

PHILLIP ISLAND NATURE PARK

VICTORIA, AUSTRALIA

Victoria's Phillip Island Nature Park, home to the famous penguin parade, is Australia's second most popular tourist attraction and a must stop, see, and experience, on every wildlife lover's wish list. On Summerland beach, at dusk, is where and when it happens. First there is one, then a few more, and then many—even hundreds—of little fairy penguins marching in from the sea to their burrows in the sand dunes after a long day spent foraging. Completely unaware of the excitement they are causing in the human species and going about their daily business, these little creatures are easily watched from the viewing stands and boardwalks, built to protect the penguins' habitat and to ensure that the 500,000 visitors that come here each year all get a good look. While the setup may seem tame and viewing as orchestrated as a theme park, the Phillip Island fairy penguins are wildlife in action at its best.

Native to Australia, the little penguins are the smallest of their species, standing at a mere 16 inches. And of the more than 26,000 penguins resid-

ing in the waters surrounding the island, 4,500 have their burrows around Summerland Beach.

The penguin parade is not the only reason to visit this park. On the western tip of the island, at Seal Rocks, more than 16,000 fur seals take up residence from October through December. And the island is also home to a large number of koalas. Visitors can wander along the treetop boardwalk at the island's Koala Conservation Centre to get a birds-eye view of the koalas high up in their favorite spot, the crook of a comfortable tree.

The island hosts a wide array of bird species. More than a million short-tailed shearwaters (also known as mutton birds) visit the island each year, covering long distances to arrive by September 25. Large numbers of migratory wading birds fly to Rhyll Inlet and wetland to forage and breed. This varied group includes colonies of royal spoonbills, straw-necked ibises, swans, and rare hooded plovers.

LOCATION: Approximately a 90-minute drive south from Melbourne.

HOURS OF OPERATION: Year-round, daily. *Penguin parade hours:* 10 a.m. to 12 p.m. *Koala Conservation Centre:* 10 a.m. to 5 p.m. (6 p.m. in the summer season).

CONTACT: *Tourist information:* Phillip Island Tourist Rd, Cowes, VIC 3922; Tel: 0359512800; Fax: 0359568394; Web: www.penguins.org.au; email: penguins @penguins.org.au.

COST: *Penguin parade:* Adult, US$20; Australian pensioner, US$14; child, US$10; family (2 adults, 2 children), US$50. *Additional parade fees:* Penguins Plus—more personal viewing, with an experienced ranger; adult, US$35; child US$17.50; family, US$87.50. Penguin Sky Box (over 16 years)—view from an exclusive, elevated viewing tower with an experienced ranger; US$50. Ultimate Penguin Experience (over 12 years, small group)—view from a secluded beach using night-vision technology with an experienced ranger; US$70. Private Penguin Parade (12 years and older)—up-close viewing from an exclusive area with personal guide; US$65.

ON-SITE AMENITIES: Interpretive center, picnic areas, restrooms, shops, cafe. Viewing platforms, ranger-led wildlife viewing tours, bush walks, car, coach, and disabled parking.

BEST TIMES: Year-round.

FIELD NOTES: To see everything that Phillip Island has to offer, a minimum of 4 days are recommended. Accommodations, tours, and activities are plentiful. For more information, options, and booking, visit www.visitvictoria.com.

MORNINGTON WILDLIFE SANCTUARY AND WILDERNESS CAMP

WESTERN AUSTRALIA, AUSTRALIA

Situated in the heart of Kimberley, at more than 885,311 acres, Mornington Wildlife Sanctuary and Wilderness Camp is the largest nongovernmental protected area in Australia and is universally acknowledged as one of the world's last wild places. Encompassing spectacular gorges and tropical savanna, it is teeming with wildlife.

The wilderness camp is the base from which this remarkable sanctuary can be explored, and where wildlife enthusiasts can take part in various guided and self-guided tours. Mornington Wilderness Camp showcases the flora and fauna of the central Kimberley region as well as highlights the groundbreaking research and conservation projects that are being conducted there. Various tours are available, allowing guests an intimate insight into nationally threatened species such as the Gouldian finch, purple-crowned fairy wren, and the red goshawk. Private tours are available to exclusive hideaways such as the tranquil pools of Fitzroy Bluff.

Owned by the not-for-profit Australian Wildlife Conservancy with the aim of preserving some of the threatened local wildlife, the camp protects amazing natural gorges, the upper catchment of the mighty Fitzroy River, sections of the rugged King Leopold Range, and various ecosystems that are home to over 200 species of birds as well as various mammals and reptiles. A stay at Mornington means you are helping the preservation cause; all proceeds going to wildlife conservation.

Visitors will find stunning scenic lookouts at Sir John Gorge. Canoeing is

available at Diamond Gorge, where rugged red cliffs tower over the cooling deep water, which is also known to be home to freshwater crocodiles—said to be of the non-man-eating variety.

In the rocky areas you may be the privileged spectator of a group of rare short-eared rock-wallabies, a secretive animal, which only a few have been lucky enough to witness. When scanning the cliff areas, look deeply into the crannies for this unusual animal. Grazing in the open areas and foraging on a variety of plant life, northern nail-tail wallabies and antilopine wallaroos are easy to spot. Quolls, dingoes, and yellow-spotted monitor lizards as well as free roaming cattle and donkeys all exist together here.

Because conservation is the mainstay at Mornington, guests are asked to take part in their efforts and to report any and all of their sightings and observations.

LOCATION: Kimberley, Western Australia. Roads are suitable for 4-wheel-drive vehicles only.

HOURS OF OPERATION: Apr–Nov, weather and road conditions permitting.

CONTACT: *Main office:* Tel: 800631946. Web: www.australianwildlife.org/Home.aspx; email: mornington@australianwildlife.org.

COST: Depends on package and choices. *Lodging* (per person, per night): from US$550.

ON-SITE AMENITIES: The camp has 10 safari-style tents, each with a large double bed and en-suite bathroom. Gourmet dinners are served at Redtails restaurant and are often followed by a presentation on the conservation programs at Mornington. Various tours led by resident naturalists, including bird-watching and wildlife, ecology, gorge, and sunset tours.

BEST TIMES: April through November.

FIELD NOTES: A minimum 2-night stay is recommended and 4–5 days are highly recommended. For the more adventurous traveler, pitching your own tent is another option available. The camp offers various activities, including bush walking, swimming, canoeing, and scenic flights.

SHARK BAY

WESTERN AUSTRALIA, AUSTRALIA

In spite of the name, the most common marine life found in Shark Bay is actually the dugong (sea cow). Although the sharks are relatively plentiful and tend to titillate with an exaggerated sense of danger, this remarkable area is much more important to conservationists for its 26 threatened mammalian species. Shark Bay is a World Heritage Site located on the western coast of Australia. The area encompasses two different bays formed by two peninsulas lying parallel to each other. Called Gathaajudu by the Malgana Aboriginal peoples, the shape and layout of Shark Bay are part of what makes the area memorable and unique.

Shark Bay is also the home of one of only two species of marine mammals that have shown a propensity for tool use. The bottlenose dolphins are taught by their mothers to use a sea sponge to protect the nose when searching for food along the sandy sea bottom. Sea otters also demonstrate this ability by using rocks to open hard shells.

Bernier and Dorre Islands serve as a refuge for five critically endangered terrestrial mammals. Four of the five mammals are not found anywhere else

on earth. The mammals that live here have been blessed by geology to have avoided contending with the major introduction of cats and foxes, which have ravaged much of Australia's endemic wildlife elsewhere.

The conservators of Shark Bay have followed the lessons learned from the island's natural isolation and have undertaken efforts to remove the few existing cats, foxes, and grazing stock. This effort, dubbed "Project Eden," has resulted in a diversified rejuvenation in the area as captive-bred animals have been introduced to the area in an effort to return the habitats to their former vibrant state.

Shark Bay may have the densest population of diverse threatened species in the world. Within the confines of the refuge are found the Shark Bay mouse, stern barred bandicoot, greater bilby, rufous hare-wallaby (mala), banded hare-wallaby, Shark Bay boodie, woylie, eater stick-nest rat, gong, and humpback whale. There are roughly 236 species of birds that have been recorded at Shark Bay, including the threatened malleefowl, rufous field wren, Dirk Hartog Island southern emu-wren and black-and-white fairy wren, and the Shark Bay variegated field wren.

LOCATION: Western coast of Australia in the Gascoyne Region.

HOURS OF OPERATION: Depends on location; some areas 24/7; others only during business hours.

CONTACT: *Main office:* Tel: 61899481208, Web: www.sharkbay.org; email: sharkbayenquiries@dec.wa.gov.au.

COST: *Entrance:* Free. Additional fees may apply. *Lodging:* Depends on accommodation.

ON-SITE AMENITIES: A full range of accommodation options is available, including hotels, resorts, and campgrounds. Shark Bay World Heritage Discovery Centre, flightseeing.

BEST TIMES: May through November. Although some times are better than others to visit, there are no bad times to visit Shark Bay.

FIELD NOTES: Allow yourself at least 2 hours to explore the discovery center. The area boasts an array of activities, including bush walking, dolphin watching, boating, fishing, snorkeling, scuba diving, windsurfing, kite-boarding, and sea kayaking. In the dolphin interaction zone, guests are permitted to feed the dolphins, which come to the beach each day, under ranger supervision. If you participate, refrain from wearing sunscreen on your lower legs, hands, and arms, so the dolphins are not affected.

ABEL TASMAN NATIONAL PARK

NEW ZEALAND

Abel Tasman National Park is named after the first European to visit what is now called New Zealand's South Island in 1642. Permanent European settlements began in 1855. The area's beech forests were logged extensively until 1942, when the park was created. Today the 54,000-acre park is noted for its golden sandy beaches and popular, scenic hiking trails. It is one of the sunniest places in New Zealand, with sunshine aver-

In the 1880s the stoat, a small weasel-like mammal, was brought to New Zealand in hopes of controlling the nonnative rabbit population. The unintended consequence was that the stoat preferred New Zealand's native mammals to rabbit and so the park has an aggressive stoat-trapping program, making it necessary for visitors to be wary of and stay clear of stoat traps.

aging 5.5 hours a day over the course of a year.

Much of the park's beech forests and natural habitats have recovered since the logging days, providing sanctuary for many species of birds. Visitors may catch a glimpse of the rare fairy penguin. Sometimes called the blue penguin because of its blue-colored feathers, the flightless bird is a diminutive relative of the much larger penguins of Antarctica. Visitors might see the wood pigeon and the noisy tui bird. Considered to be intelligent like the parrot, the tui can imitate human speech. In the wild, its noisy call includes clicks, cackles, creaks, groans, and wheezing sounds. The rare flightless weka also lives in the park. The weka, with a dark brown coat of short feathers and about the size of a chicken, is a member of the rail family and feeds on a diet of earthworms, insects, small amphibians, and lizards. Seabirds like the cormorant and oystercatcher can be seen along the park's beaches. Large colonies of fur seal live along the park's rocky shores.

LOCATION: North end of South Island, in the Nelson Region, approximately 12 miles north of Motueka town.

HOURS OF OPERATION: Year-round.

CONTACT: *Park office:* Tourism Information Center, Abel Tasman National Park, Wallace Street, Motueka, New Zealand; Tel: 006435286543; Web: www .abeltasman.co.nz; email: info@abel tasman.co.nz.

COST: *Entrance:* Free. *Lodging* (per night): Campsite, US$5; hut, US$8–$11; contact the tourism information center for information and bookings.

ON-SITE AMENITIES: Campsites and park huts, equipped with running water, toilets, and fireplaces. Park aqua taxis are available. Kayak rental companies operate from Marahau. There are no food stores or shops in the park.

BEST TIMES: December through May.

FIELD NOTES: The park is closed to vehicles. Wear good walking shoes that can stand the wet. All food must be carried into the park; however, there is a cafe at **Awaroa Lodge** in Awaroa Bay. The 30-mile-long roundtrip Coast Track is very popular and is among the most used hiking trails in New Zealand. Plan to take 3–5 days to walk its entire length. Shorter walks are available, including a 2-day option. There are camp-sites and huts along the way, and in several locations, bay crossings depend on the tide, so check with the park for timing the crossings. No bicycling or horseback riding is allowed; visit the website for tour options, accommodations, and booking.

PUKAHA MOUNT BRUCE WILDLIFE CENTER

NEW ZEALAND

The Maori people, the native inhabitants of New Zealand, have a legend that long ago Tanemahuta, lord of the forest, asked the birds living in the trees if one of them would come down and live on the forest floor. One by one, Tui, Pipiwharauroa the cuckoo, and Pukeko the hen, said no. Finally he asked Kiwi, and Kiwi said yes. As a reward for his courage and sacrifice, Tanemahuta made Kiwi the most famous and loved bird of all. Visitors to Pukaha Mount Bruce Wildlife Center can see the kiwi, New Zealand's beloved official mascot. Founded in 1958 and managed by the New Zealand Wildlife Service since 1962, the center is dedicated to saving and restoring New Zea-

land's endangered flora and fauna, including the kiwi. In addition, the center gives visitors the opportunity to see and learn about some of New Zealand's most precious wildlife treasures.

On the verge of extinction by the end of the 19th century, the kiwi is a semi-nocturnal flightless bird with bristly, hair-like feathers that lives only in New Zealand. It is the only surviving member of the genus *Apteryx*, which includes the now-extinct giant flightless bird the moa. Monogamous for life, the female kiwi, about the size of a domestic chicken, lays an enormous egg, about six times larger than a chicken egg, which the male incubates. The center has an active kiwi recovery program, and at the Kiwi House visitors can observe and learn about this fascinating creature and the center's kiwi breeding program. In addition to the kiwi, the center has other unusual and endangered New Zealand wildlife. The kaka, a medium-size parrot, is recognized as a vulnerable species by the International Union for Conservation of Nature. The kaka makes its nest in the hollow of a tree trunk and feeds on fruits, berries, and seeds, using its strong beak to shred seeds from tree cones. Visitors to the center can see kakariki, or the New Zealand parakeet, and kereru, New Zealand's wood pigeon with iridescent blue and purple feathers and a wing span of 20 inches. The center has a recovery program for the endangered takahe, a large, purple, flightless bird and the largest surviving member of the Rallidae family.

Visitors to the center can see tuatara, a "living fossil." These 32-inch-long lizards are the only surviving members of the order Sphenodontia, which roamed the earth 200 million years ago along with the dinosaurs. The greenish brown lizard with a spiny crest along its back has a number of unusual features, such as two rows of top teeth that overlap one row of bottom teeth and skeletal characteristics that are evolutionarily retained from fish. It can hear, yet has no external ears and when first born has a light-sensitive organ with a small lens and retina called a parietal eye, or third eye, which disappears as the lizard grows.

LOCATION: Between the Wairarapa and Tararua areas on the North Island, about a 2-hour drive north of Wellington.

HOURS OF OPERATION: Year-round, daily, 9 a.m. to 4:30 p.m.; closed Christmas Day.

CONTACT: *Wildlife center:* Tel: 646375800; Web: www.mtbruce.org.nz; email: info@mtbruce.org.nz.

COST: *Entrance:* Adults, US$10; children (5–17 years), US$2; children (under 5 years), free. *Guided tours* (per person): From US$20, weekends and holidays.

ON-SITE AMENITIES: Park wildlife center with interactive displays and gift shop, **Takahe Café**, Kiwi House, Kaka Feed Stations, and well-marked footpaths. Guided tours are available.

BEST TIMES: October through April.

FIELD NOTES: Wear good walking shoes and carry good binoculars. Transit buses operate between the park and the city of Masterton, approximately 18 miles to the south.

INDEX

Items listed in **bold** indicate wildlife destinations; those in *italics* indicate regions. Wildlife is listed by region.

Wild Chalet Resort, India, 276
wild dogs
    Africa, 160–62, 198–99, 208–9, 210–11
    Asia, 282–83, 284–85, 286–87, 294–95, 304–5,
        308–9, 309–10
    Australia, 330–32
wild forest reindeer, *Europe*, 236–37
wild goats, *Europe*, 239–40
wild turkeys, *North America*, 45–46
Wild Watch, 342, 343
wildebeests, *Africa*, 159–60, 160–62, 182–84,
    189–91, 192–93, 195–96, 210–11, 212–13
wildflowers
    Asia, 295–96
    Australia, 336–37
    Europe, 250–51
    North America, 26–28, 28–30, 34–35
wildlife destinations, xi–xiv
    Africa (region), 157–221
    Asia (region), 263–317
    Australia (region), 319–62
    Europe (region), 223–62
    North America (region), 1–116
    South America (region), 117–55
    See also specific wildlife (by region)
willets
    North America, 37–38
    South America, 150–51
Wilson's phalaropes, *South America*, 150–51
Wirnwirnmila Mary River Road House,
    Northern Territory, Australia, 328
wolverines
    Europe, 234–35, 252–53
    North America, 4–5, 6–7, 8–9, 10–11, 13–15,
        15–17, 39–41, 66–67, 91–93, 96–97, 99–101,
        104–6
wolves
    Africa, 195–96
    Asia, 278–79, 282–83, 284–85, 288–89
    Europe, 226–27, 228–29, 229–31, 234–35,
        236–37, 243–44, 250–51, 252–53, 255–56
    North America, 4–5, 6–7, 8–9, 10–11, 12–13,
        13–15, 15–17, 64–65, 66–67, 71–72, 88–89,
        96–97, 99–101, 103–4, 104–6, 106–8,
        108–10, 110–11, 112–13
wombats, *Australia*, 321–23, 345–46, 350–52,
    352–53

Wood Buffalo National Park, Northwest
    Territories and Alberta, Canada, 112–13
wood lemmings, *Europe*, 258–59
woodchucks, *North America*, 73–75
woodcocks
    Europe, 237–38, 240–41
    North America, 58–59
Wooded Peaks Game Lodge, South Africa,
    213
woodlarks, *Europe*, 247–49
woodpeckers
    Asia, 269–70, 308–9
    Europe, 250–51, 256–57, 259–60, 261–62
    North America, 21–22, 43–44, 71–72, 73–75,
        98–99, 101–3, 106–8, 110–11, 258–59
    South America, 132–33
World Heritage Sites, 23, 88, 110, 112, 141, 145,
    268, 325, 332, 334, 340, 348, 358
woylies, *Australia*, 358–59
wrasses
    Australia, 324–26
    South America, 127–28
wrens
    Australia, 326–28, 330–32, 358–59
    Europe, 234–35, 240–41
    North America, 28–30, 32–33, 73–75, 99–101,
        106–8, 110–11
Wyoming, USA, 90–97

Xanterra Parks and Resorts, USA, 97

yellowlegs, *North America*, 37–38, 110–11
Yellowstone National Park, Wyoming,
    Montana, Idaho, USA, 90, 96–97
yellow-throated maternas, *Asia*, 279–80
Yosemite National Park, California, USA,
    36–37
Yukon Delta National Wildlife Refuge,
    Alaska, USA, 19–20
Yup'ik Eskimos, 20

Zapata Ranch, San Luis Valley, Colorado,
    USA, 41–42
zebras, *Africa*, 160–62, 170–71, 172–73, 174–75,
    176–77, 182–84, 186–87, 192–93, 197–98,
    202–3, 208–9, 210–11, 212–13, 215–16
zibets, *Asia*, 268–69

PHOTO CREDITS

Unless otherwise specified, copyright of the works reproduced herein lies with the respective photographers, agencies, and museums. In some cases it has not been possible to establish copyright ownership. In these cases, we would appreciate notification.

Page 96: William Campbell/US Fish and Wildlife Service

Page 98: Dave Grickson/US Fish and Wildlife Service

Page 102: Phil Million/US Fish and Wildlife Service

Page 105: Larry Moats/US Fish and Wildlife Service

Page 112: Elise Smith/US Fish and Wildlife Service

Pages 114, 116, 134, 214, 215, 311, 338, 324: National Oceanic and Atmospheric Administration (NOAA)

Pages 127, 148: Oceanic and Atmospheric Research/National Undersea Research Program (OAR/NURP)

Pages 159, 162, 165, 169, 170, 172, 174, 176, 178, 183, 189, 196, 197, 199, 200, 205, 207, 210, 212, 220, 275, 285, 336: Wildlife Pictures Online

Pages 160, 202: Linda Holody

Page 184: Inyati Private Game Reserve

Page 186: Ivory Tree Game Lodge

Page 188: Kapama Private Game Reserve

Page 191: Lalibela Game Reserve

Page 192: MalaMala Game Reserve

Page 194: Monkeyland

Page 204: Sabi Sabi Private Game Reserve

Page 218: Thomas Snitch

Page 228: John and Karen Hollingsworth/US Fish and Wildlife Service

Page 236: Mike Boylan/US Fish and Wildlife Service

Page 257: Craig Koppie/US Fish and Wildlife Service

Page 258: Jim Leupold/US Fish and Wildlife Service

Pages 277, 284, 287, 308: John Duff

Page 279: Ron Singer/US Fish and Wildlife Service

Page 342: Jonathan Munro/Warrigal Highland Rainforest Reserve

Page 360: PDPhoto.org

All other photos are in the public domain.

Inspiring Americans to protect wildlife for our children's future

Protecting wildlife through education and action since 1936, the National Wildlife Federation (NWF) is America's largest conservation organization. NWF works with a nationwide network of state affiliate organizations, scientists, grassroots activists, volunteers, educators, and wildlife enthusiasts—uniting individuals from diverse backgrounds to focus on three goals that will have the biggest impact on the future of America's wildlife. NWF's key objectives are to connect people with nature, protect and restore wildlife, and confront global warming.

National Wildlife Federation relies on Americans who are passionate about wildlife and wild places to advance our mission: protecting wildlife for our children's future. Visit **www.nwf.org** or call 800-882-9919 to join us today!

Come and Explore

At National Wildlife Federation Expeditions, our goal is to find extraordinary ways to connect you with nature, and travel is an outstanding way to do that. We can't create the trips ourselves, but we can provide a service that is just as valuable. Every year, we vet hundreds of tour companies, and review thousands of programs and itineraries, to find the best tour operators, the best destinations, and the best values. After we've selected the best trips, we ask our travel partners to designate specific dates just for NWF members. We attract great people to these tours. NWF members are curious and adventurous, and treasure the natural world. If this sounds like you, then you would find yourself in terrific company on one of our expeditions. For more information, visit **www.nwf.org/expeditions**.

T68.1208